The PLOT AGAINST IRELAND

ALSO BY MYLES DUNGAN

Land Is All That Matters: The Struggle That Shaped Irish History
Four Killings: Land Hunger, Murder and a Family in the Irish Revolution

The PLOT AGAINST IRELAND

The Forger, *Spies*, Conmen and Terrorists Who Conspired Against Irish Home Rule

MYLES DUNGAN

HEAD of ZEUS

An Apollo Book

First published in the UK in 2026 by Head of Zeus,
part of Bloomsbury Publishing Plc

9 7 5 3 1 2 4 6 8

A catalogue record for this book is available from the British Library.

ISBN (HB): 9781035919611; ISBN (XTPB): 9781035919628;
ISBN (EBOOK): 9781035919567

Cover design by Simon Michele
Typeset by Six Red Marbles India

Printed and bound in Great Britain by Clays Ltd, Elcograf S.p.A.

MIX
Paper | Supporting responsible forestry
FSC® C018072
www.fsc.org

Bloomsbury Publishing Plc
50 Bedford Square, London, WC1B 3DP, UK
Bloomsbury Publishing Ireland Limited,
29 Earlsfort Terrace, Dublin 2, D02 AY28, Ireland

HEAD OF ZEUS LTD
5–8 Hardwick Street
London EC1R 4RG

To find out more about our authors and books
visit www.headofzeus.com
For product safety related questions contact productsafety@bloomsbury.com

For Shane Kenna (1984–2017) and Gabriel Doherty (1968–2024). Peerless historians.

And…

For Gwyneth Williams, Ollie and Sadie Fallon, Sophie, Ben, Charlie and Freddie Collins, Leo, Noah and Ella Dungan and Zoe Karwig. Future historians?

'But when they see that, under the pressure of Irish disaffection, you have lost the nerve, or the fibre, or the manliness to uphold the integrity of your Empire, will they not apply the lesson to themselves and many of them say, "now is the time for us to shake off this connection and stand alone and independent in the world"? ... if you fail in this trial, one by one the flowers will be plucked from the diadem of Empire and you will be reduced to depend on the resources of this small, over-peopled island.'

The Marquess of Salisbury, speech to Exeter Conservatives, April 1892

'For the Tories, Ireland historically has been a pawn in other power games or an irritant to be denied.'

Professor Diarmaid Ferriter, *Irish Times*, 3 May 2024

Contents

Introduction xi

Prelude: *Felo de se*: The Strange Death of William Mackey Lomasney xxi

Part I: Genesis

1 *Status quo ante bellum*: Fenians, Home Rulers and Land Leaguers 3

2 Bombing Britain 21

3 The War of the Three Kingdoms: Ireland and the Growth of the British Secret Apparatus 42

Part II: Exodus

4 The Bombshell 75

5 The 'Jubilee Plot': Fishing for a Red Herring 95

6 The 'Bloody Puddle': The Special Commission Convenes 129

7 The Captain, the Forger, the Spy and the Bagman 154

8 The Strange Pilgrimage of Richard Pigott 172

9 'A Thing, a Reptile, a Monster': The Exit of Richard Pigott 199

10 From Checkmate to Stalemate: Endgame at the Commission 226

Part III: Revelations

11 Theatre of the Absurd: The Wardour Street Snake Pit 255

12 The Reluctant Archivist: William Henry Joyce Colludes with 'The Forger' 277

13 The O'Shea Divorce: Plan C? 293

14 Loose Ends 312

Acknowledgements 319

Bibliography 321

Image Credits 329

Notes 331

Index 353

Introduction

'We are in a state of bloodless civil war.'[1]

The Marquess of Salisbury to W. H. Smith, 5 February 1889

'From top to bottom it is an organisation of the meanest and most squalid vices ... directed by the very scum of humanity.'

The Times, on the Irish Parliamentary Party, 1 June 1887

'A front and flank attack was made in 1887 and 1888 upon the whole Irish movement, which has never been paralleled in the history of political agitations.'[2]

Michael Davitt, *The Fall of Feudalism in Ireland* (1904)

It was always difficult to persuade the inhabitants of a smallish island on the fringes of Europe of one unpalatable truth: colonized peoples were not wholeheartedly in favour of British global dominance. It was overwhelmingly nonconsensual. For the last decade or so, where Britain is concerned, it appears that the realities of colonial history have been retreating in the face of 'sunlit upland' revisionism. The statue of Cecil Rhodes still looms above the entrance to an Oxford building belonging to Oriel College, though a 'contextualizing' plaque has been added, acknowledging that the arch-imperialist 'caused great loss of life'. Up to 20,000 African men, women and children, to be imprecise.

We can blame blinkered twenty-first-century wistfulness for the recurrent illusions of a 'glorious imperial past'. Or we can ascribe this baffling nostalgia to a certain lack of familiarity with the realities of the British colonial project, and a dearth of self-awareness about how the nation that painted the global map red in the eighteenth and nineteenth centuries is often perceived – its history at least – in its former possessions.

Because the British Empire was not created by the overwhelming desire of indigenous populations in Asia and Africa, North America and Ireland, to be 'civilized'; to delight in the language of Shakespeare and the King James Bible; to be exposed to the otherworldly benefits of Anglicanism; or to be tutored in the skills of competent civil administration. The Empire (the use of the upper case feels almost mandatory) was fashioned by overwhelming military power; by a talent for nurturing a collaborative class in each of its territorial acquisitions; by an abundance of surplus British and Irish males who could be moulded into passable bureaucrats; and by a ruthless attachment to the French axiom '*j'y suis, j'y reste*', which roughly translates as, 'what we have we hold'.

The tenacity with which Britain retained its first colony immediately to the west – the earliest incursion dating from the late twelfth century – would later be reflected in its determination to preserve the integrity of its other scattered possessions. The defection of Ireland from the Empire would be 'the thin end of the wedge'. The country was small and poor, but its location, so menacingly close to Britain, made continued ownership imperative. Faced with a determined Irish nationalist uprising (assisted by the French) in 1798, Britain had responded with an overwhelming display of military power. Thirty thousand corpses later, the 'iron fist' was followed by a display of blunt force trauma politics, when the quasi-independent Irish parliament in Dublin was obliged to abolish itself. Ireland was thrust into the arranged marriage of the 'United Kingdom of Great Britain and Ireland' with the passage of the Act of Union in 1801. The British establishment even compensated their brethren in the exclusively Protestant 'Patriot Parliament' in Dublin, by allocating Ireland a hundred seats in the House of Commons at Westminster. This was a 'privilege' never enjoyed by any of Britain's other colonies and would have profound consequences. Sporadic and hapless attempts by militant nationalists (in 1803, 1848 and 1867) to break free were batted away by the resourceful colonizers without even breaking sweat.

Ironically, despite being radically dissimilar, the 1868–74 administration of William E. Gladstone shared at least one overwhelming objective with the Marquess of Salisbury's administration that took office in 1886. Gladstone had surprised the British body politic in 1868 by declaring that 'my mission is to pacify Ireland'. Salisbury assumed office with a similar intention. However, the methodologies of these storied figures – one the standard bearer for a brand of liberalism that still bears his name, the other a champion of imperialistic atavism – underscores the different connotations of the word 'pacify'. Gladstone's interpretation eventually led him to support Irish devolution. Salisbury's imperialism took him, and his Tory government, in the opposite direction. His object was to pacify Ireland by crushing, once and for all, any hankering after legislative independence. That way lay anarchy and the end of the Empire. Salisbury viewed Irish waywardness as 'an evil dream',[3] dispelled only by stiff and regular doses of punishment. He even credited Ireland with having awoken 'the slumbering genius of English imperialism'[4] as Britain extended its sphere of influence in Africa and Asia during his prime ministerial tenure.

The serpent had appeared in Salisbury's Garden of Eden in the mid-1880s. Rather unexpectedly, it was 'the enemy within' that posed the threat. The democratization of British politics in the nineteenth century, through the three great franchise-extending parliamentary reform bills of 1832, 1867 and 1884; the introduction of the secret ballot in 1872; and the creation of a vibrant and critical newspaper sector after the relaxation of the so-called 'taxes on knowledge' in the 1850s, had the unintended consequence of enabling Irish democratic impulses, and of shifting Irish dissent and devolutionary instincts from bloody rebellion by tiny groups of conspirators into the realm of a constitutionalist 'politics of the possible'. What ultimately emerged was a cohesive nationalist political movement under the leadership of the aloof and charismatic Charles Stewart Parnell. His followers were known as 'Home Rulers'. They were members of the Irish Parliamentary Party, but, above all, they were 'Parnellites'. In the words of the great Trinity College Dublin historian T. W. Moody, 'they were the militant expression of a great national upheaval, a mass movement deriving its strength from an unprecedented combination of political and agrarian forces'.[5]

When the mathematical logic of the franchise expansion and boundary changes of the 1884 Reform Act played out in the general election of 1885, devolution for Ireland suddenly entered the realm of the practical, or, some optimists even claimed, the inevitable. The emergence of a sizeable and monolithic cohort of Irish nationalist MPs played havoc with the certainties of British politics. An Irish party now held the balance of power and could dictate the character of the 'British' government. That government had grown accustomed to Irish nationalist dissent withering on the vine: imploding or finding expression in violent insurgencies that easily succumbed to military force. The Parnellite threat was an imperialist's nightmare.

Gladstone found himself dependent on Irish nationalist support to govern and 'converted' to the cause of Home Rule for Ireland and the repeal of the 1801 Act of Union. For convinced imperialists, this really was the 'thin end of the wedge'.

Fortunately for them and their counterparts in northeast Ulster, crisis was averted with the collapse of Gladstone's devolutionary enterprise in June 1886. His Home Rule Bill was defeated by thirty votes in the House of Commons. But what if that narrow escape was only a temporary reprieve? Would the malevolent forces of Irish separatism (which now included the Gladstonian Liberals) regroup? How could the clearly senile and traitorous Gladstone, the political saboteur Charles Stewart Parnell and his feral acolytes be driven from the field? How could the union (and by extension the Empire) be preserved? Ultimately a benign solution was arrived at. Acquiescence, after all, could always be bought, in this instance with a series of Acts of Parliament enabling the transfer of Irish land from its aristocratic owners to impatient tenants. But that was a medium- to long-term project, scarcely envisaged when the Tories took office in July 1886. In the short term, calamity was to be averted by a series of questionable, quasi-legal or blatantly illicit stratagems designed to strangle constitutional Irish nationalism. It was a project enthusiastically underwritten by the Tory political establishment and its infant security apparatus, as the latter developed its milk teeth.

Unnerved British imperialists hatched a multi-faceted plot against Irish self-determination. A trident was aimed at the heart of Irish devolution: an establishment coup, as subversive as any conspiracy ever devised by Irish revolutionaries. In the words of Paul Bew, it was 'an attempt to criminalise a popular political movement'.[6] As a strategy, despite its signal failures, it worked well enough to allow a breathing space after which the more benign alternative, 'killing Home Rule with kindness' (i.e. buying the loyalty of Irish tenant farmers by turning them into peasant proprietors) could be deployed.

As it later turned out, the Conservative doomsayers were proved right. Within four decades of the partial victory of Irish republicanism in achieving independence – though not a republic – in 1921, the British Empire had been dismantled from within and without. A decade later both Britain and Ireland aligned themselves with their natural hinterland in continental Europe. In 2016, Britain, however, dazzled by the light of those beguiling 'sunlit uplands', chose a different course.

The *dramatis personae* of *this* narrative include a pornographer and forger; a shadowy civil servant charged with the conduct of an extensive but furtive intelligence operation; a largely fabricated 'plot' to murder the reigning monarch and the most powerful agents of the British state (orchestrated by a small army of *agents provocateurs*); a British newspaper proprietor intent on discrediting and destroying a legitimate political movement; an engaged and patrician prime minister devoted to the preservation of union and empire and unconcerned about the methods used to achieve his objectives; a killer involved in one of the most brutal murders in nineteenth-century Ireland; an alleged Royal Irish Constabulary 'death squad' doling out vigilante justice; one of the most effective British spies in the United States of America; some of the least effective spies in the long, and often tortured, history of British intelligence operations; the shady patrons of a Soho public house devoting their energies to 'black ops'; the coincidental and mightily convenient deaths of three significant protagonists; agents of an emerging British security apparatus; the all too familiar rivalries within that apparatus; a languid but formidable British political grandee, nephew of the incumbent prime minister; a celebrity London lawyer involved in some of the most sensational cases in Victorian England; a peerless, haughty and deeply flawed Irish political leader; an investigative journalist, committed socialist and amateur detective willing to conduct interviews at gunpoint; British cabinet ministers pursuing a political conspiracy (while maintaining their deniability); an infamous cuckold on a mission of revenge; as well as sundry swindlers, perjurers, informers, liars, conspirators and terrorists. All against the backdrop of the infamous 1888 Whitechapel murders in London.

The central thesis of this narrative is that there was an all-encompassing, loosely co-ordinated British government conspiracy – simultaneously blatant and covert – to undermine Irish constitutional nationalism. It may appear to some readers to overreach. Surely 'The Master of Hatfield' (Salisbury) was, in his opposition to Parnell and the Irish Parliamentary Party, merely indulging in appropriately robust politics to buttress his efforts at preserving the integrity of the United Kingdom? After all, it was not as if his Irish political antagonists wore kid gloves in their own dealings with his administration.

The three main components of the establishment plot – the

three prongs of the trident – if viewed in isolation, might lend credence to that analysis. However, when we view 'in the round' the Tory government's coalition with *The Times* newspaper in its crusade against 'Parnellism', the clandestine espionage operation employing *agents provocateurs* to discredit legitimate Irish nationalist aspirations, and the 'black ops' propaganda campaign launched at a time when the phrase itself had barely come into its own, it is more difficult to dismiss the idea of a 'plot against Ireland' merely because there exists no 'paper trail' that conclusively proves its existence. Where is the conclusive documentary evidence of an official British policy of extrajudicial reprisal during the Anglo-Irish war of 1919–21? But who now takes seriously British denials of the existence of such a policy? Few of the principals of the plot of the late 1880s were foolish or arrogant enough to commit the details of their stratagems to paper. However, defectors such as the disenchanted civil servant William Henry Joyce, or the dismissed Metropolitan Police sergeant Patrick McIntyre, while not entirely trustworthy, bore convincing witness to aspects of the plot. Evidence for a conspiracy is more circumstantial than documentary – weighty, but often open to more benign interpretations.

How should we treat this data?

A law student was once asked by a teaching professor for his opinion on the use of circumstantial evidence in legal cases. 'Am I prosecuting or defending?' was the canny response. In the case of *The Times* and its political collaborators, there is enough documentary material and an abundance of circumstantial evidence to point towards a conspiracy aimed at destabilization of the Irish Home Rule alliance.

This largely covert grand strategy of the Conservative and Unionist administration of the Marquess of Salisbury played out between 1887 and 1889. In the words of one of Salisbury's biographers, Robert Taylor, the Tory prime minister's Irish 'mission' 'was to reinforce the feeble crumbling pillars of the Empire from inevitable decay and the growing threats to its position from an increasingly hostile outside world'.[7] As the strategy evolved, Tory administrative machinations of the 1880s were as imperious and cynical as the extra-parliamentary Conservative/Unionist assault, from 1912 to 1914, on the democratic passage of the third Home Rule Bill. Ironically, some of the rhetoric used in the latter instance by the Tories while in opposition – suggesting rampant governmental arrogance and rank tyranny – could retrospectively be applied to the conduct of the Salisbury administration itself towards the Irish Parliamentary Party in 1888.

The battering ram was the Special Commission, appointed in 1888 to investigate the allegations contained in the 'Parnellism and Crime' series which had appeared in *The Times* the previous year. Its ultimate purpose was to remove Home Rule from the neighbourhood of acceptable politics. It was, once again in the words of T. W. Moody, 'not a device to further the interests of justice so much as the instrument by which a Conservative government … hoped to overwhelm its political opponents'.[8] The tribunal itself lurched from utter tedium to high drama and was, at times, witness to exchanges worthy of Victorian vaudeville.

There was much cloak and dagger activity on both sides. Most of this was legal, much was questionable, some verged on the farcical, and some was blatantly unethical or unashamedly illicit. It provided splendid opportunities for the opportunist. It was, *ex post facto*, defended as a sacred cause and attacked as an underhand conspiracy.

But it was a defining moment in Anglo-Irish relations, 'a rhetorical onslaught on the notion of Home Rule for Ireland … a public expression of the Irish incapacity for self-government',[9] according to historian Margaret O'Callaghan. The mentality behind the creation of the Special Commission; the parallel clandestine operation to discredit Parnell and his lieutenants; and the convenient 'exposure' of the half-cooked 'Jubilee plot', amounted to a coup beyond even the delivery by bribery and intimidation of the Act of Union almost a century before. That this attempted coup was only partially successful (and it did achieve some of its objectives, despite nationalist bravado claiming otherwise – the report of the Special Commission, for example) is beside the point. It was a cynical crusade, even in the view of that archetypal Tory unionist Lord Randolph Churchill. The man who devised the slogan 'Ulster will fight, and Ulster will be right' during the Home Rule crisis of 1886 was, during the entire *Times*-inspired controversy of 1887–9, utterly disparaging of a government (his own party) that outdid itself in its efforts to discredit Irish constitutional politics and politicians, and daub the map of Ireland with the legend 'Here be monsters'.

Whatever it was, it was not cricket. More of a no-holds-barred Eton wall game.

The Plot Against Ireland will highlight an inescapable consequence of political evolution, one that has present-day resonance. Even by the mid-1880s more than a whiff of gunpowder clung to the leadership of Irish separatism. It was no easy task for the then largely house-trained protagonists of the movement for Irish devolution to distance themselves from some of their militant affiliates. It was even harder to convince partisan British sceptics that any genuine *cordon sanitaire* existed between Irish parliamentary nationalists and their extremist Fenian first cousins – especially if it suited the doubting Thomases, and their own extended family of Cecils and Balfours, to believe otherwise.

Unlike many other bloody conflicts in the 200-year struggle to preserve the integrity of the British Empire, the body count in this skirmish was very low. This was not, however, dictated by any respect for the axiom *primum non nocere* ('first, do no harm'). The Home Rule movement was not a murderous and mutinous enterprise, so there was no necessity for a savage Indian Mutiny-type riposte.

A John Tenniel cartoon in *Punch* from 9 April 1887 portrays Salisbury as the mythical Sisyphus pushing the 'Irish Difficulty' rock uphill, the implication being that he would be required to repeat the process *ad infinitum*. Tenniel, who was not greatly enamoured of Irish nationalists, might profitably have depicted a few obnoxious creepy-crawlies emerging from under the rock. But his readers would hardly have been enthralled with the symbolism.

PUNCH, OR THE LONDON CHARIVARI.—April 9, 1887.

SALISBURY SISYPHUS.

"UNENDING TASK!" . . . .

"SWIFT ROLL THE YEARS, AND STILL THE CEASELESS ROUND,
THE TOILSOME PRESS UP THE PRECIPITOUS GROUND,
THE SULLEN SLOW ASCENT, THE SWIFT REBOUND!"

Prelude

Felo de se: The Strange Death of William Mackey Lomasney

London Bridge, 13 December 1884, 5.45 p.m.

It was already dark when they shunted their small rowing boat onto the choppy waters of the Thames from the Southwark shore. To the north, the dome of St Paul's Cathedral was barely visible through the thickening London smog. It was a cold mid-December evening and the stone-arched London Bridge, which loomed overhead, was busy with rush hour traffic.

William Mackey Lomasney, Peter Mallon* and John Fleming were three men on a mission.[1] Lomasney, nicknamed 'The Little Captain', a bookseller from Detroit, was in charge. A native of Cincinnati, he was a veteran of the American Civil War and the Fenian Rising of 1867. He was noted for his diffidence, possibly dictated by the fact that he spoke with a pronounced lisp.

Appearances, in his case at least, were deceptive. His retiring

*There is still an element of uncertainty as to the presence of Mallon. While he was apparently one of the three men who hired the boat, there is some speculation that he may not have been on board when the device exploded prematurely. However, according to John Devoy, there were four men involved in the operation, all of whom perished. (John Devoy, *Recollections of an Irish Rebel* (New York, 1929), 212.)

manner did not extend as far as tolerance of Britain's denial of Irish independence. 'No man in the Fenian movement ever did more desperate things.' He was 'a fanatic of the deepest dye,'[2] according to John Devoy, who knew a great deal about such matters. The British Secret Service had been tracking Lomasney's movements for more than a year.[3] Before travelling to Europe, the painstaking bookseller had conducted his own experiments with dynamite in an isolated area on the shores of Lake Michigan. The results had impressed him, but the exercise might not have made him cautious enough when it came to the potential instability of his chosen weapon.

None of the three boatmen was especially well equipped for steering their small vessel broadside onto the waters of a river swollen by winter rain. They had hired the boat near London Bridge, shortly before setting out on their assignment.[4] Few, if any, of the pedestrians crossing London Bridge would have noticed the approach of the three men. No one in the carriages traversing the bridge would have paid the slightest attention to them either. It was not as if a rowboat was an unusual sight on London's coronary artery.

This apparently insignificant craft, however, was quite different from the other boats plying their trade along the river. Its cargo was lethal. As well as three determined Irish-American bombers, it was also carrying a cache of explosives sufficient to destroy, or at least severely damage, London Bridge. It also had the potential to kill or injure anyone unfortunate enough to be crossing the Thames between the City of London and Southwark when the bomb went off. Upwards of 8,000 people and 900 vehicles an hour travelled via London Bridge during the course of the average business day. Unless the bomb was primed to go off in the early hours of the morning, there was a high chance of civilian casualties. The 13th of December was a significant anniversary in the Irish revolutionary mythos. It was the occasion of the tragic Clerkenwell prison bombing in 1867, when, in an abortive attempt to rescue an American Fenian, an overstuffed barrel of explosives

had destroyed part of the prison wall, levelled half the adjacent street and killed twelve innocent Londoners.

The cover of the *Illustrated London News* of 20 December 1884 offered a speculative visual account of what happened next. Half a dozen pedestrians and a couple of carriages are depicted traversing the bridge as the boat reaches the first pier on the southern side of the river. A single gas lamp illuminates the area between two of the arches. A sudden explosion and a flash of light at water level causes the pedestrians to flinch, take cover or shield their eyes. Horses, panicked by the unexpected blast, are being brought under control by their drivers. Lomasney, Mallon and

Fleming's large supply of lignin dynamite, intended for more than one Thames bridge that night, had detonated prematurely. The high explosive went off at around 5.45 p.m., as one of the bombers attempted to lodge it in a drain hole. But the Metropolitan Police had got there first. Tipped off by a Paris-based Irish-American double-agent, the resourceful Whitehall spymaster Edward Jenkinson had ordered that all drain holes be covered with a thick metal grating. This glitch in their plans was to cost the three bombers their lives.

'A deafening explosion occurred,' went the account in *Reynolds's Weekly*, 'and at the same moment a sheet of flame shot up from the southern side of the river.'[5] The explosion caused minimal structural damage. The human cost, however, was more severe. All three of the bombers died. Two of the three were atomized and their remains were never found. The other, whose mutilated corpse was beyond identification, ruined someone's Christmas Day when it was discovered floating in the Thames on 25 December. Before becoming aware that all three bombers had lost their lives, Edward Jenkinson, in charge of anti-terrorist security at the Home Office, contemplated resignation and described himself as 'dreadfully discouraged and downhearted' that the defences of such a prime target had been breached. 'I wish I were clear of it all,' he confided to the Lord Lieutenant, Earl Spencer.[6]

Some days after the premature explosion, a London landlord informed the Metropolitan Police that, on searching the lodgings of some American gentlemen who had been missing since 13 December, he had discovered a cache of dynamite. It was only after a search of their rented premises that the police were able to identify the victims of the London Bridge calamity as the relatively obscure John Fleming, one of the more extreme members of the militant Irish-American separatist society Clan na Gael; US Civil War veteran William Mackey Lomasney; and his brother-in-law Peter Mallon. For some time, because of the absence of any evidence to the contrary, the Metropolitan Police had assumed that the bombers were able to make a clean getaway.

Knowing better, 'their associates,' according to the Kerry-born Metropolitan Police CID detective John Sweeney, 'anxious to annoy and hoodwink us, kept circulating reports that one or other of them had been seen alive in London or America'.[7]

A reward of £5,000 'was offered for the discovery of the perpetrators of the outrage'.[8] It went unclaimed, although Inspector Sweeney did waste some weeks watching a house in Bermondsey, identified as Fleming's abode by a conman anxious to claim some of the 'blood money'. Sweeney was able to confirm the death of Lomasney only in 1888 after locating the man's sister in a house in London. She pointed out his coat. It had been hanging, untouched, behind her front door for four years.[9]

Lomasney, Mallon and Fleming left a four-shilling safety deposit with the owner of the boat. It was never redeemed.

PART I
GENESIS

1

STATUS QUO ANTE BELLUM

Fenians, Home Rulers and Land Leaguers

Ribbonmen, Fenians and Land Leaguers

This story really begins in the aftermath of the Great Famine, with the creation of a dangerously Anglophobic Irish diaspora in the United States of America. Irish-America, perennially in search of retribution for 'the Great Hunger', was either on the fringes or at the heart of every radical development in the Irish nationalist narrative, from the second half of the nineteenth century until the 1916 Rising and beyond. To the cause of Irish separatism, Irish-America offered money, leadership, organization, encouragement and threats of the withdrawal of vital funds in the face of inaction. But above all, they offered money.

Two beneficiaries were the radical republicans James Stephens and John O'Mahony. Their new militant separatist movement – founded in 1858 and pledged to secure independence by force of arms – was known in Ireland as the Irish Republican Brotherhood (IRB) and in the USA as the Fenian Brotherhood. The umbrella term 'Fenianism' would dominate the netherworld of militant Irish extreme nationalism for the next two generations. Much of the early leadership cadre of the IRB, men such as the wild-eyed and hirsute John O'Leary, the courteous intellectual Thomas Clarke Luby, and the dogmatic novelist Charles Kickham, author of the rural melodrama *Knocknagow*, were either former Young

Irelanders who had 'risen' in 1848, or had been in sympathy with that movement. Slightly younger than some of those elder statesmen was the dynamic revolutionary figure Jeremiah O'Donovan Rossa, born in Rosscarbery, Co. Cork in 1831.

O'Mahony and Stephens were quickly at odds. Stephens, an autocratic egotist, 'self-opinionated and dogmatic',[1] viewed the American Fenians as a mere adjunct, a support group for its fraternal Irish ally and a prop for his self-regard. The Fenian Brotherhood was a cheerleading group with an open chequebook. O'Mahony saw things very differently. Because his organization was paying the piper, he demanded a say in the selection of the tune. At the first convention of the Fenian Brotherhood in 1863, O'Mahony demanded equal status with the IRB and an end to the dominance of Stephens. However, by the conclusion of the American Civil War in 1865, in which thousands of its members participated, the Fenian Brotherhood split into two antagonistic factions and, with divided forces, organized separate unsuccessful invasions of Canada.*

In an attempt to secure funds from the Fenian Brotherhood (and wrest back some control from O'Mahony), Stephens visited the USA in 1864 and, while there, in order to enhance his dented credibility, made the rash promise that 1865 was to be the 'year of action' for the IRB. However, 1865 came and went with no more dramatic occurrence than the suppression by Dublin Castle of the Fenian propaganda outlet *The Irish People*. The closure of the newspaper was accompanied by the arrest of its staff (including O'Donovan Rossa) and the incarceration of Stephens himself in Richmond Bridewell. He was replaced, *pro tem*, as IRB Head Centre (commander-in-chief) by a thirty-three-year-old Irish-American veteran, General Francis Frederick Millen, a native of County Tyrone, who was despatched to Ireland by John O'Mahony.

*After a disturbingly successful invasion of what was still British North America in June 1866 the colony, within a year, became the Canadian Confederation, giving the Fenians a counterintuitive claim to being the Fathers of Modern Canada!

Millen, 'a raw-boned man with long arms and long oval face, a long straight nose, and lightish sandy complexion',[2] was less than impressed by the state of military readiness of the movement,[3] but was now expected to lead the IRB in Stephens's absence. However, Millen's tenure lasted barely a week. Even though he was housed in a prison cell, the obdurate and egotistical Stephens was adamant. Millen was instructed, in a pencilled note from Richmond Prison, to return to America and not to set foot in Ireland again except at the head of a Fenian expeditionary force. Millen meekly complied with Stephens's brusque order. A few months after his return to New York, either traumatized by his Irish experience or, more likely, determined to monetize the knowledge he had acquired of the workings of the IRB, he presented himself at the British Consulate, met with the Consul General, Edward Archibald, and embarked on an intermittent twenty-three-year career as an agent of Her Majesty's Government.

Left, along with the other employees of *The Irish People*, to face the music at his trial in Dublin, O'Donovan Rossa received a life sentence. He endured three years of extreme privation in various British prisons. His punishments included having his hands cuffed behind his back for thirty-four days. His harsh treatment resulted in a permanent spinal injury. In January 1871 Rossa, in a general amnesty, was one of several Fenian prisoners released on condition that they remained outside the UK until the expiry of their sentences. He launched himself into an alcohol-fuelled life of controversy, bloody-mindedness, perversity and retribution.

In a development that was little noted at the time, but would assume much greater significance two decades hence, the main beneficiary of the suppression of *The Irish People* was the Dublin journalist Richard Pigott. His newspaper, *The Irishman* – which he purchased in 1865 for £700 – also took the IRB line, and its circulation now increased exponentially in the absence of the Fenian movement's own journal.

The year 1866 became the new 'year of action', but it too came and went with no military commotion beyond drilling and war games. By 1867, O'Mahony's Irish-American lieutenants, led by US Civil War veteran Thomas J. Kelly, had had enough. Stephens was deposed and a cadre of Irish-American military veterans took over the planning for a Rising in 1867.

The oft-postponed event finally took place over a few days in March 1867, and, while it was more vigorous than the efforts of the Young Irelanders in 1848, it was so chaotic and ineffectual that it is even possible Stephens might have done just as well. While Stephens was able to flee to Paris, some of the men who had ousted him were not so fortunate. Kelly was arrested in Manchester in September 1867, and it was a botched (albeit successful) attempt to effect his release that provided the IRB with one of the two enduring legacies of a dismally unproductive rebellion. Kelly was being transported in a prison van when it was stopped by a group of Fenians. A Manchester police sergeant, Charles Brett, was accidentally killed. Kelly escaped, but three Fenians, William Philip Allen, Michael Larkin and Michael O'Brien, were later identified and charged with Brett's murder. They were hanged on the walls of Salford Jail on 23 November 1867 before a crowd estimated at around 10,000. Thereafter the three men entered Irish revolutionary folklore as the 'Manchester Martyrs'.

Three weeks later the IRB attempted to 'spring' another Irish-American Fenian leader, Ricard [*sic*] O'Sullivan Burke, and a more junior Irish colleague, Joseph Casey,* from Clerkenwell Prison in London. Using a charge of gunpowder concealed in a street seller's barrow, the IRB blew a hole in the wall of the prison on the afternoon of 13 December 1867. The explosive charge was utterly disproportionate to the requirements of the job in hand. An eighteen-metre section of the prison wall was obliterated, as were many of the tenement houses in Corporation Lane adjacent to the prison. Twelve people died in the explosion. Michael Barrett, a Fenian activist from County Fermanagh, who lived in

*Casey, along with his brother Patrick, goes on to play a murky role in this narrative in a subsequent incarnation in Paris.

Glasgow, was the only person convicted of involvement in the Clerkenwell bombing. He was hanged on 26 May 1868 outside Newgate Prison. His execution was watched by a crowd of around 2,000 Londoners, who were reported to have sung songs as diverse as the anthemic 'Rule Britannia' and the popular music hall ditty 'Champagne Charlie'. It was the last public execution to be carried out in Britain.

Some consequences are inevitable, others are unintended, a number are simply bewildering. In launching these two rescue attempts – which it should be remembered were a function of dismal revolutionary failure – the IRB had not intended to stir the conscience of one of the two leading politicians of mid-Victorian Britain, William E. Gladstone. Astonishingly, however, not only did they do so, but they extracted a significant and unplanned concession from the Liberal leader when his party defeated the Conservative government of Benjamin Disraeli in the December 1868 general election. As he entered 10 Downing Street, for the first of his four terms as prime minister, Gladstone announced, to much disbelief, that 'my mission is to pacify Ireland'. In pursuit of this objective Gladstone introduced legislation to end the primacy of the (Protestant) Church of Ireland as an 'established' state church (1869), and followed that up with remedial land legislation (1870). At the same time, an amnesty campaign led by the distinguished Irish barrister, journalist and politician Isaac Butt – who had represented a number of Fenians at their post-uprising trials – made headway in securing the release of several IRB prisoners, although in some cases this resulted in their deportation.

With nothing pressing on their dance cards – a reprise of the Fenian rising of 1867 being a very remote prospect – many ordinary IRB members worked with Isaac Butt MP in his capacity as leader of the Home Rule League, to have Irish representatives of a more moderate nationalist hue elected to Westminster. The League made a promising outing in the election of 1874 (which restored Disraeli and the Tories to power) by returning sixty MPs of varying shades of nationalist green. Present in this 'big tent' were several IRB members and quasi-Fenian 'fellow travellers'. While not exactly doctrinaire – had they been ultra-orthodox they would not have taken seats at Westminster – they assumed their places in parliament with the intention of forcing the new Tory government to pay rather more attention to Ireland than Disraeli had planned.

John O'Connor Power, MP for Mayo, was an IRB Supreme Council member. Joseph Gillis Biggar, MP for Cavan – acerbic, colourful and a former Belfast pork butcher by trade – was inducted into the IRB after his election to parliament.[4] Neither man stood for election as 'Home Rulers' in order to absorb the atmosphere of tradition, privilege and entitlement on the Westminster backbenches. To the dismay of the rather emollient Butt, both men began a concerted campaign of obstructing the business of the House by means of the filibuster. Once they remained on their feet, they 'had the floor' and could monopolize the business of the chamber.

In 1875 O'Connor Power and Biggar were joined in their campaign of obstruction by the newly elected MP for Meath – he won his seat in a by-election – Wicklow landlord Charles Stewart Parnell. Parnell was the grandson of an American admiral (Charles Stewart) who had wrought considerable destruction on the British Navy during the War of 1812. Parnell had inherited an acute Anglophobia from his American mother, Delia. This was accentuated by his undistinguished career at Cambridge University, from which he was 'rusticated' (sent down) after a drunken brawl.

Parnell's obstructionism brought him to the attention of 'non-conformist' Fenians, such as the land agitator Michael Davitt and the journalist James J. O'Kelly, neither of whom had much truck with the puritanical solipsism of 'orthodox' Fenian traditionalists like John O'Leary and Charles Kickham. Both Davitt and O'Kelly were keen to harness the energies of constitutionalists of a radical nationalist stripe. Their stimulus influenced an 1878 *rapprochement* from the exiled Fenian John Devoy, now a journalist with the *New York Herald*. Devoy had become the dominant voice in the Irish-American nationalist body Clan na Gael, which 'became, largely through his efforts, the principal rallying point for Irish-American separatists'.[5] The Clan, founded in 1867, had effectively eclipsed the largely moribund and divided Fenian Brotherhood by the late 1870s. Devoy, in October 1878, penned an anonymous cable, primarily intended to appeal to the patriotism of Parnell. This pledged Clan na Gael support (and by implication that of the IRB, which the Clan sustained financially) for a new and radical Irish constitutional movement that would not only champion the cause of Irish separatism but would work on behalf of the country's beleaguered tenant-farmers in a campaign for peasant ownership of the land.

The so-called 'New Departure' never amounted to a formalized agreement. To even call it an understanding is a misnomer. Parnell made no recorded response to the initiative, but neither did he indicate his rejection. Kickham and O'Leary, representing the purist republican tendency within Fenianism, wanted nothing to do with constitutional nationalists. Neither did they relish an alliance with agrarian interests. To Kickham, land agitation was a distraction from the drive for an independent Irish republic. Even worse was the prospect of a sated and contented peasantry in the event of a successful campaign for the '3 Fs' – fair rent, free sale and fixity of tenure.

Most rank-and-file IRB members, however, made their own decisions when it came to 'lending' their support to constitutional politicians. Many found little difficulty in allying themselves with the radical nationalists who now began to coalesce around Parnell's leadership. Others, who agreed with O'Leary's sentiment that 'nine out of ten Irishmen entering the British Parliament with honest intentions are corrupted',[6] chose the lonelier and more subversive option.

Such personal political choices were complicated by the sudden primacy and urgency of the issue of land tenure. Despite the possibility, since the 1850s of achieving a measure of land reform by legal and democratic means – Charles Gavan Duffy's Tenant League was a case in point – the violent agrarian secret societies of the pre-Famine era had not opted for a torpid retirement. The so-called 'Ribbonmen' – enforcers of the illicit decrees of the mythical 'Captain Moonlight' or his brother in arms 'Rory of the Hills' – had held on to their weapons and held fast to their traditional methods of conducting business, which often included murder, assault and intimidation. In the fractious environment of the 1880s a new nomenclature emerged. 'Ribbon/Fenianism' was now spoken of where the adherents of agrarian secret societies collaborated with, or were armed by, individual members of the IRB, despite the hostility of Kickham and other ideologues on the Supreme Council.

Between 1879 and 1882 the nation's 'Ribbon/Fenians' were busy. Their services were called upon with violent frequency as Ireland went through the tumultuous months of the First Land War.

When, in 1879, renewed famine threatened in County Mayo, there was a determination that the response to this subsistence crisis would be more belligerent than had been the case during the calamitous Great Famine of the 1840s. Hunger stalked the west of Ireland after three years of excessive rainfall, bad harvests and the economic consequences of the worldwide depression that began in the USA with the bank-induced 'panic of 1873'. The intervention of the Mayo-born ex-IRB member Michael Davitt was crucial. By associating himself with any form of militant political activity, Davitt risked being returned to an English jail. He had only recently been paroled (for Fenian activities) after an incarceration of more than seven years. In the aftermath of an anti-landlord meeting at Irishtown, near Claremorris, Co. Mayo, on 20 April 1879, Davitt became one of the founders of the rather paradoxically named *National* (my italics) Land League of Mayo. This was established in Castlebar on 16 August 1879.

Davitt wrote the new organization's manifesto. Its most memorable slogan was the line 'the land of Ireland belongs to the people of Ireland'. This quickly morphed into the more epigrammatical and abiding motto 'The land for the people'. The latter mantra was central to the three-year campaign, launched on 21 October 1879 in Dublin, with the founding of the Irish National Land League. Parnell became president of what promised to be a radical agrarian movement. Davitt acted as the organization's secretary. One of the great backroom 'fixers' of Irish nineteenth-century nationalism, Patrick Egan, took up the position of treasurer. Egan, a successful Dublin baker, was a former Fenian (he became IRB treasurer in 1872) who had been expelled in 1876 for allying just a shade too closely with Isaac Butt's Home Rule League.

For three years the Land League assumed some of the characteristics of an iceberg. Above the surface of the water, it made some effort (though never too strenuously) to remain within the law. Beneath the waterline, however, all manner of 'outrages' – the *mot du jour* of the Anglo-Irish *apparatchiks* of Dublin Castle – were being perpetrated by militants within the organization. Parnell, setting aside many of his personal scruples, turned a blind eye to the activities of the League's hard men. By 1880, however, he proposed a compelling, though hardly original, alternative to violence and intimidation. In a pivotal speech in Ennis, Co. Clare on 19 September 1880, Parnell asked his audience, 'What are you to do with a tenant who bids for a farm from which another has been evicted?' The loudest response came from those shouting, 'Shoot him!' or 'Kill him!' Such violent sentiments reflected the views of a substantial portion of the League's membership. Parnell, however, coolly offered an alternative, more peaceable, strategy. This involved the placing of opponents 'in moral Coventry'.[7] One of the earliest victims (in the winter of 1880) of this passive-aggressive approach was Captain Charles Cunningham Boycott, land agent of Lord Erne in Mayo. A neologism was born.

In the summer of 1881, Richard Pigott lost his newspapers. The hedonistic proprietor of *The Irishman*, swamped by debts incurred while living the life of a 'squireen' – a well-heeled minor aristocrat – was forced to sell out. Tiring of the incessant attacks on the Land League from the 'left' in the pages of Pigott's quasi-Fenian newspaper, Patrick Egan used £3,000 of League funds to buy him out. His presses in Dublin's Middle Abbey Street were used to print the League's own weekly newspaper, *United Ireland*, edited by the young *Freeman's Journal* reporter William O'Brien. Under the terms of the agreement, Pigott was debarred from establishing a rival weekly title. He was no longer a factor in nationalist journalism.

However, he found a host of other ways to make a nuisance of himself. As did O'Donovan Rossa.

Looking on from exile in New York, enraged by the punitive measures being taken by Gladstone's Liberal government and Dublin Castle against the land agitation, Rossa identified volunteers from within his organization, the United Irishmen of America, who were willing to retaliate by wreaking havoc on Britain. The threat of coercive legislation in the form of the 1881 Protection of Person and Property Bill galvanized Rossa and his 'skirmishers'. The passage of the Liberal government's bill – which circumvented *habeas corpus* legislation by permitting the imprisonment without trial of suspected agitators – was given more urgency by the first in a series of bomb attacks on targets in Britain in January 1881. This was the opening salvo of a four-year campaign carried out by the United Irishmen in tandem (or in competition) with rival Clan na Gael bombers, who were slower out of the starting gate. It was financed using money raised by Irish-American contributions to the 'Skirmishing Fund' of the *Irish World* newspaper, owned by extreme nationalist Patrick Ford. The Irish-American saboteurs would not relent until after 'Dynamite Saturday', a series of daring attacks on the Tower of London, Westminster Crypt and the House of Commons on 24 January 1885. Almost twenty devices were successfully triggered by the 'dynamitards' before the campaign finally fizzled out.

Gladstone, back in power since 1880, introduced his second

Land Bill on 7 April 1881, in the hope of ending the Land War. While it was a significant improvement on his 1870 legislation, its flaws ensured the continuation of the anarchy in rural Ireland. While it, essentially, gave effect to the long-sought '3 Fs' and introduced Land Courts to arbitrate between landlord and tenant on what precisely was meant by one of the 'Fs' – fair rent – it did not apply to tenants who held leases, nor did it apply to those who were in arrears of rent. Parnell indulged himself and his party in an ornamental show of opposition to the remedial legislation. Tenants were advised to boycott the Land Courts until the League could test their efficacy. This apparent ingratitude, allied to the ongoing violence (around 4,000 'outrages' were reported in 1881), was the last straw for an incensed Gladstone, and, encouraged by his hawkish chief secretary for Ireland, William E. Forster, he ordered the arrest of Parnell and the other leaders of the League under the terms of the all-embracing Protection of Person and Property Act.

On 13 October, a fateful date as far as the deeply superstitious Parnell was concerned – he had an aversion to the number 13 and to the month of October – Superintendent John Mallon, head of the Dublin Metropolitan Police's 'G' Division (the Castle's political police) arrested the Irish Party leader and brought him to Kilmainham Jail. There he would reside in relative comfort (a private cell, regular exercise, externally sourced food, uninhibited communication with his fellow prisoners) along with prominent Irish Party and Land League members such as the ebullient James O'Kelly, the industrious William O'Brien (who continued to edit *United Ireland* from his cell) and the Land League secretary Thomas Brennan. Just as O'Brien was able to get his 'copy' out of Kilmainham, Parnell had no difficulty in maintaining a correspondence with his mistress of twelve months, Katharine O'Shea, estranged wife of the ambitious and reptilian Clare MP Captain William Henry O'Shea.

Anticipating his arrest, in an interview in Wexford on 9 October, when asked who would replace him if he was jailed,

Parnell had replied insouciantly, 'Ah, if I am arrested, Captain Moonlight will take my place.' And so it proved. Chaos reigned in rural Ireland. The incidence of homicide in the latter half of 1881 almost tripled (from 7 to 20); cases of firing at the person also increased threefold (from 21 to 63); and firing into dwellings effectively doubled (from 62 to 122).

On 18 October the incarcerated leaders, including a reluctant Parnell, issued the 'No Rent Manifesto' from Kilmainham. This demanded of Irish tenants that they withhold payment of all rents until their leaders were released from jail. It led to the government's proscription of the Land League. Its work was continued by the Ladies Land League under the uncompromising leadership of Parnell's sister Anna. The 'No Rent Manifesto' only made matters worse in rural Ireland. Tenants who were reluctant to take part in what amounted to a political rent strike were often boycotted, assaulted or even murdered by some of the more extreme elements of a rapidly disintegrating, and now illegal, Land League. When it became clear that Gladstone's rent arbitration courts were recommending reductions of up to 30 per cent (the average was between 15 and 20 per cent), tenant-farmers began to flock to them. The League's 'long spoon strategy' was in tatters, as was much of its credibility.

It was the swaggering cuckold Captain William O'Shea who, by default, found himself at the centre of the process of negotiation that ended the impasse. A period of covert diplomacy culminated in what became known as the 'Kilmainham Treaty'. The self-aggrandizing O'Shea, always eager to profit from the relationship between his wife and the leader of his party (of which he was well aware; the Irish Party leader was a permanent resident of Katharine O'Shea's home in Eltham in south-east London), offered himself as an intermediary between Parnell and Gladstone, as did the President of the Board of Trade, the Birmingham MP Joseph Chamberlain, leader of the Liberal Party's radical wing. Chamberlain and William Forster, although cabinet colleagues, cherished a profound loathing for one another. This made Chamberlain's participation in the 'backdoor' negotiations even more satisfying for the Birmingham MP. An agreement emerged from O'Shea's shuttling between Kilmainham and Westminster. Gladstone agreed to introduce legislation to remedy the defects of his Land Act insofar as it applied to those in arrears. Lessees were left to their own remedies. No Liberal government would intervene legislatively in an agreement between two contracting parties.

For his part Parnell agreed to do his utmost to end the anarchy prevailing in rural Ireland. This meant having recourse to the shadowy P. J. Sheridan, a Land League organizer and Fenian much sought after by the Royal Irish Constabulary. Sheridan, who travelled the country during the Land War disguised as a Roman Catholic priest with the unimaginative name of 'Father Murphy', was suspected of having worked the taps on more than his share of the carnage in the countryside. The fact that he was now expected to turn them off seemed to confirm to many (including William Forster) that he had been the inspiration for much of the mob violence. This unofficial concordat was too much for Forster, who resigned as Irish chief secretary. It was too much for many of Parnell's supporters as well, but for entirely different reasons. The concessions made by the Irish leader went too far for his more extreme allies. It was only the intervention of an entirely new group of ultra-nationalist conspirators that forestalled a potential confrontation between Parnell and a substantial cohort of his supporters.

On 6 May 1882 the Invincibles announced themselves to the wider world with a sickening act of savagery.

William Forster's replacement as chief secretary was Lord Frederick Cavendish, the forty-five-year-old brother of Lord Hartington, leader of the conservative or 'Whig' wing of the Liberal Party. The popular Cavendish was also husband of Gladstone's favourite niece, Lucy Cavendish, and a protégé of the Grand Old Man. He was an 'amiable, high-minded,

and industrious' public servant who had conquered a speech impediment while carving out a career for himself in politics.[8] Barely installed for a day in Dublin Castle, and having just met his vastly experienced under-secretary for Ireland, Thomas H. Burke, he noticed the latter strolling in Phoenix Park as he travelled in his carriage for his first evening in the chief secretary's residence. Burke, whose capable but firm hand during the Land War had not endeared him to Irish agrarian activists, had chosen to walk along Chesterfield Avenue to his own residence, unaccompanied by any police escort. When Burke politely declined the offer of a lift from the chief secretary, Cavendish chose to alight from his carriage and accompany his new colleague on his stroll. It proved to be a fatally unwise decision and ensured that the names of the two men have been inextricably linked for almost a century and a half.

The Invincibles, a small, extremist splinter group within the wider Fenian movement – of which figures like Patrick Egan and P. J. Sheridan were suspected of being founder members – had already failed, on several occasions, to assassinate William Forster. On 6 May 1882 they were intent on 'redeeming' themselves by ending Burke's life. Using imported surgical knives, they achieved an even deadlier outcome than they had anticipated. When the murderous attack on Burke began, within sight of the Viceregal Lodge (now Áras an Úachtaráin, the home of the Irish President), Cavendish intervened in defence of his colleague and was butchered along with the under-secretary. The Invincibles discovered only later that they had hacked to death the newly appointed chief secretary as well as his deputy. It took almost a year, and some resourceful manipulation by Superintendent John Mallon, to secure convictions against the killers, five of whom were hanged in May/June 1883. When Mallon's investigation began to bear fruit in early 1883, and a series of arrests were made, Patrick Egan* and P. J. Sheridan discovered that they had urgent business elsewhere. Both fled to the USA.

Parnell, although condemning the slaughter in Phoenix Park, also vigorously opposed the response of the Liberal government, a punitive Crimes Act that went beyond the scope of the Protection of Person and Property Act of 1881. In resisting this latest bout of coercion, the Irish Party leader was able to recoup some of the cachet he had lost in acquiescing to the terms of the 'Kilmainham Treaty' described by the Invincible P. J. Tynan, whose support Parnell could safely do without, as 'a most cowardly and disgraceful surrender to the enemy'.[9] The uneasy coalition that was the Irish Parliamentary Party remained intact and on course. But on course for what exactly?

This quickly became apparent when the Irish National League (INL) replaced the Land League and became the rallying force for moderate Irish nationalists. The INL was, essentially, an administrative extension of the hierarchical and centrally controlled Irish Parliamentary Party, rather than a grassroots organization like the Land League. Parnell pulled the strings, with the compliance of a small cadre of lieutenants (William O'Brien, Justin McCarthy, Timothy Harrington, John Dillon, Tim Healy and Thomas Sexton), although not all his subalterns –

*It has been suggested by Mallon's biographer, Donal McCracken, that Egan was enabled to escape the clutches of the Dublin Metropolitan Police (DMP) because he was tipped off by Mallon himself, to whom he had been supplying information. Resident Magistrate William Henry Joyce, who supplied two tons of files to *The Times* for use against the Parnellites in the Special Commission, also believed that Egan was 'one of Mallon's contact men'.

most notably the morose John Dillon and the excitable Tim Healy – were slavishly enamoured of their autocratic leader.

Parnell's opportunity to advance the cause of Home Rule came with the fall of the Liberal government in June 1885. Because of a major overhaul of constituency boundaries arising from the Reform Act of 1884, a general election could not be held until November that year. A Tory caretaker administration, under the 3rd Marquess of Salisbury, took office. The 4th Earl of Carnarvon, that precious rarity, a Tory politician with an open mind on Irish Home Rule, was appointed Lord Lieutenant. Carnarvon's 'belief in self-government and imperial federalism',[10] gleaned from his experiences as Colonial Secretary (1866–7 and 1874–8), meant that his views were well in advance of those of his irreconcilably unionist cabinet colleagues. However, it suited Salisbury to appoint as viceroy a known Hibernophile who would distance himself from the coercive policies of his Liberal predecessor, Earl Spencer, and who might even be capable of securing Parnell's support for the Tories in the coming general election.

Carnarvon and Parnell met secretly in London in August 1885. Subsequent accounts of the tenor of the meeting differed, but Parnell was sufficiently encouraged by what he heard from the viceroy to recommend to Irish voters in Britain that they support the Tories in the November general election. The outcome of that poll saw the Irish Parliamentary Party in an enviable position. Having won eighty-six seats (an increase of twenty-three over their 1880 election result), Parnell could put either the Liberals or the Tories into power. Persevering with the logic of his electoral support for the Conservatives, and banking (wrongly, as it transpired) on Carnarvon's influence within the cabinet, he opted to put Salisbury into 10 Downing Street. However, it soon became apparent that the Master of Hatfield did not share Carnarvon's broadmindedness when it came to Irish devolution. Coincidental with Parnell's growing disenchantment with the Tories was Gladstone's Damascene conversion to Home Rule. This began to bubble upwards in late 1885 with hints of a change of heart from his son Herbert. Then the Grand Old Man himself confirmed the *bouleversement*. Courtesy of the votes of eighty-six Irish MPs, he duly became Prime Minister again on 1 February 1886. By 8 April he had introduced the Government of Ireland Bill, offering limited devolution to Ireland.

The Home Rule Bill, as it was known colloquially, aroused vituperative and sanguinary opposition among Ulster Protestants, caused near apoplexy among the ranks of the Whig section of Gladstone's party and, perhaps more surprisingly, also incurred the wrath of a significant element of the radical wing of the Liberals. When Gladstone finally revealed the specifics of the legislation to the cabinet in early April, Joseph Chamberlain, president of the Local Government Board, resigned from his ministerial position and, from the backbenches, led the Liberal Party's radical wing in opposition to the proposals. The legislation failed in June in the House of Commons by thirty votes, with ninety-three Liberals going through the 'No' lobby and helping a united Tory party bring down the curtain on Gladstone's third excursion on the Treasury benches.

In the subsequent general election, the second within six months, Salisbury was returned to power with a majority of 116 seats.* With Home Rule not even in the proximity of the backburner, and with the economic depression of the 1870s reasserting its grip on Irish agriculture, militant agrarian unrest sparked back into life. Parnell went into internal exile with Katharine O'Shea in Eltham, while the so-called 'Plan of Campaign' visited a renewed version of Land War anarchy on rural Ireland. The Tories, determined to eradicate even the aftertaste of Home Rule and stamp out the mayhem being unleashed by the inheritors of the defunct Land League, prepared to flex their coercive muscles.

Then *The Times* intervened. Appalled at the Home Rule 'near miss' – a notion that ignored the reality that, even if Gladstone's bill

*When the new informal grouping of ex-Liberals, known as Liberal Unionists, was added to the Tory total.

had emerged unscathed from the Commons, it would have been made to walk the plank in the Tory-dominated House of Lords – the newspaper made common cause with the Conservative Party defenders of empire. In a thirty-year journey, *The Times*, owned by the Walter family, had traced an arc from outspoken criticism of government (e.g. the follies of the Crimean War) to largely unqualified support for establishment policies.

Acting as Sancho Panza to the Tory party's Don Quixote, no windmill was safe as the 'newspaper of record' threw in its lot with Salisbury's government in a rancorous propaganda war against Ireland.

2

BOMBING BRITAIN

'There is yet another party, which may be called the Dynamite faction ... they content themselves by making war upon society in general, and inciting dupes to commit crimes which they would never have thought of themselves.'[1]

Philip H. Bagenal, *The American Irish and their Influence on Irish Politics* (1882)

'... the curtain was rung up, and throwing aside the mask forever, I stepped into the witness box and came out in my true colours, as an Englishman, proud of his country, and in no sense ashamed of his record in her service.'[2]

Major Henri Le Caron, *Twenty-Five Years in the Secret Service* (1895)

New Law Courts, London, 5 February 1889: the Special Commission on Parnellism and Crime

It was day forty-four of testimony before the *Times* Commission. The previous forty-three days had been an onslaught of melodrama, monotony, spectacle and verbiage. No one was aware of it at the time, but there were still eighty-four days to go. During that time there would be an abundance of supplementary tedium, alongside moments of genuine drama. This day would offer a masterclass in the latter. It was to be the first day of evidence from a surprise witness that *The Times* hoped would definitively link Charles Stewart Parnell and his associates with Irish-American terrorism and with the bombers who had plagued England and Scotland.

Waiting to testify on that cold February morning, in front of interested parties, reporters and the few onlookers whose curiosity had not been stifled by the sustained banality of the proceedings, was the most successful British agent to have penetrated the upper reaches of Irish-American radicalism. His success was easily quantifiable, because he was still alive. He had spied on the wider Fenian movement for more than twenty years and lived to tell his tale to the Special Commission on Parnellism and Crime.

This enterprising British spy had begun life as the humble Thomas Beach from Colchester, one of the thirteen children of a rate collector. He had stolen his sister's collection of pennies (destined for the far more deserving religious missions of Africa) to enable him to escape England. The pennies got him as far as Paris. There he remained for a short while before making for his intended destination, the USA. He had been known as Henri Le Caron, a pseudo-Frenchman, for most of the last three decades.

Now, as the usual daily participants gathered for another session exploring the putative crimes of the Irish Parliamentary Party, Beach/Le Caron waited for the attorney general, Sir Richard Webster, to unpack more than two decades of invaluable espionage (from the British point of view) or twenty-one years of abject betrayal (from the Irish-American perspective). Already in his late fifties, Le Caron presented a dapper figure to the audience in the New Law Courts, and to the world at large. His face had about it a pinched asceticism. The Special Commission portraits by resident artist Sydney Prior Hall depict a figure who was reminiscent of the images created by Sidney Paget of the entirely fictional, but equally compelling, Sherlock Holmes. Unlike Arthur Conan Doyle's clean-shaven detective hero, however, Le Caron sported a neat but substantial handlebar moustache. He was 'short and slightish in build; erect – like a soldier – and imperturbably cool', with 'a lofty forehead, and smallish alert eyes'.[3] The policeman who would later become his personal bodyguard, Kerry-born CID Inspector John Sweeney, described them as 'ferret eyes'.[4] He would need to keep his alertness on tap over the next five days, given the inquisition he was about to face. The attorney general, who would take him through two and a half days of direct evidence, posed no threat. But it would be a different story entirely when Parnell's counsel, the unnerving Sir Charles Russell, began to cross-examine.

Asked to identify himself as he stepped into the witness box, he appeared to inform the tribunal that his baptismal name was 'Thomas Willis Beach'. Speaking confidently, 'he paused at each of his three names, pronouncing them with slow, distinct emphasis, and nodding his head as if to punctuate them' according to *Daily News* reporter John MacDonald.[5] His pronunciation was obviously not slow or distinct enough, because the recording stenographer had misheard. His correct name was Thomas Billis Beach.*

Beach would spend the next two and a half days divulging some of the secrets accumulated in more than two decades of his infiltration of Fenianism in the USA. He also exposed leading Irish-American republicans and their Irish partners – what he described as 'the murderous alliance'[6] – to undesirable publicity. Assuming that he was a credible witness, the membership of this lethal conspiracy included Charles Stewart Parnell, whom 'Le Caron' had met in the House of Commons in 1881. The Irish Party leader had, according to Beach, adopted an extremist attitude at that meeting, referring to the financial aid coming from the USA as 'the sinews of war'.[7]

After a further two and a half days of cross-examination from Russell, Beach (Russell stoutly refused to use his assumed name of Le Caron) would trip 'lightly, smilingly out of the witness box'[8] into months of concealment from men who would have delighted at the opportunity to skewer him for his 'treachery'. He chose not to accept the assurance of the Chicago Clan member John T. McEnnis (an acolyte of Alexander Sullivan), that 'it is my deliberate conviction that Le Caron could come back to Chicago

*His full name has often appeared as Thomas Miller Beach.

and live here, and never a hand would be lifted against him'.[9] Those same hopeful assassins would have been pleased when, five years after his dramatic and unexpected appearance at the Special Commission, still in hiding from the agents of Clan na Gael and the IRB, he was killed, not by an assassin's bullet, but by peritonitis brought on by a ruptured appendix.

Splits, crevices and Sayre's law

> 'A bird never flew on one wing.'
>
> Scottish-Irish proverb

> 'One dollar for bread, nine dollars for lead.'
>
> Clan na Gael slogan

By the 1860s, 1.6 million people of Irish birth lived in the United States of America. During that decade, Irish-America became the second wing of Irish radical nationalism.

It was the talented, bibulous Irish writer Brendan Behan – himself a member of the IRA as a teenager in the late 1930s – who piquantly observed that the first item on the agenda of any Irish radical movement was 'the split'. The Irish Republican Brotherhood (IRB), in both its American and its Irish incarnations, conformed elegantly to Behan's maxim. Volatile egos, as much as ideological differences, provoked the opening of deep, and potentially homicidal, fissures in the organization on both sides of the Atlantic. In the USA the sundered elements of the Fenian Brotherhood vied with each other to invade Canada, capture Britain's premier colony and ransom it back to the UK government in return for Irish independence. In Ireland, the divisive figure of James Stephens – an IRB founder and paranoid narcissist who demanded complete personal fealty – guaranteed a semi-permanent state of disunion between his loyalists and the more democratically inclined acolytes of the organization's Supreme Council. In the wake of the failed Fenian rebellion of

1867, the level of Irish republican discord and internecine bitterness thoroughly validated Sayre's law.* This axiom holds that, 'In any dispute the intensity of feeling is inversely proportional to the value of the issues at stake.' In other words, the less important the conflict, the greater the levels of mutual antagonism.

Into this fractious environment came a new organization, Clan na Gael. The name translated literally as 'the family of the Irish', but in the English language it went by the name of the United Brotherhood. In the early history of the Clan the use of the word 'family' would have been appropriate only had it been preceded by the adjective 'dysfunctional'. It was founded in 1867 on the birthday (20 June) of the Irish patriot and leader of the 'men of 1798' (the United Irishmen), Theobald Wolfe Tone. There were times when Tone, had he been alive, would not have been flattered by the intended homage.

By the middle of the 1870s the Clan claimed a membership of 11,000. One of the new organization's aims was to reconnect the divided strands of Fenianism. Instead, while coming to dominate Irish-American militant nationalism, it would anticipate Behan's maxim and split into two warring factions of its own.

While a divided Irish-American republican movement might, on the face of it, operate to the benefit of their opponents in the British intelligence services, the level of animosity between the various factions forced British spymasters to cultivate assets in each, often with the aid of the American private detective agency founded in 1850 by Glasgow-born Allan Pinkerton. While the likes of Le Caron had his uses, this did not extend much further than the confines of the 'Triangle' faction of Clan na Gael mostly centred on Chicago and dominated by Alexander Sullivan and Kentucky-based Michael Boland.

The Clan was established along Masonic lines, right down to a set of hand gestures ('placing the right hand carelessly under the

*Named after the sage Wallace Stanley Sayre (1905–1972), US political scientist and professor at Columbia University.

left breast of the vest') designed to facilitate recognition of fellow initiates. This 'General Hailing Sign of Recognition' was adopted in 1876, when it was discovered that the previous gesture – the passing of the hand down the cheek – was already being used by the Ancient Order of Hibernians and by two Massachusetts detectives 'now operating against that order'.[10] The Clan also boasted a code of secrecy that was captured in the oath to be taken (while blindfolded) by each new member. This document concluded with the words, 'Once a member of this order you must stand by its watch words of secrecy, obedience and love.'[11] Sadly, however, the inductee was unlikely to witness very much of the promised affection. The Clan also adopted a simple 'letter shift' cipher code that can hardly have been devised with the intention of hoodwinking anyone above the age of six. Thus the 'United Brotherhood' (UB) became the 'VC', 'Ireland' was represented as the ludicrous and infinitely penetrable 'JSFMBOE', and the Republican Brotherhood became the 'SC'.

Despite these fatuous rituals, codes and practices, by the mid-1870s the Clan had established itself as the most influential Irish nationalist body in the USA, capable of funding extremist anti-British undertakings and of bankrolling the IRB. Within the Clan itself the main motive force was one of the pivotal figures of late nineteenth- and early twentieth-century militant Irish nationalism, the New York-based journalist John Devoy, who at one point in his career edited the *New York Herald*. Devoy, born in 1842, had joined the IRB in his early twenties (after a brief spell in the French Foreign Legion) and had been given the task of recruiting into the organization Irish soldiers serving in the British Army. He also played a part in the 'springing' of IRB leader James Stephens from prison in November 1865. In 1867 Devoy was sentenced to fifteen years' imprisonment with hard labour for his Fenian activities. The harsh regime he experienced in the British prison system permanently damaged his eyesight. In 1871 he, along with several other Fenian prisoners, including the mercurial Jeremiah O'Donovan Rossa, was released on condition that he agree to terms of exile from Ireland equivalent to the unelapsed duration of his original sentence. In New York, Devoy joined the relatively newly established Clan na Gael and, as a member of its Revolutionary Directory, acquired the status of Irish republican 'royalty' in 1876, when he plotted the spectacular escape of six Fenian prisoners from Fremantle Prison in Western Australia, on board the American schooner *Catalpa*.

Devoy resigned from the Clan when he established the New York-based *Irish Nation* newspaper in 1881. Not long after the *Irish Nation* folded in 1885 (the paper was bankrupted by a crippling libel suit), he became embroiled in a vendetta with the Chicago-based troika, 'The Triangle', led by Alexander Sullivan, that had taken control of the Clan in his absence. This feud culminated in the 1889 murder of one of Devoy's supporters in Chicago, Dr Patrick Cronin, as the internecine warfare of the Clan spilled over into violence. Sullivan, a paranoid egotist with a 'taste for high Western boots and pearl-handled pistols',[12] was questioned about Cronin's murder but was released for lack of evidence. Under the financially corrupt leadership of Sullivan and his acolyte Michael Boland – there were credible allegations of high-level embezzlement of organizational funds – the Clan 'became very much an American political machine, securing jobs for supporters and amassing power and prestige for Sullivan'.[13]

However, it was the Clan's fractious relationship with Jeremiah O'Donovan Rossa that was central to the sporadic bombing campaign in Britain in the first half of the 1880s, and which was one of the factors that spawned the establishment conspiracy to subvert Irish constitutional politics.

Rossa, whose involvement with the Clan waxed and waned, after a serious brush with alcoholism and several failed attempts to provide for himself and his family, found his *métier* when he established his idiosyncratic newspaper, *The United Irishman*. The newspaper was described by Devoy as 'the queerest Irish paper ever published. It was a purely personal organ, giving his own views on everything.'[14] Each edition (it was sustained by subscriptions, referred to by Rossa as 'rent' – his subscribers being his 'tenants') largely consisted of a series of essays by Rossa himself.

Through the pages of the *United Irishman* and his additional columns for the main New York Irish nationalist newspaper, Patrick Ford's *Irish World*, Rossa espoused the cause of retribution through 'Fenian fire' – 'the light that must blaze before we can see Ireland's freedom'.[15] A dynamite campaign aimed at targets in Britain was to be underwritten by a 'Skirmishing Fund' raised by contributions from like-minded Irish-Americans. 'You must strike England to her knees,' Rossa wrote in the *Irish World* in 1876, 'before she lets go her hold, and it is to strike her in this manner the skirmishing fund is started'.[16] The *Irish World* itself became banker to the fund in 1876 and Patrick Ford was both zealous and jealous in his supervision of the monies collected from ardent Irish nationalists. With the normalization of what amounted to terrorist tactics, Irish-American republicans crossed a significant Rubicon. While they might convince themselves that their targets were made of bricks and mortar and that their objectives were to instil terror and give pause to the British government in its dealings with militant Irish agrarianists, republican bombs were no more selective in the casualties they inflicted in the 1880s than they were a century later. British civilians would inevitably become collateral damage in this new version of Irish revolutionary warfare. Modern science, in the form of dynamite, would come to the aid of outmatched Irish militants. As the Irish-American journalist and senior Clan member John Finerty observed, 'in this struggle, this vendetta, which England has now distinctly challenged, SCIENCE … must match itself against STRENGTH … in this our battle for vengeance and for liberty, one skilled scientist is worth an army'.[17]

While Devoy had no difficulty with the notion of an Irish-American bombing campaign in England, he deprecated the fact that Rossa consistently broke cover, gleefully announced his bloodthirsty intentions and revelled in the successes of his adherents. On at least one occasion Rossa claimed credit for an accidental explosion in which his agents played no role whatsoever.* He also claimed, on hearing that Queen Victoria had slipped and hurt her foot on a Windsor Castle staircase, that one of his agents had soaped the stairs![18]

Rossa's erratic behaviour, his over-reliance on alcohol, his impatience with what he saw as Clan posturing and inaction and his egocentric grandstanding would ultimately result in a Devoy/Clan takeover of the Skirmishing Fund in March 1877 and Rossa's expulsion from the Clan. By 1878 the 'Skirmishing Fund' became the much blander-sounding and less menacing 'National Fund'. However, instead of assuming total control of the Irish-American bombing campaign initiated by Rossa in 1881, the Clan, slow to take decisive action and somewhat reluctant to unleash its own dynamitards, was forced to take a back seat to Rossa and his loyalists (the United Irishmen of America)** as the impulsive radical unleashed his own private army of 'skirmishers' in a series of attacks on targets in Britain.

Rossa proved to be rather more than a sottish extremist romantic talking the revolutionary talk but unwilling to walk the insurgent walk. He announced that he had engaged the services of a Russian explosives expert with the persuasive name of 'Mezzeroff' (he turned out to be a New York liquor salesman named Richard Rogers, rather than a fearsome Russian anarchist)[19] and he established the Mansonitor Manufacturing and Experimental Chemical Company. This was responsible for the 'Brooklyn Dynamite School'. There, willing students paid $30 for a month-long initiation into bomb-making. They could then volunteer to travel to the UK and put their newly acquired skills to the test, which some later did. A number of those, in turn, recruited local trainees in Britain, and assembled bombs in ad

*On board the British HMS *Doterel*, which sank in 1880 in the Straits of Magellan with the loss of 145 lives.

**Rossa, whose expulsion from the Clan followed the establishment of the rival United Irishmen of America faction, ultimately contrived to fall out even with this organization, although it was fashioned in his image and likeness.

hoc 'factories' (bedrooms, bathrooms and kitchens) using readily accessible ingredients in combination with imported American explosive material. Rossa took great pleasure in reflecting that the huge security advantages of the British state (which included a large standing army) could be nullified by a determined cadre of semi-skilled Irish-American bombers operating in conditions of strict secrecy. The Clan was ultimately forced to play 'catch-up' with their blowhard maverick rival. 'Dynamite! Dynamite! Let every Irishman and Irishwoman put a bit of it in their pocket and become a walking revolution,'[20] Rossa declaimed in the *United Irishman*. His bellicosity, barely tolerated or outrightly deplored within Clan na Gael's New York leadership, was also deprecated by the leadership of the IRB, which distanced itself from the campaign as soon as it began. James Stephens refused to acknowledge the skirmishers as genuine Fenians. John O'Leary, based in Paris, reacted with horrified astonishment to Rossa's well-aired pronouncements, which he described as 'desperate nonsense'.[21]

Irish-America's tendency towards mere bluff and bluster came to an explosive end on 14 January 1881. Scepticism, generally morphing into outright cynicism, surrounded the capacity of Irish-American militants to match their actions to their bloodthirsty pronouncements. The *New York Times* captured the mood perfectly in an editorial, accusing Rossa and his acolytes of being 'lazy patriots'. 'Undoubtedly,' the newspaper opined, in a piece dripping with self-righteous sarcasm, 'they hate England and would like to produce an occasional inexpensive explosion, whereby a few Englishmen might be killed, but with whiskey and cigars at their present price, they have too much sense to spend their money in such unprofitable work.'[22]

As it transpired, the *New York Times* could not have been more wrong. Aided by a stifling fog, in January 1881 Rossa's dynamite missionaries set off an explosive device at a military barracks in Salford, near Manchester. This action was also the most tragic of the campaign in that it cost seven-year-old Richard Clarke his young life. Initial reports, and a modicum of wishful thinking, suggested that the explosion had been caused by a faulty gas main. However, the Salford Chief Constable was in no doubt about the source of the blast, and that it was 'likely to be repeated in this or similar districts where it is known that numbers of so-called Fenians, Land Leaguers, Home Rulers and the like reside'.[23] The choice of Salford as the first target of Rossa's skirmishers was no coincidence either. Fourteen years before, Allen, Larkin and O'Brien had been hanged on the walls of the town's jail. Rossa was a firm believer in symbolism as well as savage bombast. Neither was he in the least perturbed at the possibility of a violent British reaction against any of the 800,000 or so Irish inhabitants of England, Wales and Scotland. Indeed, he hoped for such an antagonistic response as a way of radicalizing the Irish in Britain. After the Salford operation, Rossa became 'Jeremiah O'Dynamite' among his peers. There is a certain irony in the nickname, as Rossa's 'skirmishers' did not have access to dynamite and were still using gunpowder. The invention of dynamite and the development of explosive technology had made political terrorism less of a hit and miss affair. It was no longer essential for a terrorist bomber to get close to a target, light a short fuse, hurl, hope and then attempt a getaway. Improvised explosive devices could now be planted in advance and primed to detonate without the attentions of the bomber. Rossa's acolytes, however, by and large operated at a more primitive level and were just as likely to be apprehended 'red-handed', blow themselves up or be caught after their makeshift bombs – dubbed 'infernal machines' by the Victorian press – exploded.

Ironically, one of the Clan members most opposed to the activities of the skirmishers was William Mackey Lomasney, who was living in Paris at the outset of Rossa's campaign. There he met, among others, the leader of the Irish Parliamentary Party, Charles Stewart Parnell, who, political chameleon that he was, managed to convince the Detroit bookseller that 'he means to go as far as we do in pushing the business'.[24] Lomasney's opposition to the activities of the skirmishers was not based on principle. He was more concerned with the quality of their work, which he deemed 'farcical'[25] and a 'burlesque'. 'The amount of folly and bungling,' he wrote to Devoy, 'in connection with these events is simply disgraceful.'[26]

Clan na Gael did not react well to the Salford bomb, its condemnation having as much to do with antagonism towards its instigator as with any scruples about damaging British property or endangering British lives. Devoy's Clan was apparently powerless to control Rossa's destructive tendencies, and its leadership chafed at his smug bravado.

The Clan would soon imitate Rossa's disastrous tactics. Lomasney, while deriding the Salford explosion in his letter to Devoy from Paris, was himself in Europe to identify potential British targets for a Clan bombing campaign.[27] He also had a generous 'float' of more than $5,000 to smuggle arms into Ireland and to stockpile explosives in Britain. The skirmishers may have stolen a march on Devoy, but the Clan (under new Chicago management shortly after the commencement of the 'skirmishing' campaign) had no intention of allowing itself to be outshone for long by the garrulous and vainglorious Rossa. However, until the Clan could put a dynamite strategy in place, the 'skirmishers' had the field to themselves.

A failed April 1881 attack on London's Mansion House was followed by an underwhelming assault on Chester Barracks, on 5 May, which caused minimal damage. The under-resourced skirmishers, obliged to resort to crude and ineffective improvisation, planted another unimpressive device in the main doorway of Liverpool Police Barracks on 16 May and followed that up three weeks later with a botched operation aimed at Liverpool Town Hall.

Despite the decidedly mixed results of this first wave of bombings, it had the effect of animating the Clan's grass roots. At an August 1881 convention, in the absence of Devoy, who was toiling to establish the *Irish Nation*, the autocratic Chicago-based warlord Alexander Sullivan assumed the presidency of the organization. He did so amid a wave of delegate enthusiasm for the allocation of much of the Clan's substantial resources towards continuing the campaign begun by the under-funded 'skirmishers'. Sullivan, when the IRB refused to row in behind the American-inspired bombing campaign, cut off that organization's financial support from the USA. Devoy, who was 'daggers drawn' with Sullivan for most of the latter's involvement in Irish affairs, described the Chicago lawyer as 'the cross-born offspring of an English cad, born in a British camp, nursed in a British barracks with a Union Jack flying over it, fed on British rations and educated in British schools. There is nothing Irish about him except his name which does not properly belong to him.'[28] Sullivan was not, however, a good person to have as an enemy. He had burned down his own shoe shop in 1868 in order to collect the insurance money and, eight years later, killed the principal at the school where his wife worked 'for questioning her honour'.[29]

Sullivan, in copper-fastening his control of the organization, put the Clan on a war footing. Patrick Ford initiated an 'Emergency Fund' in the *Irish World* to defray the cost of the Clan's commitment to a dynamite crusade against prominent British targets. The new fund, however, was nowhere near as well-subscribed as its infamous predecessor, suggesting that the appetite of Irish-America for dynamite – once the reality of the bombing campaign had replaced empty but satisfying rhetoric – was, temporarily at least, on the wane.

However, despite Sullivan's apparent hawkishness, there then followed a hiatus of almost eighteen months* during which threats and posturing supplanted action. While the punitive new 1882 coercion bill, introduced in the wake of the Phoenix Park murders, led to increased Irish-American calls for explosive retribution, it was not until five months after the passage of the Prevention of Crimes (Ireland) Act that the bombing campaign resumed

*Apart from an ineffective device placed on railings adjacent to the Mansion House in London on 12 May 1882.

in earnest in January 1883. However, the three devices set off in Glasgow on 20 January – fourteen people were injured and one of the devices caused a severe power cut across the city – were, once again, the work of graduates from Rossa's Dynamite School, led by one of its most resourceful alumni, Thomas J. Mooney (aka James Moorehead). Eight weeks later the skirmishers returned to London and unleashed two more devices in Playhouse Yard, the headquarters of *The Times* newspaper, and at the offices of the Local Government Board in Whitehall. The latter blast, which went off at 9 p.m., was powerful enough to shake the nearby House of Commons. Both explosions were seen as a form of retaliation for the trials of the Invincibles, then taking place in Dublin. The Clan, many of whose ordinary members supported Rossa's campaign and contributed significant sums for the purchase of explosives, was in danger of being eclipsed by the activism of its idiosyncratic rival. Alexander Sullivan, anxious to deliver on his bellicose rhetoric of August 1881, and aware of murmurings of discontent within the wider Clan at the organization's perceived lack of aggression, was working on a plan for a sustained assault on some prominent English landmarks. Unfortunately, one of the men with whom he chose to share the details of these plans was his fervent acolyte, the French-born Braidwood, Illinois physician* Henri Le Caron.

Le Caron's career as one of Britain's most important nineteenth-century intelligence assets had begun in 1866. A veteran of the American Civil War, he had befriended the former Union General John O'Neill, a thoroughgoing Fenian and the military planner behind Irish republican designs on Canada. O'Neill, unaware that he was associating with the English patriot Thomas Billis Beach – rather than a French republican sympathizer –

*This is how Beach/Le Caron described himself in his evidence to the Special Commission (the Special Commission, Report of the proceedings before the Commissioners appointed by the Act, vol. 2, 146). However, he has also been described as a dentist and as an apothecary/chemist.

informed Le Caron of his plans. These were then shared in a series of letters with Beach's father, who, through his local MP, apprised the Home Office of his son's potential as an informant. Beach's services were enlisted on a return visit to England. He was to be 'handled' by the Irish-born Home Office bureaucrat Robert Anderson. Thus began an association that lasted more than twenty years and produced reams of invaluable intelligence for the British government, including the betrayal of one of the Fenian invasions of Canada,* in which, as an imaginative cover, Beach/Le Caron himself participated. In his Special Commission evidence, he gloated that, through his efforts, the invasions that had taken place in 1866 and again in 1870 had both been 'lamentable failures'.[30]

In the 1870s Le Caron moved on to membership of Clan na Gael, and by the end of that decade he had slipped effortlessly into the inner cabal of Alexander Sullivan, as the shady Chicago lawyer tightened his grip on the organization, before his seizure of power as president in August 1881. For almost a decade Le Caron – who was being paid up to $1,200 a year by Britain for the risks he was taking – played cipher to Sullivan's ruthless belligerence. He covered his tracks creatively by registering as an enthusiastic supporter of a Clan bombing campaign. Sullivan brooked no opposition to his hegemonic management of the Clan and maintained his dominance of the secretive body for many years, with the connivance of Le Caron. In his memoir, *Evening Memories*, the *United Ireland* editor William O'Brien MP encapsulated the aura of danger and threat that surrounded Sullivan. O'Brien described him as 'strong-browed and strong-jawed about whose bloodless lips and sharp white teeth there played a certain pitilessness which all his softness of voice and

*Yet another invasion (there were five in all) was betrayed by an Irish-American Civil War officer, General Charles Carroll Tevis – of whom more anon – a high-level Foreign Office spy within the Fenian Brotherhood for more than twenty years.

studious airs of deference could not change to anything but cold self-control'.[31]

One of Le Caron's tasks as a high-level Clan representative was to liaise with Patrick Egan in Paris in the spring of 1881. During that European visit, Beach/Le Caron also met Parnell in the House of Commons. The precise nature of their conversation would be raked over, and disputed, at the *Times* Commission in February 1889. There is, however, no doubt whatever about the fate of any confidential information on the Clan's entry into the bombing war, imparted by Alexander Sullivan to Le Caron. Anything of note was communicated to Robert Anderson at the Home Office in London. This included a missive at the end of 1882 warning Anderson, without any specifics, that the Clan, trailing a distant second in the wake of Rossa's bombers up to that point, was about to unleash its own bombs on selected and vulnerable British targets.

The Clan's debut – masterminded by the flamboyant Irish-American physician Dr Thomas Gallagher (who affected a gold-topped cane and a Custer-like mane of hair) and which included a young Tom Clarke, later one of the signatories of the 1916 Proclamation – was a dismal failure and resulted in the capture of several conspirators. Gallagher, Clarke and three other dynamiters were sentenced to life imprisonment after one of the members of the team, William Lynch, testified against his comrades. According to the Special Irish Branch detective Sergeant Patrick McIntyre, in a series of revealing reminiscences* in *Reynolds's Newspaper*, this was the only dynamite conspiracy that was not 'got up' by *agents provocateurs*.[32] McIntyre's 1895 newspaper memoir followed the publication in 1894 of *The Reminiscences of Chief-Inspector Littlechild*. John George Littlechild, a Special Irish Branch colleague of McIntyre, makes no such allegations

*But not *entirely* trustworthy, as he had an axe to grind. McIntyre had been demoted over an apparently trivial matter (not reporting back to Scotland Yard when completing a job a day early) and resigned from the force.

of widespread official complicity in dynamite conspiracies.[33] The same is true of a later memoir (1904) by Inspector John Sweeney.

The Clan was finally 'blooded' on 30 October 1883, when two devices exploded in London Underground tunnels near today's Paddington and Charing Cross stations. The devices had been thrown from moving trains by two (still unidentified) Clan bombers. The bombs caused a wave of panic and, in the case of the Praed Street/Paddington bomb, injured seventy-two commuters, many of whom received serious burns. Afterwards, the effectiveness of the bombers' actions could be gauged by the fact that thousands of Londoners avoided using the Underground for a prolonged period.

The Clan launched another successful assault, this one on a luggage cloakroom at Victoria station, on 25 February 1884. The apparent inability of the police to interdict supplies of dynamite entering the country or to capture those responsible for the atrocities (except for the accused at the Gallagher/Clarke trial) ratcheted up the sense of threat and panic among Londoners in particular. Tensions were not eased when, on 30 May 1884, the Clan set off two bombs in St James's Square near Pall Mall. One of the targets was the Junior Carlton, a popular venue for Tory MPs, where twelve people were injured by an enormous blast that seriously damaged the building. The date of the Junior Carlton attack was significant. It took place the morning after the Epsom Derby. The bomber, Philadelphian Luke Dillon, son of Great Famine emigrants, had high hopes that his device would kill or injure inebriated Tory politicians recovering from their post-Derby excesses. Dillon was one of the few Irish-American bombers known to have safely made the return journey from Britain to the USA. He 'ascribed his survival on "active service" to the fact that he always worked alone while wearing a belt of explosives which he was prepared to detonate with his ever-present cigar if he faced capture'.[34]

A far more significant coup that day, however, was the bomb that tore through the offices of the Special Irish Branch in Scotland Yard and damaged the adjacent public house, The Rising Sun. Had the bomb gone off fifteen minutes earlier it might have killed the Kerry-born Met detective John Sweeney, who had just stepped out of the office. 'The very desk at which I had been working was blown to pieces,' Sweeney wrote in his memoir.[35] The Rising Sun's landlord, imaginative salesman that he was, gathered up the broken glass from the windows of his establishment and sold these celebrity shards as souvenirs. He also charged threepence per head for the privilege of viewing the wreckage of 'the very headquarters of authority'.[36] The explosion destroyed most of the records on their adversaries that the Branch had been painstakingly accumulating. This audacious attack against the very force that had failed, for the moment at least, to terminate the Clan's morale-sapping campaign, did little to enhance the reputation of the plain-clothes section of London's finest. More damaging to the Clan's cause than anything inflicted by the Met was the loss of William Mackey Lomasney and his accomplices in the abortive attempt to blow up London Bridge in December 1884. After that reverse, which was followed by several other arrests and trials, the Clan's campaign began to falter.

It did not, however, go out with a whimper.

The 24th of January 1885 has gone down in British policing history as 'Dynamite Saturday', and as a 'red letter day for the revolutionaries'.[37] The coup, which was the work of a Philadelphia-based unit, seemingly uncontaminated by *agents provocateurs*, took the Home Office secret service completely by surprise.[38] The Clan's ambitious targets on that day were the Tower of London, the House of Commons and the Westminster Crypt. All were successfully breached. In the case of the Tower, James Gilbert Cunningham, recently arrived from the USA, posed as a tourist and gained entry to the highly vulnerable and much visited attraction. He wore a voluminous overcoat, large enough to conceal a bomb. This he placed unobtrusively behind a gun carriage after slipping away from a guided tour. The device exploded prematurely, shortly after Cunningham had rejoined the tour, and injured sixteen people. Dozens of tourists were successfully evacuated before a fire took hold in the aftermath of the explosion. No one, however, was allowed to leave the precincts of the Tower. Orders had been issued* that exit gates were to be locked. Cunningham, after some brief questioning, was arrested and his lodgings were searched. A detonator was discovered, and Cunningham was charged.

While the police were investigating the Tower of London device, two other Clan militants, Harry Burton and Luke Dillon, also posing as tourists, made their way into Westminster Palace, one dressed as a woman and with explosives concealed in much the same fashion as Cunningham. They figured, correctly, that a woman would not be searched. The primary target was the House of Commons. A supplementary attack on the Westminster Crypt was intended as a diversion, designed to draw away the police and ensure the success of the attack on the more strategically important of the two intended targets. The crypt bomb was spotted before it went off and a police constable attempted to carry it out of the building. Instead, he tripped on the stairs leading up to street level and the device exploded, knocking the courageous constable unconscious.

A few minutes after the first blast, the second bomb was triggered in the 'Aye' lobby of the Commons' chamber. The explosion caused thousands of pounds worth of damage – the Peers' Gallery, for example, was devastated. In two pieces of serendipitous symbolism, Gladstone's seat on the Treasury bench was destroyed, and the blast irreparably split an ornamental engraved shield, sundering the images of the Irish harp and the English Crown. More galling for the Metropolitan Police was the fact that Dillon and Burton managed to escape before Westminster was locked down.

The Commons blast resulted in no injuries because the House was not in session – hence the ability of Dillon and Burton to gain

*By Inspector Frederick Abberline, who would go on to become one of the lead investigators of the Whitechapel/'Jack the Ripper' murders in 1888.

entry as tourists – but the psychological damage was incalculable, all the more so as a 'disgusted' Edward Jenkinson, the Home Office counter-terrorist chief, had issued a warning to the Met in December 1884 that the Houses of Parliament were to be targeted.[39] *United Ireland* gloated that, 'On the shoulders of John Bull himself the whole thing lies'.[40] The Clan had violated the 'mother of parliaments' and attacked not only the bricks, mortar and fittings of the House of Commons but British democracy itself. It was a clear demonstration of the ability of the organization to breach security in even the most secure location. It presaged even more 'spectaculars', as a nation on tenterhooks awaited the next bombing.

But the rest was silence.

'Dynamite Saturday' was the last Irish republican attack of its kind in England until the Irish Republican Army's 'mainland' bombings began almost a century later.

Why did the campaign come to a sudden end after successfully penetrating some of England's most famous landmarks? The allocation of over a thousand police officers to the protection of buildings and individuals probably had something to do with it.[41] The cessation is also attributed by some to the enhanced prospect of Home Rule after the November/December 1885 general election. The major extension of the franchise in 1884 and Parnell's command of a disciplined political machine offered opportunities that would be jeopardized by dynamite or cross-dressing bombers.

However, attrition must also have been a factor. Between 1881 and 1885 twenty-three 'dynamitards' were captured and jailed – nine were associated with the Clan na Gael phase of the campaign – and three were killed by the premature explosion of their own device. Old-fashioned police work, unmediated by the Home Office intelligence apparatus, had led to the capture of Cunningham, the Tower of London bomber, and the subsequent apprehension of Harry Burton. The 'Irish Brigade' of the London CID was beefed up with the addition in 1883 of two inspectors, two sergeants and eight constables, all from Irish-Catholic backgrounds.[42] As the intelligence and investigative operations of the security forces in Britain – with a substantial contribution coming from Le Caron in the USA – began, over time, to achieve a greater measure of success, the supply of prospective bombers thinned. The shortest sentence handed down by British courts to anyone caught in the act; associated with an arms dump; or involved in the importation of dynamite, was seven years. Four of those convicted received fifteen-year sentences and thirteen were sent to prison for life. Was the game worth the candle?

The campaign of 'Fenian fire' ended abruptly (although few on either side were prepared to acknowledge at the time that it was over), but its impact prepared the way for reflexive public acceptance of the truth of an alleged plan to renew the dynamite campaign in 1887. It was not much of a stretch for Britons to accept the bona fides of the authorities in their startling revelation of what became known as the 'Jubilee plot'. Upwards of a hundred injuries and the tragic death of a seven-year-old boy made them susceptible to the 'exposure' of what appeared to be an altogether more heinous undertaking, replicating the Catesby conspiracy of 1605.

If the Clan had managed to damage an empty House of Commons, what would be the price of a return visit to the nearby Westminster Abbey when the monarch herself was present?

3

THE WAR OF THE THREE KINGDOMS

Ireland and the Growth of the British Secret Apparatus

'We hold Ireland by force and by force alone, as much today as in the days of Cromwell.'[1]

Home Secretary William Harcourt
to William Gladstone, 28 December 1883

'In the whole series of dynamite plots, the hand of the spy, or *agent provocateur*, is clearly visible.'[2]

Former Special Irish Branch detective Sergeant Patrick
McIntyre, *Reynolds's Newspaper*, 1895

Birkenhead Railway Station, 11 April 1884

It was Good Friday morning, and, rather like Christ himself, John Daly – 'the most bloody-minded fanatic since Guy Fawkes'[3] – was not going to have a great day.

The veteran Fenian walked into a welcoming committee of plain-clothes policemen as he strode onto the platform of Birkenhead railway station to buy a newspaper to read on the train back to Birmingham. Quite what he was doing there was, arguably, a source of some bewilderment to the man himself. He knew he was about to be entrusted with a package by an associate, but the exchange could just as easily have taken place in Liverpool, rather than across the other side of the River Mersey. Why take the scenic route?

While Daly had not expected to find himself in Birkenhead that morning, the small army of policemen who were there to greet him certainly did. They had not shown up in force serendipitously. Neither was it by chance that they included in their number the enigmatic Irish-born secret agent Nicholas Gosselin.

Daly was due to meet a fellow Fenian, the Liverpool publican Daniel O'Neill. The two men were well known to each other. Both had attended the funeral of Charles Kickham together in August 1882. O'Neill, however, unbeknownst to Daly, had been 'tapped' by the British secret police and was working for anti-Fenian 'spymaster' Edward Jenkinson, Gosselin's boss. O'Neill had supervised the passage of a consignment of Clan dynamite from the USA to Liverpool. This delicate smuggling operation had, for their own purposes, been facilitated by Jenkinson and Gosselin. The plan was for O'Neill to hand the explosives over to Daly in plain sight on the Birkenhead station platform. The publican would then make himself scarce. On the morning of 11 April 1884, the clearly nervous O'Neill presented his friend, as planned, with several tightly wrapped brown paper parcels. These were small enough for Daly to put into the pockets of his greatcoat. Whether Daly himself knew exactly what he was expected to carry back to Birmingham was a moot point back in 1884, and remains so to this day.

O'Neill was allowed by the waiting observers to go on his way. Only when there was a decent amount of separation between the two men did Gosselin order the Birkenhead police to pounce. Daly, knowing he was about to be apprehended, attempted to dispose of the parcels, making 'a desperate effort to get his hands into his overcoat pockets, but did not succeed.'[4] Daly resisted but was quickly overpowered and handcuffed, to the astonishment of the dozens of onlookers on the station platform. When questioned, he gave his name as 'John Denman', thus conforming to the cliché that anyone masquerading under an assumed name should retain their genuine initials. When Gosselin opened the brown paper parcels he discovered, labelled as banal household objects ('glass' and 'pens'), several detonators and a number of high-explosive grenades.

All of which came as no surprise to Gosselin.

Newspaper reports of the arrest claimed that Daly's plan had been to gain access to the galleries of the House of Commons and drop his 'grenades' onto the government front benches. That, at least, was the version of his intentions that the authorities disseminated. It was also the received wisdom that was communicated that day by Edward Jenkinson to a delighted Home Secretary, William Harcourt.

John Daly had been expertly 'set up' and the pressure was off Jenkinson, for the moment at least.

The Three Kingdoms

Between 1641 and 1653 Ireland was one of the locations for what became known as the 'War of the Three Kingdoms'. The kingdoms in question were England, Scotland and Ireland, and the competing forces included supporters of the monarchy, the Westminster parliament and their various allies. Most of the engagements in this war took place in Britain, but Ireland also came in for more than its fair share of the hostilities.

In the 1880s Ireland was the backdrop to another conflict of three warring dominions. No such exalted figures as Oliver Cromwell or King Charles I participated in this second 'War of the Three Kingdoms', which was a tawdry turf war, fought out between the securocrats of Dublin Castle, Scotland Yard and the Home Office in Whitehall.* While the first 'War of the Three

*Or, more specifically in the case of the Home Office, one of the great bureaucratic survivors of anti-Fenian espionage, Robert Anderson, postman to Henri Le Caron.

Kingdoms' encompassed regicide, civil war, ethnic cleansing and a major transfer of Irish land, the sequel boasted only petty jealousies, risible ineptitude and administrative stasis.

British anxiety around issues of security in the 1880s was not just a function of the perceived Fenian threat. There was a real fear that European political violence – which reached its apogee with the assassination of Tsar Alexander II in 1881 – would spill over into Britain, a nation that hosted several European political refugees advocating assassination in their own countries. In his memoir, John Sweeney devotes almost as much attention to the surveillance and arrest of anarchists, such as the Italian radicals Giuseppe Farnara and Francis Polti, as he does to the pursuit of Fenian suspects. Administrative concerns sprang from an awareness that the security service of the time, as opposed to detectives involved in 'ordinary' criminal investigation, was dangerously understaffed. There was also a paucity of useful confidential information on the threat from Irish-American terrorism, a shambles exacerbated by the amount of bogus intelligence emanating from the British east coast consulates. While some of the information being transmitted from New York and Philadelphia was genuine, much of it was unfiltered nonsense being purveyed by marginal Irish-American figures in search of some handy cash.

One of the missions of the highly assertive William Vernon Harcourt, on his elevation to the role of Home Secretary in 1880, was to rectify these egregious failings. Many of the methods he employed would not have met with the approval of some of the more progressive members of the Liberal cabinet, but their likely objections were purely hypothetical, because Harcourt mostly chose to keep his colleagues in the dark about precisely what he was up to.

At the centre of the internecine bureaucratic conflict that coincided with the planting of a series of destructive Fenian* bombs was Edward George Jenkinson, beneficiary of a Harrovian

*'Fenian' being shorthand for the activities of Rossa's 'skirmishers' and the more refined and complex operations launched by Clan na Gael from 1883.

education and a former Indian police administrator. Jenkinson arrived in Ireland in 1882 as the relatively humble private secretary to the new Lord Lieutenant, Earl Spencer. It was a position that failed to measure up to his expectations or his capabilities. However, the Phoenix Park murders, which advanced the careers of a number of suitably placed officials – other, obviously, than the murdered chief secretary and his deputy – smoothed Jenkinson's pathway to a challenging new posting, one commensurate with his talents, though not, perhaps, appropriate for someone with the uncertain state of health that had driven him from India in the first place.

The original choice of the Dublin Castle administration for the newly created position of Assistant Under-Secretary for Police and Crime, aka Spymaster General, was Sir Henry Brackenbury, military attaché at the Paris embassy and former head of the Cyprus police. His reign, however, was a short-lived embarrassment and earned him the nickname 'Black Brack'. Within months of arriving in Dublin, he applied for a position on the staff of the British military expedition bound for Egypt to suppress a nationalist uprising. He was sacked by an irate Lord Lieutenant, Earl Spencer, in July 1882.

That was when a chastened establishment turned to Edward Jenkinson. Spencer already had enough evidence of his private secretary's nous to realize that the talents of the former divisional commissioner of Jhansi and Oudh provinces were being wasted monitoring the Viceroy's appointments diary, organizing his correspondence and counting the spoons after a Viceregal Lodge banquet.

Edward Jenkinson took on the thankless task of suppressing agrarian secret societies while keeping a weather eye on the IRB. One of the principal factors recommending him for the job was the probability that, as the once-bitten Spencer told Gladstone, 'he will not leave his post'.[5] The bar was being adjusted downwards.

Jenkinson was introduced to Gladstone by his Lord Lieutenant as 'cool, helpful and energetic ... He may be a little impetuous sometimes.'[6] Impetuous he certainly was – he was also egotistical and tactless – but, while far from a paragon of Victorian *noblesse oblige*, his resourcefulness and his energy as a secret policeman were undeniable. As was his ability to justify – to himself at least – a recurrently questionable *modus operandi*. Jenkinson, judging that his felonious enemies had few if any scruples, was himself rarely burdened by any veneration of legality.

Jenkinson, however, never quite managed to surmount a lofty distaste on the part of the British body politic for the craft into which he now threw himself. It had taken British society decades to accept even the idea of a detective force investigating ordinary crime. The notion of espionage as an adjunct of national security was still anathema to many (the days of Sir Francis Walsingham were part of a distant Tudor past). Jenkinson was beset by a prevailing Victorian aversion to secret police work. Such disagreeable activities were seen as an unseemly continental phenomenon, appropriate only for the likes of foreigners such as the French and the Russians.

Jenkinson's job was made somewhat easier by the fact that, initially at least, it was assumed that he would be confining his activities to Ireland. What was thoroughly objectionable in Britain (the recruitment and payment of spies and informers) was perfectly acceptable, even desirable, in Ireland. Later, when he was transferred from Dublin to London – where he sought to establish a security force along the lines of his Irish operation – his brief was to vanquish the Irish-American skirmishers and bombers. The direct and very obvious threat to life, limb, liberty and chattels gave him more leeway than he might otherwise have enjoyed and, *pro tem* at least, served to overcome any patrician scorn for covert intelligence operations. Such ingrained disdain, however, as Jenkinson would discover, was merely in limbo. It would soon reassert itself.

Jenkinson dealt with any fastidiousness about spies, felon-setters, double-agents, infiltrators and other reprobates by simply ignoring bourgeois Victorian repugnance, and doing much as he wished. Recognizing that to function entirely within the confines of Dublin Castle's immediate jurisdiction (i.e. the island of Ireland) would be an inadequate response to terrorism, Jenkinson's growing network of informers and *agents provocateurs* spread first into Britain, and thence to Paris and the United States. He relied on the surveillance of suspects, information from infiltrators, intelligence from paid informers, communications intercepts and *agents provocateurs* – whose function was to entrap unwary revolutionaries in fictional plots. Jenkinson was Machiavellian in his approach to intelligence; the end (national security) justified the means (frequently illicit).

None of which caused much difficulty as long as Jenkinson was based exclusively in Dublin Castle. When he was transferred – by an increasingly desperate Liberal administration frantically seeking an end to the Irish-American bombing campaign – to the Home Office, his methods became problematic. In London he encountered new levels of both accountability and friction. He faced opposition from entrenched police interests, especially Scotland Yard – the only force in Britain directly answerable to central government – in his desire to see Ireland and Britain treated as a single intelligence entity, with, of course, Edward Jenkinson as espionage overseer. He wanted his imported Royal Irish Constabulary (RIC) undercover officers to scrutinize the activities of known Irish republican figures in Britain, rather than merely to assist Scotland Yard and local metropolitan forces in the monitoring of the terrorist threat. When it came to the 'permission' or 'forgiveness' approach, Jenkinson generally opted for the latter and conducted operations in Britain under the noses of police forces, for which he often expressed unbridled contempt. Ultimately his corrosive megalomania would prove to be his undoing.

He was particularly dismissive of Scotland Yard, even after the creation in 1883 of the Met's Special (Irish) Branch (SIB) on the 'special' Irish date of 17 March. This administrative response to 'Fenian' dynamite was established under the command of

Superintendent Adolphus 'Dolly' Williamson, with a complement of twelve detectives. The SIB, Jenkinson felt, enjoyed far too cosy a relationship with the London press and leaked like a sieve. Jenkinson was also convinced that SIB detectives were corrupt and 'on the take'. 'There is hardly a man among them who does not take money,' he wrote to Earl Spencer.[7] This mistrust meant that Jenkinson was reluctant to share information with Scotland Yard. Jenkinson's priority was 'slow policing', the covert surveillance of suspects in order to widen the net and capture as many co-conspirators as possible. Officers of the Met, however, saw this template as being illogical. They worshipped the short-term kudos of 'the collar'. And they could easily justify refusing to take the longer view by invoking the threat to life and limb posed by the suspects the assistant under-secretary preferred to keep under observation. For his part, CID director and Metropolitan Police assistant commissioner James Monro – one of Jenkinson's two *bête noires*, the other being Robert Anderson – took grave exception to the presence of a secret force of RIC policemen (as well as a small army of civilian spies and informers) operating in his bailiwick, but outside of his control.[8] For his part Jenkinson complained that Monro 'has encouraged his men to follow the RIC men about and to report about them … Monro does not object to the RIC only, he objects to <u>all</u> Service agents.'[9] *Quis custodiet ipsos custodes?*

After a bomb wreaked havoc on the offices of the SIB in May 1884, Jenkinson complained to William Harcourt about 'confusion and want of system at Scotland Yard',[10] sentiments that hardly would have endeared him to his Met colleagues. He could be just as scathing about the performance of regional British forces as well. 'The English detectives are utterly useless in this particular kind of work,' he told Harcourt in December 1884, 'and it is quite impossible to establish any system because there is no central authority over the police.'[11] This was not a challenge that he had been obliged to overcome in his work in Ireland. There he was only required to deal with two forces (the RIC and the

Dublin Metropolitan Police), and he had quickly come to enjoy uncontested authority.

Extending some of his questionable methodologies to Britain was highly controversial. At times it was almost impossible for anyone, other than Jenkinson, to distinguish between legitimate counterintelligence and the fervid entrapment operations initiated or approved by the spymaster himself. Jenkinson rarely met an *agent provocateur* or an entrapment plot that he didn't like. It would have been unwise for Jenkinson to acknowledge just how many of the policing 'coups' that attended the Rossa/Clan bombing campaigns were mere mirages. However, in the words of the definitive IRB biographer Owen McGee, 'most Irish-American dynamite teams of the mid-1880s were either created by *agents provocateurs* or involved spies'.[12]

The probable truth, as expressed by Michael Davitt in *The Fall of Feudalism in Ireland*, was that 'many of these outrages ... were deliberately planned by agents of the English secret service'.[13] Lest there be any doubt about Davitt's credibility, his informant was Edward Jenkinson himself, with whom, by 1888, he was working closely to undermine *The Times* in the Special Commission. The spymaster underwent a radical change of heart in his views on Irish nationalism well before he was forced out of his Home Office responsibilities in 1887.[14] Although it did not diminish his professional effectiveness, or affect the way he conducted his work, Jenkinson, towards the end of his career in espionage, began to develop a more nuanced approach towards moderate Irish nationalists than did his political overlords or his contemporaries in the netherworld of anti-nationalist intelligence. This was amplified after he became surplus to requirements following the Tory takeover in 1886.

The double life of 'Red Jim'

One of the most colourful of Jenkinson's felon-setters was 'Red' Jim McDermott. Born in Dublin in 1843, he fought for the Papal

Army and later became embedded in the murky world of New York politics – he was said to have avoided a murder charge owing to the influence of a party 'Boss'[15] – before joining the Fenian Brotherhood in the USA. Posing as a nationalist firebrand, he addressed the inaugural convention of Rossa's United Irishmen of America in Philadelphia in June 1880 with bloodthirsty rhetoric. He promised his audience, in a rabble-rousing speech, 'not a cent for blatherskite, but every dollar for dynamite'.[16] In 1883 McDermott, armed with a letter of introduction from Rossa and a cover story that he was a freelance journalist, turned up in Dublin and sought an interview with Davitt, who at the time was incarcerated in Richmond prison. The Land League founder quickly saw through all seven of McDermott's veils and perfunctorily dismissed him. That same day McDermott, who had aroused suspicions when he presented himself at the offices of the Irish National League and *United Ireland*, was followed to Dublin Castle, where he met with his 'handler'.[17]

Despite these semaphoric warnings, 'Red Jim' succeeded in entrapping several Cork Fenians (with dynamite provided by Dublin Castle)[18] into a bombing operation against targets in Liverpool that resulted in lengthy jail sentences for several of the 'conspirators'.

He then tried his luck in Paris, where he attempted to entice two avowed nationalist militants into participating in a bombing operation in England. Patrick Casey was a cousin of James Stephens, and the elder brother of Joseph Casey, who had intervened in the arrest of Ricard O'Sullivan Burke in 1868. Eugene Davis was a poet and journalist. This seduction was never destined to be a profitable enterprise. Casey, despite his Fenian pedigree, was already 'in service'[19] according to Michael Davitt – by which he meant that this relative of the founder of the IRB was a British agent, not a domestic retainer. Davitt regarded Casey as a treacherous fantasist. 'When sober he talked sense; when in the other condition he led those who listened to him to believe that all the revolutionary bodies in Ireland, America, and France took their inspiration or plans from this *soi-disant* desperado.'[20] Davitt also dismissed Eugene Davis as 'a well-educated but hopelessly useless creature … he was a kind of *Quartier Latin* café loafer'. Just as Casey and Davis had been taken in by McDermott's apparent revolutionary credentials, Red Jim had succumbed to the fictions of two 'revolutionary bummers or camp-followers … [who] had succeeded in creating the impression in London, Dublin, and New York that they were indispensable intermediaries in all transactions which should be kept secret from the knowledge of British authority'.[21] Self-appointed transactional intermediaries they were; indispensable they were not.

McDermott's scheme backfired when Cork republican James O'Malley, who had managed to escape the net when the Liverpool bombing conspiracy was exposed, discovered that McDermott was now plying his tradecraft in Paris. O'Malley persuaded Davis to invite Red Jim to the port of Le Havre. There the Corkman succeeded in drugging McDermott, but not in preventing him from escaping and taking ship back to New York.

McDermott next appeared in the summer of 1883 in Montreal. There he kept his hand in by attempting to hoodwink Canadian-based Irish extremists. His calling card was a heady plot to

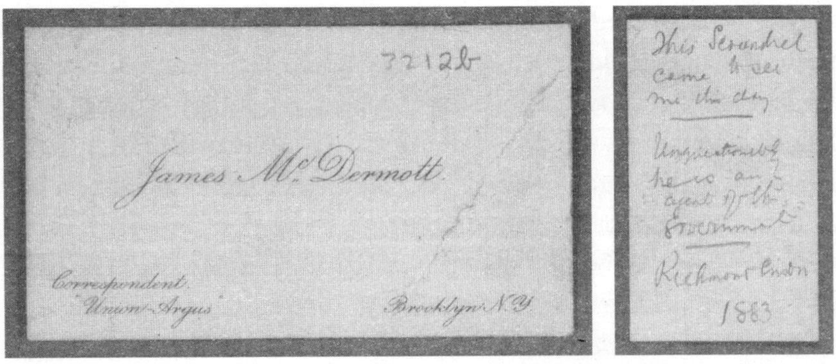

The business card presented to Davitt in Richmond prison and his reaction to Red Jim's request for a meeting.

organize 'dynamite clubs' whose zealous members would blow up public buildings in the province of Quebec. Astonishingly, the British Consulate in New York sought permission from the Canadian authorities to supply McDermott with dynamite. Far less astonishingly, the Canadians 'absolutely refused'.[22] While in Quebec he was exposed as a British agent by Davitt and the *Montreal Evening Post*.[23]

And that, surely, should have brought down the curtain on Red Jim's duplicity. However, O'Donovan Rossa, by now aware of the treachery of his erstwhile protégé, somehow managed to reassure McDermott that he did not credit any of the allegations of treachery being made against him. McDermott was invited to return to the USA to patch things up with his colleagues in the United Irishmen of America. Naïvely, Red Jim succumbed to this overture and abandoned Montreal for New York. On his return to Manhattan, he arranged to meet Rossa in Ryan's Liquor Saloon on Chambers Street. But there was to be no emotional reconciliation. Instead, two IRB assassins (Reardon and Shortt), sent from Ireland to avenge the Cork/Liverpool fiasco, burst into the bar and started shooting. McDermott was hit by one of the flying bullets, but it only grazed him. He used up another of his nine lives in making his escape. One of the two would-be assassins was arrested and charged, but, in the spirit of 'whatever you say, say nothing', there were no witnesses whatever, in a crowded bar, to his alleged crime, and he was acquitted.

Bizarrely, it may well have been the case that, even at this stage, Jenkinson was still not quite ready to retire his 'asset'. He opted to try to rehabilitate Red Jim by smuggling him to Britain and staging a 'show' trial to restore McDermott's shattered credibility as a fire-breathing bomber.[24] McDermott, apparently sporting gold spectacles as some sort of ostentatious but impractical disguise, returned to Britain under the alias 'Peter Quigley'. He was arrested on arrival, lodged in Walton prison and put on trial. The ruse failed miserably. A sceptical judge and a suspicious press led to the dropping of the charges and the spiriting away of Red

Jim by Nicholas Gosselin to a new life on the Continent.* Rossa, ever anxious to reunite with his erstwhile protégé, offered a reward of $5,000 to 'whoever will hand over the body, dead or alive' of the fugitive double-agent.[25]

Jenkinson's reward for his ill-advised loyalty to the incorrigible McDermott was a blackmail attempt from Red Jim based on documents in his possession. The former spy claimed that these proved several illegalities encouraged by his Dublin Castle handler.

To the very end Red Jim McDermott was blessed with, in the crudest Irish parlance, 'a neck like a jockey's bollocks'.

'Mrs Tyler' and 'Major Yellow'

Not all of Jenkinson's 'sting' operations were crowned with even Red Jim's level of success. Some of his agents were as clueless as they were self-confident that they would escape detection. A case in point was his despatch of a female agent into what was assumed to be the maw of the dynamite conspiracy in Dublin, a city that, in fact, remained relatively uncontaminated by this form of violence. This 'female emissary of the Home Office',[26] as she was gleefully described by Irish Parliamentary Party (IPP) MP Tim Healy in the House of Commons, called herself 'Mrs Tyler'. She materialized in Dublin in July 1884 posing as a young widow. She checked into the fashionable Gresham Hotel on Sackville Street and, according to Michael Davitt's detailed account of the episode, she was 'eloquent in her admiration for

*He briefly resurfaced in Newcastle upon Tyne in 1890 and sent a pained letter to Davitt challenging him 'to make good your statement that I was ever employed by anyone to organize, or that I did organize, dynamite or other outrages in Ireland or England'. This was on foot of a series of articles published by Davitt in *Labour World* in October 1890. Should Davitt be able to stand up his allegations McDermott hollowly promised to contribute one thousand pounds to the 'Parnell defence fund'. (Davitt papers, TCD, MS 9441/3213.)

extreme revolutionary movements', and appeared to have money to spend on 'the cause'.[27] However, she fooled no one and became the victim of the most humiliating form of counter-intelligence, a practical joke.

'Mrs Tyler' was advised that, because of her undying devotion to dynamite diplomacy, she would be introduced to an Irish-American bomber who happened to be on his way to London to provoke 'an adjournment' in proceedings in the House of Commons. She asked to meet this dyed-in-the-wool Irish patriot and promised to accompany him to London to enhance his cover story, since 'no one would suspect him while in her company'. She was promised an audience that very night. At around midnight a mysterious cloaked figure was introduced to her. In order to avoid detection, he could not remain in her company long, but he thanked 'Mrs Tyler' profusely for her generous offer to accompany him to London as his resident decoy.

Pressing home her advantage, 'Mrs Tyler' then issued an invitation to 'all the Dublin leaders of the active policy' to join her for a private dinner in her room at the Gresham. She was assured that at least eight of the most fervent Dublin desperadoes would attend her soirée. In fact, the assembly the following evening consisted mainly of intrigued journalists posing as extremists. 'Mrs Tyler', to their communal delight, plied them with the best champagne while declining to touch a drop of alcohol herself. As the 'Fenians' drank copiously, making quite a dent in Jenkinson's budget, 'Mrs Tyler' sought to persuade them that the House of Commons itself would be a surprisingly easy target for their bombs. She promised to shelter anyone who would undertake 'such a glorious task and take him, or them, to Italy for safety afterwards'.

Shortly after that enticing offer was dangled before the counterfeit terrorists, a frenzied accomplice of theirs dashed into the room declaring that 'Mallon and the "G" men' had surrounded the hotel. This caused apparent consternation among the ranks of the ersatz dynamitards. Fearful that she was about to lose her prey to the plodding detectives of the Dublin Metropolitan Police, 'Mrs Tyler' tried to calm her nervous guests. She agreed to go downstairs and ascertain the extent of the danger. On her return, she was easily able to reassure her guests that there was no threat. Before the evening broke up, the 'bombers' persuaded 'Mrs Tyler' to part with £20 towards the escape of a skirmisher then being held in a London prison.

The farcical episode was duly recorded in a letter written by the pranksters to the chief secretary, George Otto Trevelyan, in which the government was accused of using *agents provocateurs* to inveigle the unwary into political crime. The £20 note was graciously returned but no attempt was made to reimburse Jenkinson for the champagne.

Almost as unsuccessful, and equally embarrassing, was the advent in the summer of 1884 of the Jenkinson agent described by Davitt as 'Major Yellow'. He was, in fact, a former colonial policeman named Captain Darnley Stewart Stephens, who arrived in Paris to carry on the work interrupted by the enforced retirement of Red Jim. 'Yellow' had established his credentials for cold-bloodedness in colonial Africa when he 'hanged two natives with his own hand'.[28] As had McDermott before him, Stephens contacted the 'indispensable' Patrick Casey and Eugene Davis. Plots to bomb the Palace of Westminster and Windsor Castle were hatched over glasses of absinthe and cognac, again at the expense of Jenkinson. When the conspirators gathered in the Shamrock Bar on rue de Duras they were often carefully scrutinized by another customer who sat in a corner and drank alone. This was the Scotland Yard detective Inspector Maurice Moser, who had been sent by the Met's Criminal Investigation Department to keep an eye not so much on Casey and Davis as on Jenkinson's new man in Paris. Stephens did manage to entice Casey and Davis to England – where he planted a fake bomb on a Kent railway line. This caused rather more consternation than the counterfeit device itself merited. It was an oil can wrapped in a parcel with a fake 'fuse' attached. 'Yellow' later attempted, unsuccessfully, to entice Irish Party members into dialogue with him in the lobby of the House of Commons. After these escapades an irate Jenkinson sacked Stephens for his history of drunken excess. This, however, was far from the end of his espionage career.

Both Stephens and Moser were working for new employers when the Tories began their own campaign of felon-setting in the second half of the decade.

The 'framing' of John Daly

The Irish-American bombing campaign, while it did little for the façades of a number of British public buildings, certainly enhanced the career of Edward Jenkinson. Once the 'skirmishers', and later the more effective agents of Clan na Gael, began hitting their targets, something akin to panic settled on Whitehall. The British administration had expected a sustained assault along these lines immediately after the Clerkenwell bombing of 1867. A small dedicated unit, with the Irish-born 'Fenian hunter' Robert Anderson at its heart, had been established in anticipation of the reign of 'Fenian fire'. When that threat had not materialized, frugality always being the order of the day, the new unit had been stood down. Anderson, however, would outlast his bureaucratic antagonists for long enough to become one of the inspirations for Joseph Conrad's *The Secret Agent*. In the opinion of at least one expert, he 'probably kept his Home Office job for years by virtue of a largely imaginary spy network in America, until Jenkinson rumbled him'.[29] He certainly misled his superiors when it came to the provenance of the Salford bombing of January 1881, which, he claimed, was not a 'Fenian outrage at all ... not a single informant either here or in Ireland has connected the Salford case with Fenianism'.[30]

William Harcourt, the Liberal Home Secretary from 1880 until June 1885, was unimpressed with Anderson's abilities and frustrated at his boundless talent for subterfuge. In March 1883 he wrote to the Lord Lieutenant, Earl Spencer, that 'I have much difficulty with Anderson of the Home Office who has been too much accustomed to act on his own hook and who bottles up what little information he possesses – and it is mighty little – and fiddles about with the Irish Police in London.'[31]

While based in Dublin Castle between 1882 and 1884, Jenkinson was forced to tolerate Anderson – for whom he had no personal or professional regard – as his London-based Home Office liaison. But that arrangement was rendered superfluous after the spymaster, in the spring of 1884, became his own Home Office liaison. A panicked Harcourt begged Earl Spencer to release the assistant under-secretary from his duties in Dublin so that he could combat the Fenian bombers who were terrorizing Britain and leaving the Liberal government wide open to allegations of incompetence and lassitude. Jenkinson was installed in Room 56 of the Home Office building in Whitehall – he left the Crime Special Branch in Dublin Castle in the capable hands of RIC Inspector Samuel Waters[32] – and was in a position to name his price. One of the incidental items on his shopping list involved the assigning of Anderson to an unpromising career as secretary to the Prison Board.

Of much greater importance to Jenkinson than a hollow bureaucratic victory over Anderson – who continued to 'handle' Le Caron – was direct access to the Home Secretary, William Vernon Harcourt. He was obliged to liaise with 'Dolly' Williamson, head of the Special Irish Branch (SIB), but exchanges with the SIB tended to be a one-way street.

Jenkinson's sweeping administrative powers, in practice, left him in charge of security operations in Britain and Ireland. In practice, but not in theory. Crucially, government reluctance to apprise the House of Commons of this new reality meant that Jenkinson's Home Office position was never formalized.

In August 1883, when his responsibilities had required him to move constantly between Dublin and London, he had approved a crucial staffing appointment. This meant that the inscrutable Cavan-born Nicholas Gosselin, a 'spook' to the manner born, who cultivated the public profile of an earthworm, became Jenkinson's effective 'second in command' with responsibility for counteracting Fenian activities in the north of England. The first major rabbit to emerge from the hat of the Jenkinson/Gosselin double act was the controversial arrest (described previously) of John Daly in April 1884.

Edward Jenkinson had known all about Daly's movements for months, long before his 'leave of absence' from Dublin Castle took him to Room 56 in the Home Office. Before Daly even set sail from the USA, Jenkinson had been tipped off by one of his American informants, John P. Hayes of Philadelphia. Daly, a native of Limerick, had joined the IRB in 1863 at the age of eighteen and became a Supreme Council member in 1869. By the 1880s he was an accomplished clandestine arms importer who made occasional trips to the USA to encourage Clan na Gael to continue its role as an arms exporter. On one of those trips he took it upon himself to criticize O'Donovan Rossa's dynamite campaign and found himself at the wrong end of a duelling challenge from the irascible Corkman. Since it was no longer the eighteenth century, and Daly had no desire to kill or injure an Irish republican legend, he elected to return to Britain in 1883, but not before Hayes had alerted Jenkinson to his movements.

Daly, from the time of his arrival in October 1883, was followed by Jenkinson's agents in accordance with the spymaster's 'maturing crime' template. After a brief spell in London, Daly settled in Birmingham in the home of fellow IRB member James Egan. There Gosselin and a bevy of undercover RIC detectives continued to stalk him, albeit without revealing their surveillance to the local police force. While Daly eventually realized that he was being followed, the same could not be said for the Birmingham police, in the early days of the operation at least. In the course of the painstaking seven-month surveillance Gosselin also succeeded in recruiting the Liverpool publican and long-time associate of Daly, Daniel O'Neill, as his agent. O'Neill was to prove crucial in what transpired.

If Daly was a genuine 'bomber-in-waiting', he went about maintaining a low profile in an extremely unorthodox fashion. Although he appears to have had little or no talent as a performer, he prevailed on the proprietor of the Birmingham Concert Hall to allow him to tread the boards as 'O'Brien the famous Irish storyteller'. Daly made his debut, and his valedictory, on 20 December 1883 at a benefit concert. Daly the *seanchaí* outstayed his welcome, lost his audience with a display of spectacular ineptitude and his act was curtailed by the dropping of the curtain. Quite how getting 'the bird' from a music hall audience assisted his alleged mission remains a mystery.

With Jenkinson's patience running thin – Daly having shown no signs of evil intent, other than towards Birmingham's guiltless music hall patrons – matters finally came to a head in April 1884 when a consignment of explosive material, despatched by the Clan, arrived in Liverpool (with the connivance of Jenkinson's office) and was taken in care by Daniel O'Neill. Gosselin's newly recruited spy then summoned Daly from Birmingham to Liverpool.

Shortly afterwards the Limerick IRB man had his Good Friday date with destiny on the platform of Birkenhead railway station.

Daly's arrest might simply have been down to the success of a patient surveillance operation. That was certainly what Jenkinson claimed in his triumphant letter to Harcourt on 12 April in which he announced that the Liberal cabinet had just had a narrow escape. His agents, he claimed, had saved the Treasury bench from a dynamite attack in the Commons itself. However, in his intimate and informative correspondence with his former mentor, Earl Spencer, Jenkinson was much more forthcoming about the methods used to entrap Daly. Thanks to O'Neill, Jenkinson and Gosselin had been aware of the impending arrival of the bombs found on Daly in Birkenhead. However, that information they kept to themselves as the bombs were successfully smuggled past customs officials in Liverpool. The success of that part of the Clan operation was vital to the 'sting' being planned by Jenkinson and his capable subordinate. It may even have been the case that the 'grenades … had been purchased in America with money supplied by the Irish police'.[33]

Now came the tricky part: persuading Daly to turn up at a venue crawling with law enforcement officers and getting him to accept delivery of the explosives. In his self-congratulatory letter to Spencer, Jenkinson offered more detail of the undercover element of the operation than he had to Harcourt on the same day. 'Our difficulty,' he observed to the Lord Lieutenant, 'was to get the things passed to Daly and then to arrest him with "the things" on him, without throwing suspicion on our own informant.'[34]

At the end of his trial, Daly was sent down for life. Jenkinson and Gosselin appear to have had no doubt that Daly was behind a spectacular political assassination plot. And the circumstantial evidence of Daly's intentions, while not conclusive, are compelling. Twice he reconnoitred the Strangers' Gallery of the House of Commons. Presumably he was not there to assess the quality of the debates. However, there is also a wealth of circumstantial evidence that the Birkenhead arrest was a blatant example of felon-setting, with Daly as dupe and O'Neill as *agent provocateur*, in a conspiracy hatched by Jenkinson to burnish his reputation with his new employer, the Home Secretary. This was certainly the view of the Birmingham Chief Constable Joseph Farndale in an 1887 memo dealing with the incarceration of Daly's host James Egan (sentenced to twenty years penal servitude[35]). Farndale alleged that the evidence against Egan was 'very slight indeed', and accused Gosselin and Jenkinson of 'entrapping the man into crime or arranging a crime so as to ensure detection and correction'.[36] In a riposte to Farndale's memo Gosselin issued 'a most emphatic contradiction' to the 'vague accusations' of the Birmingham chief constable and pointed out that Harcourt, 'from first to last … knew every move I made and no particle of information was withheld from him'.[37] This does not, of course, exonerate the Secret Service from suspicion of entrapment. It merely adds the name of the Liberal Home Secretary to the list of those privy to the details of an operation that certainly gave off more than a whiff of entrapment.

O'Neill did not entirely escape the consequences of his treachery. He was later kidnapped and 'tried' by the IRB. However, in a final irony, he benefited from the extent of Jenkinson's infiltration of the IRB in Ireland and in Britain. One of O'Neill's inquisitors was another Jenkinson double-agent. After interrogation, the man who had betrayed John Daly was permitted to walk free. Not long after his release by the IRB he was spirited away by the spymaster to a new life in Australia. He was later tracked down there by the IRB, but again he managed to convince a potential assassin that he had not betrayed Daly.[38]

The 'Gentle Torpedo': Millen *redux*

When it comes to the rogues' gallery of spies and informants who plagued militant Irish nationalist and republican insurgencies from the 1798 rebellion to the War of Independence, Francis Frederick Millen deserves his own waxwork statue. As we've already seen, the Tyrone native offered his services to Her Majesty's Government, via Edward Archibald in the New York Consulate, as early as 1866. It is not certain whether he became surplus to requirements after the failed Fenian uprising of 1867, or whether he continued to supply Archibald with information gleaned from his continued association with the Fenian Brotherhood, and Clan na Gael, in the 1870s.

Michael Davitt, during his short career as a self-styled 'amateur detective',* compiled a revealing dossier on Millen's activities. Davitt identified the general, for reasons that remain tantalizingly

*In the preparation of the Irish Parliamentary Party case before the Special Commission in 1888/9. The information Davitt gathered – especially in Paris in 1888 – and his informed speculation, can be found in a little black notebook, 'Notes by an amateur detective' in the library of Trinity College Dublin, Davitt papers, MS 9551.

obscure, as 'the Gentle Torpedo' in the notes compiled during his Special Commission investigations (mostly in Paris) in 1888/9.[39]

Millen's rank of 'general' was held in low esteem by fellow Fenians who had served in the Union or Confederate forces during the American Civil War. He was, essentially, a 'soldier of fortune' whose military experience had been gained in the armies of Mexico and Guatemala. He was viewed as an 'inexperienced, theatrical, "banana-republic"-style officer'[40] by many of his contemporaries. In the early 1870s the military 'gamekeeper' turned journalistic 'poacher' when he began writing for the *New York Herald*, a journal that employed several Irish-American zealots, including John Devoy. The *Herald*, however, was a broad church, home also to the Anglophile correspondent Chester Ives, who viewed Irish-American nationalists in much the same light as would the members of an Orange lodge. Ives, with whom Millen was closely involved, edited the Parisian English-language newspaper the *Morning News* and had a fine pedigree in the peddling of anti-nationalist propaganda (often in the form of bogus interviews) intended to associate Irish nationalist politicians with extremist positions. 'Fake news', like success, has many fathers.

Millen was distrusted by the nominal leaders of both warring factions within the Clan – John Devoy and Alexander Sullivan. However, these inveterate antagonists had stepped away from any formal positions of authority in the Clan in 1881 and 1882, respectively,* leaving the organization in the hands of the corrupt Kentucky lawyer Michael Boland. Millen managed to make himself useful to Boland, thus giving him access to vital information and enhancing his capacity for betrayal after the Clan's transition to the dynamite strategy from 1883 to 1885.

Millen's genius for gross disloyalty and his relentless pursuit of financial reward led to his reinstatement on the secret payroll

*Devoy to devote his attention to his newspaper the *Irish Nation*. Sullivan to assume the presidency of the Irish National League of America and to play a more active part in US national politics.

after he showed up at the British legation in Mexico City in April 1885, armed with letters from O'Donovan Rossa to underscore his potential as an asset. He offered to resume his double life. Millen was described in a despatch to the Foreign Office as 'Age about 50, height about 5ft 10, rather thin. Hair brown, somewhat curly, military visage, clean shaven except long moustache – pearly grey eyes of peculiar appearance, blue grey.'[41]

This second coming as an informer of the Mexican general was communicated to Jenkinson in May 1885. He was identified by the British chargé d'affaires Lionel Carden – an ingenue when it came to matters Irish – as 'General F.F. Millen, who was formerly head of the military department of the Fenian organisation'.[42] Thereafter he was referred to, even in secret Foreign Office correspondence, as 'X'. In response, in a lengthy memorandum Jenkinson outlined half a dozen onerous terms and conditions 'that will be required from the General* in order to satisfy H.M. Government.'[43] When he finally got sight of Jenkinson's memo in early September, Carden concluded, on the basis of his extensive debriefing of the aspiring spy, that Millen was not going to pass muster, and that 'the information as given to me by XXX will not satisfy the requirements of the memorandum, and will be considered as deficient in the detail which I apprehend would be of most interest to Her Majesty's Government'.[44] However, Jenkinson's coyness about collaborating with a Foreign Office asset was short-lived. The two men met in Paris in mid-November 1885 and began a fruitful relationship that may have continued even after Jenkinson was edged out of office by the new Tory government in 1887. There is no record of their conversation, but there can be little doubt that Jenkinson enquired about the status of the bombing campaign – Millen's knowledge was 'more general than particular'[45] – since it had been ten months since 'Dynamite Saturday'. He would also have been anxious to discover the real

*In every instance even this vague identification of the potential spy fell victim to strikethrough.

extent of Millen's influence within the Clan. Did he have enough authority to stay Boland's hand should that 'shyster lawyer' (Devoy's description) decide to renew the export of dynamite to Britain?

Millen's November 1885 journey to Paris set the British government back a handsome $401.14 (about $13,000 today). This included a side trip to Chicago to pump a (not entirely) unsuspecting Alexander Sullivan for information. The Mexican Army general, unstinting in his self-care (he allowed himself a generous $15 for 'miscellaneous expenses' on board the ship taking him from New York to Le Havre)[46] would cost the spymaster many dollars more in the years ahead – and would condemn Jenkinson's successors to numerous sleepless nights. He was to become the supposed mastermind behind a fiendish enterprise that was, in truth, one of the greatest feats of misdirection in the chequered history of Anglo-Irish relations, the 'Jubilee plot'.

The warring kingdoms

Crucial in any consideration of British intelligence operations against Irish extremists (and moderates) in the 1880s are the relentless turf wars conducted between the agencies who vied with each other for credit in ending the Irish-American bombing campaign and in 'exposing' the so-called 'Jubilee plot' in 1887. The expression 'secret service' is often applied to British or Dublin Castle espionage activities against Fenian violence and 'outrage'. However, because there were multiple agencies involved, it can be something of a misnomer. There were times, during that fraught decade when the wider 'service' – encompassing Dublin Castle, the Home Office, the Foreign Office and Scotland Yard – was so secretive and self-serving that the right hand did not know what the left hand was doing. Whatever the potential for acute embarrassment, it often seemed that the cloistered spymasters preferred the risk of screwing up to the exasperation of mutual collaboration.

In the first half of the decade, with Jenkinson as spider in chief at the heart of the web, much of the inter-agency animosity was channelled in his direction. A generous helping of this hostility came from James Monro. Monro, a dour and intensely religious Scot, took over the Criminal Investigation Department (CID) in June 1884 and was irked by the walls erected by his colleague/rival and designed to separate Room 56 from Scotland Yard. The bad feeling was mutual. The Monro entry in Jenkinson's end-of-term report card to Earl Spencer in December 1884 was to the effect that the CID chief 'has not much energy or originality'.[47]* Both men had made their reputations in India; both were competitive and ambitious; and each cordially loathed and constantly belittled the other. In an unpublished memoir, Monro railed to his family against 'the machinations of Mr Jenkinson'.[48] He bitterly resented Jenkinson and his London espionage operations in particular. 'He not only collected intelligence regarding London,' Monro complained vociferously, 'but he acted upon it, without any reference to the London police, by means of a number of Irish police whom he had, without any authority whatever, stationed in London.'[49] Monro might have been prepared to concede 'the provinces' to Jenkinson and Gosselin, given that his formal jurisdiction went no further than the boundaries of the Met, but, as far as the police chief was concerned, responsibility for the security of the capital city, whether from East End gangs, European anarchists or Fenian bombers, belonged to Monro's detectives alone.

By the middle of 1885 Jenkinson's luck was beginning to run out. Harcourt came down firmly on Monro's side in the espionage turf wars. Deprecating the fact that the Dublin Castle/Home Office spymaster consistently withheld information from Monro, in a meeting in May 1885 Harcourt railed at Jenkinson that 'it is all jealousy, nothing but jealousy. You like to get information and

*This, however, was mild in comparison to his assessment of Spencer's cabinet colleague, the Home Secretary William Harcourt, who was described as 'childish and unreasonable'.

keep it to yourself. You are like a dog with [a] bone who goes into a corner and growls at anyone who comes near him.'[50]

By the summer of 1886 Monro had the upper hand. One of his officers came across a list of names and addresses of Jenkinson's private army of touts and agents, led by a dubious operator named Winter (alias Dawson).[51] Not only was this private army observing Irish-American suspects of whom Monro had not been made aware, it was also maintaining surveillance on suspects who were already being watched by CID detectives. Furthermore, in May 1886, Monro was able to tell Charles Warren, Metropolitan Police Commissioner, that 'the men employed by Mr. Jenkinson have, during the past week, been employed in watching [my] men and that the operations are directed towards the officers of Scotland Yard in the discharge of their legitimate duties'.[52] There was no comeback from that charge.

Monro organized a punitive trawl of this private network. Jenkinson's 'assets' were detained en masse. Sergeant Patrick McIntyre put their number at twenty men and two or three women, some of whom were being paid to encourage rank-and-file National League members in London to acts of violence. 'It is distinctly creditable to the young Irishmen in the League,' wrote McIntrye, 'that they held themselves aloof from outrage when they were being egged on by men who only joined the League for the purposes of associating it with dynamite conspiracies and other criminality.'[53] The new Tory Home Secretary, Hugh Childers, found in favour of Monro when the inevitable confrontation took place between the spymaster and the CID director. Jenkinson was required to remove his private army from the streets, public houses and alleyways of the capital city.[54] The timing of the altercation was significant. It had now been more than a year since 'Dynamite Saturday', and Jenkinson's influence and utility were declining in accordance with the square of the distance from the explosive Clan coup of 24 January 1885.

Then there was Jenkinson's parallel animosity towards Robert Anderson. '[He] is not the 19th [*sic*] part of a man,'[55] he railed to his confidant-in-chief, Earl Spencer, in 1888. Anderson was barely clinging to relevance himself in the Home Office. His remaining credibility was based on the steady trickle of information being supplied to him from the USA by Le Caron. Anderson made free with the intelligence – to have kept it to himself would have reinforced his insignificance – but guarded his source jealously. Jenkinson, however, was anxious to identify this long-standing spy at the heart of the Clan who appeared to rival the newly reactivated Millen in seniority. In his autobiography, *Twenty-Five Years in the Secret Service*, Le Caron wrote of his suspicion that Jenkinson (he is referred to coyly as 'a certain public official')[56] sent an agent to Illinois to seek out Anderson's source, whose intelligence he coveted and whose defection to the Jenkinson camp would permit the permanent removal from the spider's web of his London handler. Jenkinson's animosity towards Anderson was further stimulated by the realization that the latter was, for his own protection as much as anything else, edging closer to Monro. Both of them were Protestant millenarianist fundamentalists and both were at odds with the more secular Jenkinson in matters other than religious zealotry.

This was, in part, because Jenkinson, by the mid-1880s, had come to the conclusion that the Irish Parliamentary Party had shed any connection with political violence. He was regularly briefing cabinet members, such as William Harcourt, to this effect. A twenty-page memo to Gladstone in December 1885 doubtless reinforced the Grand Old Man's drift towards the advocacy of Home Rule.[57] Gladstone's marginal highlighting reveals a politician on the cusp of an historic démarche. Anderson and Monro, the former in particular, had an almost visceral loathing of Irish nationalist politics in any form and remained committed to diehard unionism. With the final demise of the Gladstone administration after the failure of the Home Rule Bill in June 1886, Anderson and Monro were more likely to get a hearing from the members of the new Tory administration than a secret policeman whose views on the legitimacy of Parnellite ambitions were very unwelcome.

Paradise lost

At the height of Jenkinson's reign, he had, in theory at least, local police forces at his beck and call, and he employed up to thirty RIC officers in Britain. All of which cost money. Analysis by Professor Eunan O'Halpin of Trinity College Dublin of the intensity of secret service activity from 1878 to 1895 indicates a huge increase in expenditure during Jenkinson's tenure in London. More than £60,000 (roughly £6.5 million today) was expended from 1883 to 1886 – mostly on anti-Fenian espionage – compared with just under £60,000 for the other seventeen years of the period surveyed. In comparison, British spending on spies and informants during the two most violent years of the War of Independence (1920 and 1921), a period of far greater 'terrorist' threat, totalled just under £110,000, which is around 85 per cent of the sum spent during Jenkinson's tenure in Room 56 (when adjusted for inflation).[58] Jenkinson's expenditure on his own operations amounted to roughly half of that £60,000 figure.[59]

Just as – to paraphrase Enoch Powell – all political careers end in failure, such is also the case with many who choose espionage as their calling. Should the spymaster preside over a series of abject intelligence fiascos, they are likely to be dismissed for incompetence. Should their covert and unpublicized successes ensure peace and stability, the need for a hard-pressed exchequer to continue to fund their activities will often become a subject for vigorous debate. Thus it was with Edward Jenkinson. While he was knighted by an apparently grateful monarch in 1888, the Order of the Boot came first, in 1886, when the new Tory administration of the Marquess of Salisbury decided that he was not only surplus to requirements, but was showing signs of incipient megalomania in clamouring for an increase in his powers with the creation of a new 'Intelligence Department'[60] based in the Home Office.

Jenkinson, scourge of Irish nationalist extremists, had, as already noted, become a Parnellite sympathizer who vouched for the constitutionalist bona fides of moderate Irish nationalists. These were assurances that his new Tory overlords simply did not want to hear. After almost two years of a dynamite-free Britain, ignoring Jenkinson's caveats that he had merely 'scotched the snake, not killed it', the Tories discovered that they could do without this Liberal appointee who was on a journey to the 'dark side': a victim of Irish nationalist 'Stockholm syndrome' a century before the term gained currency. He was allowed to resign but his departure amounted to constructive dismissal. The preference of the new Tory administration was for the less charismatic and more orange-hued combination of Robert Anderson and James Monro – the former making an unexpected comeback, the latter cresting the greasy pole after months of infighting with his implacable rival in Room 56.

Jenkinson's formal and time-limited appointment to his assistant under-secretary position in Dublin Castle had ended even before the Tories assumed office in the middle of 1886. He was retained in the Home Office itself until December of that year, at which point he was permitted to resign, a date in early January 1887 being deemed appropriate for his departure.[61] Immediately before his defenestration, in an extreme gesture of bitterness and paranoia, Jenkinson – despite a specific instruction from Home Secretary Henry Matthews that they should be preserved in the Home Office[62] – destroyed all his secret files before vacating Room 56. Edward Jenkinson's distrust of any espionage operation, other than one ordained and monitored by Edward Jenkinson, was given vivid expression by this wilful act of sabotage. He made sure that neither Anderson nor Monro would inherit his undercover operatives – not that either man expressed any interest in doing so. He would justify, to himself at least, the destruction of his records by insisting that he could not be certain that the identities of his covert loyalists would remain confidential. However, an instinct for self-preservation cannot be discounted either. Among the documents that he reduced to ashes there was almost bound to be at least some evidence of his incitement of hazardous and illicit entrapment operations.

*

Ultimately Edward Jenkinson was a law unto himself. He operated in the twilight zone between legitimacy and illegality. He bypassed, misinformed or simply lied to his political superiors, although he kept his mentor, Earl Spencer, abreast of activities of which the 'Red Earl' might well have preferred to remain in ignorance. He boasted to Spencer in 1885, for example, that, 'in the IRB nothing of importance can be done we should not know of, and in some places the organization [*sic*] is almost under our management and control'.[63] His agents and informers successfully infiltrated the IRB in Ireland and in Britain, and his reach extended across the Atlantic to the extremists within the Clan and the United Irishmen of America. He even benefited from the widespread opposition within the IRB to the Irish-American bombing campaign and hinted in a letter to Spencer in September 1884 that allowing 'a very serious outrage' to take place might lead to the total alienation – and by extension increased collaboration with the authorities – of Fenians on both sides of the Atlantic.[64]

To some extent Jenkinson became a victim of his own success as well as of his innate arrogance and his maturing political sensibilities. By the time of the establishment of the Tory government, after the fall of the Home Rule Bill in June 1886, there had been no bombings for more than a year. The Tories felt secure enough to do without the services of an increasingly egotistical, powerful and unaccountable intelligence chief of evolving nationalist inclinations. Jenkinson's conviction, and consequently his advice, that 'the peace of Ireland depends upon the influence and position of Mr. Parnell',[65] was wise counsel, but was anathema to the Tory leadership. Within months of his dismissal, Jenkinson had, in effect, switched sides and was offering practical assistance to Irish constitutionalists who were under threat from a vengeful Tory administration. Robert Anderson was far more likely to offer intelligence that accorded with Tory preconceptions and fed into their precooked policy decisions. Therefore Anderson was back in, and Jenkinson was out.

The undervalued Robert Anderson had now come into his

own. Anderson, notwithstanding the necessity to collaborate with the Scotland Yard SIB (and he would soon take over Monro's position as head of CID), treated anti-Fenian espionage as his personal fiefdom. The Liberal Home Secretary, William Harcourt, had captured the essence of Anderson's personality when he observed that 'Anderson's idea of secrecy is not to tell the Secretary of State'.[66] With Jenkinson now safely out of the picture, when Anderson was approached by *The Times* to make an anonymous contribution on Irish-American militancy for a series of articles to be called 'Parnellism and Crime', he, somewhat reluctantly, according to his own untrustworthy account, agreed.[67]

If he had thought twice about where this could lead, he might well have reconsidered.

PART II
EXODUS

4

THE BOMBSHELL

'A villainous and barefaced forgery ... this unblushing calumny'.[1]

Charles Stewart Parnell,
House of Commons debate, 19 April 1887

'The allegations of crime were almost all indefinite; the method was by allusion, suggestion, innuendo, and the combination of ingeniously selected pieces, to form a crude and hideous mosaic.'[2]

John Morley,
Life of Gladstone (1908)

Richard Pigott – the second act

The sale of his newspapers in 1881 was supposed to have neutered Richard Pigott. He should have folded his tent and faded into obscurity. He should have been able to live modestly but comfortably on the proceeds of the handsome nest egg from the purchase of his three titles by the Land League. Patrick Egan had paid a high price to be rid of him. But when his most persistent debtors were satisfied, and a few more bottles of Kingstown Yacht Club champagne were quaffed with his cronies, the nest egg quickly turned into a cold omelette. His sideline, the sale of pornographic material, was not sufficiently lucrative to keep the former proprietor of *The Irishman*, *The Shamrock* and *The Flag of Ireland* in the manner to which he had become accustomed. Desperate

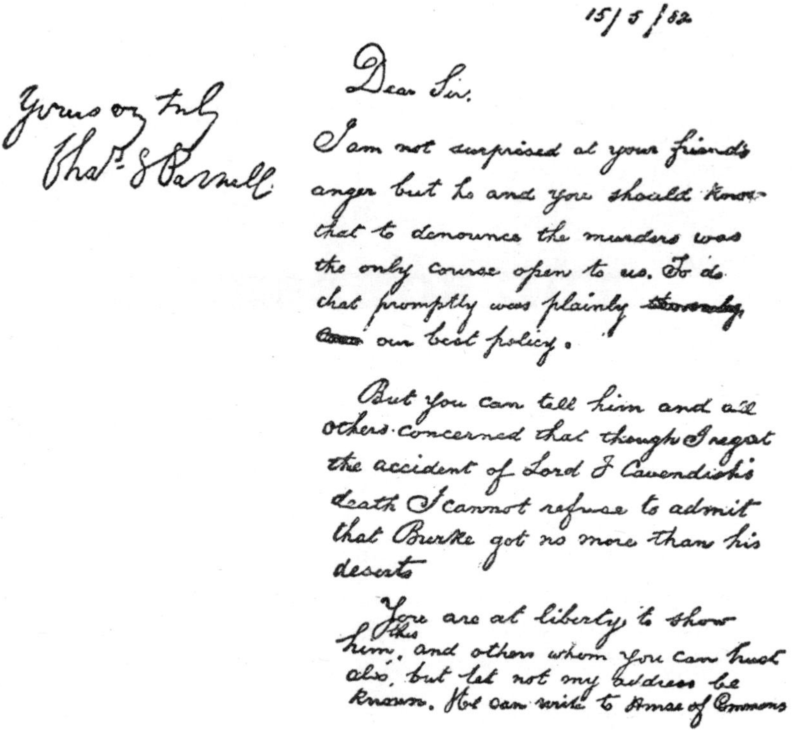

15/5/82

Dear Sir,

I am not surprised at your friend's anger but he and you should know that to denounce the murders was the only course open to us. To do that promptly was plainly our best policy.

But you can tell him and all others concerned that though I regret the accident of Lord F Cavendish's death I cannot refuse to admit that Burke got no more than his deserts

You are at liberty to show him, and others whom you can trust also, but let not my address be known. He can write to House of Commons

Yours very truly
Chas. S. Parnell

The Times, *'facsimile letter', 18 April 1887*

times called for desperate measures. The IRB had always been good to him. Its members and supporters had dutifully shelled out at least a penny a week for one or all of his newspapers. He had allied himself to the irreconcilable wing of the Fenian movement and fulminated in print against the audacity of the Land League in distracting the Irish peasantry from its obligations to practise bloody revolution. But there was no longer any income from that source. Neither could he moderate his rhetoric and offer his pen to the militant agrarian movement or its freshly house-trained political wing. That ship had sailed. Instead Pigott made a vault from extremist nationalism to virulent unionism. He discovered that there was a decent living to be made from signing on as a writer for bodies with names like the Irish Loyal and Patriotic Union. He could, almost, make a living for himself and his four children producing pamphlets that exposed the iniquities of the Land League and the Parnellites, none of whom he had much time for anyway. The feeling was mutual.

He also discovered how gullible his new patrons could be in their anxiety to impeach Irish agrarianism and nationalism. But vitriolic polemics had a short and unprofitable shelf life. Acquiring incriminating evidence of the crimes of the constitutionalist leaders of 'moderate' Irish nationalism would be far more lucrative. He made promises to his loyalist patrons that he could get the goods on members of the Parnellite officer corps and was encouraged by their enthusiastic response. He would be compensated for his time. He would be amply rewarded when he produced something of substance that would undermine the credibility of a party that had come within a handful of votes of getting Home Rule through the House of Commons.

But what if there was nothing there? What if there *were* no incriminating documents linking Parnell, Dillon, O'Brien, Biggar, Healy, Sexton or Egan to some of the murderous atrocities of the Land War and the Irish-American bombers? Unsubstantiated allegations would not fly indefinitely. Pinning felonies on the likes of P. J. Sheridan or fellow agrarian radical Matthew Harris would not suffice either. The 'hard men' were already priced in. It was the moderate salesmen of separatism who needed to be tainted.

How to do it? Pigott's answer was breathtakingly simple. He would simply create evidence where none existed and then claim his reward.

Which is precisely what he did.

The Times, 18 April 1887

It was buried in the middle of page eight, a journalistic bomb hiding in plain sight. It had been primed to ignite under the imperious Charles Stewart Parnell, 'Uncrowned King of Ireland' according to his reverential supporters. *The Times* had already planted three earlier devices and all had turned out to be damp squibs, but there was little doubt that the latest was more potent. When he first noticed the piece, one senior government supporter pushed his breakfast to one side and observed: 'There goes Home Rule, and the Liberal Party too.'[3] He wasn't the only Gladstonian to lose his appetite that morning. Tories, on the other hand, feasted on their kippers with extra gusto.

The Times had been in the business of news since 1785. Back then, for the first three years of its existence, it was published as the *Daily Universal Register* before adopting the more user-friendly title on 1 January 1788. Its original owner, John Walter, had once spent time in Newgate Prison for libel, a badge of honour for a newspaper proprietor. *The Times* had been an enthusiastic supporter of the Great Reform Act of 1832. Its first bona fide war correspondent, Dubliner William Howard Russell, had been excoriated by Queen Victoria herself for his critical and damning coverage of the Crimean War. On the debit side, the newspaper had initially opposed the repeal of the Corn Laws, and had been unenthusiastic about government intervention in the Great Famine of the mid-1840s. Two more proprietors by the name of John Walter (his son and grandson) had followed the founder. The paper's circulation had increased from a meagre 2,000 a day at its inception, to 5,000 at the time of the Battle of Waterloo, to 60,000 by 1855. This coincided with the final relaxation of government tax and excise barriers to entry to the newspaper business. The regime-changing legislation quickly led to the numerical dominance of new players, like the upstart *Daily Telegraph*. By 1887 *The Times* was 'experiencing financial difficulties, caused by its old-fashioned administration, its antiquated production methods and the competition of the new journalism'.[4] But it still wielded a profound influence among the chattering classes; 'to them *The Times* was like the Holy Writ'.[5] Few doubted anything the newspaper chose to print.

But in all that time – more than a century – of obeisance to various eighteenth-century administrations; followed by decades of thundering disapproval of their excesses and blunders; before a final reversion to an almost universal assent to government undertakings, *The Times* had never carried a photograph or a documentary facsimile (once the technology permitted of such innovations) on its tightly printed pages.

Which made the issue of 18 April 1887 ground-breaking and historic.

However, the motivation that day, in publishing the photographic copy of a controversial and damning letter, had not merely been to break new ground. More relevant had been the determination to curtail the growing power and influence of Parnell and the Irish Parliamentary Party (IPP), the party that had inveigled Gladstone into committing contempt of empire.

The Times was not fond of the Irish leader and his *amour-propre*. It was even less enamoured of the often unruly cohort of political disciples who trailed in his wake. The newspaper's antipathy had been accentuated by the recent success of the IPP in converting the Liberal leader, William Gladstone, to the cause of Irish Home Rule. In the opinion of John Walter III, and his young editor George Buckle – only thirty-two years of age in 1887 – that way lay perdition. Devolution for Ireland, of even the blandest kind, would be an inevitable prelude to the loss of the painstakingly accumulated, and enormously lucrative, British Empire.

Hence the willingness of editor and proprietor to embrace technical innovation in the higher cause of chauvinism and imperialism. Walter and Buckle had in their possession something precious: what they believed to be conclusive proof of the perfidy of the leader of the Irish parliamentary rabble. *The Times* intended to flaunt it.

The facsimile of this politically ruinous letter – clearly written by an amanuensis, but apparently signed by Parnell in his distinctive hand – read as follows:

Dear Sir,
I am not surprised at your friend's anger but he and you should know that to denounce the murders was the only course open to us. To do that promptly was plainly our best policy.

But you can tell him and all others concerned that though I regret the accident of Lord F. Cavendish's death I cannot refuse to admit that Burke got no more than his deserts.

You are at liberty to show him this, and others whom you can trust also, but let not my address be known. He can write to House of Commons.

Yours very truly,

Chas. S. Parnell[6]

The text, assuming the signature was genuine, clearly linked Parnell to the savagery of the 'Invincibles' in their slaying of Cavendish and Burke.

Now *The Times* had unimpeachable documentary evidence of the menacing extremism at the heart of Irish separatism. The knives that had felled Burke and Cavendish might not have been wielded by any of the eighty or so MPs aligned to Parnell in the House of Commons, but their leader's imprudent correspondence now revealed the complicity, in an act of brutal political violence, of a party that spuriously claimed to be 'constitutionalist'. *The Times* had finally exposed a submerged truth, one that its own leader columns had long proclaimed. The IPP was about as wedded to constitutionalism as was the militant IRB, or the bombers of Clan na Gael.

Later that day a crucial vote would be taking place in the House of Commons on a robust new Tory coercion bill designed to deal with a surge in agrarian violence in the more ungovernable parts of rural Ireland. The *Times* exposé could not have come at a better time for the new chief secretary, the languid and aristocratic Arthur Balfour, nephew of the Marquess of

Salisbury.* Assuming the facsimile letter was genuine – and *The Times* would not have published it had they believed otherwise – Balfour was entirely justified in the measures he was proposing to stiffen British resistance to Irish rural anarchy.

Of course, the appearance, on that morning, of the damning Parnell letter in *The Times* was merely a happy coincidence for the prime minister's nephew.

The publication of the 'facsimile' letter had not fallen from a clear blue sky. The clouds had been gathering for more than a month. On 7 March 1887 – coincidentally, or not, the date on which Arthur J. Balfour became the new Irish chief secretary – *The Times* had begun the publication of a series of articles designed to highlight what it condemned as the spirit of lawlessness at the core of Irish parliamentarianism. The title chosen for the series, 'Parnellism and Crime', needed little elaboration.

'The Thunderer' had in its sights the most electorally successful Irish nationalist party of the nineteenth century. Of the 105 seats allocated in the House of Commons to Irish constituencies, the Parnellites had been safely ensconced in 85 since the July 1886 general election.**

Far more alarming, to *The Times* at least, than a cohesive and highly centralized nationalist party in Ireland itself, was the nurture of its principal objective, Irish self-government, in the corridors of Westminster. As the Government of Ireland Bill wound its way through the House of Commons in the spring of 1886, the Tories raged, and *The Times* fulminated. Neither, as it transpired, need have concerned themselves unduly. Even if the legislation had not failed by thirty votes, it would not have been passed by the House of Lords.

*Dubbed 'Arthur Golfour' by *United Ireland* because of his devotion to that sport (although he was just as fond of tennis) and erroneously considered by many Irish nationalists – before they came to grips with him – to be something of an effete and ineffectual dandy.

**Albeit one of those seats, held by T. P. O'Connor, was in a Liverpool constituency.

So one might be tempted to wonder why *The Times* went to the bother of taking a sledgehammer to the Irish separatist nut? Home Rule was a dead letter; Parnell had retreated into a thoroughly domesticated semi-retirement in the Eltham home of his mistress Katharine O'Shea; Gladstone was on the cusp of his eighties; and the American-inspired bombing campaign had imploded.

The answer lay, in part, in an unprecedented unionist insecurity – accentuated by the 'near miss' of the first Home Rule Bill. But the primary reason why the journalistic pillar of the Tory establishment took aim at Irish separatism was because it could. *The Times* was motivated, and emboldened, by its acquisition of a cache of incriminating documents – of which the facsimile letter was the most damaging. Even if *The Times* had not already been philosophically predisposed to unmask the evils of Parnellism, a scoop was a scoop.

Of lesser importance was the re-emergence of agrarian tensions in Ireland since the mid-1880s, an effective renewal of the 1879–82 Land War. The drawn-out process of land reform, initiated by Gladstone's 1881 Land Act and subsequent amending legislation, allied to a highly credible measure of land purchase (the Ashbourne Act) introduced by the caretaker Tory administration in late 1885, had gone some way to ameliorating the dismal social and economic condition of rural Ireland. The spirit of desperation and defiance that had given rise to the foundation of the Land League had eased. But it had not dissolved entirely.

On 23 October 1886, in response to renewed agricultural crisis conditions, an article appeared in *United Ireland*, the newspaper now controlled by the Land League's successor, the Irish National League. In a piece headed 'A Plan of Campaign', the Irish National League secretary, Timothy Harrington, a Kerry journalist, outlined a strategy by which, he suggested, collective and mutually supportive action by tenants could force further rent reductions from recalcitrant landlords. The 'Plan of Campaign' as the tactic, rather unimaginatively, became known, involved the pooling on an estate of unpaid rents in the event of the refusal of mitigation. This would then be used as a 'fighting fund' to assist evicted tenants. The residue would be paid over to the landlord when, rueful and defeated, he finally crawled back to his united tenantry and agreed to an abatement.

At least that was the theory. In some instances the plan actually worked; in others it failed. But in a significant percentage of the more than 200 estates where the 'Plan of Campaign' was put into effect, it resulted in violent confrontations between the agents of intractable landlords and increasingly militant tenants. Advocacy of the 'Plan' would lead to frequent jail terms for influential Irish parliamentarians such as John Dillon, William O'Brien and Harrington himself. One major internal difficulty faced by these agrarian radicals was the (largely unexpressed) opposition to the campaign on the part of Parnell himself. The IPP leader, who had ably exploited the agrarian agitation of the early 1880s, had no desire to see the country descend into another season of murder, mayhem and 'outrage'. His alliance with the Liberal Party was likely to unravel if Captain Moonlight returned.

To *The Times* this was a compelling case of *déjà vu*. The mother of parliaments, in the view of 'The Thunderer', had already spent a disproportionate amount of time attempting to contend with Irish anarchy. The IPP had frequently earned the opprobrium of late Victorian society. Now the respectable classes were about to be treated to irrefutable proof with which to justify their hatred of the Parnellites and their sadly misguided Gladstonian partners. The latter, once the evidence was presented, would, it was presumed, quickly disown their former allies.

In 1887 John Woulfe Flanagan was thirty-five years old, one of eleven children of a wealthy landed Roman-Catholic family from County Roscommon. The young Flanagan, after gaining a double first in Classics at Oxford, was called to the English Bar in 1877. He seemed destined to emulate the career of his distinguished father, who was an Irish Land Court judge. But in 1886 his life took a grievously wayward turn when he became a journalist instead. At least he started at the top, when he joined the staff of *The Times* that year. He never left. Flanagan spent the rest of his working life at the *Times* headquarters in Printing House Square.

The increasing professionalization of journalism in the late nineteenth century meant that it was no longer *de rigueur* for a reporter, or even a leader writer, to share the political bias or the editorial line of his newspaper. He was merely required to be capable of mimicking whatever partisan stance was required. Such compositional gymnastics was not, however, required of John Woulfe Flanagan. Although from an old Roman-Catholic family, he was a committed unionist who was very comfortable with the loyalist Printing House Square ethos. So when he was given the task by his editor, George Buckle, of preparing a series of articles examining the connections between Parnellism and agrarian violence, he set to his task *con brio*.

In reality, as will become apparent, the articles were something of an afterthought, a literary scaffolding erected by a newspaper that had good reason to be nervous about its source material. The first three 'Parnellism and Crime' articles are described by the newspaper's own history (not the least self-serving autobiography ever written!) as '*pièces justificatives*' for the 'indictment' that would follow.[7]

A leading article introduced the series, with what *The History of The Times* sententiously describes as 'a note of solemn indictment'.[8] Here Flanagan castigated the great British public – and, by extension, his own readership – for its 'flabby tolerance of evil' in its attitude towards the activities of 'Mr. Parnell and his allies'. He then went on to suggest of the members of the Irish Party, rather gruesomely, that in times 'more robustly conscious of the difference between evil and good, their heads would have decorated the City gates'. The central thesis of the series was unequivocal. The Irish National League, successor of the Land League, 'depends upon a system of intimidation carried out by the most brutal means and resting ultimately upon the sanction of murder'. Regular condemnations of agrarian violence by Parnell and his lieutenants were brushed aside as arrant hypocrisy. Worse, 'they inflame rather than calm the evil passions of their hearers'.

The anonymous leader – the work of Flanagan (the articles themselves did not carry his by-line either) – lashed itself into a frenzy of vituperation before making the claim that *The Times* would produce 'volumes of evidence' so that all charges of murder, intimidation and outrage are 'proved up to the hilt'.[9]

Flanagan, trained at the Bar, was making his impassioned opening submission to a fresh and alert jury of public opinion as they sat in their railway carriages or devoured their breakfast eggs. However, as with many a rhetorical *tour de force*, the evidence to support the verbal pyrotechnics was scant. Flanagan may have begun in poetry, but what followed was pedantic, incendiary and uncorroborated prose. More than 3,000 words later and the insertion of the knife had not even begun to approach the promised 'hilt'.

The first feature, 'A Retrospect: Ireland', added little to the sum of human knowledge. It underlined the unprincipled pragmatism of politicians (Liberal) in jettisoning their unionist beliefs in pursuit of power, set out the (undisputed) separatist intentions of the Parnellites, and reheated some of the more hair-raising speeches of leading agrarian radical activists such as Thomas Brennan, P. J. Sheridan, Michael Boyton, Matthew Harris and P. J. Gordon. In the last instance it undermined its own case by pointing out that the most bloodthirsty comments 'have been repeatedly published', hardly a prudent course of action for those engaged in a seditious conspiracy. The entire piece was long on indictment ('we charge that the Land League chiefs based their movement on a scheme of assassination') but lamentably short on supportive facts to underpin the argument. Flanagan was largely recycling common knowledge.

As *The History of The Times* observes, while 'no evidence was cited to show direct participation by the leaders of the League', the 'inflammatory utterances' were 'put in immediate juxtaposition with the crimes that seemed the natural consequence of such violence of language'.[10] Rarely has the word 'seemed' been forced to work so hard. Flanagan's case was, therefore, based on a dubious syllogism: Land League activists made inflammatory speeches from public platforms; violent acts often followed violent rhetoric; therefore Land League activists were responsible for maiming and murder. References by Brennan, Sheridan, Boyton and others to 'twenty feet of rope' or 'five [dollars] for bread and twenty for lead', had also frequently been condemned by Parnell, Joseph Biggar and other Irish parliamentarians – but *The Times* had already discounted those denunciations as hypocrisy.

Reaction to the opening *Times* salvo was muted. Even *United Ireland*, Parnell's 'in house' newspaper, from whom a few peevish responses might have been expected, studiously avoided any comment, until it was drawn out of its lair by the 'facsimile' letter in April. Except for a brief and inconsequential flurry on 10 March,[11] there was not a single reference made to the virtual stillbirth of the 'Parnellism and Crime' series in the House of Commons until 18 April.

The second article in the series, 'A Retrospect: America', published on 10 March, concentrated much of its fire on the mercurial Patrick Ford, advocate of 'scientific warfare'[12] against Britain, one of the motive forces behind the dynamite campaign and utopian socialist editor of the New York-based Irish-American newspaper, the *Irish World*.

Flanagan was unconvincing in his efforts to tar Parnell with an *Irish World* brush. On behalf of the Land League, Parnell had accepted financial contributions from the newspaper's readers – to the tune of almost $350,000. This was far in excess of the amount raised by the Skirmishing Fund. The Irish Party leader also attempted (with difficulty) not to alienate the *World*'s American editor by excessive criticism of the more venomous chaff contained in his journal. But that did not constitute an endorsement of the Skirmishing Fund. Furthermore, by the time 'A Retrospect: America' was published, Ford had begun to adopt more centrist economic and political policies, and was an enthusiastic supporter of the constitutional pursuit of Home Rule. *The Times* was visiting its innate intransigence on political figures who were themselves more susceptible to change.

The second article also exhumed the evidence of the informer James Carey at the Invincible trials in 1883. Under examination, Carey, himself a leading Invincible, had highlighted the role of servants of the Land League, like P. J. Sheridan and Frank Byrne (secretary of the Land League of Great Britain) in the Invincible conspiracy. Byrne, he claimed, had provided the surgical knives used in the Phoenix Park murders. However, in his efforts to establish guilt by association, Flanagan was citing allegations that had been in the public domain for so long they had already begun to rust. He signed off the second article by promising, a few days hence, to lay bare the 'ligaments that knit the so-called "constitutional movement" [with] … notorious dynamiters and assassins'.[13] A small, and rapidly diminishing, cohort of even the *Times*-reading public waited with partially bated breath for these lethal sinews to be exposed.

What should have been the *coup de grâce* was published on 14 March 1887. It was melodramatically entitled 'A Study in Contemporary Conspiracy' and began by asserting that 'Mr. Parnell's "constitutional organization" was planned by Fenian brains, founded on a Fenian loan, and reared by Fenian hands … assassins guarded it about, and enforced the high decrees of the secret conclave within by the bullet and the knife.'[14] Flanagan also played his ace by introducing *Times* readers to the ruthless leader of the Clan na Gael organization in the United States, Alexander Sullivan, former president of the Irish National League of America. Flanagan asserted that the Clan, under Sullivan, 'planned and executed all the most diabolic of the dynamite outrages perpetrated in this country since the spring of 1883'.[15] The IPP had never disavowed its Irish-American proxies, therefore, according to *The Times*, it shared responsibility for the actions of Sullivan's agents.

The underlying reality of this transatlantic relationship was, however, the constant struggle by the Parnellites – via the despatch of delegates from the Parliamentary Party to the conclaves of their Irish-American supporters – to moderate the policies, the rhetoric and the work of the Irish National League of America (an organization under the sway of the Clan), while keeping funds flowing from west to east. Emissaries such as Michael Davitt, John Redmond and Justin McCarthy tried to minimize the potential for embarrassment of blood-curdling statements from the American League, or the columns of the *Irish World*.

At the conclusion of the third article, Flanagan announced with a final flourish: 'We suspend our studies of Parnellism. They do not affect to be complete. They are made on a cursory examination of a small portion of the published evidence.'[16]

Therein lay the dilemma for *The Times*. The evidence as already published – and here collated by *The Times* – had failed to annihilate the Irish National League or its parliamentary alter ego. A rehashing of that evidence by *The Times*, even in such a concentrated form, was hardly likely to bring about what almost a decade of suspicion and allegation had failed to achieve. *The Times* loudly concluded by reaffirming that the Parnellites were 'in trade and traffic with avowed dynamiters and known contrivers of murder'.[17] If the reader, however, were to ask for solid proof, the answer could only have been the perennially unsatisfactory 'trust me, I'm a journalist'. The real quandary for *The Times*, however, was that practically nobody was listening. The newspaper's strident and earnest assertions amounted to little more than white noise.

The three articles had probably succeeded in rousing the animosities of the average *Times* reader against the great Irish unwashed. But the nationalist Irish themselves – among whom were numbered relatively few *Times* readers – were largely unmoved. No Irish reader seriously believed that the Land League could have functioned without the exercise of physical, psychological or moral sanctions. Equally unmoved was British public opinion. While disposed to acknowledge the credibility of the newspaper's central charges, middle England was otherwise engaged. *The Times*, in making its allegations, was reverting to a previous electoral cycle. Much had happened since 1883. This included a stunning electoral success on the part of the Parnellites in 1885 (eighty-six seats), largely repeated in 1886 (eighty-five seats), and the acceptance by one of the two main parties in British politics that it was time to begin doing business with the IPP. It would take more than a few warmed-over horror stories to offset British apathy.

In truth, the 'Parnellism and Crime' series was fuelled by a conservative pathology that did not readily admit of the notion of political change. Whatever the murky past of members of the IPP, or of their former associates, by 1887 it was committed – some might have said 'chained' – to a constitutional settlement of Irish political grievances. This had already been acknowledged by the Liberals, a party as capable of change as were the Parnellites. The stumbling block was a largely intractable and unimaginative Tory mindset that refused to see beyond the *status quo ante bellum*, the war in this instance being the 1879–82 Land War. *The Times* had advised Gladstone and the Liberals that they should recognize the accuracy of the contents of 'Parnellism and Crime' and act accordingly, or 'regard them as calumnies'.[18] What the newspaper did not suggest was a third option: that the Liberals, while largely acknowledging the justice of many of the charges in *The Times*, could simply choose blithe indifference over outright recognition or denial.

All this was by way of tedious and tendentious prologue to the detonation of 18 April. By then *The Times* badly needed a coup that would seize the attention of the British body politic.

In the 'facsimile' letter, the newspaper got precisely what it was looking for.

After a hiatus of four weeks, on 12 April *The Times* resumed its assault on the Parnellites with an article entitled 'The National League at Work'. In this piece boycotting was assailed as 'that terrible instrument of oppression', and Gladstone's 1882 observation that 'the sanction of boycotting is murder' was exhumed. The criminality of 'the conspiracy' was updated to include instances of violence arising out of the newly wrought 'Plan of Campaign'. In the more raucous parts of the country the Irish National League was described as 'the *de facto* government', and radical priests ('contumacious ecclesiastics') were upbraided for offering their support to agrarian carnage. The piece concluded with a rhetorical question: 'Can there be a deeper infamy than to tolerate tyranny such as this?'[19]

So far, so familiar. Both nations continued to doze. Then, six days later, *The Times* did as it had long threatened to do. The facsimile letter, reportedly written on 'stout white notepaper', was reproduced in all its chilling cynicism. The faint of heart were issued a nineteenth-century version of a trigger warning, albeit with a certain righteous glee:

> We do not think it is right to withhold any longer from public knowledge the fact that we possess and have had in our custody for some time documentary evidence which has a most serious bearing on the Parnellite conspiracy, and, which, after a most careful and minute scrutiny, is, we are satisfied, quite authentic.[20]

Careful scrutiny, but, as it turned out, not quite minute enough. For the moment, however, the impeccable reputation of *The Times* gave it a moral authority that Parnell could not hope to challenge. He was loftily invited by the newspaper 'to explain how his signature has become attached to such a letter'. As definitive proof that the signature was, indeed, that of the Irish Party leader, doubters were invited to satisfy themselves 'by comparing the handwriting with that of Mr. Parnell in the book containing the signatures of members when they first take their seats in the House of Commons'.

Whatever about the authenticity of the signature, *The Times* – which claimed that the letter had been written to Patrick Egan in an attempt to pacify hardline nationalist elements alienated by the 'Kilmainham Treaty' – made at least one misstep in the covering material. The newspaper cited the reluctance of Parnell to have his address known, and referred to 'a belief prevailing at the time that Mr. Parnell was so impressed by the danger he had incurred by denouncing the assassinations as to have applied for the protection of the police on the plea that his life was in peril'.

No such application had ever been made. The canard was a malicious piece of gossip circulated by Captain William O'Shea, the husband of Parnell's mistress/common-law wife, Katharine O'Shea. While *The Times* might well have come by O'Shea's claim from someone other than its initiator, the inclusion of this particular piece of misinformation, given the original source, suggested that the captain was lurking somewhere in the shadows.

On 8 May 1882, in his first speaking opportunity in the House after the Phoenix Park killings, Parnell had, in condemning those responsible for the murder, remarked that:

> The crime has been committed by men who absolutely detest the cause with which I have been associated and who have devised that crime and carried it out as the deadliest blow which they had in their power to deal against our hopes.[21]

The Times, retrospectively, dismissed this 'benevolent construction' as Parnellite cant, despite the obvious damage done to the cause of Irish constitutional nationalism by the surgical knives of the Invincibles. The newspaper then invited the Parnellites to step into the ring. It reminded its readers that 'these charges … are protected by no privilege of parliament or other artificial shelter'. It was open to those accused to seek to 'recover damages in a Court of law'. This challenge was captured graphically in a John Tenniel cartoon in *Punch* magazine. The artist portrayed *The Times* (represented by a helmeted knight with its distinctive clock-face logo as a shield) sitting on horseback and throwing a gauntlet before a similarly accoutred but pensive Parnell. The caption, predictably, read 'The Challenge'. *Punch* also reminded Parnell that:

> The gauntlet's down, in tourney days
> The Knight who failed the gage to raise
> Had courted instant shame.[22]

If the account of Katharine O'Shea is to be relied upon (far from a given), then it was she who pointed out the *Times* article to the Irish leader before he left their house in Eltham for Westminster. On reading the piece, he displayed, she insisted, an air of insouciance, remarking to her in their cosy private language, 'Wouldn't you hide your head with shame if your King were so stupid as that, my Queen?'[23] Given Parnell's phlegmatic temperament, the anecdote – augmented with the information that a copy of the piece was later pinned to the gates of their home – has a ring of truth. However,

THE CHALLENGE.

she does get the date wrong (7 March as opposed to 18 April) and also claims that Parnell was back in Eltham that same evening. Since he was speaking in the House of Commons until almost 1.30 a.m., that would not have been possible. Furthermore, in his evidence to the Special Commission, and in his first speech in the House after the appearance of the facsimile, Parnell claimed that he did not 'take' *The Times*.

The ever-loyal Timothy Harrington MP also laid claim to having been the first to show the article to Parnell. He observed that, when he did so, the Irish leader calmly, and almost indifferently, traced his finger along the 'S' of his signature and remarked that 'I did not make an "S" like that since 1878'.[24] As we will see, this was untrue.

Parnell's apparent *sang-froid* – composure being his default position – was counterbalanced by an air of acute panic on the part of his political associates. Parnell was persuaded that a statement of denial, to be made to the House of Commons, was urgently required. But the wheels of the 'Mother of Parliaments' ground slowly, and a Parnellite *apologia* was not a priority for the dominant Tories. The second reading of Balfour's Crimes Act was the earliest opportunity for a riposte and, by then, anything Parnell said would be too late for the early editions of the morning papers of 19 April, most of which would be responding to the fallout from the 'facsimile' letter and manufacturing excuses for being scooped. After Gladstone, the Liberal leader, had concluded his demolition of both the necessity for, and the terms of, the new Tory coercion measures, Parnell rose to speak. It was approaching 1 a.m. As he did so, the languorous chief secretary stirred himself on the Treasury Bench. The chair recognized Balfour, who responded to Gladstone's denunciation of his bill as Parnell fumed on the opposition benches, watching the clock and awaiting his turn.

He finally got his opportunity to speak at ten minutes past one on 19 April. He decried the *Times*'s facsimile as a 'villainous and barefaced forgery' and an 'unblushing calumny'.[25] Thereafter, however, he became bogged down in an uninformed (and disingenuous) discussion of graphology and phraseology. He claimed the 'anonymous fabrication' of his signature looked utterly unlike his own 'cramped hand'. This was not a very promising terrain upon which to build a defence. It was, at best, misdirection, at worst an outright lie. When Michael Davitt had seen the letter procured by *The Times*, he had noted the 'staggering similarity of the signature'.[26] Far from there being 'only two letters in the whole name which bear any resemblance to letters in my own signature as I write it' – as Parnell claimed in his early-morning address to the Commons – there was an undeniable resemblance between his handwriting and the signature on the fourth page of the incriminating letter. His own party had little option other than to believe and support their beleaguered leader. A somewhat self-pitying aside towards the end of his speech, to the effect that 'I have suffered more than any other man from that terrible deed in the Phoenix Park', did him no favours with his anxious Liberal allies. The assembled members of the party, of which Lord Frederick Cavendish had been a popular member, might have observed, ruefully, that Parnell's 'suffering' was hardly on a par with that of the victims of the Invincibles' knives. On the Conservative side of the House, however, his pronouncement, where it was not entertained in stony silence, was greeted with derision.[27] The Marquess of Salisbury (a member of the House of Lords) was certainly not impressed. On 20 April he told his listeners at a meeting in Swansea that Parnell was 'tainted with the strong presumption of conniving at assassination'. In Scotland Joseph Chamberlain gleefully told his audience that the *Times*'s piece was Parnell's 'death warrant'.[28]

In journalistic parlance, this one was going to run and run.

5

THE 'JUBILEE PLOT'

Fishing for a Red Herring

'Liberty is a most excellent thing, but the kind of liberty which is to be enjoyed on the top of a barrel of gunpowder with a lighted match just on the point of being applied to it is a somewhat insecure and questionable blessing.'

The Times, 24 November 1883

'No agent of the British government would become intentionally an *agent provocateur*; but in those days it needed both vigilance and shrewdness to avoid blundering into a false position which would have involved that reproach.'[1]

Robert Anderson, *The Lighter Side of My Official Life* (1910)

'It was clear that a plot of a far-reaching character had been set on foot but there were many reasons for believing that it had been organised by the British government's Secret Service money.'[2]

Former Special Irish Branch detective Sergeant Patrick McIntyre, *Reynolds's Newspaper*, 1895

Westminster, 5 November 1605

The basement vault under the House of Lords had already been searched once. It was found to contain only an innocent pile of wood and a servant, John Johnson, delegated by his employer,

Thomas Percy, to take care of the firewood. The reason for the search was that the authorities had been spooked by a letter delivered on 1 November to the Catholic peer Lord Monteagle. This warned him to avoid attending the opening of parliament. Monteagle had brought the letter to the attention of Robert Cecil, 1st Earl of Salisbury, the power behind the throne and the man responsible for the security of the British state. Cecil had taken the warning seriously.

When the name of Thomas Percy, a notorious Roman-Catholic agitator, was invoked, the king himself, James I, ordered a more thorough search of the 'undercrofts' of the House of Lords. When the search party returned to the basement chamber being rented by Percy, they found John Johnson *in situ*, still diligently guarding his master's precious firewood. On closer inspection, however, when the faggots were moved aside, thirty-six barrels of gunpowder were discovered underneath. Johnson was immediately arrested and interrogated. Even under torture, he refused to identify his associates. It was not until 7 November that his sadistic but insufficiently scrupulous inquisitors thought to search their tormented prisoner's clothing and found there a letter addressed to a 'Mr. Fawkes'. John Johnson was Guy Fawkes, papist fanatic delegated by a group of Roman-Catholic conspirators to 'light fuse and retire': to obliterate the Houses of Parliament in an enormous explosion that would kill the king, his closest advisers and the Protestant political leadership of the country, and thus (so it was devoutly wished by the plotters) hasten the return of Romanism.

The militant Catholic conspirators, led by Robert Catesby, were disillusioned with the new king. They were frustrated at the lack of any Catholic relief measures and had decided that direct action was necessary. Their conspiracy, however, was dogged by ill luck and incompetence.

Guy Fawkes, after days of determined resistance, eventually succumbed to his torturers and named his fellow conspirators. Many of them died in a shoot-out at Holbeche House in Staffordshire. The surviving plotters received the traditional death for traitors in seventeenth-century England: they were 'half-hanged' from the gallows, eviscerated, then drawn and quartered in public. But this was not to be the fate of Fawkes. He was so weakened by his torturers that he had difficulty even ascending to the gallows. When the rope was put around his neck to 'half-hang' him Fawkes found the strength to leap off the scaffold and break his own neck. His body was subsequently quartered, and his remains were sent to 'the four corners of the kingdom' as a warning to others.

In recent years some historians have begun to question the 'received' version of events, arguing that the plot was really devised and provoked by Robert Cecil himself to copper-fasten the king's antagonism towards Catholicism. This conspiratorial alternative version of events claims that Cecil was a felon-setter who blackmailed Catesby into organizing the plot and who shepherded in the subsequent legislation stripping Catholics of the right to practise law, to become officers in the Army and Navy, or to vote in local or parliamentary elections – measures similar to the Penal Laws introduced in Ireland at the end of the seventeenth century. It's all rather circumstantial and debatable, and the thesis is generally rejected by historians of the period.

But history was to repeat itself. Almost.

Two hundred and eighty-two years after the failure of the Gunpowder Plot, members of another militant fraternity, mostly, but not exclusively, Roman Catholic, would be accused of targeting the reigning monarch, her cabinet and the political leadership of the United Kingdom in a deadly bomb plot. One of the alleged targets of this conspiracy was Robert Gascoyne-Cecil, 3rd Marquess of Salisbury, direct descendant of James I's chief minister. While there is a huge question mark over his ancestor's use of *agents provocateurs* to cement Protestant domination of Stuart Britain, there is no doubt whatsoever about Robert Gascoyne-Cecil's administration's collusion in a bogus conspiracy to undermine the legitimate claims of Irish nationalists to legislative independence.

The Gunpowder Plot was real. The 'Jubilee plot' was a sham.

'Greek fire'

'The whole undertaking was shrouded in mystery.'[3]

Henri Le Caron/Thomas Beach, *Twenty-Five Years in the Secret Service* (1895)

'This member of the Council came to me to request my assistance to raise two thousand dollars to enable them to do some work. They claim that they intend celebrating the Queen's birthday, and that one hundred and fifty men are prepared to work with Greek fire with which they are at present supplying them.'[4]

Luke Dillon to John Devoy, 7 February 1887

'The "Jubilee illumination" was declared to be a series of dynamite outrages which the American Irish were preparing as a cynic [*sic*] and cruel protest against the general joy in Victoria's fifty years of sovereignty. It had absolutely no foundation in fact whatever. There was not one iota of reality to substantiate the fright, but the dove-cote at Scotland Yard was fluttered, and detectives absolutely worked over the whole of America and France to find a foundation for their blood-curdling romances.'[5]

Sullivan supporter John McEnnis, *The Clan-na-Gael and the Murder of Dr. Cronin* (1889)

An *agent provocateur* is rather like a magnet. Once he or she – generally the former – has been activated by their handlers, their job is to attract as many dupes as possible into their magnetic field. When they are demagnetized, their prey drops smoothly into a collection bag, ready to be transferred to the courts, there to be convicted of crimes into which they were lured by the devious *agent*. Some might have become involved in such enterprises without the intervention of the magnet, some might not. All, other than the whistleblower who had provoked the entire undertaking, end up in jail. Or worse.

The use of *agents provocateurs* was an integral part of British security policy in Ireland in the nineteenth century. Sometimes this was hard to prove, because the appearance of the felon-setter in a court of law to testify against his gulls was often unnecessary. In a mass trial of a group of suspects, a convenient informer, threatened with the gallows or a long term of imprisonment, could often be found to make the transition to 'approver' and become a state witness. This allowed the *agent provocateur* to blend into the background and to become 'the one who got away', a fortunate member of the conspiracy who somehow managed to escape the clutches of the law. He might not even have outlived his usefulness if he managed to allay the suspicions of his former co-conspirators. 'Red' Jim McDermott was a case in point. He had a relatively long career in what could be a short-lived profession. Of course Robert Anderson observed unctuously in his self-serving memoir that, 'no agent of the British government would become intentionally an *agent provocateur*'[6] – except, obviously, for the many British agents, from Red Jim McDermott to Frank Millen, who did precisely that.

By the summer of 1887 Queen Victoria had been on the throne for fifty years. Newly beloved – this was due as much to her longevity as to her often lugubrious personality – such a landmark event would not be allowed to pass unnoticed by her loyal Conservative government. She was, after all, Empress of India, the ruby in the crown of the vast British Empire. No longer as cloistered as she had been for decades, after the premature death of her consort, Prince Albert, the monarch was expected to play an enthusiastic and public role in the month (June 1887) of festivities arranged to mark her Golden Jubilee. That would mean thirty days of headaches for those charged with the protection of Her Majesty – already the subject of multiple assassination attempts – Henry Matthews, the Home Secretary; Sir Charles Warren, the militaristic Metropolitan Police Commissioner; and the assistant commissioner in charge of CID, career policeman James Monro. Basking in the shadows, in saturnine anonymity, was Robert Anderson, Monro's deputy, newly restored to 'secret service' operational duties after the eclipse of Edward Jenkinson.

A crisis was imminent. Monro would take care of it. Robert Anderson would take advantage of it.

The unwitting Parnellites were to be woven into the fabric of an entrapment operation the breathtaking scale of which, if successful, would dwarf any previous 'stings'. At its core were a highly politicized civil servant and two Irish-American double-agents doing the bidding of the British unionist establishment. If the *Times* letter didn't see off Parnellism for good, then the combined machinations of Robert Anderson, Frank Millen and Charles Carroll Tevis – with the soundless (and deniable) approval of the prime minister himself – certainly would.

It is important to establish one salient fact when it comes to the 'Jubilee plot' of 1887. (This was the melodramatic terminology applied by the British press to another apparent Irish-American assault on Queen Victoria's domain.) The dastardly Clan was rumoured to be ready to resume the wave of bombing that had been in abeyance since 'Dynamite Saturday'.

There was indeed an intent on the part of the Triangle faction of Clan na Gael (rebranded as the Irish National Brotherhood) and allies within the Fenian Brotherhood/United Irishmen of America in New York to resume the bombing of British targets in 1887. A number of letters to John Devoy from followers of his who were opposed to the renewal of the campaign make this clear.[7]

At a secret meeting of the Sullivan/Boland faction of Clan na Gael in August 1886, it was decided, in a roguish euphemism, to offer 'a pyrotechnic display in honour of Queen Victoria's Jubilee'.[8] There had been a rapprochement between Sullivan's bloc of the Clan and the 'skirmishers', now led by the New York journalist Patrick Sarsfield Cassidy, a senior figure within the Fenian Brotherhood.[9] Funds were being raised for dynamite by the Irish National Brotherhood. The New Yorkers would supply the volunteers and the operational nous.

Would such a renewal of terrorism attract support from the IRB? The attacks of the early 1880s certainly had not. Senior Clan figure General Francis Frederick Millen was sent back to Europe to find out if, this time, the IRB was inclined to action. Millen travelled in early 1887 to Paris – where he may well have had a final meeting with the recently ousted Jenkinson – to re-establish a link with the Supreme Council that Alexander Sullivan had done much to weaken. Millen, who was not received with any great enthusiasm by the IRB Supreme Council, consulted and reported back. The IRB was not open to a resumption of the dynamite campaign. Surprisingly, however, Millen most certainly was. The Mexican general – now on a decent retainer as a British secret service informant – was suddenly and inexplicably an enthusiastic advocate of a conspiracy to disrupt the Jubilee celebrations. His previous opposition to the use of dynamite against British targets – often expressed in the Councils of the Clan – did not appear to have survived his journey across the Atlantic. And, as he was so positive about the value of a renewed campaign – and everyone is entitled to change their minds – why not plan and execute it himself? Millen, a 'dove' during the Clan's previous flirtation with dynamite, was given the job of planning the Jubilee-year operation from a base in France.

But was everything, however surprising, quite as it seemed?

Millen made for an odd saboteur. Throughout the abortive efforts to disrupt the fiftieth anniversary of Queen Victoria's accession to the throne, he *appeared* to take the lead, and the heat, in an operation that was doomed from the outset. He was portrayed in official circles and in the London press as the mastermind behind the conspiracy. Had he, racked by his betrayal of the 1867 Fenian rising, become a fully committed terrorist by 1887? Or was he collaborating with elements of the British securocracy (Edward Jenkinson followed by Robert Anderson) in a scheme designed to hook a number of ill-starred 'marks' who would then be scooped up by the forces of law and order? And, as an adjunct to his services as an old-fashioned *agent provocateur*, was he also engaged, at Anderson's bidding, in a parallel operation to entrap leading Parnellite politicians along with the militant Irish-American dupes?

On the balance of probability, the latter appears to be the case. The collapse of the Jubilee conspiracy had less to do with Fenian cluelessness (although there was plenty of that in evidence) than with the intrigues of the man given responsibility for its execution. Millen ensured that it would fail; that it would do so without any bothersome consequences for himself; and that it would, in the process, irretrievably blacken the reputation of the Irish Parliamentary Party.

It was a tall order, even for a seasoned *agent provocateur*, and Millen almost managed to pull it off.

After assuming control of the 'pyrotechnic display in honour of Queen Victoria's Jubilee', Millen, masquerading as the Teutonic 'Mr Muller' and accompanied by family members, was sent back to Europe by the Clan/Fenian Brotherhood (FB) on 10 April 1887, with a fighting fund of $5,000. Millen also profited financially – as he so often did – from his involvement in the enterprise, drawing funds from the New York Fenians, the Chicago Clan, his employers at the *New York Herald* and the British secret service allocation. At the same time, at least according to information supplied by Thomas Beach, Millen was accompanied to Europe, under separate cover, by '24 tins of explosives in the shape of what is known as Greek fire'.[10] This mythic alchemical ordnance never quite materialized, other than in the bowl of a suburban London toilet.

It did not take long for advance details of this latest Irish-American operation to reach Scotland Yard. Credit for the leak of this information has generally been ascribed to Beach. However, 'Le Caron', despite his association with Alexander Sullivan, was hardly privy to the entire blueprint. Frank Millen, on the other hand, as the *de facto* adjutant of the enterprise, had a detailed knowledge of the plans, and the Mexican general was now working for Robert Anderson.

Millen may even have originally concocted the bones of the scheme in collaboration with Edward Jenkinson, in the last months of the latter's Home Office tenure.

Either way, whether informed by Beach or Millen, or some combination of both, Robert Anderson, in the last of his three 'Behind the Scenes in America' pieces for *The Times*, on 1 June 1887 alerted his readers to the forthcoming apocalypse. In the article he made certain to connect every stick of dynamite, in advance, to the leadership of the Irish Parliamentary Party. Exploiting his inside track, Anderson predicted – anonymously of course – that a revitalized Fenian Brotherhood in New York would resume 'active operations' within weeks.

> The 'active operations' intended are … a series of dynamite and incendiary outrages to startle the nation amid the peaceful rejoicings of the month which has just begun.[11]

Thus were readers of *The Times* forewarned of the 'Jubilee plot'. The stage was being set for another Irish nationalist dynamite campaign.

One of Millen's first ports of call upon his return to Paris in April 1887 was his old acquaintance the rabid American Fenian and US Civil War veteran General Charles Carroll Tevis, dedicated representative of the American brotherhood. However, once again, appearances were deceptive. Tevis, probably unbeknownst to Millen, was even more of a soul mate than the Mexican general suspected: he was also a long-serving fellow double-agent, in the pay of the Foreign Office since 1866. He had, coincidentally, offered his services to Her Majesty's Government within months of the defection of Millen himself. Tevis, like Le Caron, had betrayed one of the Fenian invasions of Canada.

The operational details of the new Clan/FB bombing campaign, apparently targeted at the British monarch, were being hatched in Paris, by two British spies.

As well as Tevis, Millen folded Patrick Casey into his intrigues. This was equally problematic. Casey was also 'in service', enjoying his own slice of the secret service vote while fulminating drunkenly against Brittania's overlords and their treatment of Ireland. A junior member of this coven was Richard Pigott, who by 1887 was in effect a government agent. Michael Davitt's Parisian inquiries (to be considered later) uncovered the fact that Millen and Pigott met regularly in a Parisian hotel. While Millen can have had little doubt about the apostasy of Pigott, he was probably unaware of Casey's role as a double-agent, and there is no evidence that he saw Tevis as anything other than what he purported to be, an extreme Irish-American nationalist.

There is also a lack of clarity about how much the Met's CID chief, the fundamentalist millenarian James Monro, knew about the actual status of Millen when he got wind of the Clan/FB operation. Was Robert Anderson being parsimonious in the information he was forwarding even to his immediate superior? Anderson's espionage career had received the kiss of life when Monro appointed him as his CID deputy in 1887, so the Irishman was heavily indebted to the Scottish assistant commissioner of the Met. Would he have concealed from his patron the double role of Millen (whom he had inherited from Jenkinson), in much the same way as he had always protected the identity of Le Caron from his superiors?

In his 1910 memoir, *The Lighter Side of my Official Life* – which is anything but the stylish soufflé suggested by the title – Anderson remarks that 'one of the principal agents in [the Jubilee] plot was taken into pay on behalf of the government'.[12] This unnamed double-agent had been recruited 'during a disastrous interval' before the appointment of James Monro as head of the newly created 'Section D' (also known as the 'Special Secret Branch') of the CID in 1887. Millen's 'disastrous' recruiter was, of course, Edward Jenkinson. While the warring spymasters regularly engaged in shady – and arguably felonious – schemes, Anderson was apt to be more forgiving of his own depravities than those of his predecessor.

What Anderson did not tell the readers of his memoir is exactly when it came to his notice that the supposed architect of the Jubilee plot was, once again, a British asset. He was well aware of Millen's previous defection in 1866, having been privy to the intelligence coming from the Mexican general before the abortive Fenian insurrection of 1867. But in early 1887 Millen became Anderson's 'mole within Fenianism'.[13] Having assumed Jenkinson's Home Office responsibilities, Anderson would have been informed that Millen had returned to the fold in 1885. Assuming Anderson was in possession of that information in early 1887, at what point did he inform his boss that Millen was working for the British government and was not callously intent on blowing up Queen Victoria at her Jubilee service in Westminster Abbey?

The late historian Shane Kenna, who made an admirable career of tracking the exploits, internecine animosities and political impact of the wider IRB/Fenian/Clan na Gael movement, is in no doubt – others are not quite as emphatic – that Anderson, for a while at least, kept this rather important nugget of information to himself. 'Considering the presence of at least three British agents in this conspiracy,'* Kenna has written, 'the supposed jubilee plot was inspired, funded and operated by an intelligence network, with Scotland Yard left in the dark. The assistant commissioner James Monro continued to play the part of the fool in this conspiracy.'[14] Kenna also alleges that the Home Secretary, Henry Matthews, was unaware that Millen was being paid for his services from the secret service fund. That may well have been the case, but several other senior administration figures, including Julian Pauncefote, permanent under-secretary at the Foreign Office, and the prime minister, the Marquess of Salisbury, *were* privy to the

*The operative phrase here is 'at least'. Kenna is referring to Millen, Tevis and Le Caron. The equally well-informed Owen McGee tentatively adds two other possible double-agents to the mix: Michael Boland, co-leader of the Clan Triangle faction, and Patrick Sarsfield Cassidy of the Fenian Brotherhood/ United Irishmen of America. (McGee, *The IRB*, 105, 124.)

information that Millen was a British agent. We can be certain that Salisbury was up to speed, because he double-jobbed as Foreign Secretary after the sudden death in 1887 of the previous incumbent, Stafford Northcote (Lord Iddesleigh). All the Jubilee-related consular intelligence concerning Millen came across his desk, as it had done during the 1885/6 interregnum when the Tories were in office for six months, with Salisbury also operating as his own Foreign Secretary of the Tory caretaker government. He assumed that office shortly after Lionel Carden dangled Millen before Jenkinson in April/May 1885. Until Jenkinson and the Mexican general met in Paris in November 1885, all the correspondence relating to Millen's apostasy came through the Foreign Office, ended up on Salisbury's desk and resulted in instructions being carried out at the Secretary of State's instigation – in the best tradition of Cecil/Burghley-inspired espionage.[15] So, since the summer of 1885 the prime minister had known that Millen was a double-agent. Two years later, aware of Millen's pedigree, the prime minister made no attempt to curtail the *agent provocateur*'s activities. However, in allowing the conspiracy to proceed, like a controlled explosion, Salisbury was complicit in the efforts to grab the bigger prize, that of undermining the legitimacy of the Parnellites. This was the added value that Millen offered. He was not simply the means of averting an Irish-American crime wave – of which he himself had been the source. With good planning and a certain amount of luck he could implicate some of Parnell's lieutenants in a dynamite plot.

If Anderson, temporarily, withheld the important information from Monro that Millen was on *their* side, he did so in pursuit of his own political agenda. The more apolitical Monro, despite his unionist instincts, did not fully share Anderson's extreme anti-nationalist politics. Thus, it would have suited Anderson to keep the CID chief in the dark until Millen had begun the process, as he later did, of attempting to implicate a few well-chosen Parnellites. Anderson also had a pedigree when it came to pulling the wool over the eyes of his bosses. He had, for example, managed to keep hidden a network of RIC spies based in Britain in the early 1880s, in the pre-Jenkinson era.[16]

Monro, however, appears to have discovered the truth by May 1887. He found out not only that Millen was a double-agent but also that Edward Jenkinson's fingerprints were all over the machinery of the plot. In a November 1887 memo the assistant commissioner indicated that, 'before [Millen's] schemes of outrage were proposed to his confederates in New York they had been communicated to the gentleman who preceded me.'[17] Jenkinson was being unceremoniously lobbed under the wheels of an oncoming omnibus. However, just as Monro had never trusted Jenkinson, neither did he trust the intentions of his surrogate, Frank Millen. He would treat the Jubilee conspiracy as a bona-fide threat, even if it was being directed by a British espionage asset.

In May 1887 Monro sent the recently retired policeman Inspector James Thomson, accompanied by his wife Martha, to monitor the movements of Millen in the French coastal resort of Boulogne, as close to England as the General dared travel for the time being. In choosing the Thomsons, however, Monro may have settled on the wrong surveillance team. Thomson also worked for Anderson. His presence in close proximity to Millen (the Millens and the Thomsons became extremely friendly) begs the question: was Thomson spying on Millen on behalf of Monro, or was he 'handling' the general at the instigation of Anderson? This was all happening at the same time as the 'Behind the Scenes in America' series, penned by Anderson – but whose authorship had been kept from Monro – was being carried by *The Times*. The anonymous author of the articles seemed, as we have seen, to be well-informed about the imminence of a Clan/Fenian dynamite campaign.

Whether or not he was completely in the picture, Monro was becoming exceptionally nervous about Millen's activities by May 1887. The assistant commissioner was, first and last, an orthodox policeman. He lacked the instincts of a Machiavellian spymaster such as Jenkinson, or even the slightly more cautious, but equally manipulative, Anderson. The *modus operandi* of Jenkinson was to allow matters to play out, to feed militants enough rope to hang themselves and, in the process, to implicate collaborators as the conspiracy developed. Jenkinson was a risk-taker who preferred to gauge the full extent of a conspiracy before pouncing. Monro was more hidebound and conventional in his approach. He shared the sanctimonious Victorian distaste for the ostentatiously clandestine. If he believed that a crime was about to be committed, then it was up to him to prevent it, rather than to sit back and watch it play out. With this end in view, in June 1887 Monro took a step that Jenkinson would have deprecated. He broke cover and sent Chief Constable Adolphus Williamson to Boulogne to advise Millen that Scotland Yard was aware of his activities. The general was warned not to set foot in England or he would risk immediate arrest. In his own account of the encounter in *The Lighter Side of my Official Life*, Anderson implied that Monro had apprised Williamson of Millen's 'contract' with Her Majesty's Government. Notwithstanding Millen's ambivalent status, 'Dolly' advised the Mexican general that 'the bargain made with him [by Jenkinson] was now repudiated'.[18]

A somewhat farcical aspect of this encounter in Boulogne was the background presence of the Thomsons. They were still cultivating the Millens and were obliged to feign ignorance of their familiarity with this forceful and intimidating visitor from London. However, even that risible encounter was later eclipsed in absurdity by the experience of another of Monro's agents, Kerry-born Inspector William Melville of the Special Irish Branch. He was sent to Paris to keep a watch on Millen when the latter abandoned Boulogne shortly after the heart to heart with Williamson. Melville – who would go on to have a distinguished career in espionage himself (commanding the precursor of MI5) – was a fluent French speaker. So successful was he in his assignment that he became tutor to one of Millen's daughters!

*

Meanwhile the foot soldiers who were expected to carry out the actual Jubilee explosions were on their way from New York to London. If the Clan's object had ever been to outshine Guy Fawkes, that plan was negated by the dismal failure of the designated New York active service unit to board a Liverpool-bound boat in time for the day of the Jubilee celebration in the Abbey. The three saboteurs – J. J. Moroney (alias 'Joseph Melville'), Thomas Callan and Michael Harkins – had failed to account for the possibility that all the berths on their favoured sailing vessel might have been taken. They finally arrived in England on 21 June – the day of the service in Westminster Abbey – after managing to get three berths on board the SS *City of Chester*.

Moroney, a New Yorker, was a personal friend of Alexander Sullivan. Callan was a forty-six-year-old labourer from Lowell, Massachusetts, and Harkins was a thirty-year-old grocer from Philadelphia.[19] All three men were armed with Smith and Wesson revolvers and, between them, carried one hundred pounds of dynamite and $1,200. At least one accomplice, Joseph Cohen – also suspected by some of being a British agent, the plot positively glistened with them[20] – was already waiting for them in London. By coincidence, a few days before their arrival in England, the bibulous and attention-seeking printer Patrick Casey, a man with, to say the least, divided loyalties, confirmed in an interview in the London journal the *Morning Advertiser* that the Clan/FB bombing campaign was about to resume.[21] So – thanks to the newspaper warnings of Casey and Anderson – Moroney, Harkins and Callan would not be working completely in the shadows.

For Millen there was a sting in the tail in the arrival of the three bombers. According to Le Caron, Moroney had been sent to Europe to replace Millen on account of 'his bungling ... with a large amount of money and distinct orders to show some value for it'.[22] The Sullivan faction of the Clan did not think it was getting its money's worth from the Mexican general.

Monro, meanwhile, could not be certain that Millen had

taken to heart Williamson's heavy hint of early June. The CID chief, unwilling to depend on Millen's potentially ambiguous loyalties, obsessed over the possibility of an actual Jubilee plot, i.e. one that would target the Westminster Abbey ceremony on 21 June. He vacillated between the embarrassment that would attach to aborting the event and the infamy that would follow a successful Irish-American coup. Monro, with his distinct brand of Calvinist religiosity, was certainly not a gambler, but he chose to risk perennial notoriety (and death by dynamite). He allowed the Jubilee service to go ahead after numerous searches of the Abbey and adjacent buildings. However, while he, with considerable trepidation, was present at the event himself, he would not permit any of his family members to attend. In an unpublished memoir he wrote that, 'I prayed, and to the end resolved to do nothing, but trust in God, who had ever helped me, would do so now.'[23] On this occasion an omnipotent deity, as well as, perhaps, the lack of berths on a transatlantic sailing vessel, validated his decision to hazard the lives of the reigning monarch, her cabinet and the great and good of late nineteenth-century Britain.

For his part, Millen, the Green Pimpernel, was engaged in another stratagem. This should remove any ambiguity as to whose interests he was serving; it certainly was not those of the Clan. Michael Davitt believed that, while Millen was based in Boulogne his activities (carefully monitored by the Thomsons) were a sham. When Davitt interviewed Charles Carroll Tevis in Paris, 'General Z', Davitt's codename for the Foreign Office double-agent, told him that he (Tevis) had kept Millen under surveillance in Boulogne himself (whether on his own account or on behalf of the Foreign Office is unclear). In a highly revealing diary that he called 'Notes by an Amateur Detective', Davitt wrote that Tevis 'asserts that he [Millen] remained at B[oulogne] all the time *he was pretending he was preparing things in England*' (my italics).[24] Millen, who had been advanced £500 by Patrick Sarsfield Cassidy, was doing very little to earn the money paid over by the New York

Fenian. While maintaining the fiction that he was coordinating the activities of the small task force in London, he was working to Anderson's parallel agenda of Parnellite entrapment. Millen was about to spring the trap by introducing three prominent Irish nationalist politicians to two would-be bombers whose movements were being monitored by the London Metropolitan Police.

While Millen waited in Boulogne, and later in Paris, for the dynamite and the dynamitards to arrive in England, he occupied his time by engineering an unanswerable narrative of Parnellite collusion with the impending bombing campaign. As he could have had no expectation of moderate nationalist support for his enterprise – having already failed to engage the extremists of the IRB – what happened next can only have been done at the behest of Anderson. In Anderson's world, if no concrete evidence could be produced to connect Irish nationalist MPs and American terrorists, then it was not because such evidence did not exist. It was merely because it had not yet been uncovered. Therefore, in the best tradition of British-sponsored felon-setting, it could be manufactured with a clear conscience because the real 'Jubilee plot' was not an explosive event, or series of events, concocted by Michael Boland, Alexander Sullivan, Patrick Sarsfield Cassidy *et al.* It was a counter-intelligence operation implemented by elements of the British police and Home Office – which did not include James Monro – with the connivance of the prime minister/Foreign Secretary. The 'dynamite' of the real 'Jubilee plot' was metaphorical. It was not designed to assassinate the monarch; it was intended to explode the credibility of the Irish Parliamentary Party.

Since he was unable to visit London himself, Millen pressed into service his two adult daughters, Kitty and Florence (Kitty was living in London at the time). Knowing that Moroney was on his way to London, Millen sent letters of introduction to one 'Joseph Melville' (Moroney's alias) to three Parnellite MPs, William O'Brien, Matthew Harris and Joseph Nolan. These were delivered to the House of Commons by his daughters on 14 July, but not before Monro, courtesy of the French police, had sight of them. The Millen sisters returned to the Commons the following day – coincidentally while their father was meeting Richard Pigott in Paris – and were escorted around the Palace of Westminster by a charmed Joseph Nolan.

Monro did channel Jenkinson on occasions. Even he saw that it was far too early to swoop. Kitty and Florence Millen were mere pilot fish. Monro would wait for the sharks to appear.

On 4 August they showed up. Moroney/Melville, accompanied by Michael Harkins, visited Nolan – rapidly acquiring the status of useful idiot – at the House of Commons. O'Brien and Harris had wisely evinced no interest in meeting with them. Like Kitty and Florence Millen before them, the two would-be bombers were escorted around the Palace of Westminster by the Louth MP.

Was this a reconnaissance mission? Perhaps. Was Nolan fully aware of the identity of the two men to whom he had just been introduced, and the possible nature of their visit? Highly unlikely.

Millen's attempt to associate three Parnellite MPs with the activities of the man identified as 'Melville' indicated where his true loyalties lay. Enlisting either the sympathies or the practical assistance of O'Brien, Harris and Nolan would not have been an integral part of the Clan's original Jubilee scheme. Boland and Sullivan were deeply suspicious of the Parnellites and would have wanted no truck even with the more militant elements of Parnell's coterie of MPs (to which O'Brien and Nolan certainly did not belong). So in making his approach to the three men, Millen was not representing the interests of the extremists who had sent him to Europe. When the question '*Cui bono*?' is posed, there is only one obvious answer. The beneficiary of any illicit liaison between terrorists and nationalist politicians was the Salisbury administration and the unionist cause.

In April 1888 Joseph Nolan appeared before a Select Committee of the House of Commons. The North Louth MP admitted giving 'two ladies' the 'grand tour' in July 1887 but was reluctant to accept that they were the daughters of Frank Millen (by then publicly 'exposed', by Monro, as a notorious dynamitard). Regarding the visit of 'Melville' (J. J. Moroney), Nolan denied that he was aware of any connection between his guest and Millen, and dismissed 'Melville' as one of 'a number of Irish-Americans who have visited me at the House'.[25] If Nolan, despite his denials, actually harboured any suspicions of the bona fides of the two Irish-American visitors, he would have been dismayed to discover that the tour was being closely monitored by Scotland Yard detectives. One of those, Constable William Foley, followed Moroney back to his lodgings. It is ironic that the Irish-American nationalist had chosen to live in Gladstone Street, in Elephant and Castle, south-east London. On 7 August Inspector Patrick Quinn of the Special Irish Branch paid Moroney a visit. The Irish-American was asked to account for his presence in London and 'told the tale' that he was raising finance for the promotion of a new invention designed to prevent lightning strikes from setting fire to oil wells. Quinn's line of questioning would have left Moroney in no doubt that he had been well and truly 'rumbled'. This, however, did not appear to faze him in the least.

One thing was certain about 'Joseph Melville', aka J. J. Moroney: the man did not stint himself. During his adventure in London, whatever his precise purpose, he lived, in the Irish phrase, *ar dhroim na muice* ('on the pig's back'). He shared the high life with a companion known only as 'Miss Kennedy'. She was an elegant woman who, whatever else she might have been, was not Moroney's wife. 'Miss Kennedy' was a Boston milliner whom Moroney had met in Paris. The two dined well and saw the sights together, effortlessly playing the part of wealthy tourists. If Moroney, masquerading as 'Melville', was in London in the expectation of reconfiguring a number of its prominent features with dynamite, he made no effort to adopt a low profile. He and 'Miss Kennedy' were often to be found dining in the fashionable Metropole Hotel, draining the finances of the Clan/FB.

As Inspector Quinn's unsubtle hints had failed to send packing the *soi-disant* inventor 'Melville', Monro tried the Williamson gambit again. This time he despatched the Scottish detective Chief Inspector John Littlechild to disrupt Moroney's idyll. This the grizzled veteran did by approaching, challenging and berating the Irish-American publicly in the dining room of the Metropole. Asked to account for himself, Moroney repeated the cock and bull story he had narrated to Quinn. Littlechild loudly accused him of lying and warned him – as if Moroney could have been unaware of the fact – that he was under constant surveillance. Shortly after Littlechild withdrew, Moroney and his *innamorata* followed suit. Their dinner was spoiled and their annoyance at being the cynosure of all eyes in the dining room had ruined their appetites.

Shortly thereafter the unhappy couple perked up considerably and left London, though not for Paris or the USA, as Monro had anticipated. Instead, they journeyed west, to Dublin, and thence south-west, to Killarney, where even more of Patrick Sarsfield Cassidy's money was spent on jaunting cars, expensive meals and a tour of the Ring of Kerry. They then returned to London and – finally satisfying Monro – travelled to Paris, where Moroney met Millen on 9 September 1887. There both men were carefully watched by whatever the collective noun is for a group of undercover detectives. Millen advised Moroney (with some jubilation, one suspects) to return to the USA because his cover had been well and truly blown and he was now no more useful in England than the general himself. A chastened Moroney did as advised. Any potential challenge to Millen's authority had evaporated.

By the time Moroney and 'Miss Kennedy' boarded a transatlantic liner for New York, Monro, despite his best efforts, had, frustratingly, not been able to establish Moroney's identity, or the precise nature of his mission. The assistant commissioner now pulled an ingenious if underhand stunt. His agents had reported that 'Miss Kennedy' had been busy in Paris. Before their departure Moroney's travelling companion purchased large quantities of expensive lingerie. This, Monro was also aware, had not been declared to customs agents. The devious assistant commissioner, anxious to make as much trouble as possible for the homeward-bound travellers, wired US Customs that an international lingerie smuggler was headed in their direction. The luckless 'Miss Kennedy' was detained on arrival in New York. Her bags were searched and her 'smalls' confiscated. Monro then leaked to the American press – he was a constant and consummate journalistic source – that the companion of this underwear smuggler was himself someone of interest to the UK police. Suddenly New York reporters were just as preoccupied with 'Joseph Melville' as with his travelling companion. It did not take long for the *New York World* to discover that 'Melville' was James J. Moroney, confidant of Alexander Sullivan and holder of senior positions in Clan na Gael and the American National League. Monro dutifully acknowledged in his unpublished 1903 memoir that he allowed the New York press to do his work for him in uncovering Moroney's identity.[26] A short time later encrypted letters written to 'Melville'/Moroney from the USA were discovered in London. These, when deciphered, told the tale of a dynamite conspiracy involving Moroney and Millen.

With Moroney out of the picture (and out of Monro's reach) the execution of the Clan's renewal of the bombing campaign was now in the hands of Joseph Cohen – whose existence had also been uncovered by the resourceful Constable Foley – as well as Moroney's former travelling companions Thomas Callan and Michael Harkins. Cohen could be counted out immediately – whether or not he was a double-agent – because he was terminally ill with TB. On 19 October 1887 he died in a lodging house owned by a Mrs Elizabeth Keys. When the landlady discovered Cohen's body, she also found a large sum of money, and a revolver under his pillow. Shortly after Michael Harkins arrived to claim Cohen's effects, the suspicious landlady alerted the police. The Met were already onto Harkins, who was living in Islington. He was arrested and was interrogated by Monro himself. Harkins insisted that he had met Cohen in a pub and hadn't known him for long. He weathered whatever questions and insinuations Monro threw at him and had to be released when the Met could come up with nothing more incriminating than a *Daily News* clipping, found in his pockets, about a forthcoming visit to Birmingham by Irish chief secretary, Arthur Balfour.

After his release, Harkins never lacked for company, as he was followed twenty-four hours a day by CID detectives. He was rearrested a couple of days later after Monro, with the help of the Pinkerton Agency, was able to connect him to a private mailbox in Philadelphia associated with the Sullivan faction of Clan na Gael. Harkins, however, was no more forthcoming during a second interrogation.

Monro then took the unprecedented step of 'going public' with his suspicions by exposing the Irish-American 'plot'. This was achieved not with his customary quiet leak to the press but in the most public of forums: a coroner's court. His motivation in using such an unorthodox setting, or so he subsequently claimed, was to avoid potential embarrassment to the government because of his growing certainty that Jenkinson had been the instigator of the entire enterprise. In a 'secret' 4 November 1887 memo he wrote:

> I was mainly influenced by ... the origin of the plot. It seemed to me undesirable in the extreme to prosecute the agents of a plot where there was even the semblance of justification for asserting that in its inception the govt. was privy to it.

At the end of his lengthy memo (twenty-one handwritten pages – top-secret reports were rarely typed unless the rapporteur knew his way around a typewriter) comes the gratuitous 'you're welcome':

> To have permitted the plot to ripen, taking measures only to ensure the apprehension & punishment of the criminals, wd [*sic*] have involved comparatively little cost of thought or effort or money, while the result would doubtless have

> impressed the public with a belief in the zeal & efficiency of the Police. But the policy I have adopted and steadily pursued, tho' [*sic*] of course a thankless one so far as the public is concerned, will, I venture to hope, receive the approval of the government.[27]

One can almost sense, 140 years later, the gracious bow and the pause for a round of applause. Monro was letting his superiors know that he had ventured all in defending the reputation of Her Majesty's Government. He could have adopted a *fiat justitia ruat caelum* ('let justice be done though the heavens fall') approach, but he chose instead to risk the reputation of the Metropolitan Police in order to avoid the imputation that any agent of the government would stoop to the practice of entrapment.

Monro made his pre-emptive strike at the City and Southwark Coroner's Court on 26 October 1887. An inquest into the death of Joseph Cohen had been hastily arranged. Monro was in attendance, accompanied by a cohort of British and American newspaper reporters. The pressmen had been advised that sensational developments were to be expected. These began to unfold almost as soon as the coroner, Samuel Langham, commenced proceedings. Monro begged the court's permission to be heard. From that point onwards, Langham lost control of his inquest and it became a Monro command performance.

Monro, in a fervent monologue, informed the curious spectators that Joseph Cohen was no ordinary tubercular American. He was 'an agent of the Clan na Gael society, the head of which, General Millen, was in London during the Jubilee celebration'. 'His London agent,' the assistant commissioner continued, to a baffled but fascinated audience, 'is named Melville.'[28] Quite what all this had to do with establishing the cause and the circumstances of the death of Joseph Cohen eluded the coroner. Langham made a number of futile attempts to curtail Monro's soliloquy, but this did not cease until the senior policeman began to question the coroner's witnesses! These included Melville's and Cohen's landladies, as well as members of the Metropolitan Police. Also in the courtroom, closely guarded by detectives, was Harkins, who, when questioned by Monro – as Langham sat on his hands – continued to insist that he was unconnected to any Irish-American conspiracy. He did, however, admit to knowing 'Melville' and to having accompanied him on his tour of the House of Commons with an Irish Party MP. He failed to identify Nolan, other than observing that their tour guide was a tall man with fair hair.

Unfazed, Monro obliged Harkins by doing the job for him. Entirely contrary to the rules of evidence, Joseph Nolan MP was named by the assistant commissioner as the mysterious tour guide. Harkins did not help his cause when he made the preposterous claim that his acquaintance with 'Melville' had begun when the latter had capriciously accosted him 'because I looked like an American'.[29] The redoubtable Chief Inspector Littlechild did Harkins no favours either when, in a further irrelevant if dramatic sidebar, he produced a revolver that had been taken from the witness the day before. It was apparently germane to the inquest in that it was the same model as the one that had been found in Cohen's room after his demise.

Culpably overlooked towards the close of the proceedings was the testimony of the doctor who certified that Cohen's death was due to natural causes. A verdict consistent with the only appropriate evidence, that of the physician, was duly rendered. The pressmen, however, had their sensational story – the *New York Times* headline the following day was 'A dynamite plot spoiled' – and Monro, by his own lights at least, had achieved his object. What exactly that was, he summarized in his unpublished memoir, written for family members, in 1903:

> The next day all the papers commented in a bewildered fashion on the inquest and what it meant. Of course they did not know what it meant, and the Radical organs saw in it some deep political design to injure the Liberal Party. But what I wanted was to encite [*sic*] public attention to

> the danger of the plot going on, and I succeeded in so doing.[30]

He had hijacked a coroner's inquest to make the British public aware that there were bombers in their midst once again. While Monro's rationale can probably be taken at face value, the same cannot be said for the motivation of the arch unionist Robert Anderson, who would have been delighted 'to injure the Liberal party'. Someone ensured that Millen manufactured a connection between two (as yet unconvicted) terrorists and at least one Parnellite MP. Millen's letters of introduction ensured that the Moroney/Harkins tour of the House of Commons could be represented as a terrorist reconnaissance mission, enabled by an Irish MP. If Anderson himself had not instructed Millen to forge a relationship between Moroney, Harkins and three Irish MPs (only one of whom fell for the ruse) then he would have approved wholeheartedly of whichever of his 'secret' colleagues came up with the scheme.

The names of 'Joseph Melville' and Frank Millen had not been adduced in evidence at Southwark Coroner's Court. They had been inserted into the record by Monro himself. In doing so, according to the *New York Times*, 'Commissioner Monro clearly showed by his questions that he believes a plot existed to kill Mr. Balfour.'[31] He also gratified Anderson by connecting 'Joseph Melville' to Joseph Nolan. The North Louth MP cannot have been enjoying all the attention.

The blocked toilet and the exploding oven

Cohen was dead, Moroney had been forced back to the USA and Harkins was in police custody. However, thus far, no supply of dynamite had been discovered. This rather spoiled the arc of Monro's narrative. It took the plot of a Whitehall farce to rectify that deficiency.

Unlike Moroney, his travelling companion, Thomas Callan,

had managed to elude the Metropolitan Police. He was lodging in a house in Baxter Street in Islington, north London, owned by a Maria Bright.

A blocked toilet, a small child who took his recreation in dustbins and an explosion in a suburban domestic oven proved to be Callan's undoing. Even in the world of revolutionary terrorism, truth can be stranger than fiction.

Spooked by the Cohen inquest and the fear that Harkins would succumb to police interrogation, Callan – who was in possession of the explosives that Monro had not been able to find – decided to dispose of the incriminating cache of dynamite. He had the frankly staggering notion of flushing the lot down Maria Bright's toilet. This, inevitably, became blocked, and Callan was forced to own up to his indiscretion, without admitting what it was that he had been seeking to dispose of. Mrs Bright, a London landlady woefully untrained in the use of high explosives, failed to identify the foreign substance (which looked like caked lime and cement) that had blocked her privy. It was recovered from the toilet and deposited in her dustbin.

There matters might have rested had it not been for the exertions of a spirited child, Benjamin John, who lived next door to the Brights and who had a penchant for exploring waste bins. Locating a block of what appeared to be wet mortar in Mrs Bright's bin, little Benjamin brought it into the John family kitchen and attempted to dry it out in the oven. Within minutes there was a loud explosion, and the oven door blew off its hinges. Ironically this emerged only retrospectively, as Mrs John, possibly fearing for her curious child, failed to report the incident. Callan was only caught when he attempted to change money in a bank branch, using notes that matched serial numbers the police had already linked to Moroney. A letter in his possession also tied him to his fellow plotter. It was when the investigation reached her Islington home that Mrs John volunteered the details of her son's misadventures.

Thomas Callan and Michael Harkins were tried at the Central Criminal Court on 1 February 1888. They were charged with conspiring with 'Joseph Melville', Joseph Cohen and other persons to cause explosions. They were convicted and each was sentenced to fifteen years' penal servitude.

And that was probably that. Except for the intriguing possibility of a 'Sixth Man'. Because there is a final shadowy Irish-American accomplice who may also have been involved in the Jubilee enterprise. However, if this co-conspirator, known only as 'Stack' (aka Dunne), was indeed involved, then he was yet another 'plant' working for the British secret service. Stack's name appeared in the House of Commons register as a 'visitor', which suggests further possible efforts at the entrapment of additional Parnellite MPs, to be paraded alongside Nolan. Monro raised the name of the mysterious Stack as a possible terrorist in his evidence to a Commons select committee summoned, somewhat belatedly, to tighten up the regulations around the admission of 'strangers' to the Houses of Parliament. The assistant commissioner described Stack as 'a gentleman known to [Joseph Nolan] who had been successful in life and who was over in England on a trip'.[32] Visiting Americans were like flies to Nolan's flypaper.

Stack, or so claimed Monro, had clear links to the Clan and had spent time in London and in Ireland in 1887/8. Monro told the committee that Stack had been 'interviewed' in Ireland in January 1888 by CID Inspector Patrick Quinn. He was, however, in no hurry to return to the USA, even as the trial of Callan and Harkins was imminent. Hardly the sign of a co-conspirator anxious to escape the clutches of the law.

Monro seemed keen to fold this mysterious Irish-American republican into the Clan/FB operation. However, a number of Scotland Yard ledger payment entries for 1890 suggest that 'Stack' was not all that Monro claimed. From 7 February 1890 there are a dozen entries referring to weekly payments of £2 being made to 'Dunne (Stack)' with the supplementary information that these are 'fresh payments'. On 7 May 1890 there is a final entry: 'Dunne allowance and passage money to America – £12.'[33] Another Scotland Yard document for the period, the Chief Constable's register, is dotted with references to 'the suspect Stack' or 'the informant Stack'. This suggests that he began as the former and graduated to become the latter. It is possible that Monro's reference to Stack before a House of Commons select committee in April 1888 was designed, as in the case of the widespread advertising of Millen's involvement, to provide some cover for Stack's continued service as a British asset on his return to the USA. Monro was certainly aware of Stack's status, because the assistant commissioner's name is entered alongside Stack's in the Chief Constable's register.[34]

There are two distinct phases of the 'Jubilee plot'. Phase one ('Jubilee 1.0') involved Monro's paranoid delusion, sparked by information from Le Caron, and channelled through Anderson, that the dynamitards would strike on 21 June at Westminster Abbey. That was almost certainly never on the cards, even had Moroney, Harkins and Callan managed to board their first transatlantic vessel of choice in New York. The surveillance difficulties required to infiltrate Westminster Abbey a couple of days before the Jubilee service would have been insurmountable. However, with the Jubilee celebrations scheduled to continue until 4 July, 'Jubilee 2.0', the bombing of other targets was potentially viable.

With so many spies, informers, *agents provocateurs* and charlatans adding their tuppence halfpenny to the conspiracy (e.g. Millen, Tevis, Patrick Casey and possibly Joseph Cohen), it is clear that the plot was not intended to succeed by those participants in the employ of the British secret establishment, whatever result might have been envisaged by those actually committed to anarchy (Moroney, Harkins and Callan).

The failure of the Clan/FB operation brought down the curtain on the Irish-American bombing campaign of the 1880s.* Moroney and Millen, forewarned at the instigation of Monro to expect

*There was a further scare in 1896. It was also initiated by an *agent provocateur* and involved P. J. Tynan. (Nicholas Gosselin to John Satterfield Sandars, 13.8.96 PRO 30/60/13/2.)

retribution, succeeded in avoiding any legal sanction. However, there remained the possibility of dangerous ramifications for one or the other on their return to base. It would have been apparent to Sullivan and his acolytes, as well as to their New York allies, that someone had betrayed the mission. Since Harkins and Callan were serving lengthy jail terms, they were clearly not the culprits. That left the dead Cohen, or the extant Moroney or Millen, as the most obvious candidates.

As far as the British secret service was concerned, Moroney, who was not a double-agent, could shift for himself. Were suspicion to fall on 'Melville' it would even work to Britain's advantage. Millen, on the other hand, needed to appear 'more sinned against than sinning'. Returning to New York with a cock and bull story of having been warned off by a Scotland Yard detective would have turned their asset into an object of suspicion. A pre-emptive strike in the form of an aggressive Scotland Yard show trial at the Cohen inquest gave Millen some cover. Monro, at the Southwark Coroner's Court, highlighted Millen's Moriarty-like character as the spider at the heart of the web. In outing Millen as the brains behind the plot, Monro did the double-agent a service. Whether or not this was one of the intentions of the melodramatic exposure of the conspiracy is moot.

But the revelations at Southwark Coroner's Court kept Millen alive for most of the next two years.

Alexander Sullivan, Michael Boland and Patrick Sarsfield Cassidy may have intended for Queen Victoria and her cabinet to become the victims of an actual 'Jubilee plot'. Edward Jenkinson probably encouraged Francis Millen to sow the seeds of his (Jenkinson's) 'Jubilee plot' to generate several high-profile arrests that would discourage any new ground-level recruits to a renewed dynamite campaign. However, Jenkinson did not last long enough to reap the benefits of his duplicitous enterprise. Robert Anderson certainly intended Parnellism to be a casualty of *his* 'Jubilee plot'. In the final analysis the only real victims (other than Mrs Bright's toilet and Mrs John's oven) were Millen's 'dupes': Thomas Callan, who served a long prison term and Michael Harkins, who, physically broken by his incarceration, died shortly after his release.

There were no dynamiters in attendance at the Jubilee service. The threat had been illusory. The shrewd Superintendent John Mallon became aware of the events of the summer of 1887 shortly after the 'plot' was foiled. In retirement, the former head of 'G' Division read Anderson's memoir, *Sidelights on the Home Rule Movement*, with some interest and much scepticism. When he came to Anderson's account of the 'Jubilee plot', Mallon wrote a terse marginal comment. This was to the effect that 'Millen humbugged them'.[35] Mallon was not a fan of Anderson's. He told his biographer, journalist Frederick Bussy, that the Dublin-born spymaster 'talks a good job'. There is no doubt that Millen, financed by no fewer than four different employers, but assiduously working only for one, had succeeded in humbugging any number of guileless souls.

It may well have been the case that, on 21 June 1887, Queen Victoria was in more danger from the foolishness of a highly respectable Anglican clergyman than from the Clan. This gentleman offered to sell his tickets to the Westminster Abbey Jubilee service in an attempt to raise money for the publication of a *Te Deum* he had composed in honour of the event. The Home Secretary, who viewed the attempted sale as a possible case of 'constructive High Treason' (something of an overreaction), wrote, 'what a chance for a dynamiter to get a quiet pot shot at H.M'.[36]

'H.M.' weathered the experience without a scratch.

The complicity (or otherwise) of the Master of Hatfield

> 'Is it not just conceivable that there is no remedy that we can apply for the Irish hatred of ourselves? … Ireland must be kept, like India, at all hazards: by persuasion, if possible; if not, by force … To conduct Irish affairs on any principles is difficult

enough; but to govern a population which does not wish to be governed by you, on the principle of implicitly attending to its wishes, appears to be about as hopeless a task as ever politicians undertook.'[37]

The Marquess of Salisbury, *Quarterly Review*, October 1872

'It has transformed a chimera into a burning issue.'[38]

Salisbury, on Gladstone's conversion to Home Rule, December 1885

Where, in this maelstrom of felon-setting, conspiracy and character assassination, was Robert Gascoyne-Cecil, 3rd Marquess of Salisbury to be found? Was the prime minister/Foreign Secretary blissfully ignorant of everything that was being done on behalf of his administration? Was he on the periphery and merely receiving occasional nuggets on a 'need to know' basis? Or was he at the very heart of the commotion being created by the agents of an administration that owed its very existence to antagonism towards Irish Home Rule?

While no political leader can hope to become acquainted with every detail of the policies being enacted in their name, they bear ultimate responsibility for those policies. In that sense alone Salisbury must be held accountable for the unsavoury efforts of his administration to demonize Irish constitutional politicians.

Which is not to suggest that he merely adopted a disengaged approach, declining to involve himself in the intricacies of the various ploys designed to delegitimize Home Rule. While he was not Conan Doyle's master conspirator Professor James Moriarty, with tendrils extending into every undertaking, neither was he a semi-detached King Henry II, throwing out leaden hints that he desired to be rid of a turbulent priest.

Salisbury's own daughter, his biographer, Lady Gwendolen Cecil, has noted that her father obsessed about the issue of Irish Home Rule, even at times when it was 'almost universally looked upon as outside the field of practical politics'.[39] In an anonymous article for the *Quarterly Review* in October 1883, at a time when Ireland was focused primarily on land issues, he expatiated on the theme of what he characterized as 'disintegration'. This was a state of general political anomie that, in his view, pervaded the UK at that time. In applying this trope to Britain's colonial relationship with Ireland, he was uncompromising:

> If Ireland is not with us, she is against us ... The coast of Ireland, in unfriendly hands, would be something more than a pistol held to the mouths of the Clyde and the Mersey and the Severn. And we must not dismiss such extreme conditions from our minds as possibilities which cannot be realised. We shall have speedily enough to choose between them and the reconquest of Ireland if once Home Rule be granted.[40]

Although Salisbury is due some credit as 'the grudging initiator of a quiet social revolution in the Irish countryside',[41]* his opposition to Irish self-government – already discussed in the context of the preservation of empire and also predicated, more reasonably, on the divisiveness of the issue within Ireland itself – was underpinned by an extreme attachment to Anglo-Saxon ethnicity. This achieved its ultimate expression in a notorious speech – of 'calculated virulence',[42] according to his biographer Andrew Roberts – on 15 May 1886 in St James's Hall in London in which 'the racist overtones were unmistakable'.[43] In disputing Ireland's claim to devolution – with the Home Rule Bill wending its way through parliament – he contended that 'you would not confide free representative institutions to the Hottentots, for instance'. Self-government, he added, 'works admirably when it is confided to people who are of Teutonic

*This is a reference to the land purchase legislation of his administrations from 1885 to 1892.

race … it does not work so well when people of other races are called upon to join in it'.[44]

Sir William Harcourt was being overly charitable when, based on the expression of such sentiments – which were, after all, neither spontaneous nor extempore – he described Salisbury as the 'Mrs Malaprop of politics'. In the same speech Salisbury went on to offer his 'alternative policy' to Irish self-government, which was 'that Parliament should enable the Government of England to govern Ireland … honestly, consistently, and resolutely for twenty years'.[45] This was later paraphrased, by friend and foe alike, as 'twenty years of coercion'.[46] He also advocated the removal of a million Irish people to Canada, causing future Liberal chief secretary for Ireland John Morley to refer to the address as the 'manacles and Manitoba' speech. His remarks, made to a sympathetic audience, would 'dog him for a decade'[47] – he steadfastly insisted that the speech had been misinterpreted – but it left few listeners in any doubt about his antipathy to Irish nationalist aspirations. This found full expression in the years that followed in the series of overt and covert operations carried out with his authority – verifiable in the case of, for example, Tory collaboration with *The Times* and the recruitment of Frank Millen – or with his tacit approval.

This, after all, was the Tory grandee who alleged in an 1887 speech that 'a gentleman who intimately knew Mr Parnell murdered Mr Burke' and that Gladstone 'accepts in political brotherhood men upon whom the presumption of conniving at assassination rests'.[48] Once in power Salisbury was in a position to support efforts to confirm those robust claims, or, through judicious felon-setting, to conjure them into reality. A political leader who had 'a mania of keeping things secret and working by back-channels'[49] and was capable of claiming that a government 'not squeamish about forms of law, or particular about hanging the wrong man occasionally, might very possibly succeed in weaning the Irish peasantry from their inveterate affection for the blunderbuss',[50] was not one to baulk at the employment of a few capable *agents provocateurs*, such as Millen, despite any prevailing misgivings about the ethics or legalities of entrapment.

Irish nationalists, quoth the Master of Hatfield, would be required to 'take a licking',[51] and he was just the man to administer it.

6

THE 'BLOODY PUDDLE'

The Special Commission Convenes

'It appears that … your great organs of public opinion in this country are to be permitted to pay miserable creatures for the purpose of producing these calumnies.'[1]

Charles Stewart Parnell, on *The Times*,
House of Commons, 18 April 1887

'To attain the ends of the anti-Home-Rule conspiracy, the creators of the commission and the accusers of Mr. Parnell attempted to indict the Irish nation as represented by its leaders and their political and party organizations.'[2]

Michael Davitt,
The Fall of Feudalism in Ireland (1904)

'A unique operation of historical stock-taking.'[3]

John MacDonald, *Daily News Diary of the Parnell Commission* (1890)

The House of Commons, 24–31 July 1888

Parliamentary invective is rather like the sporting javelin: a potentially lethal weapon that falls harmlessly into no-man's land. Politicians on opposite sides of the House of Commons trade savage barbs. They then meet in the Members' Bar for a convivial drink.

However, there was little conviviality in evidence when Charles Stewart Parnell MP and Joseph Chamberlain MP locked horns in the House of Commons in late July 1888. The javelins launched by the two irreconcilable politicians were not merely intended to outdistance each other, they were intended to find their targets and to maim. There is no enemy worse than a former ally, and any bonhomie that ever existed between the two men was well in the past.

Some small part of Parnell's contempt for the Birmingham radical was probably a function of his innate lofty aristocratic disdain for lesser mortals. Most of his aversion to Chamberlain, however, was dictated by previous wounding battles; by the latter's central role in the rejection of Gladstone's Home Rule legislation; and by Chamberlain's almost provocative endorsement of a figure even less beloved of the 'Chief', Captain William Henry O'Shea. Chamberlain, a much-diminished figure after his defection from the Liberals over Home Rule – seen by many insiders as a blatant power grab that failed to dislodge Gladstone from the party leadership – had crossed swords with Parnell in the past. In 1884 he had devised a 'Home Rule light' scheme – the Central Board project – which his cut-price Hermes, William O'Shea MP, had presented to an unreceptive Parnell. When the Irish Party leader batted away the plan, O'Shea had culpably misrepresented his leader's position to Chamberlain. The Birmingham West MP, then president of the Board of Trade, had proceeded on the assumption that he had secured Parnell's support. When he discovered that this was not the case, the inevitable rancour between the two men had been amplified with the assistance of O'Shea's distortions and half-truths. O'Shea and Chamberlain had mended fences, but the antipathy between the latter and Parnell had endured and festered.

At the age of fifty-two, the twice-widowed Chamberlain had recently found love on a diplomatic mission to the USA. Ever the self-assured dandy – he was always dapper in appearance, sporting a monocle and an orchid in his buttonhole – he had managed to beat off all-comers and become engaged to the twenty-three-year-old Mary Endicott, daughter of the Secretary of War in the Grover Cleveland administration, and 'a bright particular star'.[4] Chamberlain was in ebullient form on his return to Britain in the spring of 1888. He wrote to his fiancée on an almost daily basis. His ebullience, however, did not stretch as far as a *rapprochement* with the Irish Party leader.

Instead, in July 1888 both men raked over their differences in a series of set pieces prompted by Parnell's renewed demand for a parliamentary select committee to investigate the *Times*'s allegations against him. Just below the surface of enforced parliamentary civility, where even a mortal enemy must be described as an 'honourable gentleman', a reservoir of mutual bile separated the two men.

Chamberlain, it was common knowledge, was working behind the scenes to deny Parnell his wish for a parliamentary select committee and instead to have a judicial commission – a potential Star Chamber – appointed to investigate the allegations. However, he consistently denied any attempt to sway the government. Instead, in a Commons speech on 24 July 1888, he channelled Mark Antony in his praise of Brutus by referring to a time when the two men had been on friendlier terms, during the early 1880s. Chamberlain observed unctuously that:

> I formed a judgment of the hon. Member for Cork, of his character, of his motives, of his honesty, of his sincerity, and of his patriotism, that will not allow me easily to accept the charges which have now been made against him.[5]

Parnell lay in the long grass for a week and on 30 July, during the debate on the committee stage of the Special Commission legislation, he launched a vitriolic *ad hominem* attack on 'the right honourable member for Birmingham West'. He accused Chamberlain of having sheltered behind certain Irish members in his pursuit of political advantage. This was a veiled reference to Chamberlain's baffling association with O'Shea, who, the Chief was convinced, was behind the 'facsimile letter'. Parnell then accused Chamberlain of breaching cabinet confidentiality. He concluded by dismissing the Birmingham MP's qualified endorsement of his integrity in the most scathing terms:

> I care very little for the opinion of the right honourable gentleman, I have never put forward men to do dangerous things which I shrank from doing myself, nor have I betrayed the secrets of my colleagues in council … If this inquiry be extended into these matters – and I see no reason why it should not – I shall be obliged to make good my words by documentary evidence which is not forged.[6]

Parnell's 'one may smile and smile and be a villain' diatribe was followed by intermittent chants of 'Judas, Judas' from Irish MPs whenever their leader paused for breath.[7]

A seething and 'deeply wounded'[8] Chamberlain responded to Parnell's invective the following night (31 July 1888), but the rift that had opened between the two former allies had now widened to a chasm. In that night's letter to his fiancée, Chamberlain referred to Parnell's attack as 'venomous' and observed that the entire episode 'shows how excited these Celtic gentlemen are getting now that there is a chance of their being found out'.[9]

Thereafter Chamberlain maintained a relatively low profile as the scaffolding of the Special Commission was put in place. This was dictated, in part, by his return to the USA in the winter of 1888, to marry Miss Endicott. But when the commission failed to achieve the anticipated objective – the shredding of Parnellism – he would rejoin the fray, lurking in the shadow of Captain William Henry O'Shea, while his creature sought to destroy the 'marvellous legend of Parnell'.[10]

'The irruption of Frank Hugh O'Donnell':[11] *O'Donnell v. Walter* and another*

The *Times*'s 'revelations' of 18 April 1887 had served a dual purpose. The newspaper was guaranteed an increased readership for the remainder of the series, which began on 13 May with the first of Anderson's three articles entitled 'Behind the Scenes in America', based on almost a decade of letters from Henri Le Caron. But there was also an upside for Balfour and Salisbury. Given the contents of the series thus far, the government could now more easily justify the introduction of new Crimes Act legislation. Ireland, it was clear from the facsimile letter, was a den of murderers in cahoots with their political collaborators. A firm hand was required, and Arthur Balfour would supply all five digits. For his part, Parnell, continued to protest his innocence. Whether or not anyone chose to believe him largely depended on their political affiliation.

These entrenched positions also factored into the reason why the Irish leader did not take the obvious step, if he had indeed been defamed, of taking legal action against *The Times*. The newspaper had taunted Parnell, inviting him to initiate court proceedings if he felt that he had been wronged. It drew the obvious inference from his inexplicable refusal to press his case. There was, however, nothing inexplicable about Parnell's forbearance. He was plainly on a hiding to nothing. If he sued the newspaper in Dublin, which he was entitled to do, his inevitable victory would have been hollow. But to initiate a suit against *The Times* in London would have led to an equally predictable defeat there. Legal action on Parnell's part could serve no political purpose. The sides were at a standoff and, gradually, the controversy began to sink into the quicksand of political apathy.

Enter Frank Hugh O'Donnell.

The former MP, a 'brilliant but irritable eccentric',[12] 'whose unimportance was surpassed only by his self-regard',[13] had

* The 'Walter' in question being John Walter III, proprietor of *The Times*.

been an ally of Parnell during the 'obstruction' era of the mid-1870s. However, Parnell's subsequent elevation did not sit well with O'Donnell, who did not see himself as a subaltern to his younger colleague. The capricious and egotistical O'Donnell – nicknamed 'Crank Hugh' by the viperish Tim Healy – had finally parted company with the Irish Party when his constituency disappeared after the 1884 electoral realignment and Parnell had neglected to provide him with an alternative.

He had managed to maintain a low profile since the end of his parliamentary career, mainly by living in Germany and Italy. However, after an unsatisfactory response to a letter sent to the newspaper and published on 17 June 1887, he concluded that he had been libelled by *The Times* in the 'Parnellism and Crime' series. The fact that he was not mentioned even once in the articles failed to soothe his dented ego. It may, in fact, have exacerbated his chagrin. He became 'an irascible Quixote, insulted by the windmill'.[14] Unlike his former party leader, who had far greater provocation to take legal action, O'Donnell sued *The Times* for defamation. In his memoir he is opaque as to his motivation. He writes almost as if his extraordinary intervention was the work of some mysterious third party. 'The attacks of *The Times* upon the Parnellites had the unexpected result of forcing me to bring an action for libel against the mighty newspaper,'[15] he observed in his two-volume political apologia, *A History of the Irish Parliamentary Party*. Whatever his motivation, O'Donnell's intervention raised a hare that had only recently gone to ground.

Phoenix-like, the original controversy rose from the ashes, but in a fashion that redounded exclusively to the benefit of the defendant in the case of *O'Donnell v. Walter*. The proceedings, which came before the Lord Chief Justice, Lord Coleridge, began on 2 July 1888, lasted four days and ended in abject humiliation for O'Donnell. His bizarre intervention led – in a political environment where conspiracy theories were bread and butter – to allegations that O'Donnell was a 'stalking horse' for *The Times*, and that his lawsuit was 'a collusive action instituted for ulterior purposes'.[16] The newspaper – or so went the received wisdom – had been gunning for someone, anyone, to take a lawsuit so that it could introduce into the public domain some new and damning material that would finally sink the Parnellites. The 'stalking horse' conspiracy theory was then given some oxygen with the introduction, in court, by *The Times* of a raft of allegedly incriminating documents that had come into its possession.

The newspaper, of course, did not have to concern itself with issues of potential defamation where this new material was concerned. Once it was read into the court record, with the acquiescence of the judge, it enjoyed absolute privilege. It could also be quoted in full, and without legal consequence, in the following day's newspapers. *The Times* had been in possession of many of these 'new' documents for more than a year. They had been held back in anticipation of a lawsuit from Parnell and were to be used as ammunition to justify the original alleged libel. Now that it was clear that Parnell did not intend to sue, *The Times* was anxious to get this material into the public domain. O'Donnell's suit provided the newspaper with an ideal opportunity.

O'Donnell claimed in his memoir that 'Parnell presided over the whole direction of the case.' Because the book was published in 1910, Parnell was not around to respond. But back in July 1888 he issued a statement insisting that 'he absolutely declined to give any assistance whatever to Mr. O'Donnell'.[17] However, the Irish Party leader did appear at the trial, although, according to O'Donnell, he did not wish to testify. The distinguished British barrister Sir Edward Clarke KC (solicitor general 1886–90) claimed in his memoir that, since Parnell 'was at this time living with Mrs. O'Shea at Brighton … he might well wish to avoid the risk of their relations becoming the subject of public discussion'.[18] Parnell's interest in the case may have extended no further than the opportunity it afforded him to accompany O'Donnell to the offices of the *Times*'s solicitors (Soames & Co.) and to inspect the facsimile letter in person as well as the new tranche of documents.

Attorney General Sir Richard Webster, taking advantage of the custom that allowed Crown law officers to maintain a private practice, led the case for *The Times*. By taking on the brief he managed to convey the inescapable impression that the Salisbury administration and the 'newspaper of record' were in lockstep. Webster, with no real necessity to raise any serious defence against the flimsy charge of defamation, took the walkover in his stride and read out in court a further cache of letters which, if genuine, would have damning implications for Parnell, Patrick Egan and James O'Kelly MP, among others. He refused to reveal the source of the correspondence. 'His clients would decline to give the names of the persons from whom they got them.'[19]

Had anyone read *The Times* of 5 July 1888 as it recorded, verbatim, the proceedings in court the previous day, they would have been unaware of a significant anomaly. The *Times* court reporter was not to know that there was an odd misspelling of the word 'hesitancy' in one of the letters read out by Webster. In this terse communication, apparently sent in January 1881, Parnell appeared to be upbraiding Patrick Egan in the following terms:

> Dear E, – what are these fellows waiting for? Our best men are in prison, and nothing is being done. Let there be an end of this *hesitency* [my italics]. Prompt action is called for. You undertook to make it hot for old Forster and Co. Let us have some evidence of your power to do so.[20]

While *The Times* ignored the misspelling, their opponents were gleefully aware of it. Suspicion had hardened into certainty. The letters on which *The Times* based its case were forged, and the Parnellites were morally certain that they could now identify the forger. It was an orthographical error that would come back to haunt the newspaper. Parnell was emphatic in his claim that the missive was a fake: 'I denounce it as an absolute forgery. I never wrote it; I never signed it; I never directed it to be written; I never authorized it to be written, and I never saw it.'[21]

*

On the same day that Parnell was dismissing the new cache of *Times* documents before the House of Commons, the Lord Chief Justice was giving similarly short shrift to Frank Hugh O'Donnell's defamation case. 'It seems to me,' Coleridge stated, inserting the dagger directly into O'Donnell's ribs, 'that he never was a very intimate associate of Mr. Parnell or of the persons with whom he conducted his affairs … Why he intervened and what his object was he alone knows.'[22] The jury duly found for *The Times* without leaving the courtroom.

O'Donnell had done Parnell no favours by restoring the issue of the facsimile letter to the daily news cycle, and by inviting invidious comparisons between his own gung-ho approach to the protection of a reputation that had not been maligned, and the failure of the Irish leader to launch a defamation suit of his own. *The Times* took great pleasure in reprinting the observations of influential European newspapers, such as *Figaro* and *Le Temps*, that 'he has not prosecuted for defamation the journal which has so seriously calumniated him'.[23]

On 9 July, four days after *O'Donnell v. Walter* ended, Parnell gave notice that he would seek the appointment of a select committee of the House of Commons to investigate the veracity of the allegations of *The Times* against him.[24] This demand was rejected out of hand by the leader of the House, W. H. Smith. The Tories did, however, have an unattractive alternative proposal. Rather than appoint a committee to investigate the damning allegations against one of the most prominent members of the House, Smith offered instead to indict the entire Irish Parliamentary Party (with some extra-parliamentary collaborators thrown in for good measure) for the 'crimes' of which they had been accused in the *O'Donnell v. Walter* case. A Special Commission, chaired by three judges, would pass judgement on the bona fides of an entire political movement. As Michael Davitt, one of those 'indicted', observed pungently: 'It was virtually the tender to Mr. Parnell of a halter with which to execute himself.'[25]

But was it better than nothing?

The Special Commission

> 'The erection of the Special Commission of 1888 stands out as one of the ugliest things done in the name and under the forms of law in this island during the century.'[26]
>
> John Morley, *Life of Gladstone* (1908)

> 'Ministers and their allies were determined to discredit Home Rule as well as its chief apostles, and to accomplish this end they sought to prove that the New Departure represented nothing more than the old methods of intimidation and rebellion in Irish history.'[27]
>
> L. Perry Curtis, *Coercion and Conciliation in Ireland* (1963)

According to John Morley, former *Pall Mall Gazette* editor, Liberal MP, and biographer and confidant of Gladstone, *O'Donnell v. Walter* 'stirred Mr. Parnell from his usual impassiveness'.[28]

The precise nature of any parliamentary or public inquiry would be decided by the leader of the House of Commons, W. H. Smith, who, through his bookselling business, was on friendly terms with the proprietor of *The Times*, John Walter III. Subsequent allegations of collusion between the government and the newspaper were given substance when Smith was forced to reveal to the Commons that, while the Special Commission bill was being discussed at cabinet, he had been visited by his 'old friend'[29] John Walter. The House was then asked to believe that the two men had not even discussed the elephant in the room.

Spurred by his personal animosity towards Parnell, and angered by the chants of 'Judas, Judas' from the Irish Party benches whenever he rose to speak, a thoroughly embittered Joseph Chamberlain privately pointed the leader of the House towards the ultimate option, a full judicial royal commission of inquiry which, he trusted, would lead 'to the great confusion of Mr. Parnell and his friends'. In a transatlantic letter to Miss Endicott, Chamberlain outlined how his objective was to enhance not only the scale but the scope of the inquiry. It would indict

Irish constitutional nationalism. The royal commission option that he covertly proposed to Smith would 'try a revolution as well as a man'.[30] Although stoutly denying that he was the 'artful Mr. Chamberlain'[31] (the Press Association's representation of his intrigues) pulling strings behind the scenes, a series of five letters to his fiancée between 7 and 17 July 1888 reveal the extent of his machinations. They culminated in the self-satisfied claim that 'the government is inclined to take my view'. Parnell's biographer, F. S. L. Lyons, concluded that 'Chamberlain's pressure was decisive' and that one of his motivating influences was that 'he still had at his elbow the tenacious O'Shea who had by now settled into an implacable hatred of Parnell'.[32]

The extent of Chamberlain's duplicity can be gauged from his contribution to the Commons debate on 11 March 1890 on the report of the Commissioners. Despite having lobbied energetically for a royal commission, he denied that it had been his 'pet proposal' and blithely informed the House that 'I never heard of the commission until it was suggested by the government.'[33] This was a blatant lie, and one maintained in his own memoir some years later when he falsely claimed that he would have 'taken the Parliamentary Committee suggested by Parnell himself'.[34]

The 11th of March 1890 was not, however, the first occasion on which Chamberlain had dissembled on the issue. In the Commons debate on the legislation setting up the Commission, on 24 July 1888, the Liberal Unionist leader stated, breathtakingly, that 'I am sorry the Government did not grant a committee',[35] by which he meant a parliamentary select committee. The following day he boasted to his fiancée that 'I heard a great number of pleasant things about my speech yesterday which appears to have produced a great effect; One man said that in all his experience he had never seen the house listen with such rapt attention.'[36] The peacock feathers were on full display.

On 12 July – always an inauspicious day in the Irish nationalist narrative – the curtain was hoisted on the backstage intrigue. W. H. Smith pronounced the notion of a Commons select committee as 'altogether unfit to deal with the question'. However, in the absence of an appeal to the libel courts by those who considered themselves to have been unfairly maligned, the government was prepared 'To pass an Act appointing a Commission, which should consist wholly or mainly of Judges, with full powers, as in the case of other Statutory Commissions, to inquire into the allegations and charges made against Members of Parliament by the defendants in the recent action of *O'Donnell v. Walter and another*.'[37] While the offer was not quite as injurious as the swords of King William's soldiers at Oldbridge on 12 July 1690, it was, metaphorically at least, as double-edged as any weapon wielded that day. The Parnellites were obliged to accept Smith's 'take it or leave it' offer. When the terms of the legislation were published a few days later, it was apparent to the Parnellites that they would probably have been better to leave it. Far from confining itself to the issue of the alleged forgeries of *The Times*, the commission was to be a fishing expedition. This excursion, however, was to be conducted by trawlermen rather than anglers. The rubric adopted by Salisbury's government constituted an indictment of the bulk of the membership of the Irish Parliamentary Party and several of their extra-parliamentary allies. This was to be a state conspiracy trial. 'It is clear,' wrote the Tory prime minister's biographer, Robert Taylor, 'that Salisbury and Balfour were out to destroy Parnell and his party through judicial exposure as collaborators with the men of violence.'[38]

That was not exactly how it turned out. But on the day of the first reading of the 'Special Commission' bill, no one knew how the entire charade would come back to haunt *The Times* and the Tories. Sir Randolph Churchill, who, although he had resigned as Chancellor of the Exchequer in a fit of pique the previous year, was still a Tory capo, advised Smith against creating the commission. 'Prudent politicians,' warned the ultra-unionist Churchill, 'would hesitate to go out of their way to play such high stakes as these.'[39] It was not as if Churchill was unfamiliar with high-stakes politics; however, Smith chose to ignore his colleague's well-intentioned warnings. Churchill would later describe the Commission as a 'revolutionary tribunal' that was 'utterly repugnant to our English ideas of legal justice, and wholly unconstitutional'.[40]

W. H. Smith himself set the tone for the vindictive nature of the tribunal when he led the debate on the second reading of the legislation and referred to 'this great trial' before correcting himself and opting for the more neutral 'this great inquiry'. Joseph Chamberlain had done his work well. *The Times* exulted in what was, in effect, a performative validation – and an anticipated vindication – of the 'Parnellism and Crime' series. The first straw in the wind that the incumbent government and the 'newspaper of record' might have colluded in the offer of a royal commission came in the House of Commons on 20 July. Thomas Sexton MP, nationalist Lord Mayor of Dublin, asked the leader of the house 'whether any written or oral communication has passed between any Member of the Government, or any person acting on behalf of the Government, and any person acting on behalf of *The Times*?' Smith's response was a terse, 'I decline to answer any such Question'.[41]

Despite the clear and present danger inherent in the terms of reference of the tribunal, Parnell was determined (or fatalistic at worst) that there should be some reckoning. If a royal commission was all that was on offer, then a royal commission it would be. Parnell was under no illusions that *The Times* would score some points and 'reveal lamentable indiscretions of subordinates'.[42] But the probability that a number of Land League organizers – Patrick Egan, Matthew Harris and P. J. Sheridan being the most obvious candidates – would hardly emerge smelling of roses was to be weighed against the likelihood that the general public would ignore those facets of the inquiry if the facsimile document was proved to be a forgery. The second reading of the bill received the unanimous assent of the Commons. After considerable pushback at committee stage the government used the 'guillotine'/cloture to stifle any further debate and avoid any constricting amendments. 'The unscrupulous tactics of the Tories … in appealing to the forces of political fear and religious bigotry'[43] (Michael Davitt) were already in evidence, and the joint operation with *The Times* had barely begun. Ironically, after all the parliamentary palaver about Parnell's refusal to sue *The Times* for defamation, he now did just that. Before the queen's signature was appended to the Special Commission legislation, which would have pre-empted any civil legal proceedings, Parnell began a libel action, in 'neutral' Edinburgh. He sought an ambitious £100,000 in damages from the newspaper.

As Goethe, the German poet, once observed, 'Be careful what you wish for in youth, lest you achieve it in middle age.' This is generally truncated to the more generic 'Be careful what you wish for'. It was an axiom that might well have been applied to *The Times*. Despite the apparent rout of the Parnellites with the establishment of the judge-led 'Parnellism and Crime' commission, all was not well at Printing House Square. Behind the façade of smug triumph was a pervasive misgiving.

This uncertainty was what had given rise to the 'Parnellism and Crime' series in the first place.

Ironically, the doubts that led to the 30,000-word polemic bookending the sensational 18 April 1887 scoop were prompted by one of the advocates who would argue the *Times*'s case before the Commission. This was the courtly former Liberal attorney general Sir Henry James. James had served under Gladstone but had fallen out with the Grand Old Man over Home Rule and was now one of the leaders of the Liberal Unionist faction in the House of Commons.

The newspaper had come by the facsimile letter in 1886 in a roundabout fashion (see Chapter 8). After indulging in several contortions in its efforts to verify Parnell's signature on the letter – which was then confirmed by a leading handwriting expert, G. S. Inglis – *The Times* sought advice from James about the potential legal ramifications should they decide to publish the contents of the letter. The consultation took place the day before the opening of the new parliamentary session on 27 January 1887, when it was anticipated that a rigorous Crimes Bill would be introduced. *The Times* was determined to play its part in supporting the Tory legislation.

But the ambitious plan had to be scrapped.

The management of the newspaper was disconcerted when James, on being presented with what the *Times* insiders styled as 'Letter No. 2' (which would become the 'facsimile letter'), told John Cameron MacDonald, the manager of the newspaper, and Joseph Soames, solicitor for *The Times*, that this was not the first time he had seen the allegedly incriminating document. When it first had been presented to him, in the summer of 1886, he had formed the impression that the seedy Dublin journalist Richard Pigott had played some part in obtaining the letter. James advised the management of the newspaper to avoid any involvement or association with Pigott. Neither MacDonald, John Walter III nor George Buckle had ever heard of Pigott. Nor, according to the newspaper's official history, 'was it regarded of sufficient importance to require the consultation of those members of the staff of the paper who were specially conversant with Irish affairs'.[44] Despite being miffed that they had not been the first to set eyes on what they still considered to be a prodigious scoop, *The Times* kept faith with their source material in a display of 'stunning overconfidence'.[45]

It was not as if Pigott (and his reputation) was entirely unknown in London. When future Liberal prime minister Sir Henry Campbell-Bannerman was Irish chief secretary (from October 1884 to June 1885) he received a letter from Pigott. Before he responded Campbell-Bannerman was warned by his private secretary not to reply in his own handwriting because of Pigott's known penchant for forgery and double dealing.[46] However, rather than publish 'Letter No. 2' out of a clear blue sky, the newspaper decided to create some background padding to prepare its readership for the bombshell of 18 April 1887. Hence the 'reinforcement' provided by the 'Parnellism and Crime' series.

In the summer of 1888, knowing rather more about the reputation of Pigott as a wheedler, blackmailer and pornographer than when Henry James was shown 'Letter No. 2' in January 1887, *The Times* was aware of the possibility that their entire cache of documents was forged. The newspaper was in a jam from which only the government could extricate it.

Just as the 'Parnellism and Crime' series was a protective buffer erected around 'Letter No. 2' in 1887, the Special Commission itself was a desperate attempt at misdirection designed to distract from the distinct possibility that the newspaper's treasure trove would be exposed as forgeries. The prevailing assumption was that *The Times* would want to deal with 'Letter No. 2' and the additional correspondence introduced during *O'Donnell v. Walter* as early as possible in the proceedings. Were Parnell to be proven to have signed the facsimile letter, the game would be up for the party leader and his supporters. Anything that followed, assuming anyone was paying attention, would simply confirm the depravity of the Irish nationalist leadership.

So why not start with 'Letter No. 2'?

In fact, the newspaper, in the manner of a conjurer, now wanted the audience to be looking elsewhere, or to be in a boredom-induced coma, when that problematic trick was performed. Hence the preparatory litany – presented at mind-numbing length – describing the Land League's history of lawlessness and violence, and the encouragement of rural anarchy by the leadership of the Irish Parliamentary Party. With a single exception (see Chapter 7), for the first four months of evidence, no witness was presented by *The Times* in corroboration of the only element of its case that any neutral observer felt really mattered: the veracity of Parnell's signature on 'Letter No. 2'. As far as British public opinion was concerned, the violence of the Land League, and the benign neglect/covert support of agrarian outrage by Irish nationalist politicians, was already taken for granted. It was assumed that, at the very least, Irish political leaders had turned a blind eye to the rural chaos of the Land War. Many of the more engaged British observers would also have remarked, with a shrug, that it was only through the unleashing of anarchy that the Irish agrarian movement had managed to achieve its objectives in the first place. Gladstone himself had once acknowledged as much. So why was *The Times* intent on restating the blindingly obvious?

'Captain Moonlight' depicted in The Illustrated Police News, *15 December 1888*

Michael Davitt, the only nationalist figure who persevered with the tribunal from beginning to end, summarized the dilemma of *The Times* and the Tories: 'It was in order to keep back as long as possible the inevitable exposure of the known forgery by Pigott, which would explode the whole plot, that the attorney general induced the court to permit him, on behalf of *The Times* to relegate this vital part of the investigation to the very last stage of the accuser's case.'[47] Webster, who had already been humoured by Lord Coleridge in *O'Donnell v. Walter*, was now being indulged by the Commissioners.

There would be many occasions when the eye-rolling and practically comatose judges regretted their indulgence.

In all, sixty-five members of the Parnellite parliamentary party were included in the exceptionally vague 'charges' entered by *The Times*. They included Parnell himself, his principal lieutenants Justin McCarthy, Thomas Sexton, John Dillon, William O'Brien, Timothy Harrington, Joseph Biggar, John Redmond and Tim Healy. The extensive list of 'other persons' indicted alongside the MPs read like a 'Who's Who' of extra-parliamentary Irish nationalism, ranging from the moderate to the revolutionary. From the relatively innocuous James Redpath – an American journalist with avowed nationalist sympathies – to card-carrying Fenians such as P. N. Fitzgerald, James Stephens and John O'Leary. A smattering of Irish-American extremists (Devoy, Rossa, Sullivan, Millen, and Patrick Ford) were thrown in for good measure. Other notable villains were Anna Parnell and Hannah Lynch of the Ladies Land League; Patrick Egan, Michael Boyton, P. J. Gordon, P. J. Sheridan and Thomas Brennan of the Land League, as well as acknowledged 'Invincibles' such as James Mullett, John Walsh, Frank Byrne, John McCafferty and P. J. Tynan. At least two of those indicted (James Carey and William Mackey Lomasney) were dead, and one (Millen) was a double-agent in the employ of the British government.

The three judges asked to preside over the tribunal were Sir

James Hannen, President of the Probate, Divorce and Admiralty Court, and two Queen's Bench judges, Sir John Charles Day and Sir A. L. Smith. Day, a Roman Catholic, was described by journalist and MP T. P. O'Connor as having 'the face of an undertaker, black hair, black whiskers, black eyes, and the solemnity of an owl'.[48] All three were viewed as reliable Tory justices, 'by no means sympathetic with Irish nationalism',[49] who were appointed to deliver a positive outcome for the government and *The Times*. Events, however, did not work out entirely as expected. The commissioners were fair-minded enough not to oblige their political 'masters' by conducting themselves in accordance with Tory principles of equity.

The government managed to get itself into a lather with the appointment of the 'prosecuting' counsel. Attorney General Webster – described by T. P. O'Connor, as 'thoroughly thick-headed' and of having 'the unconscious partisanship and impenetrability of a thoroughly narrow-minded man'[50] – appeared to have no difficulty representing *The Times* in a personal capacity, and for a sizeable fee, in the O'Donnell case. However, he baulked at the prospect of accepting the *Times*'s brief in the Special Commission proceedings. On 3 September 1888 he wrote to the solicitor general, Sir Edward Clarke, advising him that he had asked W. H. Smith to allow him to resile from participation in the tribunal. Aware of Chamberlain's influence on Smith in the creation of the Commission, Webster told Clarke, 'every day I curse Chamberlain and the unionists for their obstinacy'.[51] Clarke himself was in no doubt that 'Chamberlain and his friends pressed hard for an inquiry'.[52] He had 'forced it upon the government in prosecution of his political and personal vendetta'.[53]

Sir Henry James, who obviously had his own reasons to be sceptical of the *Times*'s case, was also keen to bail out. But Salisbury wasn't having any of it. Any suspicion of backsliding on the part of a high-ranking government place-holder, or even a Liberal Unionist supporter, was not going to be tolerated. He warned Smith that 'the simultaneous refusal of these two men to go on would have the worst possible effect. There will be no persuading the outside world that they have not run away from the case because on scrutinising the evidence they satisfied themselves that the case was bad.'[54] The prime minister instructed Smith to hold Webster's feet to the fire. The attorney general was forced to bow to the Master of Hatfield. An equally reluctant Sir Henry James was cajoled into becoming Webster's second in command.

The two best-known advocates on the Parnellite side were the shrewd and forceful Newry-born Sir Charles Russell, a former attorney general (February–July 1886) and future lord chief justice of England and Wales. Russell, Liberal MP for Hackney South and an enthusiastic supporter of Home Rule, was about to embark on what his biographer described as '*the* great event'[55] (his italics) of his professional life. He was obliged to sacrifice a lucrative retainer from *The Times* to do so. Russell was engaged, along with future prime minister Herbert H. Asquith, to defend Parnell. Although avowedly on the same side, the Irish Party leader and his main defence counsel were frequently at loggerheads, with Michael Davitt often acting as intermediary when the two alpha males butted heads. Russell concluded at an early stage that Parnell had no interest whatever in the wider *Times* indictments and was interested only in the elements of the case that concerned his own reputation. 'He is a selfish fellow. He thinks only of himself,'[56] he complained to his biographer, the journalist and historian Richard Barry O'Brien. Parnell also had a habit of passing unsolicited notes to Russell suggesting points to be made or courses of action. Russell generally ignored them.

Some of the 'accused' (Davitt, Biggar, Healy) conducted their own defence, while the remainder of those indicted by *The Times* were defended by half a dozen additional counsel. Of paramount importance was the involvement of the London law firm Lewis and Lewis on the Parnellite side. George Lewis ('Sir' George from 1893) had long made good 'yellow press' copy. Although a thoroughly respectable solicitor himself, he was actively involved in many of the high-profile and most eye-catching cases of the mid-Victorian period. Having Lewis in your corner was reckoned to double an accused's chances of acquittal in a criminal court. He was sufficiently celebrated to have been caricatured by Spy in *Vanity Fair*; cited by Arthur Conan Doyle in the Sherlock Holmes mystery 'The Adventure of the Illustrious Client';[57] painted by John Singer Sargent; and lampooned by Gilbert and Sullivan. His contribution to the Parnellite cause in the Special Commission proceedings has often been underestimated. In the words of his biographer, 'Lewis made the cannonballs; Russell only fired them.'[58]

The commissioners slip their bonds

While the Commission might have disappointed Irish nationalists in allowing *The Times* to postpone indefinitely any exploration of their single most ruinous allegation against the Parnellites, the three justices demonstrated an unexpected degree of independence from day one. The Commission met for the first time on 17 September 1888. The task of the three justices was to try 'a social and political revolution',[59] according to John Morley. This was not a position in which many judges would be comfortable. The preliminary proceedings – the tribunal proper commenced on 22 October – should have been a relatively mundane affair. Webster was out of the country and sent a deputy to sort out any 'housekeeping' issues raised by the commissioners. Hannen, the Commission president, began by addressing both sides and elaborating on how the three justices had decided to proceed.

His exposition was not welcomed by *The Times* and 'gravely embarrassed the paper',[60] according to its own official history. Hannen observed that 'we propose in the first instance to conduct this inquiry as though it were an issue directed between those parties to try the truth or falsehood of those charges and allegations'.[61] What this meant, when translated from legalese, was that the entire onus and burden of the 'prosecution' had been transferred to *The Times*. The newspaper had assumed that the Commission would proceed along the lines of a defamation case, with the plaintiff (in this case the Parnellites) being required to prove that they had been libelled by *The Times*. Instead, the tribunal assumed the shape and weight of a criminal trial. *The Times* would be required to produce evidence of malfeasance against those named persons who were considered to have been 'indicted'. To make matters worse, the newspaper of record was expected to pay for Smith, Balfour, Salisbury and Chamberlain's anti-nationalist project in its entirety. *The Times*, though hardly an innocent party itself, was now exposed to considerable potential costs and a logistical headache. It was obliged to assemble conclusive proof to back up the vague allegations made in a series of articles that would never have seen the light of day but for doubts over the documentary 'proof' already in their possession, the Pigott papers. There would, ultimately, be almost 500 witnesses called (494) 'and the whole expense of calling them, which in an ordinary prosecution would have fallen upon the Crown, had to be borne by *The Times*',[62] the newspaper's official history lamented, six decades later. When the bills were all paid, the Tory government's opportunistic decision to refuse the Parnellites a select committee investigation cost their supposed allies in the region of £200,000 (around £31 million today), and almost bankrupted the newspaper. A secret government promise to underwrite the newspaper's financial outlay was quietly rescinded after the Pigott debacle (see Chapter 9).[63] *The Times* was left to shoulder the entire expense of the Special Commission.

The *London Daily News* correspondent John MacDonald – the *News* was a Liberal organ – was the most loyal (or slavish) devotee of the tribunal, reporting on all 128 days of speeches and testimony. His straight reportage, and his occasional analytical sifting of the evidence, was never less than interesting and was often compelling. His colourful pen portraits of many of the witnesses, who ranged from the cherubic to the psychotic, were generally on the money. His coverage of the first day of speeches and testimony on 22

October 1888 focused on 'the van of a multitude of Irishmen (and Irishwomen) about to assist at a unique operation of historical stock-taking'. His own take on the males of the species was crammed with the patronizing stereotyping of the urban English sophisticate. There were, he recounted:

> Witnesses from every class of Irish society, the Paddy of *Punch*'s shopwindows, in the flesh, in his traditional costume. He wears knee-breeches and woollen stockings. The style of his tall hat is unknown in Piccadilly. His starchless collar of blue-striped cotton falls round his lean, weather-beaten neck loosely as an aesthete's; and the swallow-tails of his baggy dress-coat of greyish brown shaggy frieze impinge upon his calves. Just as he appears at mass, or on market-days – say at Galway or archiepiscopal Tuam – while he waits, mutely, through the irresponsive hours, straw rope in hand, beside his pig.[64]

On 22 October 1888, the 'plump, industrious and somewhat obtuse'[65] Sir Richard Webster rose to address the commissioners in Probate Court No. 1. *The Times* would present its case over 128 days, the resulting evidence filled eleven thick folio volumes, amounting to almost 8,000 pages and 90,000 questions. Webster took five days (22–6 October) to open his account, during which it became clear, if any additional clarity was necessary, that the *Times*'s case was to be a scorching indictment of Irish separatism. This would be advanced by the depiction of Irish nationalists and agrarian agitators (little distinction would be made between the two) as anarchic assassins who enjoyed the wholehearted, but covert, support of Irish parliamentary representatives. Ireland was to be portrayed as a nation unfit for self-government, in even the most diluted form - as savage, uncivilized and chaotic a country as any of the newly colonized spaces currently enjoying the benefits of British civilization on the African continent.

On the first day of his strident jeremiad, Webster began as he intended to continue. He may have been a reluctant presence in Probate Court No. 1, but he knew what was expected of him:

> We shall allege that all the acts that were done were done in furtherance of a concerted and preconceived conspiracy with definite objects, with definite aims, and that the only way in which that conspiracy could be carried out ... was by the commission of crimes ... In other words, the somewhat stock phrase of 'Parnellism and Crime' is a correct paraphrase, almost a history, in three words, of what the organisation was.[66]

Before getting down to the specifics – in their hundreds – of alleged incitement to murder, hurled from Land League platforms by the likes of Joseph Biggar, Timothy Harrington, Thomas Brennan, Matthew Harris, John Dillon *et al.*, Webster made the generalized claim of 'speeches at Land League meetings, directly inciting to outrage, inciting to arson, inciting to treatment which has led to the most iniquitous results'.[67] 'The landlord garrison was to be removed altogether from Ireland,' he declared, 'because landlordism was a British garrison which barred the way to national independence.'[68]

An RIC officer named Bernard O'Malley had the distinction of being the first witness before the Commission after Webster had concluded his tirade. O'Malley was taken through his relatively inconsequential evidence (the reading of notes taken at a 'Land League' meeting in Milltown, Co. Galway on 25 July 1880 addressed by Thomas Brennan and P. J. Gordon), and O'Malley was the first of many such witnesses, as *The Times* attempted to give performative shape and expression to 'Parnellism and Crime'. He was also the first witness – but he was far from being the last – whose accent the three presiding justices found difficult to understand. Sir Henry James, who was taking the witness through his evidence, was obliged to read out O'Malley's notes himself, so that the commissioners could make head or tail of what was being said. From day one, the doyens of the Inns of Court were finding Hibernia either difficult to comprehend or downright unintelligible.

O'Malley and those who immediately followed him were merely appetizers for the main course that followed on the third day of direct evidence, 31 October. Although *The Times* had indicated its unwillingness to come to grips immediately with the Pigott letters, and especially with the incendiary 'Letter No. 2', the newspaper appeared to second guess itself by introducing a surprise witness on day three. He was someone who was very familiar with Parnell's signature and would stitch into the record of the tribunal an early confirmation that, whatever about the content of letters being offered by *The Times* over the autograph of the Irish Party leader, the signatures themselves were genuine.

The 'prosecution' was going to play one of its colour cards. The cocksure Captain William O'Shea would eventually do considerable damage to the Parnellite cause but he was to come perilously close to being reduced, under cross-examination, to the status of joker. His evidence, under interrogation from an oddly well-informed Sir Charles Russell, would also intersect with the sordid details of a campaign of dirty tricks, 'black ops' and felon-setting known only to a select few.

7

THE CAPTAIN, THE FORGER, THE SPY AND THE BAGMAN

'A sleek, odoriferous, furtive, professional pimp and go-between, an entirely contemptible and unclean thing as everyone now can see in this strong glare, one of the vermin species, a flabby muskrat needing but a prod for such a smell to arise.'[1]

United Ireland on William O'Shea,
3 November 1888

'O'Shea in box all morning and far into afternoon. Doesn't seem to like it; shaved off whiskers in order to better face ordeal. But no use. In unbroken line below him sit old familiar friends ... a trying ordeal for the once *debonnaire* [*sic*] but now decidedly damaged Captain. Some signs of quailing at first. Strong disinclination to meet the four pairs of gleaming eyes.'[2]

Punch on O'Shea's commission testimony,
10 November 1888

The Special Commission, Probate Court No.1, 31 October 1888

The brooding figure of Parnell, who was apt to show up hours after the day's proceedings had begun, was today in his seat a full fifteen minutes before the commissioners took to the bench. It was the seventh day of the tribunal. It had already set high standards for tedium. What could possibly have occasioned the dilatory Parnell to change his habits? The two RIC witnesses who had been testifying on day six had been asked to reappear to give further evidence and to be cross-examined. The squire of Avondale would not have abandoned his bed a quarter of an hour early so that he could listen to two police shorthand notetakers continue their account of the rhetorical excesses of his former Land League colleagues and associates. Only something pertaining to Charles Stewart Parnell would have overcome his customary tardiness.

The prosecution was about to spring a 'surprise', though clearly it was not much of a revelation to Parnell, hence his early arrival. When proceedings began, Webster advised the commissioners that Captain William Henry O'Shea would be favouring them with his presence that day. *The Times*, Webster advised the commissioners, had been hoping to take this witness's evidence much later, but his presence was required in Spain, where he would be detained on business for a number of months.

The news of O'Shea's imminent departure for an indeterminate period must have pleased Parnell immensely.

The normally cocksure O'Shea was palpably nervous as he took the stand. In the words of one of Parnell's early biographers, the Birmingham journalist Alfred Robbins, the captain had a 'shabby genteel'[3] appearance.

Sir Charles Russell was immediately on his feet to object to having an unexpected witness foisted upon him. He was unprepared, he insisted, to cross-examine. His objections were dismissed. When he did go toe to toe with O'Shea, however, he seemed oddly well-prepared. Neither, it appeared, was Sir Charles Russell overly surprised at this premature appearance of one the *Times*'s star witnesses.

The attorney general quickly eased the 'plump, vivacious, overtalkative'[4] O'Shea – a notorious 'gabbler and a babbler'[5] – through his narrative in direct testimony. Webster hovered over the 'Kilmainham Treaty' for some minutes to enable the witness to confirm that Parnell 'had full knowledge of criminal acts perpetrated by his associates [and] could at any time (even in jail) have suppressed the criminal agitation, of which … he and his colleagues were the authors'.[6] The argument was an old chestnut. If Parnell had turned off the tap of rural violence in pursuit of concessions from Gladstone, then, logically, he must have turned it on. The captain's real value to *The Times*, however, was as a credible witness familiar with Parnell's signature. The newspaper wanted it nailed into the Commission record – before abandoning the matter of the letters for another four months – that a close associate and former political ally of Parnell had confirmed his signature on the facsimile letter and the other documents in the possession of the newspaper. The captain duly obliged. When asked directly by Webster to identify the signature on 'Letter No. 2', O'Shea, despite disavowing any expertise in calligraphy, was only vaguely non-committal at first. 'It appears to be Mr. Parnell's signature,' he told the attorney general. When quizzed about two more of the incriminating letters (both from 16 June 1882), he was more emphatic, 'I believe them to be Mr. Parnell's,' he observed confidently.[7] Having shafted Parnell, his job done, Webster quickly concluded his examination and handed O'Shea over to Sir Charles Russell for cross-examination.

That was when things began to go wrong.

A snake on the make[8]

In October 1888, in one of his regular letters to his bride-to-be Mary Endicott, Joseph Chamberlain described Captain William Henry O'Shea as 'indiscreet and therefore a dangerous person'.[9] Few who knew the captain would have argued with that dismissive assessment, yet even the hard-headed Chamberlain often succumbed to O'Shea's charm. It was one of the captain's few endearing features. The flow of unction could be turned up or down, on or off, depending on who needed to be enchanted. When he was toadying up to the influential Chamberlain the spigot was always wide open.

Son of a wealthy professional, often reliant on the income of others, and with political connections to County Clare, O'Shea – but for the timing* – might have been a model for Anthony Trollope's 'man on the make', Phineas Finn, minus most of that fictional character's redeeming personal qualities.

O'Shea's father, Henry, was a Limerick solicitor who made a tidy fortune buying and selling 'encumbered' (bankrupt) estates after the Great Famine. William was, appropriately but ominously, named after his dissolute grandfather. Much given to affectation, Captain William Henry O'Shea pronounced the family name as 'O'Shee' rather than the more common 'O'Shay'. In 1880 he stood for election in the Clare constituency as a (vaguely) nationalist candidate and was elected to the House of Commons, along with the superannuated and far more colourful Colonel James P. O'Gorman Mahon. The latter was a white-haired veteran of the army of the tsar of Russia and an habitual duellist who styled himself 'The O'Gorman Mahon'. To ensure the elder statesman's support, O'Shea covered his election expenses. It was not the last 'shakedown' with which the junior member for Clare was associated, albeit on this occasion he was on the receiving end.

O'Shea, an incorrigible Whig, given his obvious lack of commitment to any form of radical constitutional nationalism, surprised everyone, including possibly himself, by voting for Parnell in the Irish Parliamentary Party leadership contest of 1880, the latter's first definitive show of strength. O'Shea was, on the face of it, 'an improbable partisan of Parnell'.[10] The Clare MP was already second-guessing himself when he wrote to his wife Katharine that night expressing the anxiety 'that Mr. Parnell might be too "advanced"'.[11] That, as it transpired, should have been the least of his concerns about his titular party leader. 'Titular', because as far as O'Shea was concerned, the whip was an instrument associated with equestrian sports, not Westminster politics.

*Since *Phineas Finn, the Irish Member* was first published in serial form between 1867 and 1869, we must look elsewhere for Trollope's prototype.

The captain's relationship with his wife was, to say the least, unorthodox. Katharine O'Shea, née Wood, was five years his junior and had come to regret their 1867 marriage by the early 1870s. The former Hussar was a sleek, handsome, plausible, generously moustached and amiable companion when the two first met. O'Shea was in his early twenties, Katharine Wood (one of thirteen children) in her late teens. Their marriage, however, quickly went sour. O'Shea's apparent commercial ineptitude saw him bankrupted by 1869. Thereafter he was an unreliable provider for his wife and three children, was notable for his frequent lengthy absences from the family home and was often unfaithful. The couple 'drifted respectably apart'.[12] Katharine ultimately relied on the financial support of her widowed aunt, Anna Maria Wood (or Mrs Benjamin Wood – 'Aunt Ben'). 'Aunt Ben' provided her niece with an income and a house adjacent to her own in the London suburb of Eltham. O'Shea, who had a flat in London at 1 Albert Mansions, near Battersea Park on the southern bank of the Thames, was an infrequent visitor to Eltham but was, in effect, as reliant on Mrs Wood's charity as was his wife.

Although the couple were, for all practical purposes, estranged, the captain, for public consumption at least, still relied on his wife's collaboration. He insisted on Katharine's presence at a series of salons in London hotels, most of which she was expected to organize. These hollow (for Katharine at least) social occasions were designed to advance her husband's business career, or his political aspirations, and to foster the illusion that he and Katharine were still a happily married couple. It was O'Shea's insistence that Katharine do his bidding in captivating and 'capturing' potential allies that would finally destroy the marriage. In 1880, dissatisfied with his access to the party leader whose elevation he had supported, O'Shea urged his wife to 'acquire' Charles Stewart Parnell – to ensnare him for one of her evenings at Thomas's Hotel on Berkeley Square.

Be careful what you wish for.

Within months of their first meeting – a churlish and notoriously anti-social Parnell had ignored all her letters of invitation until she turned up at Westminster in person and insisted that he see her – they became lovers, and Parnell was soon installed at Eltham. For almost ten years Parnell and Katharine O'Shea (she was never known to friends or family as 'Kitty', the appellation was intended to sting as it was a derogatory nickname also applied to Victorian sex workers) were common-law husband and wife and had three children together, albeit Katharine was still, for at least some part of that decade, at the beck and call of her estranged husband. For some months after the affair began, Katharine was, willy nilly, involved in a sexual relationship with both her husband and her lover.[13] She and Parnell made some effort to conceal their affair from O'Shea in the early months – she tried, for example, to convince her husband that her first child fathered by Parnell (Claude Sophie, who died within months) was his. In 1881, when O'Shea became aware that he had been cuckolded, he responded in the manner expected of any offended former Hussar and eighteenth-century throwback. He challenged Parnell to a duel. O'Shea may have been surprised, or taken aback, when the Irish Party leader accepted. O'Shea did not pursue the challenge, and the dawn shoot-out never took place. Perhaps he was conscious of an inauspicious precedent. The last duel fought between an Irish political leader and a more experienced opponent had not gone well for John d'Esterre, who had been shot dead by Daniel O'Connell in 1815.

In 1882 O'Shea muscled in on the secret negotiations that ended the Land War of 1879–82. Joseph Chamberlain, then president of the Board of Trade and leader of the radical element of the Liberal Party, was the intermediary on the government side. O'Shea managed to elbow out Parnell's trusted colleague Justin McCarthy – one of the few senior Irish nationalist politicians who was not languishing in jail in the spring of 1882 – as the primary nationalist go-between. O'Shea, far more anxious to please Chamberlain and Gladstone than his own party leader, may well have exercised undue influence, and exploited his knowledge of his wife's affair, in the compilation of the document that became known as the 'Kilmainham Treaty'. The correspondence around the settlement included a somewhat overenthusiastic codicil that promised to scatter roses and spray perfume on the previously rank relationship between Parnell's and Gladstone's parties.

A preening O'Shea – 'distrusted by his colleagues and weak in political acumen'[14] – secure in the knowledge that he possessed coercive leverage over the undisputed leader of Irish nationalism, became a fractious irritant to that leader's subalterns. He adopted political positions that aligned more with Liberal aspirations than with those of Irish nationalism. Barely tolerated by his party colleagues – he declined to take the 1884 'pledge' to vote in accordance with the will of the party leadership – he was roundly rejected as a candidate for the 1885 general election by the Irish National League members in County Clare. Instead, with the reluctant connivance of a hamstrung Parnell, he ran as a Liberal in a Liverpool constituency and lost. He blamed this failure on what he perceived to be Parnell's lack of enthusiasm for his candidacy. Querulous victimhood was one of O'Shea's outstanding qualities.

What followed was one of the less edifying passages in Parnell's relatively short political career. At O'Shea's insistence he was put forward, with Parnell's support, for the Galway constituency in a February 1886 by-election. Joseph Biggar and Tim Healy were so horrified at this blatant imposition of an entirely inappropriate candidate that they rushed to Galway to oppose O'Shea's nomination. Both men came perilously close to making the Parnell/Katharine O'Shea relationship public in their efforts to scotch O'Shea's candidature. Parnell's intervention, however, persuaded the two MPs to back down. With Parnell's support, O'Shea won the seat. However, he then steered his own political career onto the rocks when he abstained – unwilling to oppose the empire loyalist Chamberlain – in the June 1886 vote on Gladstone's first Home Rule Bill. Shortly thereafter he resigned his seat. He became, in Tim Healy's memorable phrase, 'this political castaway, whom all parties alike despise'.[15]

At this point, with his political aspirations in shreds – he always cherished the hope that a grateful Liberal administration would appoint him to the Irish chief secretaryship – O'Shea might well have turned on Parnell and exposed his relationship with Katharine. He chose not to do so. At least for the moment.

Why did he keep his own counsel?

The answer is relatively simple: it was not in his financial interests to tap his bottomless well of political spite. Although relatively healthy, Aunt Ben was in her nineties. Such was her level of intimacy with her aunt that Katharine was confidently expected to inherit most, if not all, of Anna Wood's considerable fortune. O'Shea, still legally married to Katharine, while not expecting to be a beneficiary, certainly anticipated some financial advantage from Mrs Wood's bequest. Exposing his spouse as the common-law wife of Parnell would jeopardize her legacy and his prospects. Aunt Ben was a true 'Victorian'. A hint of scandal and she would have cut her niece out of her will, leaving the profligate and heavily indebted William O'Shea bereft.

When the facsimile letter appeared in *The Times* on 18 April 1887, O'Shea had even less reason to expose Parnell to public scandal. *The Times* would act as a convenient proxy. He could

William O'Shea

now cheerily await the death of the ninety-six-year-old Aunt Ben while watching Parnell's career disintegrate. When his ally, Chamberlain, baited the trap for Parnell, O'Shea's cup ran over. When Chamberlain advised *The Times* to put the captain in the witness box and was asked to sound out O'Shea on the newspaper's behalf,[16] O'Shea was only too happy to give Chamberlain and *The Times* all the help he could possibly render. In return he was allowed to see the originals of the disputed letters.

By the time the attorney general had concluded his opening five-day diatribe against Irish 'outrage' in late October 1888, the captain was ready for the limelight.

The captain is challenged

Adversity is often the handmaiden of opportunity, and the appearance of O'Shea before the Commission, despite the hammer blow he had administered when identifying Parnell's signature, gave the nationalists many openings to send threatening signals to *The Times* and the government. Russell took full advantage of the opposition's unprotected goal to introduce some unfamiliar names into the record of the Commission. He offered no explanation for these apparent *non sequiturs*, and the names meant little or nothing to most observers. The references, however, were not intended for the presiding justices, the British press or the casual attenders. They were introduced as a warning to *The Times*, and to agencies such as Scotland Yard, the Foreign Office and the Home Office, that the Parnellites' investigative capability was not inconsiderable and had uncovered evidence of the work of *agents provocateurs* in the employment of Her Majesty's Government. The Parnellite intelligence operation was attributable, almost entirely, to the single-handed efforts of Michael Davitt. His research – recorded in the small black copybook that he entitled 'Notes by an Amateur Detective' – was highly instructive. The information he gleaned ensured that the leading Parnellite counsel were well-briefed on British 'black ops'. Davitt had also worked his way into the confidence of the former Dublin Castle spymaster Edward Jenkinson, now a neophyte Irish nationalist, who was an invaluable informant for the Parnellites. It was Davitt who, along with Tim Healy, insisted on 31 October 1888 that O'Shea's feet should be held to the fire immediately after his examination by Webster. Russell and Parnell both wanted to postpone the cross-examination. Davitt and Healy prevailed.[17]

Russell quickly established that the captain had been recruited as a *Times* witness by Chamberlain. O'Shea was happy to testify, he claimed, so that he could 'have an opportunity of refuting the slanders circulated about me by Mr. Parnell and his friends in regard to these letters'.[18] Parnell had not been behind the door in expressing his suspicion that O'Shea was the author/forger of the 'facsimile' letter and was immersed in the conspiracy surrounding the acquisition of the rest of the cache in the possession of *The Times*. 'Mr. Parnell and his friends had stated,' according to O'Shea, 'that I was engaged in a conspiracy to get these letters, and that it was through me that they were got.'[19] Despite O'Shea's aggrieved response to these persistent rumours, Parnell had not plucked the allegation out of thin air. There was evidence that O'Shea had some expertise in this murky field, having allegedly forged a letter from his estranged wife to Gladstone in March 1886 seeking a meeting between the prime minister and Parnell. The Home Rule legislation was in preparation and O'Shea had apparently done so – probably to ingratiate himself with a seething Chamberlain – 'in order to compromise Gladstone by an ill-judged furtive meeting with Parnell which would find its way into the papers just as the home rule bill was announced'.[20]

Russell later introduced the name of Richard Pigott, to no apparent purpose. It would have been unfamiliar to most of the observers and was dropped after a few beats. Even that dedicated follower of the Special Commission, John MacDonald of the *London Daily News*, ascribed so little significance to the interchange that he ignored it completely in his daily report.

Those 'in the know' however – an ever-widening circle – would have been aware that Russell was priming an explosive charge. Regular audience members would become much more conversant with the name a few months later. O'Shea admitted knowing who Pigott was but claimed not to be personally acquainted with the man. He was aware that Pigott's name was 'mentioned in connexion with those letters,' and 'it was said that I had entered into some combination or conspiracy to get those letters with Pigott'.[21] A co-conspirator in this alleged enterprise – the name was volunteered by O'Shea – was the former Louth MP Philip Callan, a diehard Parnell antagonist.

Another name that Russell dropped into the cross-examination was that of the Paris-based 'advanced' nationalist (and British agent) Patrick Casey. Once again, little context was offered for the apparent *non sequitur*, but the question would have ruffled the captain's plumage. He was able to insist that he was not personally acquainted with Casey but was forced to concede that Casey might have been approached on his behalf. Russell, having touched only lightly on Casey, passed on. But a *frisson* of alarm must have passed through O'Shea's ample frame and disturbed the peace of mind of any informed observer from the British secret service. This, of course, was precisely Russell's intention. Like the blithe reference to Pigott, it was a shot across the bows of the establishment side and an indication that the Parnellites had access to privileged information of their own. Because Casey was a 'notorious dynamitard', Russell would have been unlikely to have invoked his name had Davitt not made him aware that the Paris-based radical was a fraud and a *provocateur*. O'Shea may well have been telling the truth when he claimed never to have met Patrick Casey, but it was not as though he was unfamiliar with the double-agent. He had communicated with Casey, but he had used a trusted intermediary to do so. The go-between was also unfamiliar to the tribunal. He was a London-based Fenian, George Mulqueeny.

Mulqueeny's was an unfamiliar name that was not touched upon by Russell. It was, inadvisably, introduced by O'Shea himself in an unsubtle attempt to blacken Parnell's reputation. O'Shea dredged up the allegation that Parnell had paid for the escape from London of the 'Invincible' Frank Byrne, who was believed to have supplied the weapons that killed Cavendish and Burke in May 1882. Mulqueeny, according to O'Shea's testimony, had informed him that a letter existed from Byrne acknowledging 'the receipt of money from Parnell'.[22]

O'Shea was probably not expecting any follow-up questions on Mulqueeny from a supposedly unprepared Russell. In fact, Parnell's counsel devoted the next fifteen minutes of his cross-examination to an extended discussion of O'Shea's relationship with the London Irishman. The information gleaned by Davitt in Paris and London, and from Jenkinson, meant that the Parnellite legal team was aware of the importance of Mulqueeny to O'Shea, and of Mulqueeny's own back story. He was, in effect, the former MP's bagman, a willing cut-off employed by O'Shea to enable him to deal with the unsavoury characters with whom he was now associating. It was Mulqueeny who had been sent to Paris to meet Patrick Casey on behalf of the captain. O'Shea admitted compensating Mulqueeny for his trouble.

Out of the blue Russell then demanded of the captain, 'Is Mulqueeny a member of any secret society?'* O'Shea, thrown by the question, conceded that his bagman was 'an advanced nationalist'.[23] He was certainly posing as such, but, according to Michael Davitt's information, Mulqueeny was 'in police service [for] ten years'.[24] He had been one of Jenkinson's London-based informers and operatives. However, given that there was little loyalty in the murky world of London-Irish espionage, Mulqueeny also worked for Jenkinson's arch-rival, Robert Anderson,[25] who clearly placed considerable value on his services. On one occasion, Mulqueeny stole two letters of Byrne's that he sought to deliver

*In his own testimony to the Special Commission on 13 March 1889, Mulqueeny candidly admitted to having been sworn in to the IRB in London in 1881. (*Special Commission*, Book 6, 13 March 1889, 382.)

to Anderson while the latter was preaching at a Notting Hill Presbyterian church. Made aware of the presence of his agent, the normally pietistic Anderson 'brought the service to an abrupt termination' so that he could commune with Mulqueeny.[26]

In the course of his inquiries about the bagman, Russell suddenly pivoted and demanded of O'Shea if he was familiar with 'the house of a Mrs. Lynch in Wardour Street?' The fact that O'Shea conceded, without argument, that 'it is very likely that I have been there once' was suggestive of a witness who assumed that his inquisitor had solid evidence of that fact. Mrs Lynch's 'house', it transpired, was a public house, The Golden Lion, which was owned by her father, Mayoman Peter Cowell. Russell, doubtless at Davitt's instigation, was now sending the clearest possible message to the government side. The Golden Lion in Soho was home to many a plot and frequented by a 'Who's Who' of anti-Parnellite covert operatives. O'Shea claimed, implausibly, to having patronized The Golden Lion 'because a number of advanced nationalists [he refused to call them Fenians] had signed a declaration protesting against my exclusion from Irish politics'.[27] In fact, as we shall see (Chapter 11), O'Shea was almost certainly at least an occasional visitor to The Golden Lion, where he was at one with the parties (including Captain Darnley Stewart Stephens and Richard Pigott) conspiring to ravage the Irish nationalist cause and to bring down Parnell. As Russell poked and prodded, delving ever deeper into some of the witness's many dubious associates and activities, O'Shea was seen to become more nervous, frequently wiping his face and almost turning his back on his inquisitor.[28]

During the lengthy exchange on Mulqueeny, O'Shea revealed that his associate, in the course of his philanthropic efforts on behalf of the captain, had been threatened by two Irish-Americans. These he named as 'Hayes' and 'General Carroll-Thalis'. But the commission stenographer misheard O'Shea, because the Irish-American military veteran was, of course, General Charles Carroll Tevis. Mulqueeny's efforts on behalf of O'Shea (the witness stuck to the narrative of the pursuit of signatures for the supportive petition) were introducing him to some thoroughly seedy characters. Both men were associated with extremist Irish-American nationalism. Both, however, were also double-agents working for the British authorities. The 'Hayes' in question was John P. Hayes, the Philadelphia Irish-American who was one of Edward Jenkinson's agents. Tevis, as we have seen, had been a Foreign Office spy within the Fenian Brotherhood for more than twenty years.[29] Although the names of Hayes and Tevis were volunteered by O'Shea, it is possible that Russell might have introduced them both himself had O'Shea failed to do so. It is clear from his questioning that he was aware of the fraught meeting between Mulqueeny and his alleged antagonists. Russell's information was sufficiently detailed that he even suggested to the captain that the explosive meeting had taken place at the Bedford Hotel in Covent Garden.

O'Shea's evidence prompts several questions that can be addressed, at this remove, only with speculative answers. While it was true that he did achieve some sort of *entente cordiale* with Clare Fenians on the basis that 'the enemy of my enemy is my friend', we can take with a grain of salt his assertion that this arose from their conviction that he was hard done by when he was de-selected in his Clare constituency. So what was he up to? Why would a renegade nationalist politician – *persona non grata* after abstaining on the Home Rule Bill vote – ally himself with the IRB? The only thing O'Shea had in common with the 'men who considered that they could fight their country's battle on the hillside against British forces'[30] (his characterization) was a mutual antipathy to Parnell, an antagonism that, on the Fenian side, was often more apparent than real. Mulqueeny, a probable agent of Scotland Yard – and, in 1889, employed by *The Times* on a retainer of £7 a week[31] – was working diligently for O'Shea, but it beggars belief that his efforts were solely connected to the gathering of Fenian signatures on a worthless petition.

The other conundrum is, why were so many of his avowed

Fenian/'advanced nationalist' connections double-agents? Coincidence? Misfortune? Something more sinister? Patrick Casey, John P. Hayes, Charles Carroll Tevis and George Mulqueeny all figured in O'Shea's narrative. He claimed only to have a personal relationship with Mulqueeny, but his bagman had been despatched on the captain's behalf to meet the other three. All four men had some connection with Fenian, United Irishmen or Clan activities, but each was also a secret service informant. O'Shea's direct or vicarious involvement with some of the most notorious British double-agents of the 1880s adds some credibility at least to an unprovable contemporary (and abiding) assumption on the part of Irish nationalists. This held that O'Shea was a British government agent. Whether or not he was ever a paid informer – highly improbable given that he did not have access to the inner circles of Irish constitutional or militant nationalism after 1886 – he was certainly an enthusiastic collaborator with the Tory establishment.

In November 1890 he would prove himself to be a tremendously 'useful idiot' indeed.

Russell – courtesy of Davitt's investigations – was not alone in using the cover of his cross-examination of O'Shea to issue veiled warnings to interested listeners. O'Shea himself made a couple of opaque references to his marital situation and to Parnell's compromised position. In the course of a short series of questions about the June 1886 Home Rule Bill, O'Shea gratuitously referred to the fact that 'certain things came to my knowledge at that time which absolutely destroyed the good opinion I had hitherto held of Mr. Parnell'.[32] O'Shea, in the wake of his resignation as an MP, weary of waiting for 'Aunt Ben' to do the honourable thing and die, had, at that time, considered 'discovering' his wife's infidelity and suing for divorce (or possibly blackmailing the couple). He had, however, stepped back from the abyss. Sensing danger if he were to ask for elaboration from the witness, Russell pivoted away from the revelation with the dexterity of a circus performer. But

O'Shea was bluffing. He was not yet ready to risk exposing the Parnell/Katharine O'Shea relationship and torpedo any prospect of a share in Anna Maria Wood's legacy. He was still banking on *The Times* dragging Parnell's reputation through the mud without him having to lift a finger. Accordingly, as the *New York Times* put it, when it came to the cause of the rupture between the two men, 'both sides chose to leave this unrevealed'.[33]

O'Shea, however, almost stumbled into the abyss himself. He had sailed close to the wind in his direct evidence, informing Webster that, after his release from Kilmainham in May 1882, the Irish leader had called on him at his London apartment (in effect his permanent residence) at 1 Albert Mansions. When asked by an uninformed, or merely careless, Webster why he was not at his 'home' at Eltham, where his wife and children resided, O'Shea responded smartly, 'I had had an attack of gout from which I was recovering. Mr. Parnell first went to Eltham. I was unable to go there, and he came up to me.'[34] Parnell had, of course, when arriving in London from Dublin, gone straight to Eltham because it was already his English domicile. O'Shea, who, chillingly, had exercised his conjugal rights with his estranged wife while Parnell was incarcerated in Kilmainham, was as welcome in Eltham in the summer of 1882 as a visitation from cholera. One observer, Parnell's biographer Alfred Robbins, noted that, 'all through this, O'Shea was manifestly trying to repress his excitement, but his hands trembled a great deal, while Parnell looked eagerly yet gravely towards him the whole time'.[35]

Russell was also unable to shake O'Shea's crucial identification of Parnell's signature on the *Times*'s cache of letters. He circled around the captain's earlier testimony, prodding for weaknesses, uncertainty or contradictions, but O'Shea was not for turning. He had been in receipt of many letters signed by Parnell and attested once again that 'the handwriting of these letters is the handwriting of Mr. Parnell, I cannot say more than that'.[36] Russell, with no desire for him to do so, dropped the matter.

The captain left the stand well satisfied with his work. He

bragged in a typically sycophantic letter to Chamberlain the following day that he had bested Russell, 'I had him down round after round. People here seem to think that my manner of putting the case will not be disadvantageous to you.'[37] His mentor concurred, responding that, 'I have had an account from a thoroughly trustworthy source & am assured that both the manner and the matter were excellent.'[38] For its part, *United Ireland* revelled in its own invective while acknowledging Chamberlain's watching brief. The editor, William O'Brien, described O'Shea as a mouthpiece, 'who changes his masters like a cur dog … he is ready to pimp and spy to ruin the patron of yesterday'. The journal then lowered the boom on O'Shea's sponsor. 'More degraded still, if that may be so, is the character of the treacherous coward who, willing to wound and yet afraid to strike, employed so base a tool for so base an object. Now, at least, Mr. Chamberlain has fairly earned his title of "Judas".'[39] As the violent tone of *United Ireland*'s editorial polemic suggests, O'Shea's evidence had done some damage to his former allies. However, although he helped *The Times* in his identification of Parnell's signature, he also compromised his value to the prosecution cause by informing Russell that 'I believed Mr. Parnell to be absolutely free from any connivance at outrage.'[40] *Punch*, in skewering the captain's pretensions, pilloried the cloak and dagger nature of much of his evidence. 'Mulqueeny took me there in a four-wheeled cab, blindfolded,' the satirical magazine mocked, 'someone hit me on small of back with flat side of sword. Then I signed my name in red ink (they said it was blood). They all swore at Parnell; said I ought to be Chief Secretary.'[41]

The neutral *New York Times*, notwithstanding O'Shea's positive self-evaluation, probably offered the most succinct assessment of the day's exchanges. On its front page it noted that the captain's appearance 'created a good deal of a flutter in the court at the outset'. His testimony, however, had not inflicted much damage on the Parnellites. 'When he was set off prematurely the effect was simply a big and only moderately interesting fizzle. The net result of his evidence and cross-examination was to weaken the *Times*'s case.' The American 'newspaper of record' went on to observe coyly that O'Shea's testimony 'skirted the pitfall of some allusion to the real reason why Captain O'Shea and Mr. Parnell quarrelled without ever actually touching it'.[42]

Had O'Shea commanded anything like the stature of a Brutus, Parnell might well have muttered Caesar's 'Et tu, Brute' under his breath as the preening Hussar left the stand. But O'Shea was no Marcus Junius Brutus, apart from his wielding of a metaphorical knife. He was merely a disappointed place-seeker, complaisant cuckold and political performing flea who had extracted at least some measure of revenge from his potent adversary. 'Now, and for the rest of their lives,' wrote one of Parnell's many biographers, 'there could be no pretenses [*sic*] between them, but now and forever they were enemies waiting for the moment when the deathblow could be delivered.'[43]

But what deathblow? Surely O'Shea was now a spent force. His value to the establishment was exhausted; he would quickly become a relic. Nothing further would be heard from the captain, apart from the occasional pompous letter to *The Times* 'setting the record straight' on some long-forgotten, yawn-inducing wrangle.

However, Parnell was not finished with this Anglo-Irish Pulcinella. Their contest would resume a year later, not far from Probate Court No. 1.

8

THE STRANGE PILGRIMAGE OF RICHARD PIGOTT

"I suppose what he really was,' said the Baron, 'was a boulevardier who liked to swagger along with a flower in his buttonhole … they caught up with him in the end and destroyed him, as the things we hate mostly do … an elite spirit who felt he should be free in some way from the degrading conditions under which most lives are lived."[1]

Anthony Cronin, *The Identity Papers* (1979)

'Had Pigott the faintest notion of the crucial ordeal before him, all the money in the coffers of the *Times* – unscrupulous as he was – would not have induced him to go back into the box. He had no conception of what was before him, much less had he any suspicion of the crushing evidence in Sir Charles Russell's hands.'[2]

James O'Connor, *Irishman* editor, on Pigott's appearance before the Commission (1889)

Hôtel des Deux Mondes, Avenue de L'Opéra, Paris, July 1886

There was a certain poetry about the location.

However, it was more the poetry of Edward Lear than of John Milton. The fateful meeting took place in the Hôtel des Deux Mondes (Two Worlds) on the fashionable Avenue de l'Opéra in Paris. It was an unpretentious inn a few hundred metres from the Jardin des Tuileries and the Louvre. And indeed two worlds did collide on that hot Parisian day. One was the cynical demimonde of trickery, chicanery, deceit and misdirection. The other was the *monde naïf* of doomed unionist intrigue and wishful thinking. What occurred was more low farce than grand opera.

Upstairs, in a rather basic hotel room, Edward Caulfield Houston and Professor Thomas Maguire waited anxiously. Their hope was that a productive melodrama was being played out in the lobby a few flights below, an exchange that would have a profound impact on the future of Ireland as an integral part of the United Kingdom. Houston, the self-made son of a prison warder, was a young Dublin journalist whose talents had come to the attention of the Irish correspondent of *The Times*, Dr George Valentine Patton. Houston had been entrusted by Patton with much of the coverage of the dramatic Phoenix Park murder trials. But it was his ideological inclinations that had brought him to Paris. He was a committed unionist, appalled at the apparently inexorable drift towards Irish Home Rule. He had agreed to assume the role of secretary to a newly formed anti-national organization with whose policies he sympathized, the Irish Loyal and Patriotic Union (ILPU).

Houston was greatly indebted to his companion in that upstairs room, the Trinity College Dublin classicist and ILPU luminary, Dr Thomas Maguire.* He was, literally, indebted. Maguire's privileged vantage-point at what both men were hopeful would be an epochal moment had come at a steep price. He had lent Houston £850 (just under £100,000 today) for his ringside seat. Some of that money would soon change hands.

The reason for their tense vigil was an exchange of documents and cash that was about to take place in the lobby of the hotel. Houston's agent, the Dublin journalist Richard Pigott, had surpassed himself. He had identified a cache of highly incriminating documents that included letters despatched by Charles Stewart

*Maguire's demise on 26 February 1889 was one of a number of oddly convenient deaths that pepper this narrative. It meant that he was not required to testify to the Special Commission as to how a humble academic could afford to expend £850 of his own funds on Houston's Parisian adventure.

Parnell and Patrick Egan. These, Houston was morally certain, would torch the political reputation of the commander in chief of Irish nationalism. These documents would finally expose the Parnellites as little more than a front organization for terrorism and agrarian outrage. As Houston and Maguire twiddled their thumbs upstairs, the resourceful Pigott was negotiating the purchase of these explosive letters downstairs. Negotiations were taking place with a mysterious intermediary named 'Murphy'.

Houston's anxious wait ended when a corpulent and breathless Pigott returned with a bag containing a sheaf of letters. Maguire and the ILPU secretary seized upon them and began to examine them closely. Once satisfied that they were genuine, Pigott was given a cheque for £500, drawn on the Thomas Cook Paris office, to be handed over to the enigmatic Mr Murphy. Pigott was also paid 100 guineas for his sterling efforts in sourcing the treasure trove of incriminating documents. One letter in particular excited Houston and Maguire above all.

Nine months later, on 18 April 1887, it appeared in *The Times* as the *pièce de resistance* of its faltering 'Parnellism and Crime' series.

Richard Pigott being cross examined by Sir Charles Russell

From *Hard Times* to *Bleak House*: the Dickensian life of Richard Pigott

In the nineteenth-century world of teeming slums and 'rookeries', soaring infant mortality, child labour, sweeping pandemics, quotidian disease and oppressive poverty, the margin between modest economic success and utter destitution was wafer thin. Wilkins Micawber famously summarized the dilemma in Charles Dickens's *David Copperfield*:

> Annual income twenty pounds, annual expenditure nineteen pounds nineteen and six, result, happiness. Annual income twenty pounds, annual expenditure twenty pounds nought and six, result, misery.

For those who, unlike Micawber, were ill-equipped to live a life of hopeful expectation, there beckoned the debtors' prison or the workhouse, the latter being the last refuge of the desperate. It was more of a fishing net than a safety net. Once you stepped inside, it was almost impossible to escape. Many workhouses – 'pauper bastilles' – were cruciform in design. It was an appropriate shape, emblematic of the metaphorical crucifixion of the indigent occupants. Debtors' prisons – which began to disappear as dedicated institutions after the 1869 Debtors Act – were merely locked workhouses. There, in a final cruel twist, the insolvents were obliged to pay for their own upkeep while incarcerated.

For a late Victorian 'provider' to fail in business to the point of bankruptcy and penury was not simply to invite social humiliation. Public disgrace could quickly be followed by wretched poverty. The archetypal fictional failed banker, Mr Merdle of *Little Dorrit*, knew this when he took his own life. John Sadleir, the Irish MP and financier, upon whom Dickens apparently based the character of Merdle, chose the same non-fictional escape route when his Tipperary Bank collapsed under the weight of its debts – and his own criminal misappropriation – in 1856. His punishment was an unmarked grave in Highgate Cemetery, London.

Richard Pigott was aware of the precedents, of the margins and of the social consequences of pecuniary failure. He had spent several years close to the edge, juggling, embezzling, ducking and diving. He had robbed, importuned, misappropriated and cheated. He had learned to forestall and defraud Peter in order to satisfy the pressing demands of Paul. He was an excellent parent, a loving husband, a thoughtful and generous brother to his two sisters, someone who took his duties as a provider very seriously. He was also an ebullient, companionable individual who was popular among his Kingstown/Sandycove circle of prosperous, unionist friends, despite his well-advertised extreme nationalist connections. He was known as a man of principle and of considerable moral courage. At one point in his life an expression of his political beliefs earned him a spell in prison.

But Pigott was also a pornographer, an embezzler, a forger, a fraudster, a wheedling mendicant,[3] a hedonist who was unable to pay the bills for the high life he enjoyed to excess, a perjurer, a turncoat and, ultimately, a pathetic and tragic suicide. Shakespeare would have revelled in a narrative of the life of Richard Pigott. His flaws were legion and legendary.

Irish argot teems with derogatory words and pejorative phrases that could be deployed to describe what Richard Pigott became. As a late-blooming collaborator with the unionist establishment in Ireland he offered his services to William E. Forster and Robert Anderson – he was generally even more reviled than long-standing servants of the Crown. He was a *shoneen** and a sycophant, but he was also a turncoat, perceived as having abandoned previously stated principles for thirty pieces of Treasury silver. Pigott's difficulty was that the Crown was not especially interested in his services, and a reward merely on a par with that of Judas Iscariot was wholly inadequate to his needs.

*From the Gaelic *seonín*, or 'little John', as in, John Bull, aka a 'West Brit'.

The enterprise upon which he embarked in the summer of 1886 was the logical conclusion of a decade spent living beyond his means. It was a desperate endeavour, requiring an extraordinary level of dexterity and adroitness. To date he had shown little evidence of either.

But he almost pulled it off.

Richard Pigott was born in 1828 in Ratoath, Co. Meath. He came from a relatively comfortable middle-class family. His father, George Pigott, worked on a number of newspapers, including the influential Young Ireland project of the 1840s, *The Nation*.

In the early 1850s we find Pigott in Belfast working on *The Ulsterman* newspaper. By 1859 *The Ulsterman* had metamorphosed into *The Irishman* and had relocated to Dublin. Included in its rather florid prospectus was the ambition to 'make it true in every respect to the national traditions, affections and aspirations of the Irish people'.[4] The journal quickly became a mouthpiece for the newly founded Irish Republican Brotherhood, and set itself up in opposition to, and in competition with, the more moderate nationalist *Nation* newspaper, owned by Alexander Martin Sullivan. Pigott would encounter, and create, many enemies, but Sullivan was one of the earliest and most enduring. In 1862, O'Donovan Rossa wrote a scurrilous letter to *The Irishman* – which it gleefully printed – accusing Sullivan of being an informer. The editor of *The Nation* sued for libel. As Pigott jubilantly pointed out in his autobiographical and thoroughly unreliable *Personal Recollections of an Irish National Journalist*, Sullivan duly won his case and was duly awarded damages … of sixpence.

In 1865, through a series of happy accidents – happy at least from Pigott's point of view – he managed to acquire *The Irishman* for himself. The former Young Irelander P. J. Smyth had purchased the title and had steered the journal into calmer, more moderate nationalist waters. This resulted in the forsaken Fenians establishing *The Irish People*. Smyth, smelling the potential for his newspaper to turn into a money pit, walked away from the project, and handed *The Irishman* over to Pigott, for a meagre £650. Pigott's long-time associate and deputy editor James O'Connor (himself a loyal Fenian and treasurer of the Irish Republican Brotherhood) expressed doubts that Smyth ever saw a penny of the purchase money.[5]

Pigott was richly rewarded for his 'purchase' of *The Irishman* when the authorities closed down *The Irish People* in 1865, and began rounding up Fenians. Pigott and *The Irishman* were left in sole possession of the journalistic green field, at a time of distress for extreme republicanism and increased interest in the activities of the IRB. Both were good for sales. The newspaper's circulation increased to a healthy 10,000 copies weekly, according to Dublin Castle's assessment.[6]

Pigott achieved his personal apotheosis, among the members of his chosen constituency at least, when he published an article entitled 'The Holocaust' in *The Irishman* on 23 November 1867. This was a denunciation of the executions of Allen, Larkin and O'Brien, the 'Manchester Martyrs'. That week's edition of *The Irishman* was already being distributed when news of the hangings reached Dublin. A second edition was rushed into print, bearing black borders, and including a thousand-word article, apparently written by the scholar and medical man Dr George Sigerson, which denounced the verdict and the executions.[7] Pigott was charged with seditious libel on 10 January 1868 and brought before a Dublin jury on 10 February. One of the five witnesses presented by the attorney general on behalf of the Crown was John Joseph Corridan (aka Corydon), an American Civil War veteran and Fenian informer.[8]

Pigott's enthusiasm for the cause of the Manchester Fenians cost him six months in jail. He was not alone in the dock, however. His once and future antagonist, and undying business rival, A. M. Sullivan, suffered a similar fate. This was on account of a seditious article published in his newspaper the *Weekly News*. Their shared fate did not serve, however, to draw the two men closer together. When Pigott was released, he was feted at a Dublin banquet in his honour.[9] His journalistic career was at its zenith. He established two new titles, *The Flag of Ireland* and *The Shamrock*, the latter a literary publication. However, according to his *Dictionary of Irish Biography* entry, written by Professor Margaret O'Callaghan, 'it appears that even at this time he had back-channels to Dublin Castle'.[10]

And that, for Richard Pigott, was as good as it got.

When, in the 1870s, the fascination with extreme nationalist politics flagged, so did the revenues from his three weekly newspapers. He was forced to make deals with creditors, and to begin his career as a frantic financial juggler. The plates had to be kept spinning at all costs. Any loss of momentum could prove calamitous.

Cleaving to extreme Fenian orthodoxy, Pigott, an acerbic opponent of the 'New Departure', was critical of the rise of agrarianism and the capacity of the Land League to distract from the separatist aims of the IRB. 'He virtuously assailed the unprincipled promoters of such an anti-national scheme,'[11] according to Davitt. But by 1880 it was clear that Pigott had backed the wrong political horse; had arrogantly defied the agrarian zeitgeist – as exemplified by the new politics of the Land League; and had maintained an incongruously profligate and hedonistic lifestyle, typified by his enthusiastic membership of the predominantly unionist Kingstown (Dún Laoghaire) Yacht Club. It was a lifestyle that the dwindling circulation of his newspapers was no longer capable of supporting.

James O'Connor, Pigott's deputy editor, in his pamphlet *Recollections of Richard Pigott*, published shortly after Pigott's death in 1889, recorded that Pigott's income, at its height, could not have been less than £2,000 a year, but that his unsustainable taste for the high life was his undoing. 'When his profits were reduced to a few hundred a year, he lived at the same high speed as when they were a couple of thousand.'[12]

As his star faded, Pigott cut an increasingly pathetic figure, reduced to wheedling and conniving, neither very successfully. One of Pigott's survival techniques can be adduced from a letter sent to the eccentric character The O'Gorman Mahon, an inveterate duellist with a chequered past, who was standing – along with the even more dubious Captain William O'Shea – for the Clare constituency in the 1880 general election. Pigott, at the time threatened with the loss of his newspapers, wrote, requesting Mahon to place an advertisement – in the form of an address to his putative constituents – in *The Irishman* and *The Flag of Ireland*. 'I may add,' he wrote, 'that in both papers will appear from week to week up to the time of the election a perfectly impartial review of the claims of the various candidates to the representation of the constituencies which they seek.'[13] The concluding sentence is vintage Pigott. After the initial cajoling comes the implied threat, rolled up in the thinly veiled promise of positive editorial commentary, for those willing to spend some of their election finances in the advertising columns of Pigott's stable of 'influential' newspapers.

Other alleged coping mechanisms strayed well beyond a desperate canvassing for business, and into outright illegality. In those days, many charitable donations for extreme nationalist causes – including the provision of support for the families of imprisoned activists – were channelled through newspapers, principally those in Pigott's stable of publications. There were frequent allegations that a sizeable proportion of such donated funds ended up in Pigott's pocket.[14]

He also, allegedly, stole money raised by the IRB itself. This was apparently being kept in the offices of *The Irishman* by his employee James O'Connor. The Fenians, Pigott might have reasoned, were hardly in a position to report the theft to the Dublin Metropolitan Police. Neither, for some reason, do they appear to have taken any punitive action against Pigott. They were rarely as restrained in the case of suspected informers, clearly perceived as a crime of much higher magnitude than embezzlement. The disappearance of the funds resulted in James O'Connor being replaced as IRB treasurer by Patrick Egan.

Pigott also sought to be added to the Dublin Castle payroll as an informant. However, he thought better of the offer when the IRB got wind of his potential treachery.[15] Theft they might be prepared to overlook, but the sale of information to the Castle was not to be tolerated. So problematic did Pigott become that the Fenians sought to buy him out of the newspaper business on a couple of occasions in the 1870s, but they lacked the resources.[16] It was more than a little ironic that his appropriation of IRB funds must have contributed in some measure to this shortfall in their assets.

In addition to Pigott's covert criminality, he had, as a lucrative side venture, the selling of pornographic paraphernalia – books, photographs and stereoscopic lenses.[17] All these activities were required to support his Yacht Club-champagne lifestyle, his love of fine food and wine, two sons boarding at the exclusive Roman-Catholic school Clongowes Wood College, and two demanding sisters – one an invalid – in the manner to which they were accustomed.

And then there was his recusancy. As the clamour from his creditors became deafening and, in the wake of the sale of his newspapers (on which more later), the self-styled 'advanced' nationalist began to take up positions that were diametrically opposed to his erstwhile convictions. This repositioning, or reinvention, was captured in a series of crude and unattributed philippics, and an extended series of begging letters addressed to the chief secretary himself, the Liberal MP William E. Forster. Forster emerges from the correspondence as an oddly sympathetic, if somewhat naïve, individual. Pigott, for his part, is confirmed as an impecunious, cynical, double-dealing defector, of negligible political virtue. During the correspondence he resorted to his usual repertoire: offering inducements, begging for assistance and threatening blackmail.

It is hard to know if a 1904 biography of Pigott, *The Crime of the Century*, is truth or fiction. It was written by the prolific crime novel writer 'Dick Donovan', which suggests the latter, though the level of original research – which claims to include personal interviews with some of the main players – points to the former. 'Dick Donovan' was a pseudonym used by the popular late Victorian writer of detective and horror fiction, James Edward Muddock, who may have the enviable distinction, for a writer of crime fiction, of popularizing the use of the word 'dick' in the USA, as applied to the profession of private detective.

What we learn from Donovan is that Pigott, during his brief time in Belfast while working for *The Ulsterman*, began a professional and sexual relationship with a woman named only as 'Lydia'. She is described by Donovan as a petite and 'attractive' woman 'with a plump figure, a quantity of fair hair, blue eyes, regular features, even teeth and a small mouth'.[18] 'Lydia', who would enter and exit Pigott's life with mysterious regularity, was from Cork farming stock. She had, according to Donovan, abandoned her family clandestinely because 'there is every reason to believe … she had murdered her illegitimate infant by strangling it'.[19]

In Donovan's version of events 'Lydia' describes an intriguing character arc, from Belfast coquette to police informer, working alongside a thinly disguised Superintendent John Mallon (dubbed 'Molloy' in the text). Donovan alleged that information from 'Lydia' led to a raid on a Fenian 'safe house', where the Dublin Metropolitan Police narrowly missed capturing the fugitive IRB leader James Stephens. 'Lydia' was saved from being murdered by two IRB assassins only by the intervention of Pigott himself, who at the time was in good odour with the Brotherhood. For her own safety she fled to London, where she made herself useful to the authorities in that city as well.

Donovan (as does James O'Connor) depicts Pigott as a hedonist without the means to support his decadence. His initiation into the world of forgery involved the counterfeiting of signatures on bills of exchange. Most of the money thus illegally acquired was used to enhance his reputation among his peers in the Kingstown Yacht Club.[20]

Donovan also claimed that Pigott was instrumental in an attempt to murder one of his own employees, a young man he calls 'Denis Fagan'. 'Fagan' was, in fact, David Murphy, a leader of the Limerick Fenians in 1867 and a bookkeeper in the offices of *The Irishman*. Murphy had threatened to expose Pigott's thefts from the various charitable funds subscribed through his newspaper. Pigott plotted to kill Murphy, fortunately without fatal results.[21]

Pigott appears to have grown careless in his misappropriation of IRB funds and, according to Donovan, 'the Fenians became clamorous, and demanded a balance-sheet, and for the first time in his career the adventurer found himself in a real difficulty'.[22] Pigott's solution – as stark in its simplicity as in its duplicity – was to identify 'Fagan'/Murphy ('who was a young man, highly respectable, and well connected') as the embezzler. In 1886 Pigott would make a large sum of money by cannily identifying the gullibility of several prominent citizens. In the much lowlier Murphy, however, he met his match. He fatally underestimated the resourcefulness of his bookkeeper, who systematically acquired and retained documentary proof, against the inevitable rainy day, of his employer's finagling.[23] When the downpour threatened, Murphy produced his umbrella. This was in the form of incriminating correspondence Pigott had sent him. His employer decided that his only option was to rid himself of Murphy. To this end, as 'Dublin was full of patriots, who for a few pounds were ready for anything', Donovan claimed that Pigott hired 'a young and very foolish man' named Edward O'Kelley* to kill his shrewd employee.

The attempt on Murphy's life is described in graphic and melodramatic detail ('there were neither moon nor stars, and a fine rain was falling') and was as inept as the intended victim could possibly have wished. According to Donovan's account,

*Not to be confused with the man of the same name who murdered Robert Ford, killer of the American outlaw Jesse James.

Murphy survived a bullet that grazed the back of his head. He was later able to identify his assailant. Although convinced that O'Kelley had been set to his task by Pigott, the young clerk could not prove it.

Politically, from the outset of the Land War in 1879, Pigott, conscious of the predilections of his (dwindling) readership, had taken the dogmatic IRB line on the land struggle in *The Irishman*. This held that Fenians should keep their distance from the agrarian campaign because the Land League, and the issues thrown up by the Land War, were a political distraction. In the summer of 1881 Parnell and the Land League treasurer, Patrick Egan, moved against Pigott and his publications. With a dual purpose in mind, an offer was made to buy him out. This would have the effect of ending his irritating philippics, while allowing the Land League to avail of Pigott's printing press and launch a newspaper supportive of the policies of the agrarian movement. Pigott was easily persuaded to part with his three newspapers for just under £3,500.* He had little option but to agree, and, such were his enormous debts, the sum of money he received was not 'sufficient to pay the Creditors more than a small Dividend'.[24] James O'Connor believed that the three newspapers were 'not worth a fourth of the money'.[25] However, the acquisition of the presses and offices at 33 Lower Abbey Street, and a guarantee of Pigott's permanent departure from the publishing business – a condition of the sale – made it a worthwhile expenditure for the Land League. Within weeks, a staunchly pro-Land League newspaper, *United Ireland*, edited by the former *Freeman's Journal* reporter William O'Brien, was being produced in 33 Lower Abbey Street and being printed on what had once been Pigott's presses.

Pigott now became a pen for hire. The agrarian and Home Rule

*The precise figure was £3,460.16.6 for 'plant, good will, etc.' according to the accounting of the editor of *United Ireland*, William O'Brien. (O'Brien Papers, University College, Cork, UCC-WOB-PP-AA, f.81. Accounts for the Irish National Newspaper & Publishing Company.)

movements were certainly not about to pay for his journalistic services, so he quickly endeared himself to unionists by writing a series of provocative articles and pamphlets for organizations such as the Irish Loyal and Patriotic Union. These highlighted the alleged connections between nationalist politics and agrarian crime. Within four months of the sale of his titles to the Land League, Pigott wrote an article for the biannual London-based journal *Macmillan's Magazine*, in which he heralded the end of Fenianism; proclaimed the impossibility of achieving legislative independence for Ireland; and signposted the gradual erosion of support for the Land League because of its opposition to the terms of Gladstone's 1881 land legislation. The League, he averred, with some justification, was 'managed by businessmen, for businessmen' and was populated by 'professional patriots'.[26] Advertising his conversion to pragmatism, and his availability to bite the hand that had recently lodged almost £3,500 in his bank account, he urged that his fellow countrymen

> … should not give ear to the evil counsels of interested and unscrupulous guides, who are moved by no higher motives than greed of gain or lust of political power, but should avail themselves of every advantage which this Act proposes to give them.[27]

What emerged from the backdraft of the Special Commission, through a cache of letters entered into the record after Pigott's exposure as a forger, was the involvement of the Liberal chief secretary, William E. Forster, in Pigott's first attempt at journalistic double-dealing.

The correspondence, according to Pigott's account, had been preceded by a summons from the chief secretary to a meeting in his Phoenix Park residence. There, apparently, Forster had sought Pigott's co-operation, asking if the journalist could 'see [his] way to do anything that will help the Government'.[28] Pigott, predictably, acquiesced. The first fruit of this *détente* was the *Macmillan's Magazine* article that had appeared in November 1881. Thus, according to Pigott, he had 'made shipwreck of my future prosperity in the service of the Government'.[29] A not unreasonable assessment of his position, as it happens, but one – because of his cynical defection in anticipation of further government generosity – that he must have foreseen. His pivot had not gone unnoticed. *United Ireland*, operating from his former premises, was scathing in its response, denouncing the *Macmillan's Magazine* piece. 'His apostacy [*sic*] may sell a dull article to an English magazine,' wrote William O'Brien, 'and secure him the price of it. Its only effect in Ireland will be to bury Mr. Pigott's political reputation at a crossroads with a stake through it.'[30]

While the waspish retort in *United Ireland* was clearly based on Pigott's apostasy and ingratitude, it was also, in no small measure, a response to the accuracy of some of his barbs. Despite the official hostility of the Land League to the 1881 Land Act, tenants – as Pigott had claimed – were indeed flocking to the Land Courts, established under the act, to have their rents arbitrated. Pigott's characterization of the League's leadership as a self-interested bourgeois cadre of the merchant class of rural Ireland would also have hit home, given that it was dangerously close to the unpalatable truth. The tone of the article, as well as the content, ensured that Pigott thoroughly burnt his bridges and effectively announced, to a largely uninterested unionist audience, that he was for hire.

By the mid-1880s Pigott had penned a series of anti-nationalist leaders, articles and 'notes' to outlets like *St James's Gazette* (from whom he earned £132 in 1884), the London *Evening News*, the *Morning Post* and *Vanity Fair*.[31] In doing so Pigott bought into and enhanced a Tory propaganda campaign designed to stoke fears in Britain by depicting Irish constitutional politicians as criminals with British blood on their hands. During this spree as a 'dynamite revelationist'[32] (Davitt's phrase), Pigott made his most lucrative connection, when Edward Caulfield Houston and the ILPU swam 'like a new planet … into his ken'.

By 1886 the unionist establishment had more on its mind than protecting the interests of Irish landlords. The more prescient members of that class had already begun to take advantage of the opportunities afforded them by land purchase legislation and were selling up their interest to their tenants. This race for the exits, slow to gain momentum, had begun to accelerate after the interim Tory administration of Lord Salisbury had improved the terms of land purchase arrangements in the legislation introduced by the Irish Lord Chancellor, Edward Gibson, Baron Ashbourne in late 1885.

But Gladstone's conversion to Home Rule – conveniently coinciding with the December 1885 election of more than enough Parnellites to return him to power – had utterly changed the dynamic of Anglo-Irish relations. Separatists were ecstatic; loyalists were apoplectic. The defection of a large cohort of unionists from the ranks of the Liberal Party when the Home Rule Bill was put to a vote in 1886 caused the sort of realignment in British politics not seen since the days of the Repeal of the Corn Laws. In Ireland, Gladstone's extraordinary démarche, and ultimate defeat, left nationalists bruised. But the entire process had been an odious shock for Tories and unionists, where the utterly unthinkable had nearly come to pass. The moral terror induced by the relatively narrow failure of this first modest act of Irish devolution led to a determination on the part of the unionist establishment that all forms of separatism must be rooted out. To do otherwise was to expedite the disintegration of the Empire. If this necessitated the use of political artillery, mischievous propaganda or underhand tactics, then so be it.

Both the principles underlying and the principals championing Home Rule must be discredited. Casting doubts on the characters of the latter was the key to undermining the former. The parliamentarians of the Irish Party – an increasingly

Edward Caulfield Houston

accommodating cohort whose radical teeth had been pulled – were to be depicted as a dangerous criminal element still allied to the gun, the tar-barrel, the boycott and the strategically positioned vat of boiling water. One of the more unreliable agents of this campaign would be Richard Pigott.

A more substantial champion of the Empire in its hour of need was the newly wrought Irish Loyal and Patriotic Union.

The Irish Loyal and Patriotic Union (ILPU), founded in May 1885 by a group of academics, businessmen and landlords, was an attempt to unite southern Irish Liberal and Conservative voters – of whom there were relatively few – in opposition to Home Rule. The ILPU ran a slate of candidates as loyalists and champions of empire in the 1885 general election. This list included candidates with given names like Gervaise, St George and Augustus:

monikers unlikely to appeal to many voters with nationalist sympathies, though the ILPU also managed to persuade a 'Daniel O'Connell' to run on its behalf in South Kerry. However, he too was washed away, with the Gervaises and St Georges, by the nationalist wave of 1885, garnering only half of 1 per cent of the votes of the southern half of the county. Outside of north-east Ulster, loyalist fortunes did not prosper, although one candidate, Augustus Stewart in Donegal, did poll almost a thousand votes (952), just over 17 per cent of the ballots cast.[33]

Thereafter the ILPU targeted its resources on the winning of 'hearts and minds' via a series of hectoring pamphlets (released on an almost monthly basis) and a news sheet entitled *Notes from Ireland*. The polemical leaflets included turgid titles like *The Parnell Catechism: Questions and answers on the Government of Ireland Bill* (1886) and *Three months of the National League: a record of the working of the National League branches in Ireland for the months of June, July and August, 1887* (1887), alongside the pithier-sounding *The real dangers of Home Rule* (1887). The ILPU might well have been permitted to fade into historical obscurity had its secretary, Edward Caulfield Houston, not seen fit to engage the services of Richard Pigott, first as scribe, then as spy.

Gladstone's former chief whip, Lord Richard Grosvenor – who had abandoned the party over the Home Rule Bill – bears some of the responsibility. But only some.

Pigott had pestered Grosvenor (the latest in a long line of recipients of his begging letters – Isaac Butt had been one of the first) for financial assistance, with the promise of a rousing loyalist pamphlet to gladden his unionist heart, viz. an early draft of the 'exposé', *Parnellism*. Grosvenor, soon to become Baron Stalbridge, in order to get rid of his unsought correspondent, had the bright idea of palming him off on Houston. After a brief association, during which a number of anti-national pamphlets written by Pigott were published by the ILPU, the former *Irishman* editor managed to convince Houston that he, Richard Pigott – by now completely *persona non grata* in nationalist circles – had somehow become a custodian of the secrets of the Parnellites and could dish the dirt, should he be given the opportunity to investigate them. All the while, of course, having his palm crossed with silver.

He was offered a guinea a day as a retainer by Houston. The ILPU secretary, had he done his due diligence, would have supped with his fellow journalist using an extremely long spoon. Or, had he done the job conscientiously, declined to sup at all. Houston later told the Special Commission that, regarding Pigott's bona fides, he 'really did not give the question consideration'.[34] As a Dublin-based journalist, albeit a callow member of the profession, he could not have been entirely unaware of Pigott's reputation. So a charitable interpretation of the commissioning of Pigott 'to hunt down the Parnellites'[35] would be that Houston was setting a thief to catch, as he saw it, a bevy of thieves.

The Parnellites were adamant that at least some of the money used to pay Pigott for his 'research' came from the government's secret service fund. They, unsuccessfully, demanded sight of the ILPU accounts during the proceedings of the Special Commission, and withdrew from the tribunal when the commissioners ruled against them. As Davitt alleged:

> Information which reached us from more than one well-informed source affirmed that three members of the cabinet of Lord Salisbury during the years 1886–88 were parties to the Irish Loyal and Patriotic Union plot; that moneys were contributed by them, in checks [*sic*], towards the fund for the purchase of the forged letters; that the publication of the letters in *The Times* and the draughting [*sic*] of the bill which created the special commission, with its loaded-dice provisions and character, were the direct work of that conspiracy.[36]

Pigott's strange pilgrimage began when he alerted Houston to the presence of a (fictional) black bag containing incriminating letters signed by Parnell and Egan. This had allegedly been abandoned in Paris by the fugitive Invincible, Frank Byrne, in mid-flight to the USA. The 'discovery' of this potential pot of gold more than justified his guinea-a-day retainer.

Pigott's first port of call in his efforts in 1885 to 'hunt down the Parnellites' had been Eugene Davis, by then living in Lausanne, Switzerland. Davis, along with James Stephens, had been expelled from France in February 1885. Pigott went there in 1886, at the expense of the ILPU. According to 'Dick Donovan', 'Lydia' accompanied him as far as Geneva. His initial forays were funded by the generosity of the former Liberal MP for Kerry Sir Rowland Blennerhassett (£70)[37] and Lord Richard Grosvenor (£450).[38] From Davis, Pigott claimed to have learned of a letter from Parnell, written to mollify Patrick Egan, who had been angered at the Irish Party leader's condemnation of the Phoenix Park murders.

'Next followed the story of Pigott's marvellous luck',[39] according to the wry observation of the *Daily News* correspondent John MacDonald, not altogether dazzled by the Dublin journalist's great good fortune when Pigott recounted his subsequent odyssey to the Special Commission in February 1889. This included three 'accidental' meetings in Paris with an Irish-American Fenian compositor named 'Maurice Murphy' – a former employee of Pigott and a member of Clan na Gael – who seems to have spent far more time as a Parisian boulevardier than in setting type back home in the United States. 'Murphy' always materialized just when Pigott had most need of him, as if summoned by some gift of extra-sensory perception on the part of both men. Had Pigott been a novelist rather than a journalist – he was more of a *seanchaí*, a native Irish teller of tall tales – the frequency with which 'Murphy' came to the rescue of the main protagonist would have fatally undermined the credibility of his plot. The newly minted loyalist sleuth had hopped across to Paris in search of a gaggle of Irish-Americans who had arrived there and 'who might be useful to him in his researches'.[40] Lo and behold, the Americans found him instead. Pigott recounted how he was accosted in a Paris street by Murphy, whom he barely recognized.

At this first fortuitous meeting Pigott happened to drop into the conversation a reference to the intriguing letter Davis had allegedly mentioned in Lausanne. Did 'Murphy', he wondered, with all his excellent Clan/Fenian connections, know anything of the existence of this letter? Sadly 'Murphy' did not. However, his curiosity must have been aroused, because Murphy went in search of the murky note. By an amazing coincidence Murphy, yet again, bumped into Pigott sometime later and was delighted to be able to inform the ILPU agent that the letter did indeed exist, along with several other equally fascinating documents. He ('Murphy') had been permitted, by persons unknown, to have sight of them. Happily, for Pigott, and by extension for his mentors in the ILPU, the letters were available for purchase. Pigott, who was well acquainted with the signatures of Parnell and Egan, was to be allowed to examine this documentary windfall, to satisfy himself as to their authenticity. No sooner had he identified this bonanza as genuine than he notified Houston of their mutual good fortune.

Unfortunately, he was obliged to second guess himself a short time later. Damnably, 'Murphy' had been misinformed, the letters could not be sold – even to such a radical and loyal nationalist as Pigott – without the approval of the über-Clansman John J. Breslin, in New York. Breslin had established his Clan credentials when, at the behest of John Devoy, he had taken up residence in Australia to mastermind the escape of six Fenian prisoners from Fremantle Prison on board the *Catalpa* in 1876.

This temporary setback would necessitate an expensive and time-consuming journey, on Pigott's part, to New York. It was inconvenient for all concerned, and he was loath to put the ILPU to this additional expense, but needs must. Houston, given the potential rewards, agreed to the expenditure. Dick Donovan offered as a rationale for this trip, apart from the obvious extension of Pigott's idyll, the necessity to remove 'Lydia', who was privy to all his crimes, to the safety of the USA. 'She vanishes from the scene as completely as if she had been spirited away to another world,' wrote Donovan.[41]*

Pigott, or so he told Houston, duly bearded Breslin, the republican legend, in his republican den. He returned to Europe – after passing eight days in the USA – with a sealed letter from Breslin to 'Murphy' giving him permission to sell the correspondence to the eager purchaser. Pigott carried this letter on his next journey to Paris in early July 1886 but had difficulty locating 'Murphy', who, despite the potential windfall of a cash sum of £500, had neglected to provide Pigott with his address. *Mirabile dictu*, the two men bumped into each other, yet again, on a Paris street. Such a small city.

The rest of the narrative (like the entire prelude) was pure music hall fantasy. The transaction (outlined previously) took place in the Hôtel des Deux Mondes on the Avenue de l'Opéra with Houston and Professor Maguire attending remotely. It concluded with Pigott claiming to have accompanied 'Murphy' to the nearest Thomas Cook office, cashed Houston's £500 draft, handed the proceeds to his mysterious supplier and later sworn an oath – on a Roman-Catholic prayerbook in the absence of a bible – to the Parisian Clansmen that he would never divulge the identity of his suppliers and would never appear as a witness to the transaction in any court. Part of the arrangement was that neither Houston nor Maguire were, at the supplier's insistence, to be permitted to meet the obliging 'Murphy'.

This was primarily because there was no such person.

The entire mission, bar Pigott's visit to the entirely guiltless Eugene Davis in Lausanne, was a complete fabrication. Pigott had indeed made numerous trips to Paris (at the expense of the ILPU) but had passed his time there racking up his expenses, enjoying the fleshpots and incurring debts with local booksellers.

*Donovan/Muddock claimed that *The Times* went in search of Lydia with a view to having her testify before the Special Commission, 'but she could not be found'. He also claims that the Parnellites knew of her existence and would have questioned Pigott about the relationship had he been cross-examined fully. (Donovan, *Crime of the Century*, 310.)

He had also visited New York – that much was true – but had not approached within a city borough of the formidable Breslin, who would not have been at all impressed by the sudden appearance of this feckless apostate. The 'exchange' in the Hôtel des Deux Mondes was a charade worthy of the great French *farceur* Georges Feydeau himself. While there was no 'Murphy', according to Davitt, Pigott may well have prevailed upon Joseph Casey to accompany him on delivery day to a café near the Hôtel des Deux Mondes.[42] It is possible that Casey was, unbeknownst to himself, Pigott's Plan B should Houston insist on having sight of the elusive 'Murphy'.

Davitt added an additional pinch of farce to the concoction when he recounted the contents of a letter recovered from Pigott's house in Sandycove in the south Dublin suburbs after his suicide. It was from the office of the Mayor of New York and acknowledged Pigott's letter of 19 May 1886 (which allows us to date his transatlantic jolly). It promised to investigate 'the confidence men' who relieved Pigott of some of his ill-gotten ILPU gains.[43] It appears that, while avoiding an unwinnable *tête-à-tête* with John J. Breslin, Pigott had fallen among fellow thieves. The snake had been bitten.

Pigott's explanation of his good fortune in acquiring two additional caches of documents was far less imaginative. He claimed to have been identified in Parisian 'advanced nationalist' circles as a 'buyer' of Parnellite memorabilia. The second batch of letters was offered to him by a fellow collector named 'Tom Brown'. The third came from a source who declined to even leave behind an unlikely invented name.

While Houston was happy to take advantage of the renegade Pigott's past republican credentials, their association was purely a business arrangement conducted by the ILPU secretary. Having got what he wanted from his secret agent, Houston guaranteed Pigott that his name would never come to light as the purveyor of the *Times* letters – any such revelation would not have enhanced the credibility of the documents anyway. Initially, when he approached *The Times*, he did not identify the source of the first batch of letters. He burned his correspondence with Pigott and assumed that the discredited journalist had done likewise.

Not that these precautions were of any avail. Aside from Parnell, who was convinced that O'Shea was the forger, most of his party colleagues plumped for the disreputable Pigott, a man with a reputation for blackmail and extortion, as the most likely culprit.[44] Tim Healy decided to put this theory to the test. He persuaded the radical MP Henry Labouchère, owner of the magazine *Truth*, to identify Pigott as the forger in his publication. Labouchère had considerable personal wealth and could afford to risk an expensive lawsuit. Although Pigott sent a letter demanding a retraction when the allegation was printed, he did not submit a writ for defamation.[45]

Shortly after the Special Commission got underway, the most senior Dublin Castle official, Sir Joseph West Ridgeway, the Irish under-secretary, became aware that the *Times*'s case against Parnell rested on the bona fides of Pigott. In correspondence with the chief secretary, West Ridgeway warned Balfour that there might be trouble ahead. He accused *The Times* of a distinct lack of 'ordinary caution and common sense'. This was because of the newspaper's failure to make 'an enquiry here regarding Pigott's character and antecedents before or since they accepted his information'.[46] West Ridgeway had no inkling in November 1888 that, within four months, Pigott would be unmasked as a double dealer, but the forger's involvement in the 'discovery' of the *Times* letters was already being spoken about in Dublin Castle in highly disparaging terms, while the Commission was bogged down in the sodden trenches of Irish agrarian 'outrage'. West Ridgeway strongly suspected that Sir Charles Russell would make hay if Pigott was put on the stand and that, as a consequence, the newspaper's entire case would collapse. A mere six months before, the under-secretary had been exultantly confident that *The Times* would prevail.

Pigott would validate West Ridgeway's fears in October 1888, while enhancing his reputation for double-dealing. The sybaritic journalist had just been subpoenaed by George Lewis for the Parnellites (one of the factors in a subsequent subpoena from *The Times*). At the instigation of Dublin lawyer Matthew O'Brien, who at that time was working for the Parnellites,* Pigott was inveigled to travel to London to meet Henry Labouchère in his house in Grosvenor Gardens, near Victoria railway station. Gladstone himself – who might have preferred to remain in ignorance – was made aware of this questionable tryst by Labouchère in one of the radical MP's delightfully indiscreet letters.[47] It cannot have required much imagination on Pigott's part to deduce that, in accepting this invitation, he was walking into an ambush where Labouchère would accuse him of forging the *Times* letters. However, Pigott, once again desperate for money, saw a short-term solution to his difficulties. He would persuade Labouchère to part with a large sum of money in exchange for double-crossing *The Times*. When he reached London, however, Labouchère was not alone in Grosvenor Gardens. The last person Pigott wanted to see, a contemptuous Charles Stewart Parnell, was also present. The Irish Party leader proceeded to browbeat, hector and threaten Pigott, but without any positive result. Clearly the Irish Party leader was unfamiliar with Aesop's fable of the divergent negotiating tactics of the north wind and the sun.

It was only when the Parnellites' London solicitor George Lewis arrived and proposed an arrangement with Pigott that matters came to a head. Lewis's offer was not especially attractive to the cash-strapped journalist – immunity from prosecution (which the solicitor was hardly in a position to offer) in return for an admission that he (Pigott) had forged the letters. However, what did appeal to Pigott was a private offer from Labouchère

*He also went by a number of aliases, Sinclair being the one he used most frequently. He had worked for Jenkinson in New York and was, in fact, a double-agent, working for *The Times* and Nicholas Gosselin.

of £1,000 should he agree to accept responsibility for the forging of the letters. The high-minded Parnell was not to hear about the bribe, warned Labouchère. Pigott, in his dealings with Lewis, however, agreed only to a version of events in which he was the *provider* of the letters but not their forger. His sole (entirely useless) concession was that he would inform the tribunal that 'I did not believe them to be genuine' when he handed them over to *The Times*.[48] Since this was far removed from the result the Parnellites sought, Lewis terminated the negotiations.

At some point in the confrontation, however, Pigott must have admitted his guilt, because later that evening Parnell visited Davitt and announced that 'He has confessed'. Davitt, to Parnell's surprise, was anything but overjoyed. He was dismayed because he fully expected the relentlessly treacherous Pigott to take Labouchère's money; inform *The Times* that he had been suborned by the Liberal MP – with the approval of Parnell; and accept an even larger sum from *The Times* to 'disappear'. When it came to their turn to testify, the newspaper's detectives, who kept Pigott under constant surveillance, would be able to tell the Commission that the fugitive witness had been last seen entering Labouchère's house in Grosvenor Gardens. As Davitt put it, after he had sketched out this potential scenario to the Irish leader, 'Mr. Parnell's good spirits fell some degrees at this prospect, and he resolved he would risk no more interviews with Pigott, and he did not.'[49] It later transpired that Pigott, always one to keep his options open, had forewarned *The Times* of the impending meeting with Labouchère. Soames, Lewis's opposite number, seeing the advantages that might flow from the gathering, advised Pigott to go ahead with the meeting and report back. Later, when giving his evidence to the Commission, Pigott painted himself in the colours of *The Times*, insisting that, in agreeing to meet Labouchère, he had been acting in the newspaper's interests all along. While his forewarning of Soames suggests that this was the case, we can safely assume that, had the affair been handled more deftly, and had Pigott been made an offer he could not refuse, the outcome might have been a lucrative confession more acceptable to the Parnellites.

When it came to backstage sparring, Davitt must have experienced some satisfaction at the expense of Pigott and the ILPU. Aware that Pigott had used much of his time in Paris to purchase several books for resale (with Joseph Casey often acting as his agent) and had paid by way of a series of dud cheques, Davitt made the rounds of Parisian bookshops. He posed as a distraught member of the society on whose behalf he claimed Pigott had been purchasing the volumes. Exhibiting intense embarrassment for the aggravation and inconvenience they had suffered, he advised each of the bilked booksellers that they should make an immediate application for compensation from his (Davitt's) employers – the Irish Loyal and Patriotic Union in Dublin. 'What will the ILPU say,' he wrote in his notebook, 'when the bills are sent in. Ha! Ha! Ha!'[50]

Davitt, at his mischievous best, even obligingly fashioned a template letter for the use of the put-upon Parisian *libraires*. This referred to Pigott as an agent of 'your honourable association', and that 'among his other commissions for your society was the purchase of indecent literature for the use of your members'. As Pigott has been supplied 'with the choicest books in the erotique line' and as payment for same was still due, the patient *libraire* would now 'confidently apply to your distinguished association for the payment of the above sum'.[51]

The 'Father of the Land League', it appears, despite his solemn mien, was possessed of a roguish sense of humour.

9

'A THING, A REPTILE, A MONSTER'

The Exit of Richard Pigott

'What has been the result of this uprootal of constitutional practice? What has been the one result? Pigott! A man, a thing, a reptile, a monster – Pigott ... the bloody, rotten, ghastly foetus.'[1]
Randolph Churchill, House of Commons speech, 1889

'So perished Richard Pigott, a forger bold,
Who tried to swear Parnell's life away for the sake of gold,
But the vengeance of God overtook him,
And Parnell's life has been saved, which I consider no sin.'
William Topaz McGonagall,* 'Richard Pigott, the Forger' (1889)

Archbishop's palace, Dublin, March 1887

When the Roman-Catholic archbishop of Dublin, Dr William Walsh, sat down to deal with his correspondence on a spring morning in early March 1887, his heart sank when he saw a letter bearing a London postmark. It was the handwriting on the envelope that caused this momentary pang of depression rather

*The poem runs to seventeen verses, so it could have been much worse! McGonagall (whose parents were Irish) was often described as 'the worst poet in the world'.

than any animosity towards the first city of the Empire. The hand was familiar. He had received enough importuning letters from Richard Pigott to paper the walls of the archbishop's palace in the north Dublin suburb of Drumcondra.

Walsh had made the mistake of meeting with Pigott and offering some financial assistance in response to earlier missives.[2] In recent months, and especially as he became more aware of Pigott's reputation, the archbishop had adamantly refused to offer any further assistance. He was probably tempted to deposit the letter in the nearest wastepaper basket but, possibly intrigued by the London postmark, he opened it and began to read. It had been sent from Anderton's Hotel in Fleet Street on 4 March 1887.

> My Lord, the importance of the matter about which I write will doubtless excuse this intrusion on your grace's attention. Briefly I wish to say that I have been made aware of the details of certain proceedings that are in preparation with the object of destroying the influence of the Parnellite party in parliament. I cannot enter more fully into the details than to state that the proceedings referred to consist in the publication of certain statements purporting to prove the complicity of Mr. Parnell himself and some of his supporters with murders and outrages in Ireland, to be followed in all probability by the institution of criminal proceedings against these parties by the government … and I will further assure your grace that I am also able to point out how the designs may be successfully combated and finally defeated.[3]

Walsh might have wondered why *he* had been favoured with this intelligence. Was it simply because he was not Dr Edward McCabe, his irascible predecessor and the most castellated of 'Castle Bishops', a prelate who never encountered an 'advanced' nationalist whom he did not think richly deserving of castigation from the pulpit? The nationalistic Walsh was a refreshing contrast for most of the Catholics of his archdiocese.

A second letter from his concerned correspondent arrived the following day, also bearing a London postscript. Walsh did not acknowledge receipt of the letters, nor did he reply.

Two days later, if Walsh opened a copy of *The Times*, he would have noticed the trumpeting by the newspaper of a major new series on 'Parnellism and Crime'. This undoubtedly met the criterion of attempting to establish 'the complicity of Mr. Parnell himself and some of his supporters with murders and outrages in Ireland'. He could not fail to make the connection between Pigott's urgent letters and the reporting in *The Times*. Arriving at the same time as the daily papers on 7 March was yet another letter from Pigott. This one adopted a peevish tone, expressing disappointment 'at not having a line from your Grace'. He got one, two days later. On 9 March Walsh wrote advising Pigott that 'I certainly should not be inclined in any way to interfere.'[4]

That should have ended the matter, but Pigott was persistent. Two more letters, on 12 March and 1 May, both sent from Paris, made it clear that Pigott was eager to sell out *The Times* to the Parnellites with the archbishop as intermediary. This time Walsh's reply, on 3 May, was more encouraging. He was prepared to accept and to transmit a statement from Pigott 'that may be of use to the victims of fraud and slander'.[5] When it came, however, the archbishop was unimpressed. On 7 May he advised Pigott that 'I cannot see how what you have written could be of any use to Mr. Parnell or others'; he had supplied no evidence of fraud on the part of *The Times*, and anything short of that 'is, in my opinion, absolutely useless'. In response, Pigott asked for the return of his correspondence. Walsh obliged him by sending back the final two letters. If Pigott assumed that the earlier notes had been destroyed, he was mistaken. Walsh retained them. Some months later, the archbishop sent the originals to Sir Charles Russell as 'proofs of Pigott's intimate knowledge of the Houston plot'.[6]

Their reappearance on the first day of Pigott's cross-examination utterly derailed the forger. Exposed as a swindler, he never recovered from this inescapable evidence of his duplicity.

That night he wrote to his housekeeper, 'Our worthy archbishop has ruined me and my children beyond recall'.[7]

The Times takes the stand

> '… if as I suppose, Pigott is a principal witness, he is likely to be easily attacked for there is little doubt he has done many things for money in his career as a patriot, and besides his constitution is much weakened by drink.'[8]
>
> William O'Shea to Joseph Chamberlain, 28 December 1888

> 'This is no ordinary offence. It was an impeachment by one of the leading journals of the country, backed by the government, and warmly supported by one of the great parties of the state. It was made with every pomp and circumstance that the support of the government could give it, and the legal officials of the state were permitted against all precedent to press it home. Behind it are men of great wealth, some of whom are associated with it in responsibility for this gigantic fraud.'[9]
>
> *Reynolds's Newspaper*, 3 March 1889, after the suicide of Pigott

The Yeomen of the Guard, yet another delightful Gilbert and Sullivan operetta – their eleventh collaboration – was entering its fourth month at Richard D'Oyly Carte's Savoy Theatre on the Strand. One of the snatches of song performed by the company in the finale of Act I was entitled 'The prisoner comes to meet his doom'. It includes the melancholy line 'the funeral bell begins to toll'. The line was equally appropriate to the staging of a less effervescent entertainment a short distance from the Strand.

A house of cards was about to be assembled at the Special Commission. It had taken *The Times* four months to progress to this point, so it stood to reason, with such an amount of preparation, that the foundations could well support a far more solid construction. However, a flimsy house of cards it was going to be. No structure that was reliant on the integrity of Richard

Pigott could have been anything other. The truth, the whole truth and nothing but the truth – while it was a familiar concept to Pigott – was a luxury he could not afford. Everything had been built on lies; the finale would be no different.

Perhaps hoping for some assistance from the patron saint of love and happy marriages, St Valentine, *The Times* began its damage limitation exercise on 14 February 1889, when the newspaper summoned its own solicitor and 'fixer' Joseph Soames to the witness box. The *London Daily News* correspondent John MacDonald observed that 'there was an instant silence' as Soames approached the stand. 'The world had been waiting well-nigh four months for Mr. Soames: and there he stood at last, with his black box beside him.'[10]

The impressive box contained the 'Parnell letters', as they had by now become universally known. After considerable beating about the bush, Webster finally got around to asking the only question to which the eager audience in Probate Court No. 1 required an answer.

'When, Mr. Soames, were you consulted as to the facsimile letter of May 15, 1882?'

Soames, it transpired, had first seen almost the entire cache at the end of 1886. J. C. MacDonald, manager of *The Times*, had brought the documents to his office. Soames had then set about obtaining examples of Parnell's handwriting, and that of his amanuensis, Henry Campbell. Soames also testified that he knew nothing about the source of the letters until after the conclusion of the O'Donnell legal action. As to the running costs of Operation Pigott, Soames told Webster that he had paid Houston up to £3,000 to defray the expenses incurred in securing the letters. Soames had paid out the money himself, 'as I act, to a certain extent, as the treasurer of *The Times*'.[11]

On 15 February, when Russell cross-examined Soames, the supporting cast was almost as interesting as the star. The handwriting expert Inglis (who, to the chagrin of *The Times*, was never called to give evidence) loitered at one of the doorways of

Probate Court No. 1. Edward C. Houston was not far off. Parnell, whose presence was not expected – because he was rumoured to be 'dangerously ill' – turned up anyway 'with his yellowy brown topcoat thrown over his left shoulder ... to all appearances he was on good terms with himself'.[12]

But the most intriguing presence 'sat in an obscure corner by himself, almost unobserved'.[13] Almost.

Richard Pigott might well have been allowed to listen to the cross-examination of Soames had Russell not drawn attention to his presence and demanded that he withdraw from the courtroom. Pigott was forced to comply with this curt demand. John MacDonald of the *London Daily News* described how there was a lot of neck craning, 'as if everybody suspected everybody else of being Piggot'.[14] The Dublin journalist slipped out almost unnoticed. Had he been allowed to remain, he might have witnessed an exchange between Parnellite counsel and the manager of *The Times* in which the spelling of the word 'hesitancy'* in one of the published letters was highlighted.

Soames, it transpired under cross-examination, had been introduced to Pigott during the passage through the House of Commons of the Special Commission legislation. Only then had Houston divulged the identity of his confidential source, with the source's permission.

Soames's most useful contribution to the cause of *The Times* that day was his success in ensuring that the commissioners were made aware of the visit of Pigott to the house of Henry Labouchère to sue for terms with the Parnellites. Here the ground was being laid by *The Times*, should the need arise, for the exposure of Pigott as an unreliable witness secretly playing one side off against the other. It was a shrewd enough insurance policy in the event of any embarrassing evidence from Pigott. However, there

*The exchange, on 19 February, was between Herbert H. Asquith and J. C. MacDonald. (*Special Commission*, Book 5, 352.)

was no opportunity to cash in because of the cataclysm that was the forger's disastrous testimony.

Soames was followed into the witness box by the Scottish-born manager of *The Times*, John Cameron MacDonald. In his early twenties, MacDonald had reported from Ireland during the Great Famine and had narrowly missed the capture of William Smith O'Brien after the Ballingarry, Co. Tipperary skirmish that constituted the sharpest end of the Young Ireland rebellion of 1848.[15] He was also in the wrong place at the wrong time on 15 February 1889 when he faced the Special Commission and was asked to account for the insouciance of his newspaper in avoiding any due diligence exercise before placing its trust in the integrity of Richard Pigott.

MacDonald was cross-examined for the Parnellites not by Russell but by the future Liberal prime minister Herbert H. Asquith. At times the confrontation was an uneven contest between Asquith and MacDonald's highly expressive *pince nez*. These were deployed as a defensive weapon and were frequently twirled for emphasis by the burly *Times* manager as he gave his evidence. MacDonald treated his inquisitor 'with a mingled air of tolerance and amusement'. [16] He did however, betray his naivety when he admitted to Asquith that he had complete faith in the authenticity of the letters 'from the very beginning', i.e. in October 1886, before he had seen the originals.[17] Like Soames before him, MacDonald was also forced to concede that he had made no attempt to ascertain from whom it was that Houston had obtained the letters. The name of Pigott never passed Houston's lips until just before the convening of the Special Commission. He also made no bones about the fact that the publication of the facsimile letter on 18 April 1887 had been 'an appropriate moment on which to issue that letter'[18] because of the newspaper's support for the Crimes Bill then being debated in the House of Commons. No clearer connection could possibly have been made between newspaper and administration.

MacDonald's presence in the witness box was, sadly, one of his last public appearances on behalf of the newspaper. He fell ill in September 1889 and died on 7 December at the age of sixty-seven. Most obituaries claimed that the stress of dealing with the Special Commission had contributed to his demise.

Next into the witness box for *The Times*, on 19 February, was Edward Caulfield Houston. He must by then have been regretting the supreme miscalculation he had made in allowing his enthusiasm for the cause of empire to get the better of him in sending a mere parasite on a mission more appropriate to a skilled predator.

The attorney general took Houston – who appeared understandably nervous – through his direct evidence. Webster established that the young journalist had taken up his position with the ILPU – which he described as an 'anti-Land League' organization – in May 1885 and had first met Richard Pigott in August of that year. The ILPU secretary then outlined the excursions of Pigott as he ranged across western Europe like a hedonistic bloodhound.[19]

During his evidence, Houston unwittingly underscored Pigott's particular genius, or at least his native cunning. Three weeks after the melodramatic transfer of the first batch of letters in the Hôtel des Deux Mondes in Paris, Pigott contacted Houston and sought the return of the entire cache of documents. It transpired that the 'people who had given him the letters rather repented of their doing so and were anxious to get them back, and he was authorized to state if I would give the letters back they would return me the money paid for them'. This approach, by Houston's own admission, copper-fastened his conviction that the haul was genuine. Which, of course, was precisely Pigott's intention. He had read his man well and realized that Houston was susceptible to the sort of double bluff that would reinforce his (Pigott's) fragile credibility.

Under cross-examination, handled this time by Russell, Houston made the damning admission that, in November 1888, he had destroyed all his correspondence with Pigott. He offered as his motive a determination to protect Pigott's informants. However, he had no difficulty naming John P. Hayes and the Casey brothers as Parisian ports of call for Pigott, names that would have been familiar to any nervous Home Office, Foreign Office or Scotland Yard officials among the spectators on the day. James Monro was certainly au fait with Hayes's work on behalf of Jenkinson for at least two years.[20] The name of the mysterious 'Maurice Murphy' was also invoked, but Houston was deliberately hazy as to the doings of this obliging citizen, other than the fact that the unfortunate go-between had conveniently shuffled off his mortal coil, a further addition to the list of convenient deaths that inhabit this narrative.

Houston admitted to having assiduously cultivated ignorance when in the Hôtel des Deux Mondes in Paris – where he operated under the *nom de guerre* of 'Mr Wilson', almost as imaginative as 'Maurice Murphy'. He had declined to have anything to do with the supposed providers of the cache of letters. 'You were very carefully shutting your eyes?' asked Russell. 'My procedure was invariably actuated by the desire to keep myself altogether apart from these men,' Houston acknowledged. As he related the story of the securing of the now infamous 'black bag' to a sceptical Russell, his nervousness reasserted itself. 'He moved about rather restlessly; his hands, clasped behind his back, were constantly twitching.'[21] He was probably not soothed by the fact that his responses to Russell, in describing the cloak and dagger burlesque of Les Deux Mondes, were constantly being greeted by belly laughs from spectators who saw only smoke, mirrors and absurdity.

The second and third cache of letters had come Houston's way, via Pigott, after the publication of the facsimile letter. By then, Houston, having been spurned by Lord Hartington and *Pall Mall Gazette* editor W. T. Stead, had thrown in his lot with *The Times*. The newspaper then used the *O'Donnell v. Walter* case to liberate these bonus items into the public domain without any legal consequence. At around the time of the opening of the commission Houston's confidence in his agent, he admitted, had been shaken when he became aware of Pigott's flit to London and the conversation in Labouchère's house. He insisted on Pigott making a 'sworn declaration' – in effect a full confession – of what had occurred. The 'sworn declaration' seems to have been enough to restore Houston's childish faith in the veracity of his secret agent. Russell does not appear to have been moved by this touching revelation. He had some idea of the prudential value of a Piggot statement, sworn or otherwise.

When Houston left the stand it was time for the confrontation that *The Times* had been secretly dreading. No amount of horror stories of agrarian outrage in rural Ireland could further postpone the appearance of the brittle supplier of the 'Parnell letters'. The cry went up outside the courtroom for 'Pigott'. The male lead took his own sweet time in installing himself in the witness box, ready to tell his unlikely story. Had he known what was to come, he might well have decided to exit Probate Court No. 1 long before he heard his name being called and lose himself among London's teeming millions.

The details of Pigott's appearance before the Commission and his exposure as a reckless charlatan are relatively familiar territory. He took the stand at 1.30 p.m. on 20 February 1889 and Webster took him through his direct evidence. He cut an unimpressive figure: squat, bald, sporting a monocle and a large but well-kept beard. John MacDonald of the *London Daily News* (no relation of the manager of *The Times*) underscored his 'big, somewhat irresolute mouth, big fleshy nose, and smallish eyes, far apart'.[22] Michael Davitt sat in his customary seat and waited for the axe to fall as soon as the attorney general was obliged to hand over his witness to a thoroughly well-briefed and impatient Sir Charles Russell:

> Pigott's appearance would not suggest the character of an unmitigated scoundrel. Rather the contrary … the small,

> protruding eyes, fleshy nose, and flabby mouth; the thin, caressing voice, and the sly and shifty expression of the face, were keys to the character and life which were about to be dissected under the merciless hand of the man who sat watching him from the counsel's bench as a hawk would watch a doomed prey.[23]

Russell may have looked hawkish, but he was nervously conscious that his cross-examination of Pigott might well define his career. His friend and biographer R. Barry O'Brien recorded that the impending contest was playing on the barrister's mind for at least a week before Pigott took the stand, 'Russell grew restless and irritable. He looked ill … at times he remained altogether silent … his expression was grave, thoughtful, anxious; and his face and manner showed that the strain upon him was intense.'[24]

Pigott had acquitted himself adequately in his first day of evidence, when, under the gentle probing of Webster, he largely confirmed the testimony already offered by Soames, MacDonald and Houston. He 'left the box with a self-satisfied expression'[25] after a couple of hours of unchallenged testimony. This continued on the morning of 21 February, when he treated the patrons in Probate Court No. 1 to the tale of what John MacDonald called 'his marvellous luck'.[26] In the course of describing his many fortuitous encounters with 'Maurice Murphy', Pigott told Webster that the second batch of letters had been sold to him by a man named 'Tom Brown'. This provider was, presumably, well past his schooldays and was yet another example of the journalist's lack of imagination when it came to inventing fictitious names. When asked directly by the attorney general whether he had forged the letters himself, Pigott, while admitting that he was aware that such malign accusations surrounded him, denied the charge emphatically.

When it came to the discomforting London meeting in November 1888 with Labouchère and Parnell, Pigott attempted to pass off what was an obvious piece of double-dealing by reverting to the preposterous fiction that he had been working in the interests of *The Times*. During this passage of questioning, Pigott was visibly uncomfortable. 'His fingers twitched, and his voice was so broken and husky that water had to be brought.'[27] His patent discomfort was about to be amplified. As soon as Webster resumed his seat, having completed his examination, 'Sir Charles stood bolt upright.'[28]

Russell began his cross-examination with an ace up his sleeve, courtesy of the Dublin archbishop's palace, but Pigott instantly provided him with a second.

His cross-examination began in unorthodox fashion. Instead of peppering the witness with questions, Russell produced a piece of blank paper and handed it to Pigott. He asked the journalist to write a series of words. 'Livelihood', 'likelihood', his own name, 'proselytism', 'Patrick Egan' and 'P. Egan'. Then, in an apparent afterthought – one that almost a century later would become the stock in trade of the TV detective Columbo – he asked the witness to write the word 'hesitancy'.[29] Had Pigott been permitted to remain in the courtroom during the cross-examination of Soames, this request might well have prompted alarm bells to disturb what shards of composure he had left. Instinctively, Pigott spelled the word as 'hesitency', the very error that had appeared in one of the letters purchased by *The Times*. Russell then reclaimed the paper. He glanced at it before handing it over to one of his colleagues, Frank Lockwood. Under his breath, Lockwood could be heard by several spectators to declare triumphantly, 'We've got him.'[30]

Shortly thereafter Russell played his first trump card. Pigott was asked whether he had engaged in a correspondence with Archbishop Walsh. He admitted that he had, but implied that this had only begun *after* the first appearance of the 'Parnellism and Crime' series in *The Times*. The cross-examination was only a few minutes old and already Pigott had perjured himself. He assumed that he was on safe ground as Russell could not produce any of the originals of his letters to Walsh.

There he was sadly mistaken.

Walsh had not only retained those early letters but had handed them over to Russell. When presented with the conclusive evidence that he was aware of the plans of *The Times* to vilify the Parnellites and was clearly offering to neutralize the campaign of his paymasters, Pigott advanced the ludicrous claim that he should not be questioned about the Walsh letters because he was a member of the archbishop's flock. Therefore, the correspondence was subject to the seal of the confessional.[31] That produced the first communal belly laugh of the day. It was the first of many, as Russell proceeded to roast Pigott over a slow spit, making it apparent that the testimony of the witness could not be trusted and that Pigott was a liar and a perjurer.

As Russell's cross-examination proceeded into a second day, Pigott began to look as if he could do with a more congenial father confessor. His voice quavered in response to Russell's questions and barbs, before almost disappearing altogether. His face was permanently flushed, became wreathed in embarrassed smiles as he floundered, and his responses to Russell took longer and longer to emerge as 'his body and spirit alike bowed under the strain'.[32]

Russell was at his forensic best again that day (22 February), catching the witness in a series of blatant and obvious untruths. Pigott emerged as a shyster *par excellence*, an embarrassment to Irish nationalism, an extortionist and a blackmailer. The courtroom was frequently racked with gales of laughter as Pigott piled absurd lie upon lie. The ushers gave up discouraging such unseemly displays of merriment when the judges themselves joined in the laughter. The effect on the usually taciturn and emotionless Justice Day, in particular, was noted by T. P. O'Connor MP:

> Laughter literally shook his sides and was a sort of obbligato [*sic*] to the evidence of the miserable wretch on the rack in cross-examination. His whole frame shook – his eyebrows shook – his long whiskers shook … After the departure of the cause of this judicial merriment, Mr. Justice Day returned to his gloom and never smiled again.[33]

The only observers who remained grim-faced throughout were the representatives of *The Times* sitting directly opposite Pigott as his testimony 'brought down the fabric of [their] case in ludicrous ruin'.[34]

In a series of rapid-fire sallies (interrupted only by recourse to the occasional pinch of snuff), Russell pointed out to the tremulous witness the similarities between letters procured by *The Times* and the correspondence of Egan, Pigott and Parnell at the time of the sale, in 1881, of his newspapers to the Land League. Egan had retained the entire collection and had sent it from the USA. It was made apparent to all that phrases that appeared in these letters magically surfaced later in the 'Murphy'/'Brown'/A. N. Other document haul.

Pigott was forced to concede, in order to retain what little credibility he had left, that the coincidence of phraseology was 'very remarkable indeed; so very remarkable as to be extremely improbable'.[35] After this candid concession Russell then toyed with the witness by asking him repeatedly how he would go about forging a signature, should he ever feel the need to do so. He even enquired of the witness whether he thought Parnell's signature would be difficult to forge. By then the stricken journalist's frantic gesticulations were sure signs of a man who was drowning, not waving.

In any other circumstance the *coup de grâce* would have been the introduction by Russell of a lengthy and damning correspondence between Pigott and then Liberal chief secretary William E. Forster. This began in June 1881 with a sycophantic letter from the Dublin journalist. It then passed through phases of wheedling entreaties for financial assistance (Forster parting with at least £155 of his own money), job requests and threats of suicide, before, four months prior to Forster's death in April 1886, graduating to threats of blackmail. However, in the context of Pigott's testimony and the ruthless exposure of his character flaws, even the reading into the record of almost fifty letters between the two men merely confirmed what half a dozen prior *coups de grâce* had already made obvious.

Finally, Russell chose to end the agony, for that day at least. He reverted to the piece of paper on which Pigott had scrawled several words the previous day. He pointed out Pigott's unusual spelling of the word 'hesitancy'. 'Have you noticed the fact,' he asked disarmingly, 'that the writer of the body of the letter of the 9th of January 1882, the alleged forged letter beginning "Dear E" spells the word in the same way?'* Russell noted that, the previous day, Pigott too had spelled the word as 'hesitency'. Did this, asked the Parnellite counsel, not strike Pigott 'as being a remarkable coincidence'? The witness demurred, 'No, I do not think it is very remarkable,' he replied.[36]

He was in a minority of one.

Russell, in the cross-examination of a lifetime, had left no one in Probate Court No. 1 in any doubt that Pigott was a charlatan, a serial perjurer and a forger. Once he got into his stride, Russell was, in effect, shooting fish in a barrel – Davitt described the interrogation as 'a process of slaying the slain'[37] – a display of merciless harrying and harassment.

As the downcast Pigott left the courtroom, most of the audience wondered how he was going to fare when his cross-examination resumed the following Tuesday (26 February). Parnell, with a prescient lack of faith in his quarry, turned to his solicitor and warned Lewis to 'let that man be watched. If you do not keep your eye on him, you will find that he will leave the country.'[38]

Which, of course, is precisely what happened. But not immediately, and not before a period of intense and confusing preliminaries.

Pigott had no intention, if he could avoid it, of subjecting himself once again to the slow torture of a Russell cross-examination. But he was being carefully monitored by both sides; two, and sometimes three, RIC and Scotland Yard detectives were guarding/imprisoning him in Anderton's Hotel in Fleet

*The letter purported to be from Parnell to Egan urging an intensification in militant action.

Street. Furthermore, he lacked the resources for a midnight flit, and he needed to secure his financial future before his leverage evaporated. He decided that his only option was to explore the Labouchère flight path. He returned to Grosvenor Gardens on Saturday 23 February and offered to make a complete confession, in return for money and amnesty. Labouchère, wisely, sent for a neighbour, the journalist George Augustus Sala, to witness Pigott's statement. This plan, however, was stymied, when the 'confession' was sent to the offices of George Lewis, where it was read by Parnell and was returned contemptuously to the forger at his hotel. The Parnellites no longer needed Pigott's 'confession'. Thanks to Russell's ruthless hatchet work, any document bearing Pigott's signature was not worth the paper it was written on.

After this rebuke Pigott changed tack. In concert with a Dublin solicitor, W. J. Shannon, whom Soames retained, he drafted a second 'confession'. The Labouchère/Sala document was unsafe, he claimed. It had been extracted under duress (the threat of prosecution) and with the promise of a large cash sum. It was now time to toss Patrick Casey under the wheels of a steam train. The Parisian 'Fenian', he alleged, had provided him with many of the *Times* letters. He [Pigott] had forged the others. However, he clung to the truth of his (and Houston's) version of how the first batch of letters had been procured. He then stated his firm belief that the 'Casey batch' – including the facsimile letter – were genuine. The Shannon/Pigott document was then sworn as an affidavit on the morning of 25 February. Later that day Pigott either evaded the detectives who were guarding him or he – an acutely embarrassing witness, now surplus to requirements – was allowed to slip his chains. The Irish journalist Andrew Dunlop, who was covering the commission for the *Irish Times* claimed to have seen Pigott 'escape' (his quotation marks) on 22 February, the day of his last appearance before the commission. Dunlop, in his biography, *Fifty Years of Irish Journalism*, describes Pigott as being accompanied into Anderton's by his two 'keepers'. They remained inside for less than five minutes and then came out again. Pigott immediately walked across Fleet Street, at that hour densely crowded, and in broad daylight, while his two keepers remained at the door of the hotel.[39]

While this was not the precise moment of Pigott's escape – the manager of Anderton's told the Commission that the fugitive had remained in the hotel until at least 4 p.m. on Monday 25 February – it indicated that Pigott was allowed to go about his business without any let or hindrance. On the evening of Monday 25 February, he made for Charing Cross station and took the night train to Paris. From there he posted the returned Labouchère/Sala confession to W. J. Shannon and then headed south: destination Madrid.

Having adjourned while Pigott was still in the dock – it could no longer accurately be described as a witness box – at 4 p.m. on 22 February, the Commission re-convened at 10.30 a.m. on 26 February. In anticipation, the hordes had descended. More 'great and good' than 'hoi polloi'. There was standing room only in Probate Court No. 1 as a curious audience, having read press accounts of Pigott's evisceration, wanted to see what new soufflé of lies and evasions he had been able to bake over the long weekend. One luminary who was not required to stand was Catherine Gladstone, wife of the Liberal Party leader. While she did witness a memorable drama, it was not exactly the spectacle she had anticipated. When the three judges entered the courtroom and the ushers demanded 'Silence', everyone settled into their seats.

And waited.

And then waited some more.

After about five minutes of gestures, enquiring looks and puzzled shrugs, the sworn witness had still not returned to continue his cross-examination. At this point the Commission president, Sir James Hannen, intervened and demanded of the attorneys for *The Times* that they produce the witness. A muttered conversation ensued between Soames and Webster, after which a red-faced attorney general rose and, almost inaudibly, informed the Commission president that Pigott had not been seen since the previous night.

On hearing this news, Russell extended his arm in imitation of a Roman senator, demanded that the commissioners issue a warrant for Pigott's arrest and proclaimed, in a sentiment truer than even he knew at the time, that the Parnellites were the victims of a 'foul conspiracy'. Not content with the senatorial gesture, Russell followed it up by dramatically and painfully bringing his fist down on the bench in front of him with a booming thud. The business of the tribunal was suspended for an hour.

A warrant for the arrest of Pigott was issued, the execution of which was entrusted to James Monro of Scotland Yard, a 'trust' that was to prove problematic. Robert Anderson, to whom the apprehension of the fugitive was delegated, stalled the execution of the warrant. This, ultimately, would have little impact on the pursuit of Pigott, but it underscored the extent of Anderson's own personal collusion with *The Times*.

When the Commission reconvened, Soames was recalled to the witness box to deny that he had colluded in Pigott's escape. Shannon, 'a tall, black-haired, pale-complexioned man, with a softish voice and dark eyes',[40] testified to the nature of the 'confession' of the previous Saturday. Later that day George Lewis, in the witness box, dissected what little remained intact of the reputation of Richard Pigott. Had he appeared to face further cross-examination, he would have been presented with evidence that he had forged numerous money bills and that he was a dealer in obscene books and photographs, the latter sideline providing the real explanation for his many trips to Paris at Houston's expense. After a fruitless interrogation of Pigott's two sheepish police guardians – one of whom had witnessed Pigott leaving Anderton's Hotel but did not bother to follow him – the Commission adjourned for the day, allowing Parnell, Lewis, Davitt and Labouchère to step outside and acknowledge the cheers of the waiting crowd.

*

When the Commission re-convened on Wednesday 27 February, Michael Davitt, who normally attended the proceedings religiously, was absent. And with good reason. Pursuing a thoroughly educated guess, Davitt was in Paris trying to track down the fugitive forger. He was too late; Pigott was already on his way to Madrid by the time Davitt arrived in the French capital. Before his departure, however, the forger had despatched the 'confession' of 22 February to the Special Commission via the solicitor W. J. Shannon. This was the signed and witnessed version of events he had related to Labouchère and Sala, in which he confessed to having forged the entire *Times* cache of letters. 'I told Houston,' he admitted, 'that I had discovered the letters in Paris, but I grieve to have to confess that I simply myself fabricated them, using genuine letters of Mr. Parnell and Egan.'[41]

The reading of this communication to the commissioners was followed by 'a rather awkward pause'.[42] It was now clearly up to *The Times* to don sackcloth. A mortified Webster rose to offer at least some measure of embarrassed expiation. He laid into Pigott with venom: 'I desire to say nothing respecting that witness except that I presume everyone will agree that no one ought to attach any weight to any evidence he has given.' After his brief tantrum, however, Webster, on behalf of *The Times*, raised a white flag and proceeded to eat crow:

> I will now, on behalf of those whom we represent, ask permission to withdraw from your consideration the question of the genuineness of the letters which have been submitted to you, the authenticity of which is denied, with the full acknowledgement that, after the evidence which has been given, we are not entitled to say that they are genuine.[43]

It was an utterly humiliating retreat. Webster, who had been reluctant to accept the brief of *The Times* in the first place, may have experienced a tiny measure of vindication. He could barely summon the energy to deny Russell's accusation of 'foul conspiracy'. 'I desire emphatically,' to say, he asserted wanly, 'that if any foul conspiracy exists, then those whom we represent have no share in it.' The watching J. C. MacDonald must have been mentally totting up the cost of the defamation damages that would inevitably accrue to Parnell. His action could now proceed without the slightest doubt as to the outcome. MacDonald's mood cannot have been improved by the fact that the Irish Party leader (the 'contemptuously indifferent victor'[44]) was seated next to him as Webster launched into his cringe-inducing expression of regret. Joseph Soames – two spaces removed from Parnell – had 'the air of a man attending a funeral of dead reputations'.[45] Both men however, despite their dejection, must have sat up and taken notice at one startling admission contained in Pigott's confession to Labouchère. He had misled Houston about the destruction of his side of their correspondence. The ILPU secretary's letters to Pigott lived on, ensuring the potential for further humiliation of both Houston and *The Times*. Steps would have to be taken to ensure that this cache of unforged letters did not see the light of day.

The reaction of *Reynolds's Newspaper* to the exposure of Pigott looked beyond the here and now, and recognized the wider implications for the conservative establishment:

> Behind Houston, who hired the forger, are a number of men who determined to ruin the political party to whom they were antagonistic and who stopped at nothing to compass their shameful ends. These men must not be allowed to skulk behind while their tools are being made the scapegoats. Who would care to see Pigott or Houston in the dock if their high placed, titled, and wealthy employers are allowed to go scot-free?[46]

On 27 February Pigott – the sale of some rare volumes to Sotheby's having facilitated his escape to the Continent in the first place – had taken the Paris express to Madrid. Somewhere en route he adopted the pseudonym of Rowland Ponsonby, an alias rather too close for comfort to that of the former Home Rule MP for Kerry, Rowland Ponsonby Blennerhassett.* Stepping onto the platform in Madrid, he was immediately buttonholed by an interpreter who worked for the Hotel de los Embajadores, whom he agreed to take on as a guide in a city with which he was unfamiliar. For two days both men were inseparable as an apparently untroubled Pigott toured some of the city's churches and museums. However, the proceeds of the Sotheby's transaction were running out, and Pigott needed funds to enable him to disappear permanently. With this end in view, he sent a telegram to Shannon in London seeking payment of the money he claimed he was owed by the Dublin solicitor. In breaking cover in this way, he made a fatal error. Not even the procrastination of Robert Anderson could prevent the despatch of a telegram from London to Madrid requesting that the Spanish authorities arrest and detain the fugitive. At 5 p.m. on 1 March the Hotel de los Embajadores interpreter informed Pigott that police officers were in the hotel lobby and wished to speak to him. It was quickly apparent to Pigott that the game was up. He met with the detectives and asked if he could be allowed to return briefly to his room. On entering the room, he reached for a bag lying on a chair. The last seconds of his life were described thus by the newspaper he had tricked and defrauded:

> The Inspector seemed to divine Pigott's object and sprang forward to seize him. It was too late. Pigott had a big revolver in his hand, placed the muzzle against his mouth, drew the trigger, and fell to the ground a horribly mutilated corpse.[47]

It was yet another convenient death, at least as far as *The Times*

*Not to be confused with Sir Rowland Blennerhassett, who had contributed £70 to fund Pigott's Parisian jaunts.

and the authorities were concerned. Pigott's suicide – some have speculated that he was murdered to silence him, Tim Healy wrote 'Shot, indeed he was. Suicide, I doubt'[48] – probably spared him a speedy extradition process and a long jail term. But it also spared *The Times* the further mortification of a trial and the possibility of fatal collateral damage to a Salisbury administration that had bought into the newspaper's prosecution of Irish nationalism. As we shall see, the Irish official who did more than anyone to provide *The Times* with ammunition against the Parnellites, the Resident Magistrate William Joyce, was convinced that Soames had expedited Pigott's escape.[49]

But what brought Richard Pigott to Madrid in the first place? If he felt unsafe in Paris, a city with which he was very familiar, why not flee incognito to some other French city or Francophone location in Belgium or Switzerland? He spoke no Spanish, but he might have been under the illusion that Spain had no extradition treaty with the United Kingdom. Or he might have been aware that in 1878 both countries had signed a mutual agreement to repatriate absconding criminals.[50] Pigott was clearly short of funds. Why waste his dwindling resources on a night-time journey from Paris to Madrid?

Could it possibly have had anything to do with the presence in the Spanish capital of William Henry O'Shea? Or was that merely an extraordinary coincidence? O'Shea had told the Special Commission in October 1888 that he was leaving for the Spanish capital, where he had business interests. He was still there in March 1889. Furthermore, what were the odds, in a city of half a million people, that O'Shea should accidentally bump into Pigott over the short period (less than two full days) the forger spent in Spain before doing away with himself?

Because that is precisely what happened. At least according to William Henry O'Shea.

This barely credible encounter took place on the evening of 28 February, the eve of his suicide, on the day Pigott arrived in

Madrid. It will be recalled that O'Shea had told Sir Charles Russell in his evidence to the Special Commission that, while he was aware of Pigott's existence, he was not personally acquainted with the man. However, a few days after Pigott's death, O'Shea sent a gleeful letter to Chamberlain on 9 March 1889 recounting his strange experience while dining in the city's Café Ingles. Two men entered the restaurant, one of whom he suspected was Pigott, the other he took to be an interpreter. The forger asked for an English newspaper and began to read. O'Shea wrote to Chamberlain that:

> His hand trembled then he looked around the café through an eyeglass, rose suddenly, touched the interpreter on the shoulder, and left hurriedly … hearing of the suicide a few minutes after it occurred the next day, I had no doubt of the identity.[51]

Despite his testimony to the Special Commission, it is probable, based on the investigative work of Davitt, that Pigott and O'Shea were acquainted, but that the captain, taken aback by Russell's line of questioning the previous October, and having at least an inkling of the work being done by the forger, had no desire to confirm that fact to the Commission. Assuming that he did manage to identify Pigott in the Café Ingles, why did O'Shea not immediately inform the authorities? As one who relished the limelight, surely O'Shea's vanity would have been piqued at the prospect of playing a central role in the arrest and detention of the most notorious fugitive in Europe at that time. O'Shea, in his giddy 9 March letter to Chamberlain, couldn't resist putting himself at the centre of the story of Pigott's final hours. Was he actually there as of right, rather than by coincidence?

Had Pigott been promised payment by O'Shea for services rendered? Was that what took the impecunious fugitive to a city where he had no history or contacts, other than the cuckolded captain? Was he intent on extorting money from O'Shea? Either way Pigott's exposure and suicide would have a profound impact on O'Shea's future options. Parnell had now slipped the snare *The Times* had laid for him. The humiliation of the Irish Party leader – O'Shea's dearest wish – was on hold, unless O'Shea stirred himself to create the scandal that was almost guaranteed to bring down Parnell. *The Times* had failed to deliver the *coup de grâce*. O'Shea would finally have to 'screw his courage to the sticking place' and sue for divorce.

If Pigott did, in fact, meet O'Shea by design in Madrid, it was likely to have been an echo of another fascinating encounter in Paris the previous autumn.

In his idiosyncratic but compelling survey of the Jack the Ripper killings *They All Love Jack*, the actor and screenwriter Bruce Robinson ponders the oddity of Robert Anderson, newly appointed head of the Met's CID, choosing to take a European vacation in September/October 1888 while a notorious serial killer stalked the Whitechapel area of London. Anderson, pleading exhaustion, decided to take four weeks' holidays in Switzerland, barely a week after assuming his new position, and at a stressful time for his Metropolitan Police colleagues. He left London on the day of the murder of Annie Chapman, the Ripper's second victim. Under pressure to return to England, he abandoned his Swiss vacation on 30 September, the day of the double murder of Elizabeth Stride and Catherine Eddowes. However, he did not immediately return to supervise the Ripper investigation. Instead, he travelled to Paris and remained there for a short period while the London press clamoured for his return.[52] Why did Anderson defy British public opinion and fail to cut short his vacation?

Could it have had anything to do with the fact that a coincidental visitor to Paris in early October 1888 was Richard Pigott?

Both men left Paris on the same day. Did they meet? Bruce Robinson is in no doubt that Anderson was pursuing his obsession with the Special Commission and returned to London only after an 'urgent appeal' (Anderson's phrase) from the Home Secretary.

'Anderson may well have heard that there had been a murder or two in London's East End,' wrote Robinson caustically, 'but the business of destroying Parnell allowed little time for distraction, especially in respect of those forsaken sluts whose ritualized deaths, according to him, were their own fault.'[53] Pigott's presence in Paris and his possible meeting with Anderson may have been related to his changed relationship with *The Times*. By the latter half of 1888 Pigott was working not for Edward Houston but for *The Times*. He was directly involved in 'constructing formally what was to become the case against Home Rule for Tories and Irish unionists alike'.[54] This work included attempts to persuade Fenian/Clan prisoners in British jails to give evidence before the Special Commission.

Whether or not his interest was piqued by the reference in Pigott's Labouchère/Sala confession to the continued existence of a tranche of letters from Houston to the forger, Michael Davitt, the intrepid amateur detective, absented himself from the increasingly turgid proceedings in Probate Court No. 1 – the Special Commission still had eight months and seventy often tedious sessions to run – and made for Pigott's house in Sandycove, Co. Dublin, to retrieve anything of value from the suicide's papers. However, he was beaten to the punch by 'the most mysterious and romantic of the many strange people who figured directly or otherwise in *The Times* commission'.[55] This was the former Dublin solicitor Matthew O'Brien, who also went by the alias 'Sinclair' and who was an agent for the administration and, latterly, for *The Times*.

In the early days of the Special Commission, O'Brien/Sinclair had been employed by the Parnellites. It was he who enticed Pigott over to London to meet Parnell and Lewis in Labouchère's house. But appearances were deceptive: by March 1889 he was certainly taking the *Times*'s shilling. A few years before he had been working in New York for the British Consul General, William Hoare, and for Edward Jenkinson. There, he was in cahoots with 'Red Jim' McDermott.[56] O'Brien had also been involved as an *agent provocateur* in one of the decade's most high-profile terrorist cases, the arrest of Clan na Gael's Dr Thomas Gallagher in 1883. His government work had not, however, prevented him from taking on confidential tasks for Henry Labouchère. Except that, while on Labouchère's payroll, he was also working for Nicholas Gosselin and was passing on information to Soames.[57] The very model of a modern double-agent.

Ironically, none other than the almost equally duplicitous William O'Shea had the measure of O'Brien. O'Brien 'just happened' to run into Joseph Chamberlain on board a ship in the mid-Atlantic at around the time of the latter's wedding in the winter of 1888. O'Brien was able to tell Chamberlain in a 'chance' encounter that the Parnellites had extracted a confession from Pigott. He was, of course, privy to this information because it was he who had cajoled Pigott to London in the first place. Chamberlain mentioned the encounter in a letter to the captain. O'Shea warned Chamberlain that O'Brien (who had identified himself as 'Sinclair') was not to be trusted. He had, according to the captain, abandoned his wife in the USA and had later eloped with a woman from Ballinasloe, Co. Galway. What O'Shea did not know was that O'Brien had later concocted a Clan na Gael assassination plot against Chamberlain and 'warned' the Liberal Unionist leader that his life was in danger while he was in the United States. The Clan – when it became aware of this, fearing that O'Brien himself, or one of his associates, would murder Chamberlain to further blacken the reputation of Irish-American militants – hired Pinkerton detectives to guard Chamberlain, from a distance and without his knowledge.[58]

The English language is ill-equipped to embrace the irony of Clan na Gael expending even a red cent of its resources on the protection of 'Judas' Chamberlain.

Thanks to a contact of his own in the Pinkerton organization, Davitt became aware of O'Brien's treachery, but not in time to finish a distant second to the double-agent in the race to get to Pigott's house in Sandycove. Davitt was a day too late. When he arrived, the forger's housekeeper Anne Byrne* informed him that another 'gentleman' had already been through her late employer's papers. Davitt was left with meagre pickings and no idea what O'Brien had pilfered. It would now be impossible to prove the precise extent to which Pigott had been an active agent for *The Times.*

The highly successful run of *The Yeomen of the Guard* closed after 423 performances on 30 November 1889, giving way to *The Gondoliers.* This was a week after the last witness gave evidence to the Special Commission, which itself closed after 128 performances. Many of those had been reminiscent of the comic work of Gilbert and Sullivan at its best.

*Mrs Byrne, a good-hearted woman, took charge of Pigott's four young male children (the eldest was seventeen). Davitt also made generous efforts to support the children, even reaching out to his arch-enemy Joseph Soames, who contributed £10 towards their upkeep. (Davitt papers, TCD, MS 9441/3160–4.)

10

FROM CHECKMATE TO STALEMATE

Endgame at the Commission

'They only paid the Moonlighter his cattle-hocking price,
They only helped the murderer with counsel's best advice,
But – sure it keeps their honour white – the learned Court believes,
They never give a piece of plate to murderers and thieves.'[1]

Rudyard Kipling, 'Cleared – in Memory of a Commission' (1890)

'The government has lain like moonlighters behind a hedge with their faces blackened.'[2]

T. M. Healy, House of Commons, 31 July 1888

Probate Court No. 1, Special Commission, 5 July 1889

Were it not for the fact that the Special Commission had long since entered its 'watching paint dry' phase, more attention might have been paid to a Mayo witness introduced by Michael Davitt a few weeks before the summer recess. *The Times* had thrown the kitchen sink at the Parnellites by early July 1889 but had made no attempt to offer any credible rationale behind the brutal murders of five members of the Joyce family in Maamtrasna in the summer of 1882. This had led to the execution of an innocent man, Maolra Seoighe (Myles Joyce), and the imprisonment of three equally guiltless relatives. The episode had been the single worst atrocity of the Land War, so this was an odd oversight. Pinning the savage Maamtrasna murders on the Land League would have provided a much-needed fillip to the newspaper's case.

The Times – warned off perhaps by those in the know – may have had good reason to shy away from drawing too much attention to the events of a mid-August night in one of the remoter regions of the Galway/Mayo border. Davitt displayed no such reticence. When he introduced John J. Louden as a witness for the Parnellites, it was in the hope of shaking the tribunal out of its lethargy. Or, if it was already far too inert to induce such a welcome tremor, he at least hoped to send a message to Dublin Castle that the nationalist side had some dangerous insights into RIC vigilantism in the west of Ireland.

By 1889 Louden had faded from public memory, but ten years previously the Westport barrister, poor law guardian and grazier had been one of the powers behind the establishment of the Land League, along with his current inquisitor, Michael Davitt. 'He was an excellent witness,' observed the stir-crazy John MacDonald, 'as downright candid as his examiner – and he succeeded in thoroughly interesting his hearers.'[3] One of the golden nuggets from Davitt's examination of his witness was the first, and only, introduction into evidence of an enigmatic agrarian antagonist of the Land League in the west of Ireland, a mysterious cabal that Louden described as the Herds League.* This shadowy organization, which had no public profile whatever and operated along the lines of a secret society, was, however, unlike the Ribbonmen, no ally of the organization founded by Davitt and Louden, and no friend of the 'moonlighters' of County Mayo. It was, said John J. Louden, a vigilante group that staged a number of attacks on the property of well-known Land Leaguers. The Herds League, according to Louden, was 'purely and simply a murderers' organisation' and was, he believed, involved in the Maamtrasna killings. He then

*'Herds' as in herders/shepherds.

went on to link this murder gang to the Royal Irish Constabulary by claiming that its members were *agents provocateurs* working for a forty-six-year-old Sligo-born RIC Head Constable named Gerald Whelehan who had joined the force in 1864.

The rationale behind the Herds League, Louden alleged, was to discredit agrarian activists via a series of controversial killings – including the Maamtrasna massacre of August 1882 – that would then be blamed on the Land League.* Whelehan, according to Louden, operated in a netherworld of vigilantism inhabited by informers and assassins.[4] Louden himself had questioned one of those indicted for the Maamtrasna murders who had told him that 'Head Constable Whelehan had these men organized to commit murder.' He was aided and abetted by 'a man called Tracy who was mentioned to me as the author of outrages'. Tracy, Louden went on to claim, had been brought over to London to testify for *The Times* but had been withdrawn as a witness.[5] Louden's information was not entirely newly minted. In its issue of 15 October 1887, *United Ireland* claimed to have evidence that Head Constable Whelehan (a policeman who also operated under an alias, 'Gerald Whelan') had been conducting covert operations for the RIC as far back as 1875.

Both Louden and *United Ireland* were on solid ground, legally at least, where Whelehan was concerned. This was because, whether or not their allegations had any validity, the former Head Constable was not around to rebut the serious charges being made against him. In August 1887, acting on information received from an informer named James Cullinane, Whelehan had prepared

*A similar allegation was made in the House of Commons by East Clare MP Joseph Cox against a colleague of Whelehan's, Head Constable Maurice O'Halloran. (Alfred E. Turner, *Sixty Years of a Soldier's Life*, 637.) Suspicions were also expressed in briefs for Special Commission defence counsel about Castleisland Head Constable O'Donnell, who was 'strongly suspected of having planned more than one outrage himself'. (Timothy Harrington papers, 'Instructions for cross-examination of witnesses who may be called for *The Times*', NLI, MS 8579.)

an ambush for a group of moonlighters who planned to attack the house of a 'grabber' named Thomas Sexton in Ballygastel near Lisdoonvarna, Co. Clare. There is more than a hint that 'the informer Cullinane'[6] was actually an *agent provocateur* who had initiated the attack rather than the casual recipient of inside information. The assault on Sexton's home took place, but the counterattack did not go well for the waiting ambushers. Three RIC men were injured and Whelehan's skull was crushed; he died at the scene. Cullinane, who had been a member of the moonlighting assault party, became an 'approver' and gave evidence at the trial of seven men (at Wicklow Assizes, well removed from County Clare), some of whom received long prison sentences.[7]

In his cross-examination of Louden, Sir Henry James was unable to shake the witness's testimony about what seemed to amount to a death squad led by a senior RIC officer. It was a template freely and frequently adopted just over thirty years later by off-duty RIC members against prominent republicans or

Sir Charles Russell cross examines Thomas Beach (Henri Le Caron)

their fellow-travellers.* Louden was, in the words of the *London Daily News*, 'raising the curtain over a fragment of the life of contemporary Ireland, a life as strange and unintelligible to the people of London as if it were another planet'.[8]

Beach becomes Le Caron, becomes Beach, 5-12 February 1889

The startling appearance at the Special Commission of Thomas Billis Beach, aka Major Henri Le Caron (the 'Major' was his American Civil War rank), has been dealt with earlier. It was a potentially explosive coup for *The Times*, facilitated by its sometime contributor and newly appointed Scotland Yard assistant commissioner in charge of CID, Robert Anderson. Beach's appearance, according to Davitt, came as a complete surprise to the Parnellites, who had not been forewarned 'by our friends or agents in America'.[9] Beach's job was to link the Parnellite leadership to the militant activists and dynamitards of Irish-America. Sir Charles Russell's job was to underplay the extent of the witness's knowledge of the wider nationalist movement (beyond the state of Illinois) and to colour Beach as an informer, an *agent provocateur* and a cynical facilitator of dynamite plots in order to maintain his cover. To achieve his aim, Russell needed to establish the animus that existed between Irish-American extremism and Irish constitutional nationalism.

Both sides drew blood. In a boxing contest Beach would probably have won marginally on points but, in reality, both witness and inquisitor emerged relatively unscathed from what had promised at first to be a damning encounter for the Parnellites. In taking Beach/Le Caron through his evidence – a process regularly

*The killing of Cork IRA OC Tómas MacCurtain was the most obvious case in point, but, for example, the murder of Navan, Co. Meath post office official Thomas Hodgett was one of many similar extra-judicial killings that can be traced to members of the Royal Irish Constabulary. (Ultan Courtney, *Sons of Fire: the Murder of Thomas Hodgett* (privately published, 2022).)

interrupted by objections from Russell mostly concentrated on the question 'does he know this of his own personal knowledge?' – the most controversial revelation surrounded the second of two meetings in 1881 between Parnell and the undercover British spy.

Beach's testimony quickly landed on his spring 1881 trip to Europe, undertaken at the instigation of Devoy, during which he met Patrick Egan in Paris. The Land League treasurer advised the British agent, in an unguarded conversation, that Parnell was a 'revolutionist to the backbone'. Later Beach was able to confirm this alleged fanaticism for himself during a forty-five-minute meeting with Parnell in the House of Commons. The conversation was reported to Anderson within hours.[10] Parnell, in Beach's words, asked for his support in ending any tensions between the Clan and the IPP/Land League. Their objectives were one and the same. 'There need be no misunderstanding,' Parnell assured Beach:

> We are working for a common purpose, for the independence of Ireland, just the same as you are working for. Doctor, I have long since ceased to believe that anything but the force of arms will ever bring about the redemption of Ireland.

Parnell added that 'he did not see any reason why, when we were prepared, had sufficient money, were armed and organised, a successful insurrectionary movement could not be inaugurated in Ireland'.[11]

The next time the two men met was at around noon on 6 February 1889, when Parnell made a noisy and distracting entrance into Probate Court No. 1 as Beach was testifying. As Parnell seated himself, Beach 'just glanced at him, curiously'.[12] Beach's difficulty in attempting to advance the *Times*'s cause was that, while he had gleaned much gossip during his two decades in the IRB and Clan na Gael, he had not spent all that much time in 'the room where it happens'. Hence Russell's frequent interruptions with the salient question 'does he know this of his own personal knowledge?'

Much of the evidence *The Times* wished to extract from him was in the form of hearsay, to which Russell immediately took a torch.

Beach had access to, and had copied, many compromising internal Clan documents, but the admissibility of these, in the absence of the originals, was also open to challenge. This documentation often did little more than expose the masonic bureaucracy of the Clan, 'half of whose time', according to a lawyer of Davitt's acquaintance, 'seems to have been occupied in concocting ridiculous cipher circulars which could conceal as many secrets as a sieve could hold water, and in wasting the other half of their time in securing the destruction of these silly documents'.[13] Neither could Beach testify, in any meaningful way, to the relationship between Irish politicians and Irish-American militants. The only Irish 'player' with whom he had had much direct contact was Egan, largely because of the latter's 1883 flight to the USA.

On 7 February, almost three days into Beach's evidence, Russell was unleashed on the man he pointedly refused to call 'Le Caron'. It did not take Parnell's counsel long to extract from Beach the disconcerting information that the documentation he had brought with him into court – his espionage reports to Anderson from the USA – had been handed over to him by the assistant commissioner of the London Metropolitan Police. He was also forced to concede that he had been painstakingly coached. He had gone over his secret reports thoroughly with Houston before he presented himself to give testimony. He insisted, however, that the decision to end his career as 'a military spy in the service of my country' had been entirely his own. He had been unimpressed, from afar, by the case being made by counsel for *The Times* – this was 'rather hard on the attorney general,' observed Russell puckishly – and had decided to swoop in and save the day by offering his own informed perspective on the network of relations between Irish-America and the Parnellites. Just as his high-risk espionage activities had been prompted by his patriotism, so too, he insisted, was his decision to expose those activities on behalf of *The Times*. He was motivated by altruistic considerations only.

The prospect of reward played no part in his appearance before the Commission.

Bar forcing an admission that, before his 1881 House of Commons meeting with Parnell, he was aware that the *Irish* Fenians were at loggerheads with the Parnellites, Russell hardly laid a glove on Beach. He left the witness box on 12 February, 'smilingly … found a quiet corner on the solicitor's bench, right in front of their lordships, and became an interested spectator of the trial of which, for a whole week, he himself had been the hero'.[14] However, his testimony had failed to provide the expected fireworks and, in the words of the *New York Times*, was a 'complete failure', although the newspaper also acknowledged that 'his story [was] practically unshaken'.[15] The influential international newspaper concluded that 'a spy who had been on intimate terms with the plotters for twenty years was not able to adduce any testimony that raised a reasonable suspicion of their complicity. The spy's testimony really disposes of *The Times*' charges against Parnell.'[16]

'Beach' may well have decided to shrug off 'Le Caron' by testifying before the Special Commission and, therefore, ending two decades of part-time employment as a British agent in a dangerous environment. The reward from *The Times* for his testimony, notwithstanding his claims of unqualified altruism, was a stipend and a 'safe house'. However, Beach, by some accounts at least, did not relax into his new life. His appearance before the Commission ended the American phase of his espionage career, but it did not end his undercover existence, even as he entered a nineteenth-century version of a witness protection programme. He undertook some work for *The Times* and published his memoir, *Twenty-Five Years in the Secret Service*, in 1892. Thereafter, however, he became increasingly paranoid, fearing the prospect of being poisoned by agents of the Clan. He died of appendicitis complications on April Fool's Day 1894, barely five years after opting for the quiet life. Such was the misery of his last years that, when his death was reported, 'many people suspected that he had really been spirited abroad to rescue him from the terror in which he lived'.[17]

The ramifications for Robert Anderson of Le Caron's testimony were instantaneous. His name had been mentioned early in the spy's testimony, and he was criticized in the House of Commons for playing fast and loose with classified documents. Among those in the vanguard of the attacks was the former Home Secretary, Sir William Harcourt, who, in Anderson's words, 'declared war upon me'.[18] Harcourt accused Anderson of 'allow[ing] himself to be made a tout for the *Times* newspaper', betraying 'the secrets of the department' (the Home Office) and handing over his 'informers' (plural) 'to *The Times* without the consent of the Secretary of State'. Harcourt insisted that, had this happened on his watch, Anderson 'would not have remained twenty-four hours in Scotland Yard'.[19]

As the *Times*'s case wound down, Anderson pressed Webster and James to be allowed to respond to these charges by appearing before the commissioners. He was assured that he would be called, but this did not happen. Sir Henry James overruled the attorney general in agreeing to give the spymaster a hearing. Instead, in a letter to *The Times* on 20 March 1889, Anderson offered his rebuttal of the hostile narrative. This held that Anderson had been instrumental in persuading Beach to testify at the Commission. In fact, Anderson claimed, the reverse was true. When Beach had arrived in Britain in December 1888, to attend his father's funeral, he had reiterated a previously expressed desire to shrug off the 'Le Caron' persona and give evidence on behalf of *The Times*. Anderson claimed that he had attempted to dissuade his 'asset': 'I went on to speak of the terrible risks and penalties he would incur by coming forward, and I urged him strongly to reconsider his position.'

Beach, however, would not be thwarted. When, according to Anderson, with the *Times*'s cause disappearing underwater, John MacDonald, the newspaper's manager, appealed to the CID chief to help him find a witness who could attest to the 'American part of the case', he bowed to the inevitable and put Beach in touch with Houston. That, at least, was the spymaster's version of events, as recounted in *The Times* in March 1889. However, a letter of MacDonald to Anderson on 10 January 1889 strongly suggests otherwise. Beach's potential appearance before the Commission had clearly been broached shortly after his temporary return to Britain in December 1888. 'If your man is not available …', MacDonald wrote of Beach/Le Caron, 'the case will have been virtually concluded and that section of it embraced in *your* articles (my italics) no longer needful to be gone into.'[20] The letter also offers solid proof that MacDonald lied to the Commission in February 1889, when he claimed not to know who had written the three 'Behind the Scenes in America' articles.

When it came to authorizing Beach to consult their twenty-year correspondence, Anderson argued that 'the question was not whether I should assist *The Times*, but whether I should set myself to thwart the court'. He looked into a pure heart and, his conscience clear, declined to plead any form of privilege for the documents. He held 'no official position' as a secret service 'handler' and 'the letters in question do not come within the definition contained in the Official Secrets Act. They were never on record in a government office. They were never "filed" in a public department. I kept them at my private residence.' Thus did the pedantic spymaster make a virtue of his obsessive determination to be the sole conduit of Beach's intelligence.

A few months after he was smuggled into obscurity, Beach, along with Houston and Sergeant Patrick McIntyre (of the Scotland Yard CID), were to be found in Paris still 'trying to substantiate the Pigott letter'.[21] According to McIntyre – who later had a serious falling out with Le Caron/Beach – they were there at the behest of the Walter family and, in his own case, with the approval of Anderson. In a series of articles for *Reynolds's Newspaper* in 1895, entitled 'Scotland Yard: Its Mysteries and Methods', McIntyre told a convoluted tale of intrigue and double-dealing associated with the continued search by *The Times* for some version of the truth about the facsimile letter – any version that did not accord with the (now almost universally accepted) account offered by Pigott to Labouchère and Sala. The first port of call of the 'three fishers', as McIntyre describes the Parisian team, was the ubiquitous Patrick Casey, 'a man who knew all that was going on in connection with the letters', at least according to McIntyre. Casey, no doubt being plied with drink and the promise of a finder's fee, appeared to be co-operating with the agents of *The Times*. To help move things along, John P. Hayes was summoned from the USA. Once he was sure his expenses were being paid, he too turned up in Paris. But there were wheels within wheels within wheels. According to McIntyre, Casey was keeping his brother Joseph well-informed about what was going on, and:

> Joseph was repeating this information to Mr. Michael Davitt, who, in his turn, was communicating it to some of his friends in the Irish parliamentary party. It only remains to be said that one of those parliamentary colleagues was kindly supplying Mr. Soames with the whole story. Who this traitorous MP was is not for me to say. And thus the information went round and round.

Sir Walter Scott's *Marmion: A Tale of Flodden Field* anticipated the Special Commission by eighty years, but he could have been discussing the secretive underbelly of the tribunal when he wrote the lines, 'Oh, what a tangled web we weave, / When first we practise to deceive!'

The pursuit of Sheridan and Millen

Because Beach's testimony had been something of a damp squib, and because it was followed a few weeks later by the definitive discrediting of Pigott, *The Times* found itself in dire straits. All the newspaper had to offer after the humiliating exposure of the forger was a tedious resumption of the litany of Irish agrarian crime – largely a matter of public record and private apathy – which had stirred little enough interest before Sir Charles Russell had dislodged the main supporting plank of the newspaper's case. A game-changer was required, so the newspaper went in pursuit of two extremist icons who, unlike Beach, had not spent their activist careers shuffling paper and eavesdropping on inadmissible Clan gossip.

One turned out to be a canny double-dealer, at least by his own somewhat dubious account. The other was, unlike Beach, an unacknowledged British spy.

The name of P. J. Sheridan had been invoked so often at the Commission as to confer upon him a sort of celebrity status. During the Land War he had been a Land League organizer. This, from the perspective of *The Times*, was a euphemism for an instigator of agrarian 'outrage'. Parnell nominated him during the negotiation of the Kilmainham Treaty as the Land League operative who could, if he was instructed to do so, turn off the tap of agrarian violence. The convicted Invincible, Patrick Delaney, testifying to the Special Commission in the hope of amnesty, identified Sheridan as a fellow member of that cadre of assassins. His revolutionary credentials were impeccable – which made the prospect of his appearance as a *Times* witness all the more appealing.

Ever since the Invincible evacuation of 1883, when a number of activists – nominally affiliated with the Land League alone – had felt an urgent need to be anywhere but within range of Superintendent John Mallon, Sheridan had been running two ranches with over 3,000 sheep in Pueblo, Colorado. By 1886, however, it appears that sheep farming might have lost at least some of its appeal for the former Fenian. As far back as April 1884 there were hints that Sheridan was seeking alternative employment. In 1886 Sheridan made an approach, by letter, to the British embassy in Washington DC. He 'had been robbed during forced exile from Ireland' and wanted to recover some property in County Roscommon. Could he be given safe passage to Ireland to sort out his affairs?[22] Rightly or wrongly, this approach was interpreted by the British ambassador, Lionel Sackville-West, as a tentative prelude to an offer to switch sides by a 'wily and dangerous character', a well-positioned member of Clan na Gael who was a vocal supporter of the dynamite campaign and who knew – possibly literally – where many of the Land War bodies were buried. Sackville-West's assumption was that Sheridan had an ulterior motive for making a journey that appeared to have little to do with a lawsuit that 'does not seem absolutely to call for his personal presence'.[23]

Overtures from *The Times* to Sheridan began at around the same time as William O'Shea was testifying to the Commission. By then, behind the scenes, the newspaper was becoming extremely nervous about the provenance of the 'Parnell letters'. Obtaining the co-operation of Sheridan was a vital insurance policy. Hopes were high at Printing House Square as emissaries were despatched to negotiate with the jaded sheep farmer. The first ambassador was a Montreal private detective named J. F. Kirby (code name 'Mohawk'), who arrived in Colorado in mid-October 1888. Kirby carried with him glad tidings from *The Times*. In exchange for his testimony, the newspaper was prepared to pay £20,000 for Sheridan's (code name 'Henry') testimony.[24] This would be disguised as the purchase of his sheep and his farms. However, what *The Times* and the potential witness were initially unaware of was that the transatlantic messages between the newspaper and Sheridan were being passed on by a friendly New York Western Union clerk to the Parnellites. Most of these were read into the record of the House of Commons on 4 March 1890 by Timothy Harrington MP, to the discomfiture of Attorney General Sir Richard Webster. Webster emphatically denied having ever laid eyes upon any of the originals. It is highly probable that he was lying.

Although they were encoded, it did not take much to break the cipher – the 'code' mimicked the ultra-simplistic Clan na Gael-style single letter shift and was merely an alternative to telegraphic transmission *en clair* – although at least one crucial

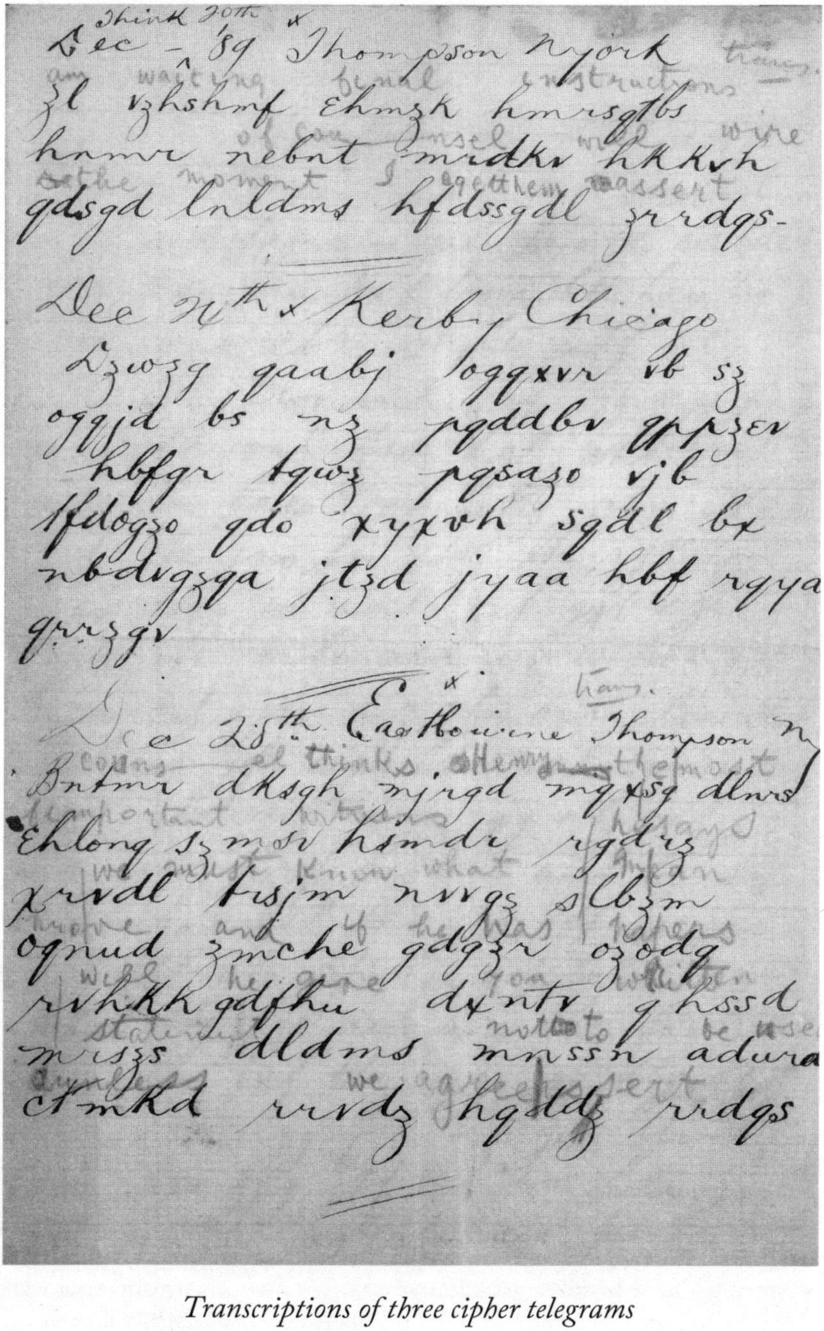

Transcriptions of three cipher telegrams

telegram* proved exceptionally difficult to decode. This was finally decrypted, according to Davitt, by 'a distinguished Irishman, a learned embodiment of all the sciences'.**

On 19 November 1888 Kirby wired Soames with encouraging news. 'Have been with Sheridan three days. He will give whole history of Land League that will convict if I buy his two ranches and 3,000 sheep, price £25,000.'[25] (The equivalent of almost £3m today.) Sheridan, or so it appeared from this cablegram, had gone 'full Pigott' and was offering *The Times* a black bag, allegedly 'containing letters of Parnell's, Dillon's, Egan's, Davitt's and others which will completely sustain *The Times*'s charges'.[26] Davitt notified Alexander Sullivan, the Chicago Clan leader, of Sheridan's potential betrayal. However, he did not risk naming the former Land League organizer as the high-level Clan official who appeared to be about to defect, instead calling him 'Buncomb' in his telegram. Davitt assumed that there was enough information in the cable for Sullivan to work out who 'Buncomb' was. In his autobiography Tim Healy claimed that 'this unwisdom caused deplorable results' and may have emboldened Sullivan to deliberately misidentify the alleged turncoat, and to commission the infamous murder of his deadly Chicago rival, Dr Patrick Cronin, whose naked body was discovered in a drain less than a month later.[27] Cronin, because of his well-publicized animosity towards Sullivan,*** had also been a possible target of *The Times*.[28]

*From 24 December 1888 (see image), which read, 'Never allow drafts to be drawn on me. Cannot accept yours. Have cabled two hundred and fifty Bank of Montreal. When will you sail? Assert.' Assert was the code name of Joseph Soames.

**Tim Healy claimed in the *Freeman's Journal* to have decoded a number of the telegrams, but it appears to have been the serviceable Archbishop Walsh who decrypted the more tricky communication after *The Times* changed its code when Healy let slip that it had been cracked. (Healy, *Letters and Leaders*, vol. 1 296.)

***Cronin was also convinced, correctly, that Sullivan's ally, Henri Le Caron, was a British spy. Le Caron, when consulted by *The Times*, described Cronin as a 'professional scoundrel and a liar'.

Negotiations between Sheridan and *The Times* were prolonged. They extended well into 1889, by which time Kirby had been replaced as negotiator by a civil servant (an employee of the British Museum) named Birch. In April 1889 the newspaper's new agent telegraphed *The Times* in a panic. His sense of dread, however, did not come close to matching the foreboding of Sheridan himself. This was because Soames, in his February testimony to the Special Commission, had blurted out some of the details of the approaches to Sheridan. As a result the former Land League organizer had, or so he told Birch, been sentenced to death *in absentia* by the Clan. Sheridan had been obliged to hire two 'heavies' with Winchester rifles to guard his life and his property, which he now insisted that *The Times* must purchase.[29] This otherwise unwelcome development, however, looked like it was working to the advantage of *The Times*. 'His life is sought;' wrote Birch,* 'hence he threatens that he will now go to London and prove *The Times*'s justification. His life is in hourly jeopardy here … He will on the stand and otherwise prove the Parnell letter, and his and others' complicity.'[30] Birch's reference to the facsimile letter, which had officially been disowned by *The Times* after the dissection of Pigott, affords us further evidence that the newspaper was still attempting to validate its authenticity.

It has been claimed by Michael Davitt, R. Barry O'Brien (who refers to it as 'a comical aspect of the case')[31] and others that, throughout the entire affair, Sheridan was leading *The Times* in a merry dance. The reluctance of *The Times*, reflected in the increasingly cantankerous urgings from Kirby, who believed he had his fish on the hook and did not want to lose him, suggests that the newspaper itself was sceptical about Sheridan's bona fides and was reluctant to spend such an enormous sum of money. *The Times*, over the course of a seduction that lasted from November 1888 until July 1889, regularly sought evidence from Kirby and/

*The cypher correspondence has also been attributed to Kirby but he appears to have given way to Birch by April 1889. (Ó Broin, *The Prime Informer*, 88.)

or Birch that Sheridan had anything useful to offer, in the form of documentation, to back up his proposed testimony.[32] While Sheridan did ultimately collaborate with Davitt *et al.*, it is possible that he only did so once his negotiations with the newspaper had been exposed to the Commission by the thoughtless Soames, and his life had been placed in danger. During the summer of 1889 he was still in talks with *The Times* but he was now passing on details of the negotiations to Davitt. William Joyce, the resident magistrate appointed to provide Dublin Castle archive material to *The Times* for the duration of the Special Commission, claimed that, after the failure of Birch to secure the appearance of Sheridan, he (Joyce) was approached to 'undertake the mission'. Joyce was personally apprised by Birch of the course of the negotiations – a campaign characterized by Joyce as 'the attempt to suborn a witness by huge bribery'. Joyce concluded that Sheridan 'was playing a part' and refused to have anything to do with what he viewed as both a corrupt enterprise and a pointless charade.[33] If Sheridan was indeed an agent of the Parnellites, the increasingly hapless newspaper had succumbed to that old saw, 'Fool me once, shame on you. Fool me twice, shame on me.'

However, the Parnellites may have had an especially compelling reason to keep Sheridan as far away from the Commission as possible. There remains a possibility that Parnell, on his release from Kilmainham Jail in May 1882, a short while before the Phoenix Park murders, was inducted into the Irish Republican Brotherhood by Sheridan.[34] Were the former Fenian/Invincible to have testified to that effect, while it would not have entirely mitigated for *The Times* the impact of Pigott's collapse, it would have caused a sensation and gone a long way to confirming the newspaper's central thesis. Michael Davitt's papers contain a hint of the extent to which Parnell might have been prepared to go to prevent Sheridan from sailing for England. A note written by Davitt's occasional sparring partner, the double-agent Matthew O'Brien (alias Sinclair), was intended for Soames's eyes only but somehow came into the possession of the 'amateur detective'. It describes a meeting that took place on

31 October in the house of Henry Labouchère at which O'Brien was present and at which the Sheridan 'problem' was discussed. Parnell, according to O'Brien's account, was adamant that under no circumstances was Sheridan to be allowed to testify; 'tell Egan,' said Parnell, 'he will understand'. Both O'Brien and Labouchère's interpretation of Parnell's enigmatic remark was that 'Sheridan should be removed if necessary'. The manner of his 'removal' was to be left to Patrick Egan.[35]

Whether through intimidation, late-onset guilt or an infinite capacity for devilment, Patrick J. Sheridan did not grace the Commission with his presence, nor did he share his detailed knowledge of the excesses of the Land War with an already indifferent British public. It has been claimed that Sir Henry James extended his (already lengthy) closing address in November 1889 in the forlorn hope that the services of Sheridan could finally be secured before the evidentiary phase of the Commission came to an end. Given the interminable and prolix nature of James's valedictory ('Sir Henry's listeners ... were tired of all this ancient history,'[36] wrote John MacDonald), in which he droned on for almost a fortnight, Sheridan has a lot to answer for.

The other target of *The Times* was the well-placed double-agent Frank Millen. The attempted seduction of the retired soldier of fortune, now pursuing a second career in journalism, began in December 1888. Inspector James Thomson, who had befriended Millen in Boulogne in 1887 on behalf of Anderson, was tapped for this enterprise, except that he and his wife, Martha, were now working for *The Times*. On 13 December 1888 Thomson cabled Soames with good news:

> The final decision of F. M. is that he is now ready to come over and give evidence on three days' notice, upon payment of £5,000 down and the remaining £5,000 to be paid to him after his evidence and cross-examination ... I think him of the utmost importance. Cable reply in full.[37]

But there was a problem. This had little or nothing to do with Millen's reluctance to betray the cause of Irish nationalism – that ship had long since sailed – but was about the refusal of his New York 'handler' to prostrate himself before the newspaper's covert recruitment drive. For several years the British Consul General in New York, William Hoare, had cultivated a productive sideline in infiltration and espionage. Quite how productive was an open question that only Hoare himself could answer honestly. Hoare was reticent on the matter. Did his reticence emanate from a natural inclination to protect his sources or, as has been suggested in some quarters, from the fact that much of his 'network' was imaginary and designed to enhance his reputation within the Foreign Office? In 1890, in a series of articles for his newly established weekly newspaper *Labour World*, Michael Davitt alleged that Hoare was a veritable ball of energy when it came to covert operations. Included in his retinue of spies, at least according to Davitt, were the two sons of the late Allan Pinkerton, William and Robert, and the infamous infiltrator of the Molly Maguires in Pennsylvania, James McParland. Hoare was also responsible for placing Matthew O'Brien in the New York Post Office, where he illegally tampered with the mails on Hoare's behalf and sent bogus letters designed to entrap potential east coast Fenian activists.[38] Nicholas Gosselin, however, had reason to be more sceptical about the New York consul, finding only one legitimate informant among Hoare's retinue when he travelled to the city in 1890.[39]

The Times despatched James Thomson to New York to meet and interview Hoare, but Thomson was curtly dismissed with a refusal on the part of Hoare to co-operate with the newspaper.[40] An infuriated Balfour sent for the New York consul in May 1889 but got no further in brow-beating Hoare in their London meeting than had Thomson in New York.

Hoare's reluctance was understandable. Millen was a useful source and, like Le Caron, would be redundant if he gave evidence on behalf of *The Times*. The extent of the government's collaboration with the newspaper can be gauged from the fact that the administration was prepared to sacrifice yet another prime intelligence asset in pursuit of the suppression of Parnellism. However, Hoare had an additional motive for his obstruction of the Tory establishment. Millen had been central to the 1887 'Jubilee plot'. He had been cited repeatedly in public by securocrats and politicians as the 'brains' behind a conspiracy to blow up Westminster Abbey, along with the queen. The alleged plot was, as we have seen, largely fictional and was driven by *agents provocateurs*, among them Millen himself. Should the discomforting truth about the spurious elements of the 'Jubilee plot' emerge during a Russell or Davitt cross-examination of Millen, it would be profoundly embarrassing for the British government. Furthermore, the far-sighted Hoare could envisage the consequential administrative need for scapegoats. He could easily visualize his own name, in red, at the top of any protective memorandum composed to cover the posteriors of his superiors. The Tory government, for the sake of the *Times* alliance, might be prepared to risk the exposure of the administration's own immersion in the 'Jubilee plot' – gambling (foolishly) that the Parnellites were unaware of Millen's duplicity. Hoare was not, and proved to be resourcefully obdurate. 'Difficulties will be removed,'[41] Soames assured a frustrated Thomson obliquely in one of the wires intercepted by the Parnellites.

And so it came to pass.

The consul was ultimately circumvented with a transfer to Hawaii, then a sovereign monarchical state, and which was 6,000 miles away. His duties in Hawaii would not tax Hoare's abilities as a spymaster. The picturesque backwater, graveyard of diplomatic careers, was not noted for its Fenian activism.

However, the spate of transatlantic telegrams had alerted the Parnellites to Millen's potential defection. As he contemplated his banishment to the archipelago in the Pacific Ocean, Hoare must have been concerned that *The Times* would exercise its option on

Millen's testimony and – courtesy of a financial inducement – summon him from New York to Probate Court No. 1.

He need not have worried.

On 11 April 1889 news reached London of the sudden and inexplicable demise of General Francis Frederick Millen. He had been found slumped over his desk by his daughter Kitty in their New York apartment. Millen, like Sheridan, would not, after all, be assisting *The Times* in making its case against the Parnellites.

Had 'difficulties' been removed – by both sides – with the exile of Hoare to Hawaii and the death of Millen? While Irish-American 'royalty' showed up en masse for Millen's funeral, there must always be a lurking suspicion that, however unlikely, his unexpected passing might have been assisted by the Clan, possibly to prevent his appearance at the ailing show trial in London, or in revenge for his betrayal of the Fenian cause, an apostasy that had been suspected by some (Devoy among them) since at least 1879. There was no published evidence of foul play but, in a narrative that boasts a number of convenient deaths, none was more fortuitous than that of Millen, soldier of fortune, journalist, dynamitard and double-agent.

One of those who attended Millen's funeral was a Major Rudolph Fitzpatrick.[42] Fitzpatrick was one of the many Irish-Americans who had formed an orderly queue in the mid-1860s to keep the Foreign Office apprised of Fenian plans for the invasion of Canada.[43] There are hints in John Devoy's correspondence that Fitzpatrick may even have been peripherally involved in the organization of the 'Jubilee plot', yet another Foreign Office asset employed at the blueprint stage of an operation where the spies and *agents provocateurs* far outnumbered the members of the active service unit.[44]

The Commission grinds on … to an eventual halt

While *The Times* attempted to shore up its cause with sensational testimony from the likes of Sheridan and Millen, the nationalist

Parnell giving evidence before the Special Commission

side was putting its own case to the commissioners. This had begun with a long and detailed history lesson from Sir Charles Russell.

April Fool's Day fell on a Monday in 1889, which, since the Commission did not sit on Mondays, allowed Russell to avoid commencing what became a seven-day marathon on such an inauspicious occasion.* The address was 'the greatest and most impressive speech ever delivered on the subject of Ireland', according to the *London Daily News*.[45] Assisted by the works of those two great historiographical antagonists, W. E. H. Lecky and J. A. Froude, which lay on the table in front of him, Russell invoked Edmund Burke's famous 1775 quote – concerning Britain's slight difficulty with its American colonies – 'I do not know the method of drawing up an indictment against a whole people', and applied it rigorously to the matter in hand.[46] He ranged from a discussion of 'Grattan's Parliament' of the late eighteenth century,

*A published copy of the speech, including an extensive index, runs to 615 pages.

through a potted history of Irish land legislation, to the Land War of the 1880s. Then he topped it off with a blistering critique of the case presented by *The Times* against the Parnellites:

> There has been thrown down before your lordships a heterogeneous, confused mass of evidence, a tangled skein, without any assistance to your lordships in unravelling it, with no order of time, no order of subject, no order of place, no order of person, and it has been left to me and my learned friends to endeavour … to extract the real issues which we submit this Commission has to try.[47]

Shortly after noon on 12 April – the day on which the death of Millen was being reported in the morning newspapers – Russell concluded with the hope that the Commission 'will remove baneful misconceptions as to the character, the actions, the motives, the aims of the Irish people, and of the leaders of the Irish people' and 'hasten the day of true union, and of real reconciliation between the people of Ireland and the people of Great Britain'. The tribunal, no doubt enervated by Russell's rhetoric, then took a break of eighteen days before the nationalists called their first witness, one Charles Stewart Parnell. Russell sat quietly while the examination in chief of the Irish Party leader was left to the future Liberal prime minister, Herbert Asquith.

In the witness box Parnell engaged upon a series of denials. Contrary to the evidence of Le Caron, he had never met the *Irish World* editor Patrick Ford. Contrary to the report of the *Irish World*, he had not referred to the severing of 'the last link' in his infamous 1880 Cincinnati speech. Neither was the Land League associated with the Fenian movement. He had not, as O'Shea had alleged, asked for police protection after the Phoenix Park murders. Le Caron's account of their House of Commons meeting was 'entirely imaginary'. And so on and so forth.

At 11.30 a.m. on 1 May Asquith gave way to Webster's cross-examination of Parnell. In his landmark biography of the Irish Party leader, F. S. L. Lyons is scathing about the attorney general's performance. 'If Sir Richard Webster had been a better informed and more intelligent man, Parnell's nine days of interrogation … might have been an unmitigated disaster'.[48] As it was, the only major error on the part of the Irish leader was a self-inflicted wound at the end of a long day of questions. Asked why he had told the House of Commons in January 1881 that secret societies had ceased to exist in Ireland, when this was palpably untrue, he replied thoughtlessly, to the astonishment of observers, 'it is possible that I was endeavouring to mislead the House on the occasion'.[49] He attempted to recover from the error first thing the following morning by claiming that, obviously, he had been referring not to Fenianism but to agrarian Ribbon societies. 'I knew at the time,' he told the commission, 'that the great Fenian organisation had branches all over Ireland.'[50]

One wonders how the description 'great', when applied to the IRB, weighed on the minds of the commissioners as they prepared their report through the winter of 1889/90.

The Special Commission report

> 'A mountain was in labour … but it gave birth to a mouse.'
>
> Aesop

> 'We find that all the letters produced by Pigott … are forgeries and we entirely acquit Mr. Parnell and the other respondents of the charge of insincerity in their denunciation of the Phoenix Park murders.'[51]
>
> Commissioners' Report, February 1890

There is an endgame known in chess as the 'Philidor position'. It comes into play when, in addition to the two kings, a single rook is defending the almost empty board against a rook and a pawn. The eighteenth-century French composer and chess connoisseur

François-André Philidor devised a strategy to ensure that the defending player, against the odds, could manage to achieve stalemate – to pull off a draw. Had the Special Commission been a chess game, *The Times* would have lost its queen (the 'facsimile' letter) in the middlegame, after a lethargic opening. However, channelling Philidor, it arguably managed to cling on until total victory was not possible for either side. That, at least, is the logic of the report of the three commissioners, a document that was neither fish nor flesh.

On 24 October, just over a year after its opening session, dialogue became monologue. It was time for closing submissions. Davitt took five days to complete his valedictory. Sir Henry James took more than twice as long (twelve days) to wave goodbye on behalf of *The Times*. He finally resumed his seat on the afternoon of 22 November. After moments of high drama interspersed with days of utter tedium – the largely soporific *Times*/Tory indictment of constitutional Irish nationalism finally petered out.

A largely indifferent nation (Britain) and its cynical counterpart (Ireland) now waited for the commissioners to parse just over a year of testimony, separate the few grains of wheat from the sacks full of chaff, and offer their views on the precise nature of the relationship between the leadership of Irish nationalism and violent extremism.

'May it please Your Majesty,' the report began, in the forlorn hope that anything that followed would gladden the heart of the reigning monarch:

> We the undersigned Commissioners, appointed under the 'Special Commission Act, 1888' to inquire into the report upon the charges and allegations made against certain members of parliament and other persons in the course of the proceedings in an action entitled O'Donnell *versus* Walter and another, having inquired into the said charges and allegations, humbly report to Your Majesty as follows:[52]

One hundred and sixty-two pages later and the Irish Parliamentary Party was home free, though not totally in the clear. The report landed softly in February 1890 and, according to Lyons, 'preserved a balance so exact as to allow each side to claim victory'.[53]

Parnell and the Irish Parliamentary Party were exonerated of charges of complicity in agrarian violence. However, the commissioners also found that 'the respondents did enter into a conspiracy by a system of coercion and intimidation to promote an agrarian agitation against the payment of agricultural rents, for the purpose of impoverishing and expelling from the country the Irish landlords, who were styled the "English Garrison"'.

This was, by and large, the job description of the Land League.

The commissioners also found that Davitt and certain members of the Irish nationalist leadership 'joined in the Land League organization with the intention by its means to bring about the absolute independence of Ireland as a separate nation'.[54]

The job description of the Irish Parliamentary Party.

As Parnell observed, it was 'just about what I would have said myself'.[55] The Gladstonian Liberals were also able to greet the report with a relieved shrug and maintain their alliance with the IPP. Just as Irish MPs had chosen to forget the abuses of governmental power evident in, for example, the Maamtrasna trial and executions, the Liberals had put the Phoenix Park murders behind them. The Tories, with far less skin in the game, were unwilling to do likewise. The Irish Home Rulers, while avowedly being held to account for sins of the recent past, were really being punished for crimes against empire, and, in the short term at least, that process would continue.

The Times could point to some 'positives' – a mild adverse finding against Davitt was about as good as it got – but those crumbs of comfort were mostly to be discovered in the months of evidence of agrarian anarchy in rural Ireland. These it had painstakingly reported in newspaper columns that were duly passed over unread by the bulk of its readership. The modest £5,000 defamation settlement paid out to Parnell was a mere down payment on the estimated £200,000 in costs incurred by the newspaper in prosecuting its (and the Salisbury administration's) case. It was a penal sum that almost bankrupted 'The Thunderer'. The third volume of the newspaper's own history bemoans the fact that *The Times* 'was left to bear the costs of what was virtually a State prosecution'.[56] But left to bear the costs it was. And those were not merely financial in nature. There had been severe damage to its standing as well. 'The paper's reputation for infallibility was gone forever',[57] and even its own historians accepted that 'the mid-Victorian legend of the inerrancy of *The Times* was exploded'.[58]

Brighter days, however, lay ahead for *The Times*, psychologically if not financially. The failure of the Tories and their 'in-house' journal to, in Burke's phrase, press home its 'indictment against a whole people' would quickly be rectified without being reversed. Within a year the gun would, once again, be trained on Parnell. This time, however, he would not be able to dodge the bullet.

From the point of view of the political establishment, the humiliating eclipse of *The Times* would be more than compensated for by the O'Shea divorce case. It would, however, be a mistake to see this outcome as a stroke of luck. A 'stroke' it most certainly was. Luck, however, had little to do with it.

PART III
REVELATIONS

11

THEATRE OF THE ABSURD

The Wardour Street Snake Pit

'He had on a filthy flannel shirt, a still more filthy white coat with the collar turned up, and a pot hat. In his hand he carried a shiny leather bag. I could not help thinking as he vanished into space, that he ran the risk of being arrested as the Whitechapel murderer.'[1]

Henry Labouchère MP (on Parnell's nocturnal surveillance activities), November 1888

'The younger generation of Irish men have simply learned that all secret societies are nothing but the hunting ground of informers and spies … all recent physical force movements were organised by the subsidised agents of the government. The object of these agents was to keep such things alive and thus to prevent their own occupation from becoming extinct.'

Former Special Irish Branch detective Sergeant Patrick McIntyre, *Reynolds's Newspaper*, 1895

'Parnell suspected me of having got the facsimile letter for the *Times*.'[2]

William O'Shea to Joseph Chamberlain, 28 December 1888

'Under the circumstances of our Secret Service when the moment of action arrives a certain amount of fiction is inevitable.'[3]

Nicholas Gosselin, 7 October 1896

Wardour Street, September 1888

The killer struck three times in Whitechapel that month. Twice in the same night. Annie Chapman was his (or her) second victim on 8 September, in Hanbury Street. Three weeks later, on 30 September, he took the lives of Elizabeth Stride and Catherine Eddowes. The city of London – or at least those who traversed the streets in the small hours of the morning – was in a state of panic. The authorities were on the lookout for a single man on foot, probably disguised and armed with a surgical knife. He had killed at least four women by the end of September 1888. He would claim the life of a fifth before 'retirement', death, imprisonment on some lesser charge or the fear of detection brought about the end of his short but traumatising dominance of east London's 'nighttown'.

Meanwhile, a short distance away, another man was stalking his prey in the alleyways of Soho. He was tall, slightly stooped, bearded and anxious to conceal his identity. Dangerously oblivious of at least some of the risks he was running – from curious policemen on the lookout for suspicious unaccompanied males – Charles Stewart Parnell's entire focus was on his own obnoxious quarry, Captain William O'Shea.

Parnell could have hired a detective to stalk O'Shea through London W1, but he preferred to do the job himself. He waited in the shadows of Wardour Street, outside number 104, a public house named The Golden Lion. According to T. P. O'Connor, 'he used to lurk about outside, strangely muffled, and watch the doors to see if the loathed one would appear'.[4] Occasionally he would be accompanied by his secretary/bodyguard, Henry Campbell, but mostly he worked alone. The Golden Lion was known to play host to a crew of Irish renegades and drunks. One of Edward Jenkinson's former minions – still keeping his hand in – was in semi-permanent residence in a room above the establishment. He attracted the wrong sort, men like Pigott, like O'Shea. Parnell was convinced that The Golden Lion was one of the main sources of the *Times*'s allegations against himself. He was equally convinced that the husband of his mistress was up to his neck in the business.[5]

Convinced of O'Shea's capacity to orchestrate a criminal conspiracy against him, with the assistance of The Golden Lion's clients, Parnell just needed to confirm for himself that O'Shea was familiar with the pub and its hangers-on. 'He prowled about London in search of evidence,' according to one of his biographers.[6] In doing so, heavily disguised, he paid little heed to the sanguinary events just a few miles from Soho, events that were dominating the news cycle in the autumn of 1888.

Nothing would have delighted the Tory establishment more than to read of the arrest of Charles Stewart Parnell for vagrancy, or on the suspicion that he was Jack the Ripper.

That old Golden Lion crowd

Its former name was The Jolly Brewer. Before 1878 it stood at 42 Wardour Street in Soho among a warren of side streets and alleyways shared with dozens of similar establishments. Ten years later its official address was 104 Wardour Street. The Golden Lion (one of ten London public houses of that name) hadn't moved, but the buildings in Wardour Street had been numerically redesignated.

The Golden Lion has long since been demolished, and the space is occupied today by Snowflake Gelato. There was, however, no room for snowflakes at that address in the 1880s. Soho then was a haven for serious drinkers. This modest public house was owned at the time by a Mayoman, Peter Cowell, who ran it with his daughter Sarah Lynch before he handed over the establishment to her and returned to the west of Ireland.[7] That much, and little else, is known about a premises that, in addition to its regulars, attracted a shadowy collection of spies, moles, snoops, informers, *agents provocateurs* and all-round anti-nationalist reprobates. It may even have welcomed a gaggle of London-based Fenians, although probably not at the same time as the cadre of loyalist conspirators.

Exhibit A, Philip Bagenal.

With a name like Philip Henry Dudley Bagenal, he would have made an unlikely Irish nationalist. His origins – he was the son of a Carlow landowner – served to reinforce his solid unionist credentials and affiliations. He manned the barricades on behalf of his tribe in a series of books and pamphlets, railing against the Land League and the Parnellites. These included *Parnellism Unveiled* (1880) and *The American Irish and their influence on Irish politics* (1882). His vitriolic pen brought him to the attention of a troika of British unionist grandees. This self-appointed vigilante committee comprising 'two peers and a commoner' – according to Davitt, who declined to name them – probably included Lord Richard Grosvenor, the former Liberal chief whip who contributed £450 to the adventures of Richard Pigott. The other 'peer' may have been Sir Stafford Northcote, recently elevated to the Lords as 1st Earl of Iddesleigh, a former Tory Chancellor of the Exchequer and Foreign Secretary in Salisbury's cabinet up to the time of his death in January 1887.

Bagenal was tasked with the recruitment of propagandists who would collate the ostensibly abundant evidence of collusion between Parnellites, terrorists, agrarian gunmen and barnburners. In doing so, although there is no evidence that he ever frequented the Cowell establishment himself, he became the fountainhead of the Wardour Street scorpions.

Exhibit B, Captain Darnley Stewart Stephens.

Davitt's 'Major Yellow' – the *nom de guerre* Stephens is given in *The Fall of Feudalism in Ireland* – was an agent who 'was sufficiently daring to be frequently indiscreet'.[8] His indiscretions allowed Davitt to discover a surprising amount about his nefarious activities. Stephens was one of Bagenal's first recruits – Sir Stafford Northcote had recommended him – although at heart he was a committed freelancer with any number of employers at any one time. These included *The Times*. Stephens was so comfortable with the ambience of The Golden Lion that he briefly made his headquarters there, renting a room from Cowell. The Mayo-born proprietor claimed to have recognized Stephens 'as a spy from the beginning',[9] an assertion dismissed by Davitt, to whom the claim was made during an interview with Cowell in Enniscrone, Co. Sligo, on 3 October 1888.

This Irish-born former secret agent of the Crown, dismissed by Edward Jenkinson for drunkenness, was 'back in the game' by the mid-1880s. When working for Jenkinson, Stephens had put up at one of the Parisian equivalents of The Golden Lion, the Hôtel d'Alma in the Rue Volney, a short walk from the Champs-Élysées. He had left the city in a hurry when some of his papers were stolen by a jilted lover. In his flight, he abandoned his wife and his hotel bill. He established himself in The Golden Lion in 1885. Nowadays his mission would be characterized as a 'dirty tricks' operation – a combination of propaganda, espionage and misinformation.

At The Golden Lion Stephens entertained guests of like mind: men who were prepared to promote any cause working to the detriment of Irish nationalism. These included visiting scholars such as Irish-American double-agent John P. Hayes, O'Shea's bagman George Mulqueeny, the hapless Richard Pigott, cuckold-in-chief William Henry O'Shea and someone described by Davitt in *The Fall of Feudalism in Ireland* as 'a late Irish MP'[10] but identified in his notebooks as Philip Callan, a former MP who attributed his 'former' status to the hostility of Parnell and who was anxious for revenge. Their mutual loathing went back to the early days of Parnell's career, when the rising star of the Home Rule party made it clear that he disapproved of Callan's frequent drunkenness. He also suspected the Louth MP of being a reliable source of leaks to his friends in the British and Irish press.[11] After Parnell's assumption of the party leadership, he had kept Callan at arm's length, until his firm grip on the constituency nominating process led to Callan's de-selection as an IPP parliamentary candidate. Whereas the likes of Stephens were intent on the demise of Parnellism, Callan was obsessed with the annihilation of the man behind the 'ism'. As a spiteful conduit of gossip and scandal, he had other uses as well.

During his extensive investigation of the squad of malcontents and bad actors based in The Golden Lion, Michael Davitt became convinced that O'Shea and Callan convened in the public house for purposes other than liquid refreshment and reflections on their manifest grievances against Charles Stewart Parnell. However, while Cowell admitted that Stephens and Callan were in cahoots, he could not, according to Davitt, be persuaded to 'remember O'Shea meeting Callan at W. St[reet]'.[12] Cowell was more forthcoming on the relationship between Stephens and Callan. They met frequently in Wardour Street and Callan even claimed to the proprietor of The Golden Lion 'that he had got Stephens a commission'.[13] From this we can assume that Callan, who was a valued servant of *The Times*, managed to convince the newspaper to add the former police captain to its growing retinue of collaborators.

In Davitt's treasured notebook, where he sought to identify the forger of the *Times*'s 'Parnell' correspondence, he inscribed the names of his three prime suspects. Numbers one and three are Pigott and O'Shea. The name of 'number two' is expertly and determinedly crossed out in pencil but is legible with a magnifying glass. It was that of Philip Callan. Does this decisive deletion suggest that Davitt exonerated the former Louth MP? It appears that Davitt may, ultimately, have had second thoughts about the extent of Callan's involvement in what he himself believed to be a far-reaching conspiracy to 'source' and publish incriminating letters, one that went well beyond the apparent solo run of Richard Pigott. But he certainly harboured well-grounded suspicions about Callan. Before the Commission had hit its stride, in November 1888, the Irish under-secretary Sir Joseph West Ridgeway confided to Arthur Balfour that 'the Parnellites are going to produce one Hayes to confess to having forged the letters at the instigation of Phil Callan and Eugene Davis'.[14] While Ridgeway was well off the mark in his speculation, his lack of confidence in the authenticity of the letters was telling, and he was alive to the possibility of Callan's involvement in the conspiracy.*

Davitt also records frequent meetings between Pigott and Callan in Wardour Street, as well as the presence of several 'Americans'. Pigott – Davitt gleaned from an interview with Peter Cowell – 'scarcely ever visited London without calling to see him [Cowell]'.[15] At least one of the American visitors was the double-agent John P. Hayes from Philadelphia. Hayes was 'a hulking scoundrel and reputed desperado ... he was a burly-looking, brutish-mannered fellow in the prime of life, [in 1888] powerful in build, and with the face of a prize-fighter'.[16] Davitt confirmed Hayes's occasional visits to The Golden Lion during an unorthodox 'interview' with the Philadelphian in Paris, where he was accompanied by Parnell's devoted amanuensis/bodyguard, Henry Campbell. Both men armed themselves with revolvers before their encounter with the Irish-American turncoat. In February 1889, Hayes, although he was supposedly a notorious member of the dynamite faction, somehow managed to visit Dublin, along with the equally Janus-like Patrick Casey. When in Dublin, this apparently extremist Irish-American nationalist openly attempted to enlist witnesses for *The Times*.[17]

Even *after* the exposure of Pigott, Parnell refused to relinquish entirely the conviction that it was O'Shea who was the forger of the *Times* letters. The Radical MP Henry Labouchère claimed that Parnell 'went to his grave the sole man who did not believe that Pigott had forged the *Times* letters'.[18] Given the level of

*The letter also indicates that someone from within the Parnellite camp was supplying Dublin Castle with information about nationalist Special Commission strategy. Ridgeway's apparent lack of awareness of the pedigree of Hayes (a British agent) is almost as revealing. Elsewhere in the same letter, however, Ridgeway appears to be in little doubt, in November 1888, that the *Times* letters were forgeries, and that Pigott was responsible for forging them.

collaboration between the members of this Wardour Street cabal of his committed enemies, it is not impossible that the Irish Party leader was right. Pigott changed his narrative almost as often as he changed his shirt. His assertion to Labouchère and Sala that he had forged the entire cache of *Times* letters must be set against his subsequent retraction, and his claim to Shannon that he forged only some of them.

During his visits to The Golden Lion Pigott could have found any number of willing allies eager to assist him in a viable scheme to discredit Parnell. It is possible that Pigott, rather than operating in isolation, was merely part of a chain of demimonde villains paid from private (and possibly public) funds – or happily grinding their axes by working gratis – to bring Parnell to grief by fraudulent 'exposures' if that end could not be achieved legitimately by covert investigation or partisan journalism.

Another regular visitor to The Golden Lion was O'Shea's obliging bagman/batman, the Victoria Docks clerk George Mulqueeny. The excursion of Mulqueeny, on behalf of William O'Shea, to the Parisian bolthole of Patrick Casey, when seen in conjunction with the supposed forger's association with the Casey brothers, points towards a rather more complex conspiracy than the lonely (if highly profitable) road taken by Pigott, to which he owned up in February 1889. Historian Margaret O'Callaghan has said of Pigott himself that his role 'went beyond simply forging and adapting old letters from Parnell, to constructing formally what was to become the case against home rule for Tories and Irish unionists alike'.[19] In fulfilling that function he was assisted by his Wardour Street co-conspirators. It is not hard to see O'Shea (abetted by his confidant Mulqueeny) as an active and enthusiastic ally in any effort to subvert Parnellism and/or destroy Parnell. In what appears to be preparation for a series of articles, in one of Davitt's notebooks – 'Synopsis of Pigott and his Patrons or the Conspiracy behind the Forged Letters' – the amateur detective links the forger to Hayes and Stephens, indicating that Pigott was not working alone.[20] Elsewhere Davitt claims that Le Caron and MacDonald 'wanted to put Casey & Hayes in [the witness] box to swear they had seen originals of forged letters'.[21] He was also of the opinion that Pigott was not the only member of the Wardour Street circle with a talent for forgery. While Stephens was tailing him in the USA, Davitt, to indicate to his tracker that he was less than rattled by this close attention, wrote an ironic lunch invitation to his pursuer. However, Davitt records that he disguised his handwriting because 'this rascal is quite capable of resorting to any means to serve his ends'.[22]

The enduring legacy of the Wardour Street cabal – produced with considerable input from Pigott – was the so-called 'Black Pamphlet', published in 1886. Its formal title was *The Repeal of the Union Conspiracy; or, Mr. Parnell, M.P. and the I.R.B.*, and it anticipated much of the content of the 'Parnellism and Crime' series of the following year. Davitt, admittedly not a non-partisan critic but certainly a well-informed one, was scathing in his assessment of the much heralded (and expensively produced) 'Black Pamphlet'. 'It was compiled', he wrote, 'chiefly from the drunken ravings of Kasey [*sic* – Patrick Casey] and other Paris "dynamiters," the "revelations" of the spy Hayes, Pigott's pamphlet, "Parnellism Exposed"* and the statements of Captain O'Shea's friend, George Mulqueeny.'[23] This work of propaganda, which connected Parnell and the leaders of the Irish Party with the Irish-American bombing campaign, allegedly cost the Tory government (which, through Irish chief secretary Carnarvon, was negotiating with Parnell at the time it was assembled) £1,000 from the secret service fund. Ninety-three pages long, *The Repeal of the Union Conspiracy* was published anonymously. It was printed by the reputable firm of William Ridgway in Piccadilly. The pamphlet was probably the work of a committee, although there are ample traces of Pigottism throughout its talking points. The pamphlet sets out its agenda (shared with the future Tory

*The actual title was 'Parnellism Unmasked'.

government) in the first paragraph. Once the facts of what it calls 'The Repeal of the Union Conspiracy' are known, the anonymous author – writing 'from inside the conspiracy' – observes, 'I have little doubt Great Britain will decide once and forever against the concession of an independent legislature to Ireland.'[24]

The 'author' – who claims to be a reformed Fenian – in the first two pages labels the ('pompously called') Parnellites as 'a foreign conspiracy, invented by felons and traitors, fed by foreign funds and carried on by a systematic combination of agitation, terrorism, and murder'. After a detailed account of the structure of the IRB, in which several Irish MPs and former Land League activists are named as sworn recruits, or as members of the upper echelons of the organization – James O'Kelly MP comes in for particular attention – the pamphlet then becomes bogged down in an account of Fenian adventures in Canada and South Africa, before highlighting the Parisian chapter of the wider IRB movement and singling out Charles Carroll Tevis (the Foreign Office spy!) as a member of the Military Council of the IRB.

The most egregious atrocities of the Land War are then recounted in some detail before the author pre-empts the kernel of the *Times*'s case against the Parnellite movement in the Special Commission, i.e. that bloodshed was prompted by Land League platform speeches. 'Consult any newspaper of the years 1880–1, and I guarantee that it is possible to trace the invariable bloody results of a platform oration from Mr. Parnell or one of his lieutenants.'[25] The pamphlet, after a detour through the Invincibles, then returns to the Parisian haunts of those celebrated 'men of action' Eugene Davis and the Casey brothers. Since Pigott often met the Caseys in Paris, references to their supposed extremism may well have been an attempt to bolster Patrick Casey's militant credentials and divert suspicion from his extracurricular activities on behalf of the British secret service.

The final chapter of this collaborative oeuvre deals with the dynamite campaign, allegedly directed from Paris, on behalf of the Clan, by the Casey brothers.[26] Apparently Patrick Casey – in fact a fully paid-up British asset, as was Tevis, who is also cited as an extremist menace – had been 'vice-president of the Invincibles'[27] and had despatched John Daly to England to assassinate the cabinet from the Strangers' Gallery of the House of Commons. The bogus Daly 'rescue' attempt is also graphically described, albeit with one of the pamphlet's authors (Stephens) modestly declining to take any credit for his role in the operation.

By 1885, the pamphlet concluded, Parnell 'definitely and finally threw in his lot with the IRB … and assassination and dynamite will resume its place in the van of Mr. Parnell's army at no distant date'.[28] With a final self-righteous assertion that 'this is the truth the whole truth and nothing but the truth', the writer(s) piously stated, 'I have done. May God save Ireland yet.'[29]

Nationalist reaction to the 'Black Pamphlet', which contained just about enough factual material to avoid being classified as imaginative fiction, was a mixture of derision, outrage and apathy. The pamphlet appeared shortly after the introduction of Gladstone's Home Rule Bill, so the attention of most Irish nationalists was elsewhere. The *Freeman's Journal* described it as 'monstrous nonsense'.[30] The pamphlet finally came to the notice of *The Times* on 6 July 1886, after the Home Rule emergency had passed. The newspaper couldn't fail to be impressed by the tenor of the tract and complimented the work of the pamphlet's 'well-informed writer'. For its part *United Ireland* saw the hand of *The Times* itself in the compilation of the pamphlet, asking 'Is there no way of bringing this scoundrel newspaper or its scoundrel proprietor to justice?' However, it also pointed the finger squarely at Bagenal as the inspiration for the work, 'supplemented by the fine Roman hand of a gentleman who claims to have been an "oathbound Fenian" but who has adopted the profession of an I.L.P.U. pamphleteer'.[31] This was a scantily disguised reference to Pigott.

Darnley Stewart Stephens himself next saw service, briefly, in

Kerry, where he was 'arrested' for importing arms. Before he could entice the moonlighters or Fenians of Kerry into a contrived conspiracy, he was stood down by the formidable General Sir Redvers Buller, VC, British hero of various African wars, who had responsibility for security in the county and was not about to extend any hospitality towards an *agent provocateur*. Or at least not this one.

Later, at the instigation of Bagenal and the Tory Chancellor of the Exchequer, Randolph Churchill, Stephens tracked Davitt on a speaking tour of the USA while attempting to source documents that might incriminate the Land League founder. He also failed in a cack-handed plot to kidnap the Invincible co-founder Captain John McCafferty, late of the army of the Confederate States of America. In February 1887 he urgently requested an 'extraction' from the United States as, according to William Hoare, the New York Consul General, while 'on a secret mission for the Irish executive' his intentions 'had in some way been discovered by the leaders of the Fenian organisations here who had threatened his life if he did not leave the country'. In fact, Davitt had been wise to his presence and purpose, hence the cheeky luncheon invitation. Lest there be any doubt about the 'legitimacy' of Stephens's mission, the Chancellor of the Exchequer had been involved in commissioning the project and, according to Hoare, Stephens travelled to the USA armed with a testimonial from the prime minister himself.[32]

Almost inevitably, on his return to England Stephens entered the service of *The Times*. Counsel for the newspaper considered putting him into the witness box but prudently thought better of it. Any value he might have had would probably have been erased had he given honest answers under cross-examination to questions about, for example, the sources of funding for the assembly of the 'Black Pamphlet'. Unless Stephens was suddenly 'sprung' on the defence, as O'Shea had been – and even that surprise had not perturbed the Parnellites very much – the well-informed Davitt was lying in wait for his erstwhile stalker.

'A bird never flew on one wing'

As well as being a familiar phrase in Irish social transactions, 'a bird never flew on one wing' is also the title of a painting by the twentieth-century Irish modernist artist Harry Kernoff. The painting depicts two men raising pints, while in the background the names of hundreds of Dublin pubs are inscribed on a remarkably detailed expanse of wallpaper.

Neither did a conspiracy ever fly on one wing, albeit its origins may have revolved around a single Soho licensed premises. Although – largely based on his own admissions – there are valid reasons to believe that Richard Pigott acted alone in conning the gullible Houston, and later the equally credulous MacDonald and Buckle of *The Times*, there is considerable circumstantial evidence suggesting that he was only one spoke in the wheel driving a much larger conspiracy against Parnell and Parnellism.

That Richard Pigott forged each of the letters he passed on to *The Times* has long been historiographical holy writ. Because of his evisceration by Sir Charles Russell and his subsequent self-incrimination before his escape to France and Spain, responsibility for the hoodwinking of *The Times* has always been laid solely at his door. However, what is usually forgotten is that Pigott's 'confession' was not extracted by skilled cross-examination by Russell while his plaything was under oath. Pigott made no admission of guilt, in person, before the Special Commission. And, as has already been pointed out, his 'confession' that he was a forger consisted of two mutually contradictory admissions of guilt, each consisting of precisely what his interlocutors wanted to hear.

Pigott was certainly not a lone wolf. His regular appearances at The Golden Lion implicate him in a much wider conspiracy. If he wanted a drink, there were many other pubs much closer to home that he could have frequented. Granted, opportunist that he was, he may have taken inspiration from the ongoing shenanigans in Wardour Street, added some of his own toxins and, 'hey presto', the appearance of a profitable cache of letters sold to *The Times*.

But it is also possible that he was merely a collaborator in the schemes supervised by Bagenal and Stephens, which included the double-agents John P. Hayes and Patrick Casey, William Henry O'Shea and George Mulqueeny, as well as the rancorous Philip Callan. One of Pigott's many narratives was that, while most of the letters sold to *The Times* were bogus, some were genuine and he had purchased these, in good faith, from renegade Fenians in Paris. His last word on the subject, the statement made to the *Times* solicitor (Shannon) two days before his disappearance, was an admission of partial responsibility only. Pigott denied having forged the 'facsimile' letter. Of course, in a signed statement witnessed by Henry Labouchère the previous day, he had, in the hope of extracting money, admitted to having forged *all* the letters. History has, quite sensibly, chosen to accept *that* version of events.

At around the time of the failure of Gladstone's Home Rule Bill in 1886, there were persistent rumours of a cache of documents abandoned in Paris by the fugitive Frank Byrne. These documents, according to those in the know, could destroy Parnell and many of his close associates. Because of the potential for profit, these were rumours that the 'Fenian' stalwarts of the Hotel d'Alma were not inclined to quash. There was brass in that muck, gold in that ink. O'Shea's despatch of Mulqueeny to Paris suggests that he too was on the trail of the phantom cache of incriminating documents. Mulqueeny's audience with Casey and his subsequent Dorchester Hotel tussle with the British agents, Hayes and Tevis, make little sense otherwise.

While there is little to no doubt that Richard Pigott forged all of the second bundle of *Times* letters – the ones unveiled during the *O'Donnell v. Walter* case – the precise status of the 'facsimile' letter has always been disputed. *The Times* newspaper's own history continued to tout its possible authenticity decades after Sir Richard Webster had conceded to the Special Commission that it was a forgery. As we have already seen, in late 1889 the newspaper was still actively working on the assumption that 'Letter No. 2' was genuine.

One of Davitt's many well-informed sources was a detective named W. J. Reynolds. Davitt gives him the alias 'Thompson' in his notebooks. Fortunately for Davitt, Reynolds was owed a considerable sum of money (£138) by the *Times* solicitor, Soames, who was refusing to pay.[33] In retaliation, Reynolds offered to swear an affidavit for Davitt exposing some of the chicanery in which the newspaper had indulged. This included the interception of letters to and from Patrick Casey in Paris; collusion between Gosselin and Soames;[34] and surveillance by Reynolds of Patrick Casey in Paris – at the prompting of Houston and Le Caron – as late as September 1889 in a vain attempt at an *ex post facto* coup that would 'stand up' some of the Pigott letters.[35] Houston still stoutly maintained, in a surprisingly jocular letter to O'Shea, sent barely a week after the abject humiliation of Pigott, that, 'the ordinary man in the street is now beginning to veer round to a belief in some of the letters. My idea is that the first batch were genuine, and that the facsimile letter wh[ich] was amongst them was a bona fide document.' He lamented the fact that the *Times*'s legal team had panicked and withdrawn 'the whole of the documents'.[36]

When it comes to the facsimile, we can be morally certain that the body of the document was a clumsily fabricated forgery and that no such letter was ever knowingly signed by Parnell.

However, in the opinion of this writer, the same cannot be said of the signature itself.

Parnell deliberately misled the House of Commons on the night of 18/19 April 1887 when he claimed that the signature on the facsimile document, dated 15 May 1882, was in a hand that he had abandoned a number of years before. In conversation with colleagues, he highlighted in particular the letter 's', insisting that 'I did not make an "s" like that since 1878.' Assuming he is referring to the highly distinctive lower case 's' of 'Chas', that statement, as we will see, is untrue.

In 1885 he was still using the characteristic raised and underscored lower case 's' on letters bearing his signature. This author has closely studied a range of letters signed by Parnell dating from 1873 to 1888.

Below is a reproduction of Parnell's signature on the facsimile letter.

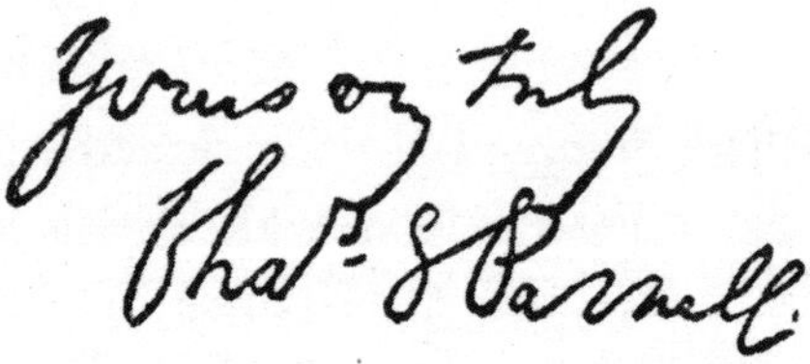
Yours very truly
Chas. S. Parnell

Compare that with the signature on a letter sent by Parnell to Irish National League treasurer, Alfred Webb in 1884, many years after he claimed to have abandoned the underscored lower case 's' of the 'facsimile' letter.[37]

Yours Very Truly
Chas. S. Parnell

The signatures appear to be almost identical. By contrast, in a letter of 1888 to the manager of the Press Association office in London, signed a year *after* the appearance of the *Times* facsimile, he had indeed changed his style of handwriting and had abandoned the raised, underscored, lower case 's'.[38]

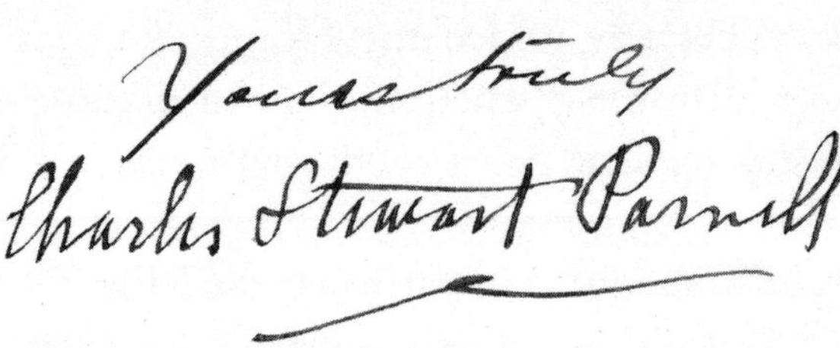
Yours truly
Charles Stewart Parnell

Was this an *ex post facto* modification designed to justify his House of Commons statement of the morning of 19 April 1887?

Parnell's personal habits come into play here. Although he could be a precise and a high-energy individual, he was lazy and sloppy when it came to his personal correspondence. He was notorious for ignoring the bulk of it, often leaving letters unopened and unanswered. He was also known to provide his trusty amanuenses (first Henry Campbell and later Henry Harrison) with blank letter paper already bearing his signature. They would then compose messages and memos to various correspondents which tallied with Parnell's intentions. He had complete confidence in both men to use the letter paper responsibly. However, he was not nearly as trusting when it came to the use that others might make of his signature. When responding to requests for autographs from members of the public, as witnessed on one occasion by his colleague T. P. O'Connor, he would carefully append his signature to the top of a piece of paper 'to prevent anything being written over the signature on that sheet of paper'.[39]

The internal evidence of the facsimile letter suggests that the signature might not have been forged by Pigott but was already inscribed when the controversial text was added.

The *Times*'s 'Letter No. 2' is an odd piece of work. It is a mirror image of a normal letter. The text is on the right-hand page while the signature is on the left. The four lines of the concluding third paragraph are squeezed into the bottom quarter of the document, prompting the suspicion that this was done to avoid having to continue overleaf where the signature was already in place and too close to the top of the page for the insertion of additional material. The definite article has been omitted before the words 'House of Commons' for what appears to be the same reason. If the text of the note had continued to the top of 'page 2', the natural assumption would be that the signature would follow immediately below. Once the text is all crammed onto 'page 1', the appearance of the signature on the facing page retains some plausibility.

Five lines into the note, three words are heavily crossed out. Why would an amanuensis, having made such an error so early in the letter, not simply have begun again on a fresh sheet? Was it because the letter had already been 'signed' before the text was written? If this is the case, is it possible that Parnell appended

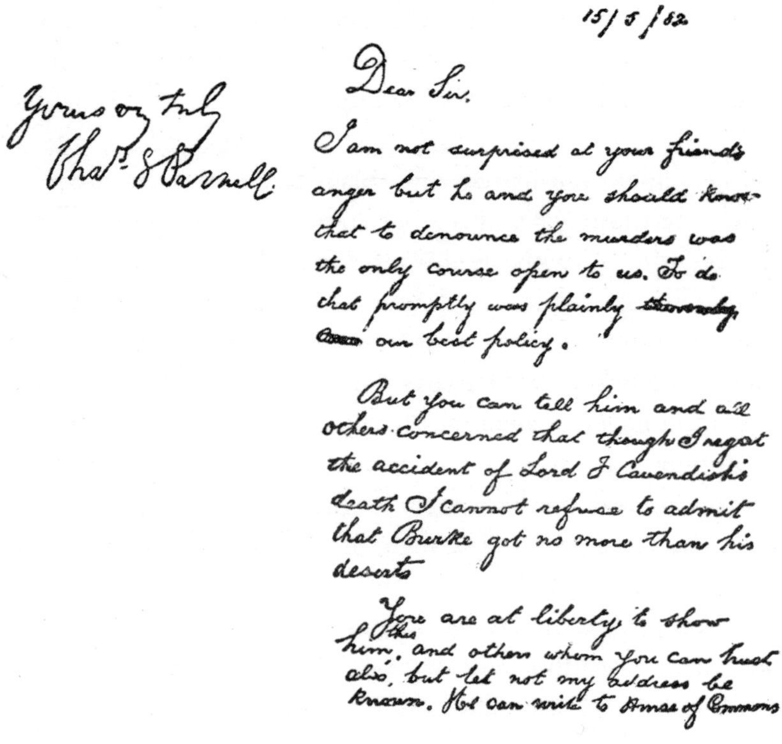

15/5/82

Dear Sir,

I am not surprised at your friends anger but he and you should know that to denounce the murders was the only course open to us. To do that promptly was plainly our best policy.

But you can tell him and all others concerned that though I regret the accident of Lord F Cavendish's death I cannot refuse to admit that Burke got no more than his deserts

You are at liberty to show him, and others whom you can trust also, but let not my address be known. He can write to House of Commons

Yours very truly

Chas. S. Parnell

his signature to a blank sheet of paper without checking to what use it had been subsequently put? This was something that he became almost paranoid about avoiding in later life.

There is one more odd inconsistency. In the forged letter that tripped him up, the one allegedly sent on 9 January 1882 Pigott misspelled 'hesitancy' and 'inexcusable'. This letter was addressed to 'Dear E', assumed to be Patrick Egan. There is, however, a further aberration that is generally overlooked. Pigott has Parnell sign off 'Your's very truly' – with an errant apostrophe between the 'r' and the 's' of 'yours'.

However, if we look again at the 'facsimile' letter, the 'yours' is spelled correctly. Pigott had several letters signed by Parnell in his possession. These were sent at the time of the purchase of his newspapers in 1881. I have checked half a dozen letters in the National Library of Ireland and in the Chamberlain collection in the University of Birmingham, all signed by Parnell. His sign-off is inconsistent. Sometimes he spells the word 'yours' correctly – sometimes with a superfluous apostrophe. On that basis it is possible that Pigott may have had examples of both in his possession. However, it is reasonable to assume that Pigott would have used the same example of Parnell's signature for *all* his forgeries. In which case they should all be consistent. 'Yours' should be spelled correctly or incorrectly in *all* of them. The 'Dear E' letter, with its errant 'your's truly' as well as the giveaway spelling of 'hesitency' is clearly a forgery. So where does that leave the facsimile letter where the 'yours' is spelled correctly?

Robert Anderson claimed in *Sidelights on the Home Rule Movement* that the text of the 'facsimile' letter was written by one Arthur O'Keeffe, an employee of the Parnellite newspaper *United Ireland*. O'Keeffe, who had strong Fenian connections, had been 'lifted' in December 1881 and lodged in Kilmainham Jail. There, according to Anderson, he became Parnell's temporary amanuensis. In a preface to the second edition of his book, Anderson claims 'to have received definite confirmation that [the 'facsimile' letter] is in the handwriting of Arthur O'Keeffe'. Unfortunately, we must either accept or reject this assurance, because he doesn't elaborate on the source of this information. Anderson speculated that Parnell's signature was obtained in advance and the letter concocted (without his knowledge) to appease Land League hard-liners disillusioned with his adherence to the 'Kilmainham Treaty'. 'Of the genuineness of the signature I feel no doubt,' Anderson wrote.[40] Despite the need to be intensely wary of Anderson's undeniable unionist beliefs and his infinite capacity for intrigue, there remains the possibility that Parnell, in Kilmainham, had pre-signed any number of letters and handed them over to O'Keeffe, at least one of which was then retained and became a much sought-after commodity some years later. The *United Ireland* employee may not have been as worthy of Parnell's trust as were Campbell and Harrison. He may even have been a bogus internee 'lifted' by the Dublin Metropolitan Police for the purposes of spying on the Kilmainham prisoners. In December 1881, at around the time O'Keeffe was taken into custody, Mallon had managed to secure some assistance from within the *United Ireland* newspaper. 'My informant who is employed in the establishment'[41] as the 'G' Division superintendent referred to his agent, was male, so he was not one of the members of the Ladies Land League who were struggling to keep the journal afloat. So either O'Keeffe was incarcerated on foot of information supplied by Mallon's spy, or he *was* Mallon's spy.

Could O'Shea have heard of the existence of this invaluable autographed sheet? Was Mulqueeny charged with obtaining it in what appears to have been a Parisian clearing house of questionable documents? Was O'Shea beaten to the punch by Pigott, or was Mulqueeny successful in his mission and was this potential landmine handed down the chain for the impoverished journalist to prime? O'Shea, whatever its true source, believed the 'facsimile letter' to be genuine and a potential 'dagger to the heart' of Parnell. This is clear from a memo written by Joseph Chamberlain of a meeting with the captain in August 1888:

> Mr. O'Shea called today. He states that he has heard from members of the Irish party in London that the first letter signed C. S. Parnell and printed in facsimile in the *Times* is undoubtedly genuine.[42]

O'Shea's narrative to the Commission, under cross-examination, was that Mulqueeny was sent to Paris to seek Casey's signature on a petition of endorsement by Clare-based Fenians. According to Davitt, however – after a conversation with Casey in Paris in October 1888 – the primary object of Mulqueeny's trip appears to have been to warn Casey against the 'swaggering fool' John P. Hayes.[43] While it is verifiably true that O'Shea did attempt to cultivate good relations with 'advanced nationalists', why would he go to so much trouble as to have Mulqueeny travel to Paris and track down Casey to persuade him to append his signature to such a document? O'Shea also used the existence of this 'petition' to justify his only admitted visit to The Golden Lion. Were both an invention to cover his association with Darnley Stewart Stephens and Pigott, while accounting for Mulqueeny's suspicious journey to Paris?

At an early stage in the *Times* campaign against Parnell, Patrick Egan, watching on from the United States and armed with numerous letters that he had received from Pigott before the Land League purchase of his three newspaper titles in 1881, wrote to Henry Labouchère pouring cold water over Parnell's growing obsession that it was O'Shea who was behind the *Times* letters. 'The fellow is incapable of playing the role of heavy villain,' Egan contended. 'I am quite convinced that the forgery part of the scheme was the sole work of Pigott.'[44]

If the former military man William O'Shea was incapable of 'playing the role of heavy villain', where does that leave the wretched Richard Pigott?

In the context of the Wardour Street scheming, an interesting insight into the understandable paranoia of the Parnellites – who could never be certain that they had not been infiltrated by agents of *The Times* (which they had, in the case of Sinclair/Matthew O'Brien) – is to be found in an exchange of letters in November 1888 involving Davitt, Charles Carroll Tevis and the future nationalist icon, Maud Gonne. The correspondence begins with an undated 1888 letter from Tevis to Davitt asking 'can you give me any information respecting a Miss Gonne … daughter of a former military attaché'.* Tevis, who had yet to meet Gonne, was enquiring on behalf of 'one of our friends who returned from Russia last night'.[45] Gonne had travelled there in 1888 on a clandestine mission inspired by her then lover, the right-wing French politician Lucien Millevoye, and may have encountered

*Captain Thomas Gonne of the 17th Lancers, who had died in 1886.

Tevis's impressionable 'friend' in Moscow. There she had certainly enraptured the *Pall Mall Gazette* editor W. T. Stead, who described her as 'one of the most beautiful women of the world'.[46] We don't have Davitt's response to this query from Paris, but it is clear from Tevis's follow-up that the canny socialist journalist was not enamoured of the reputation and the Boulangist associations of the twenty-two-year-old former debutante. Tevis, who by then had met Gonne, remarked that 'I judged her, perhaps, less severely than yourself' and assured the mistrustful Davitt that 'I did not give away any information'[47] to the eager young convert to Irish nationalism. When Gonne made direct contact by letter with Davitt in late November 1888, seeking a meeting in London, his scepticism concerning her bona fides and purpose is apparent in a note scribbled over the salutation. This reads, 'What is this little game? Probably a *Times* plot.'[48]

So paranoid and cynical was the 'amateur detective' that he suspected Maud Gonne – future muse of William Butler Yeats, future wife of executed 1916 leader John MacBride and future founder of the radical nationalist women's organization Inghinidhe na hÉireann – was a spy for *The Times*.

12

THE RELUCTANT ARCHIVIST

William Henry Joyce Colludes with 'The Forger'

'How comes the "Forger's" business to be transacted by Government officials at the Irish office?'

United Ireland, 17 August 1889

'Such a network of chicanery and treachery is not the least remarkable fact connected with the protracted tragedy deliberately planned and ruthlessly carried out by that political party whose leaders still pose as the only true exponents and guardians of constitutional rights within the United Kingdom ... there are powerful reasons of an ethical nature for throwing a searchlight upon such nefarious doings.'[1]

William Henry Joyce, RM,
'Sidelights on British Conspiracies' (1921)

When it came to the question of whether, or to what extent, the Salisbury administration should assist *The Times* in its prosecution of Irish nationalism, the government was on a hiding to nothing. It could cheer while the representatives of *The Times* waded through back issues of the newspaper to stand up the allegations made in 'Parnellism and Crime'. To adopt such a disengaged approach, however, would jeopardize the newspaper's chances of pressing home its case, and there was little doubt that the Tories would be loudly accused by the opposition of collusion anyway. Sir William Harcourt did just that in the House of Commons on 31 July 1888, even before the Commission commenced proceedings. He accused W. H. Smith of having consulted John Walter on the Commission's terms of reference. Smith's lame response – he could not deny having recently entertained the proprietor of *The Times* – was that the two men had met socially and Walter, 'an old friend', made no contribution whatever to the formulation of the investigative template for the ritual trial of the Irish nationalist members.[2] The *Pall Mall Gazette*, within days of Pigott's exposure, brought out a sixteen-page pamphlet itemizing the particulars and extent of the collusion between government and newspaper.[3]

However, it was not based on any preference for being hanged as a sheep rather than as a lamb that the Salisbury administration chose the route of collaboration. The Tories wanted to put Parnell in the dock and bid a final farewell to Home Rule. They could not depend upon *The Times* capably doing the job for them, so, like a good neighbour when a barn is on fire, they rolled up their sleeves and pitched in. 'To most of the cabinet, then, the question of assisting *The Times* became one of degree rather than kind,'[4] wrote the prime authority on Tory policy in 1880s Ireland, L. Perry Curtis. As early as August 1888, two months before the Commission began its work, Arthur Balfour was already consulting Uncle Robert on the potential for Tory collaboration. He was clearly seeking advice rather than permission. Salisbury, in response, while counselling caution, was essentially directing his nephew, the Irish chief secretary, to proceed, because it would 'be fulfilling an obvious and elementary duty'.[5]

But, at all costs, he should avoid getting caught.

Thus was activated a squadron of RIC constables, senior officers and magistrates who could, and did, offer endless hours of commentary supporting the case of *The Times*. How were these helpful witnesses so seamlessly chosen by the newspaper from an Irish security cohort that approached 15,000 in number?

Those inspired choices were mostly down to the diligent, if often reluctant, efforts of one man, Resident Magistrate William Henry Joyce.

In the wake of the humiliation of February 1889, the Salisbury administration might well have decided that now would be a good time to distance itself from *The Times*. Instead, it doubled down on its commitment to reinforce the newspaper's case. Salisbury observed loftily that all the Pigott contretemps proved was that one nationalist could forge the signature of another. It was 'The high-water mark of Salisbury's patrician insolence,' according to the Liberal scribe J. L. Hammond.[6]

In its attempt to bribe, cajole or intimidate Irish witnesses who might offer some comfort in its allegations against Parnell and his senior colleagues, *The Times*, predictably, tried to elicit the co-operation of antagonists of the Irish leader. For example, the former MP John O'Connor Power – jettisoned by the IPP in 1885 – turned them down. The newspaper, illogically, also sought testimony from avid supporters of Parnell. However, in the case of the latter, the stick replaced the carrot. Take the relatively insignificant IPP MP for Kilkenny Thomas Quinn, who was closely associated with Frank Byrne. He was threatened with a fifteen-year jail sentence in an interview with Joseph Soames. In approaching Quinn, *The Times* was aided by two renegade former IPP MPs, Lysaght Finigan and Philip Callan. However, there is no compelling evidence that the threat against Quinn (which never materialized) was sanctioned by any government official. Although it does, in the words of Tim Healy's biographer, Frank Callanan, indicate 'how far the *Times* was prepared to go in the use of the most dubious means, and the creation of a climate of fear'.[7]

As we have already noted in another context, representatives of *The Times*, including Richard Pigott ('the Titus Oates of Irish history'[8]) were admitted to British and Irish prisons to try their hand at convincing jailed bombers, and at least one Invincible, to tell all before the Commission. Among the ambassadors for

The Times were the Paris-based double-agents John P. Hayes and Patrick Casey.[9]

While exploratory prison visits could be shrugged off as inconsequential, clemency agreements could not. The newspaper's emissaries brought with them offers from the government to commute sentences – imposed by British and Irish juries – should the prisoner agree to co-operate with a prosecution being undertaken by a private commercial entity. They would be released, or their sentences would be curtailed, depending on how closely they could connect the IPP leadership, and Parnell in particular, to dynamite and to the Phoenix Park murders. John Daly (future mayor of Limerick) and Thomas Clarke (future signatory of the Easter 1916 proclamation) were two of the most prominent jailed Clan prisoners to be approached. Soames and Pigott, on separate occasions, visited Daly,[10] who declined the offer of an early release. In Clarke's memoir of his time in prison, *Glimpses of an Irish Felon's Life* (which he was hoping to revise before publication, a plan that came to naught due to the intervention of a British Army firing squad), he recounted how, on one particular day, up to a dozen Irish prisoners in Chatham jail were kept in their cells instead of 'being turned out with the others in the usual way for labour'. One by one they were taken away, usually returning within half an hour, as Clarke waited his turn. Presently he was ushered into 'a cosy little room, where I found Mr. Littlechild sitting at a table in front of a fire'. Inspector Littlechild, who greeted Clarke amiably – the detective had been responsible for installing Clarke in Chatham in the first place – seemed reluctant to come to the point of the visit. Clarke requested his nemesis to 'never mind beating about the bush' and the Section D detective began his well-practised spiel. The Special Commission was anxious to hear evidence 'from America in connection with the skirmishing movement'. The chief inspector then dipped pen in ink and announced himself 'ready to take down anything you'd wish to say'. Littlechild's transcription skills were not put to the test. Clarke rose from his chair and politely advised the CID detective:

> Look here, Mr. Inspector, if a single word of information would get me out of here to-morrow, sooner than give it to you I'd prefer to remain here till the day of judgment. Please take that as final.

Littlechild, however, was 'not to be choked off so easily'. He spent the next forty-five minutes playing both 'good cop' and 'bad cop' himself, coaxing and berating in turn a stoically tight-lipped Clarke. The veteran Fenian remained contemptuously silent.[11]

The consequences of a refusal to co-operate with *The Times* may have been fatal for another Fenian prisoner, the accomplished sportsman P. W. Nally. Nally was in prison after an 1884 conspiracy trial in which he was convicted of membership of a 'secret society of assassins'. He was offered early release from his ten-year sentence if he gave testimony that would incriminate Parnell. Like Daly and Clarke, he refused. He died in November 1891 (a month after Parnell) while still a prisoner in Mountjoy. The prison authorities announced that he had died of typhoid fever. A Dublin city coroner's inquest concluded, however, that he had been fatally weakened by punishments inflicted after his refusal to appear before the Special Commission. At Nally's funeral, his coffin was draped with the same flag that had adorned Parnell's the previous month.*[12]

Patrick Delaney, a former Invincible incarcerated in Maryborough (Portlaoise) Gaol for the attempted murder of a judge, succumbed to the blandishments of *The Times* and appeared before the Commission on 16 January 1889.[13] Delaney knew precisely what was expected of him. In his evidence he diligently connected 'Leaguers, Fenians and Invincibles together',[14] naming Egan as financier to the Invincibles and Sheridan as a fellow member, and identifying Egan's signature on a number of the forged Pigott letters.[15] However, he was undermined when he was obliged to admit under cross-examination that most of his testimony was based on hearsay.

*The Nally Stand in Dublin's Croke Park, opened in 1953, was named after him.

After being pummelled by Russell and Davitt in cross-examination, Delaney was returned to his cell in Maryborough, where he remained for most of the next two years. 'No witness created a worse impression than this unmitigated scoundrel,' wrote Davitt.[16] In November 1890 – a little over two years before his sentence expired – Australian newspapers reported, with little enthusiasm, that Delaney would soon be among them.[17] He had been released from Maryborough Gaol and, for his own protection, was bound for Britain's continent-wide Antipodean 'safe house'. He failed to distinguish himself as a member of Australian society. Under the name of Clarke he was jailed for six years for stabbing a man in a public house brawl.[18]

In addition to incarcerated Fenians who resisted cajolery and coercive pressure, there were at least two prominent officials who also declined to assist *The Times*. The refusal of New York Consul General William Hoare, and the personal consequences, has already been described.

Loyalty towards his 'touts' was the impetus behind Superintendent John Mallon's refusal to testify before the Special Commission himself. He was subpoenaed by *The Times* and travelled to London. However, he made strenuous efforts to avoid giving evidence. His biographer, Frederick Moir Bussy, wrote that Mallon 'had woven a wonderful network of informers and spies ... only by reason of his absolute loyalty to the persons who trusted him and whose very existence was literally in his keeping'.[19] However, Bussy was not naïve enough to think that this was the only reason for Mallon's reluctance to testify. He hints at a possible connection, outlined earlier, between the 'G' Division chief and Patrick Egan.[20] Were he to be cross-examined, Mallon might well have been questioned about Egan's fortuitous escape from Dublin a few hours in advance of the presentation of a warrant for his arrest.

On his arrival in London Mallon spoke to Sir Richard Webster and advised the attorney general that he would abide by an axiom with which he (Mallon), as a native of Ulster, would have been well familiar: 'whatever you say, say nothing'. He refused to testify. Webster, however, 'was inexorable'. Having failed to persuade the lead counsel for *The Times*, Mallon sought the help of the commissioner of the Dublin Metropolitan Police, David Harrel. He sent a coded telegram to Harrel that read 'Cannot give evidence. I prefer Waterloo Bridge. It is for you to protect me.'[21] Whether or not Harrel took his chief superintendent's threat of suicide seriously, he was impressed enough to instruct Mallon to hide away in the Bath Hotel in London and await his arrival. Harrel then faced down Webster and Sir Henry James after a heated argument. Pledging to take the consequences upon himself for Mallon's non-compliance with a subpoena, Harrel informed the two jurists that 'Mallon is my officer, engaged in secret service, and I forbid him to open his mouth in this case or to give you the smallest assistance.'[22]

Mallon's only function was, at the end of the meeting, to look up the time of the next train to Holyhead.

Of course, *The Times* was not obliged to rely entirely on the efforts of the Tory government to render assistance. The testimony of William O'Shea was secured by Joseph Chamberlain (then enjoying the political status of 'a prophet without honour') long before his period in exile was ended with his accession to the office of Secretary of State for the Colonies in the Salisbury administration of 1895. Chamberlain would have required no inducement whatever to impugn the reputation of Parnell, nor would his faithful lapdog.

An accessory, both before and after the fact, was James Monro's deputy in the Metropolitan Police CID. There is no doubt whatever about Robert Anderson's commitment to *The Times*, merely the extent of his involvement and how much of his work for the newspaper can be linked to his official functions. When he acknowledged his authorship of 'Behind the Scenes in America' in 1910 – which prompted a Commons debate, a threat to his pension and a rap on the knuckles from Herbert Asquith, by then prime minister[23] – he claimed that his superior, James Monro, had given his approval. An ailing Monro quickly denied this.[24] So it appears that Anderson, while making use of information supplied by Le Caron, had contributed to the 'Parnellism and Crime' series on his own initiative spurred by his antipathy towards the evolving nationalism of his fellow countrymen. Subsequently, as we have seen, while acting as head of the CID, he was integral in the appearance of Beach/Le Caron before the Commission, albeit he initially discouraged the spy from testifying. This was one of the most significant coups in the *Times*'s presentation of its case. The prospect of an immediate windfall of £10,000 (over £1 million today) and a steady annuity of £400 thereafter probably swayed Beach as much as his sense of patriotic duty. It was Anderson who negotiated the generous stipend.

Neither can Anderson have been entirely in ignorance of the level of collaboration between administration and newspaper, which renders a comment in one of his memoirs particularly amusing. In *Sidelights on the Home Rule Movement*, when exculpating himself for handing back to Le Caron the pick of their twenty-year correspondence for use in his testimony, he concurred with the complaint of *The Times*, 'that the government gave no assistance in the presentation of the case submitted to the Special Commission … I've always felt that in this respect the government failed in its duty, not only to the Commission Court but to the public.'[25]

The words 'beggar' and 'belief' come to mind.

Solid and effectively incontrovertible proof of the rampant collusion between the Tory government and *The Times* came in a book published just over ninety years after the Special Commission report. *The Prime Informer: a Suppressed Scandal* (1971) is the work of the late Leon Ó Broin, a freelance historian, novelist, translator and senior civil servant of impeccable reputation and considerable literary ability, in two languages. *The Prime Informer* first appeared in 1963 as *Comhcheilg sa Chaisleán*.

The book is based on an unpublished memoir, 'Sidelights on British Conspiracies' (a swipe at Anderson's *Sidelights on the Home Rule Movement* – the two men were not close), by the County Tyrone-born resident magistrate William Henry Joyce, a former district inspector in the RIC. Joyce's extraordinary memoir, and his astute retention of a number of supporting documents, is a detailed and entirely credible account of being co-opted to identify Dublin Castle files injurious to the cause of Irish nationalism, marrying that with policemen and magistrates who could offer vivid confirmatory testimony of the evils of Parnellism, and handing over the results to Joseph Soames. By 1910, when Anderson became embroiled in the controversy surrounding his authorship of 'Behind the Scenes in America', Joyce was at the end of his tether. Recurring health issues causing frequent absences from work, a problem with alcohol and a simmering resentment over the failure to secure what he deemed as appropriate promotions – he was forcibly retired on a reduced pension in 1902[26] – prompted Joyce to break cover and reveal his pivotal role in the efforts made by Dublin Castle and the British government to shore up the case being constructed by *The Times* at the Special Commission.

Unable in 1913 to interest the governing Liberal Party, or indeed John Redmond, in the documents he had preserved, Joyce moved well outside his unionist comfort zone and approached Eoin MacNeill, founder of the Irish Volunteers, and Sir Roger Casement, 'who considered his documents of some propaganda value'.[27] War and rebellion intervened, the latter ending Casement's interest in Joyce's trove as he suffered a similar fate to Thomas Clarke. The Anglo-Irish War, however, re-awakened republican interest in Joyce's documents and in his narrative. At the instigation of MacNeill and Sinn Féin Minister for Home Affairs Arthur Griffith, Joyce was sent to New York[28] (where his files had been hidden) to write 'Sidelights on British Conspiracies' in the Irish consulate in that city. The resulting polemic was to be used for propaganda purposes by Sinn Féin against their British antagonists. He remained a 'man of mystery' during his sojourn in the USA and 'courted anonymity in America'.[29] The signing of the Anglo-Irish Treaty and the subsequent Civil War put paid to that plan. Joyce died in poverty and obscurity in 1928, and what he believed to be the only copy of 'Sidelights on British Conspiracies' disappeared. However, MacNeill had made a copy of his own, and this was the document on which Ó Broin based his account of the covert services rendered by Joyce to an ultimately ungrateful government in 1887–8.

Was William Henry Joyce a stereotypical disgruntled employee writing an unreliable, or even fabricated, memoir? He certainly had an axe to grind, and there is at least some scope for the belief that his treatment at the hands of Dublin Castle was not altogether unfair. Unwise perhaps, given his knowledge of dark practices, but not entirely unjust given his propensity for excessive consumption of alcohol. However, 'Sidelights on British Conspiracies' has more than a ring of truth about it. In the opinion of the great T. W. Moody, 'despite his partisanship, his testimony on the main issue cannot be impugned'.[30]

As Ó Broin points out, there is a wealth of corroborative evidence for the claims made by Joyce in his memoir. A letter sent by Soames to Joyce in November 1888 confirms the nature of the professional relationship between the two men. A second letter makes it clear that Irish regional detective forces had been briefed that Joyce was their conduit to *The Times* for compromising material that could be used against the Special Commission accused.[31]

Some good investigative work by *United Ireland* in August 1889 does likewise. William O'Brien's newspaper, in an editorial entitled 'On Her Majesty's Service', claimed that the Irish Office in London was being 'used as a branch establishment of Mr. Soames'. A cipher telegram had come into the newspaper's possession. It had been sent 'OHMS Cork' on 10 July, to 'Joyce, Esq, Irish Office, Great Queen St., London S.W.' It contained some relatively inconsequential information that would assist Webster in his cross-examination of a Commission witness. Of far more interest was *United Ireland*'s speculation as to the identity of 'Joyce'. 'The evidence in our possession points with almost conclusive clearness to Removable* W. H. Joyce, known in the West of Ireland as William Hangman Joyce, from the unscrupulous savagery that helped to purchase his promotion.'[32] *United Ireland* had finally got their man. Earlier, in March 1889, they had alleged that 'All the vile agencies of Irish officialdom were employed for the "Forger"** … The most confidential documents, the most valued spies of the Government, were sacrificed to the "Forger" in the vain effort to bolster up their abominable charges.'[33] However, when it came to establishing who exactly was running the operation in Great Queen Street, half a dozen names were tossed out by the Parnellite newspaper. The 'rogues' gallery' did not include William Henry Joyce.

There is also corroboration in the Balfour papers in the form of a letter from the under-secretary, Ridgeway, to the chief secretary in May 1888. This was sent five months before the Commission began hearing evidence, nearly three months before the enabling legislation that created it, and two months before *O'Donnell v. Walter*. Ridgeway told Balfour that Soames had made a 'great haul' of Land League material in Dublin; 'the result is to make *The Times* case safe in the coming action, and if Soames is not over-sanguine, to break Parnell's reputation … Altogether the case looks very promising.'[34]

Soames, it would turn out, was radically 'over-sanguine'.

Joyce was an unwilling recruit to the cause of *The Times*. Aside from the strain placed upon him by the work he was expected to do and the demands he was obliged to meet, he was unconvinced of the merits of the newspaper's case and had no time whatever for Houston's beloved Irish Loyal and Patriotic Union. That organization, he believed, consisted of 'the lineal descendants

*A resident magistrate.
***The Times*.

of degenerates who had betrayed their country for peerages and monetary rewards, of grasping lawyers on the make, and professional and academic gentlemen on the lookout for jobs and minor honours'.[35] Joyce was 'inducted' at a meeting with the Irish attorney general, Peter 'The Packer'* O'Brien. He was told that he would have complete government support, but that his work must be done entirely in secret. He was left to speculate about the extent of the government support should the secret ever get out. Joyce was reluctant to undertake the task outlined by O'Brien but ultimately yielded to pressure to lead the collaborative effort with *The Times*.[36]

Joyce was given several civil servants and policemen to assist him in his task and was assigned an office in Dublin Castle, far from prying eyes or curious officials. He then set about contacting resident magistrates and senior police officers and beginning his trawl. 'Give them everything, Joyce,' O'Brien had instructed the unenthusiastic resident magistrate. By mid-October, as the Special Commission began to hear evidence, 'everything' consisted of two tons of files in large packing cases that were shipped to London. The contents of the boxes included files to which even the Liberal Home Secretary, William Harcourt – not noted for his generosity towards accused Irish suspects in the early 1880s – had appended remarks such as 'rubbish' and 'humbug'. Joyce was being thorough. He was not being paid to be discerning.

The boxes were then transported, as *United Ireland* much later discovered, to the Irish Office in Great Queen Street, situated between Covent Garden and Holborn. There Joyce and his covert archivists had been allocated a couple of rooms immediately above the office of Arthur Balfour. The chief secretary, although aware of what was going on, neglected to familiarize himself with the details. He needed to preserve his virginal ignorance and retain his deniability in response to questions in the

*So called because of his talent for 'packing' juries to the advantage of the prosecution.

House of Commons. There he scornfully batted away accusations that the government was offering a single iota of assistance to *The Times* – a consistent assertion that Joyce later characterized as 'a frigid and calculated lie'. Balfour, he is very clear, was 'made fully acquainted with every detail [and] he entered thoroughly and unreservedly into the business'.[37]

So paranoid were Tory ministers at the prospect of the entire operation being exposed by some enterprising newshound that, when Joyce needed to consult Home Office papers, he was required to visit the house of Henry Matthews's private secretary, where he could read files without fear of detection. Matthews did not want Joyce to be seen within a mile of the Home Office. There was no red carpet for him at Scotland Yard either. With Monro having replaced Sir Charles Warren as Metropolitan Police Commissioner (and Joyce's adversary Robert Anderson now in charge of CID), any papers the Irish RM required were removed to Monro's residence, and from there Joyce would transfer them to Great Queen Street.

Joyce had a hair-raising conversation with Major Nicholas Gosselin – now in charge of Irish secret work at the Home Office – where he learned that certain files were closed to him because the crimes involved were the work of *agents provocateurs*. Joyce even claimed that Gosselin confided in him that policemen, and police informers, had planted bombs themselves to secure convictions against some of the 'usual suspects'. 'The Gosling' cited the case of John Daly as an example. An astonished Joyce took Gosselin at his word and, therefore, with supreme irony, references to the dynamite campaign were scant during the proceedings of the Commission.

At around the time of the Piggot debacle Joyce's relationship with Balfour appears to have changed dramatically. Now that the 'Parnell letters' had burned up entering the atmosphere, Balfour took a more direct and personal interest in what amounted to a rescue operation of the drowning newspaper. This went as far as directing that inconvenient documents should be destroyed. Joyce recounted how he had come across 'one most important document, the contents of which appeared to be in direct conflict with the other papers'. He brought this to Balfour's attention. There then followed an extraordinary dumbshow in which the chief secretary mimed the burning of the document in his office fire. Joyce did as he had been directed in this subversive pantomime. 'The unpleasant incident,' he wrote, 'produced an indelible impression upon my mind of the extraordinary psychological mentality of a powerful statesman (who was then in training to be Prime Minister of England) with regard to the destruction of inconvenient papers.'[38]

When it came to the turn of Soames to testify, Joyce's greatest fear was that the *Times*'s 'fixer' would, under cross-examination, reveal the work of the supporting cast in the Irish Office and Dublin Castle. However, the question of governmental collusion was never put. Joyce attributed this welcome oversight to the close relationship between Soames and Sir Charles Russell. Counsel for Parnell had enjoyed a lucrative *Times* retainer, which he had thrown up to take on the Irish Party leader as a client.

When the Commission concluded its evidentiary phase, Joyce was able to abandon his 'occult' (his description) duties and resume the more conventional tasks of a resident magistrate. However, despite his obvious talents, he was now a potential liability to the Salisbury administration. *United Ireland* had at least some awareness of his Special Commission work. Should the newspaper train its sights on the tasks of a resident magistrate (RM), it would be hard to avoid collateral damage to the administration. Naturally, Joyce was more concerned at the ever-present possibility of embarrassment to himself. He greatly feared that his background role during the Commission could be exposed at any time.

Joyce also felt, after the onerous and secretive nature of his employment, that he was entitled to a significant promotion. Instead, he watched as officials who had been his underlings during the epic *Times* trawl were advanced, while he marked time. This was, in part, due to lengthy periods of ill health on Joyce's part. An unsatisfactory correspondence with Balfour, which continued until late 1891, did not bring the sort of preferment he expected. He sought an appointment as assistant inspector general of the RIC, which, because he was then in his early forties, he must have hoped would lead, in time, to the top job in the constabulary. Instead, Balfour and his subordinates attempted to fob him off with the insulting position of resident magistrate, second class, a position to which he was already entitled without any intervention from the nabobs.

This snub broke Joyce's spirit. He continued working as a resident magistrate in different parts of the country for another decade, but his health deteriorated further. This he attributed to the strain of the Commission-related tasks that he had performed for the government in aid of *The Times*.[39] His record of leave-taking on health grounds during his last decade in public service was abysmal (over a four-year period he was absent for almost sixteen months), and he was warned that if his work attendance record did not improve, he would be forced into early retirement. There is no doubt that his personal difficulties were exacerbated by an increased resort to alcohol in the final decade of the nineteenth century. However, he greatly resented official claims that this was 'the *cause* of my illness' (his italics). The end came in 1901, when he was forced out and allocated a 'retiring allowance' instead of a pension. Even that was reduced owing to his 'drink-ended service'.

Unable to provide for his family on his reduced emolument, he sought, and failed to find, alternative employment. He was forced to cash in his life insurance policies prematurely.

But he had not left the magistracy empty-handed. He had managed to hold on to some documents from the Special Commission period, and he had a fascinating story to tell. He set this down in 1910 and went about the task of extracting personal revenge, and at least some sort of remuneration (as described earlier) from his former political opponents. His decision to write his memorandum was prompted by a decade of ill feeling towards the Conservative Party in general, and Balfour in particular, and was fuelled by the controversy over the revelation of Robert

Anderson's (by then 'Sir' Robert Anderson) authorship of three of the 'Parnellism and Crime' articles.

Hell hath no fury like a magistrate scorned. Joyce was one RM who would not have been comfortable in the benign Somerville and Ross universe.

13

THE O'SHEA DIVORCE

Plan C?

'The instrument is changed from Pigott to O'Shea … the projected divorce suit is a political attack.'[1]

United Ireland, on the O'Shea divorce, 4 January 1890

'It is often suggested that it was Chamberlain who encouraged O'Shea into taking action through the courts. Whatever the truth might be, the unionist alliance enjoyed a short lease of life, free from the cares of Irish obstruction in the Commons. This enabled it to recover a good deal of its lost momentum.'[2]

Robert Taylor, *Lord Salisbury* (1975)

The Divorce Court, London, 16–17 November 1890

'The respondent denied that she had been guilty of adultery, as did also the co-respondent; and the respondent alleged that the petitioner had been guilty of connivance in the adultery.'[3]

The position of the respondent and co-respondent was paradoxical. They seemed to be claiming that Captain William Henry O'Shea had connived at their alleged adultery, while simultaneously insisting that no adultery had ever taken place. That, at least, was the logic of the particulars of the case, read out in the courtroom at the commencement of one of the most dramatic and important battles to come before a court since the

Katharine O'Shea

passage of the Matrimonial Causes Act of 1857 moved divorce from ecclesiastical to civil courts.

But neither respondent nor co-respondent was in court to explain this head-scratching inconsistency. They had sent a legal representative to keep a watching brief, but his hands were tied. His instructions were that he was not to intervene. Frank Lockwood QC had already told the divorce court judge, 'I do not intend to cross-examine any witnesses, to call any witnesses, nor to take any part in these proceedings.' It was clear from the outset that there was to be no defence case of any kind. William O'Shea's suit for divorce would be uncontested. After a few banalities, everyone could go home. Nothing to see here.

Not quite, as it transpired.

Captain William Henry O'Shea would still have his day in court, and it would be a field day. The eager onlookers and the transfixed pressmen sat through chapter and verse from the aggrieved husband. Only a couple of intriguing questions from sceptical jurors paused his sorry tale of victimhood and betrayal.

'Sleek and smooth and shiny, pimp and spy, from the top of his oily curls to the tip of his patent-leather boots',[4] was *United Ireland*'s description of O'Shea in the witness box as he shredded the reputation of his estranged wife Katharine and of her *sui iuris*/ common-law husband, Charles Stewart Parnell. While doing so, he carefully coloured his own actions in virginal white. O'Shea's counsel, the solicitor general Sir Edward Clarke, confidently led him through his catalogue of grievances. The Tory grandee could hardly have earned an easier fee.

With no one to contest his lies, O'Shea gleefully perjured himself. His untruths meandered from minor 'porkies', such as a reference to 'my daughter Clare' – she was Parnell's daughter and well he knew it – to more blatant falsehoods. 'It was never within my knowledge that he slept in the house [Eltham] or visited there during my absence,' he claimed unblushingly. He had been aware of the couple's Eltham cohabitation since 1881.

O'Shea's command performance, however, was a mere whining aperitif to the comic humiliation that followed, as the private lives of Katharine O'Shea and Parnell were dissected and reassembled as ribald farce. Number 8 Medina Terrace in Brighton had been their home for some time, and one Caroline Pethers was cook and housekeeper there. Her testimony quickly became the stuff of music hall comedy. Pethers told judge and jury how O'Shea had rung the front doorbell of 8 Medina Terrace when she (Pethers) knew Parnell to be in the first-floor drawing room with Katharine. O'Shea had duly been admitted to the house and had gone upstairs. A few minutes later Parnell had presented himself, Houdini-like, at the front door. Pethers was asked innocently by Clarke – who could barely conceal his merriment at the answer that he knew was coming – was it possible for Parnell to have descended via the staircase before making his exit and re-entrance?

'No!' replied Pethers, emphatically, to the delight of the assembled press, who now had some colour to add to O'Shea's dirge. However, Pethers pointed out helpfully, there was a balcony outside the room and two 'fire escape' ropes, down one of which Parnell must have abseiled to escape the cuckolded husband. Supporters of the Irish leader immediately tried to expunge the image of their aloof and dignified 'Uncrowned King' shimmying down a rope to escape the pompous ex-Hussar. For their part, the nation's newspaper cartoonists sharpened their pencils and disseminated many variations of the image. While *O'Shea v. O'Shea and Parnell* had harsh political consequences for the Irish leader, the testimony of the forthright Caroline Pethers exposed Parnell to social ridicule as well.

Even the dullest of defence barristers, on cross-examining Caroline Pethers, might have enquired of her why Captain O'Shea needed to knock at the front door of what was supposed to be his own Brighton home.

But Frank Lockwood could only look on and seethe.

The 'outraged valet'

> 'The Commission ended in a disastrous failure for the gov[ernmen]t and *The Times*. Then as a *dernier resort* the O'Shea divorce proceedings were exploited with the result of disrupting the Irish Party, followed by the tragic death of Parnell.'[5]
>
> William Henry Joyce, 1923 memorandum to the Free State government re. 'Sidelights on British Conspiracies'

The particulars of the *O'Shea v. O'Shea and Parnell* divorce case have been recounted frequently in numerous Parnell biographies, in Katharine O'Shea's own memoir and in a mountain of academic books and articles. It is beyond the scope of this work to retell the narrative of Parnell's ritual humiliation in the divorce courts in November 1890, and his fall from political grace in the months that followed. But the bare facts are as follows. After 'discovering' in early 1887, with the co-operation of his almost equally repulsive son Gerard, that Parnell and Katharine were co-habiting, William O'Shea threatened divorce. He pulled back from the brink after a series of enforced concessions from Katharine and the coincidental publication of the 'facsimile letter' in *The Times* on 18 April 1887. Rather than risk an expensive rupture with Aunt Ben, and the exposure of his own serial adulteries, O'Shea adopted the line of least resistance. He opted to allow 'Parnellism and Crime' to play out and to burn his adversary at the stake of public opinion. O'Shea was a seasoned opportunist, and here was an opportunity to see Parnell banished from politics and society, at no cost to himself.

But the abject failure of the *Times*'s case against Parnell, and the death of Aunt Ben a few weeks after the Pigott travesty, caused a rethink on O'Shea's part. If Parnell was to be defenestrated, it looked as if he was going to have to push the man out of the window himself. How to improve the odds of success? If he could take on a behemoth like Parnell with the encouragement and assistance of some key members of the unionist establishment – Chamberlain and Balfour to name but two – so much the better.

O'Shea's chagrin at the failure of *The Times* was accentuated by the revelation, shortly thereafter, of the terms of the will of Mrs Anna Maria Wood. She had finally passed away at the age of ninety-eight, on 19 May 1889. Aunt Ben's fortune was left, almost in its entirety, to her niece Katharine, but the legacy was outside the terms of the O'Shea marriage settlement. While her five children (three of whom were also O'Shea's, though he claimed all five) stood to gain from the legacy at Katharine's own death, O'Shea himself was excluded. He could not touch a penny of Aunt Ben's fortune.

The problem was that neither could Katharine.

Because her siblings challenged Aunt Ben's last will and testament – drafted and signed in March 1888 – the legacy ended up in a bitter probate action, with the funds locked away until the dispute was resolved. Her siblings maintained that Anna Maria Wood – almost completely blind at the time of her death, and whose memory by 1887, according to an examining physician, 'is most imperfect and she may lose it altogether at any time'[6] – was not *compos mentis* when she signed the new will.

One of the unlooked for consequences of this legal stand-off was the lack of available funds with which to bribe O'Shea into continued connivance in ignoring his wife's adulterous relationship. Both Parnell and Katharine were confident that he would drop the divorce petition if a sum of the order of £20,000 (the equivalent today of around £2 million) was dangled before him. Throughout 1890, when Parnell was queried by colleagues – most notably Davitt and John Morley – about the possible outcome of the divorce suit, he hid behind a 'non-denial denial' of the affair by insisting that he would emerge from the lawsuit without a stain on his character. What he really meant was that the suit would be withdrawn, thus fatally undermining its credibility. He avoided addressing the question of the inherent justification of O'Shea's petition. Parnell's evasive confidence was based on the perceived ability of his consort to raise the money to buy off her husband. When the funds failed to materialize, and it was clear that the divorce suit would proceed, Parnell insisted that it be allowed to take its course. He wanted to marry Katharine O'Shea, whatever the consequences, even if this meant an uncontested divorce that could fatally undermine his reputation. This uncompromising attitude would lead to the abject humiliation of the Divorce Court.

For her part Katharine entered a legal counter-claim designed to deter O'Shea from appearing in court. In addition to alleging that her husband had condoned and encouraged her relationship with Parnell, she also cited numerous instances of infidelity on his part, alleging that he had 'between the years 1868 and 1890 … habitually committed adultery with divers prostitutes and other women whose names except as hereinafter stated are at present unknown to the Respondent'.[7] Those who were 'named hereinafter' were three in number and included Katharine's own sister, Anna Steele, whom she accused of having had sex with O'Shea 'on or about the 13th and 14th of July 1881'. She also accused her husband of having physically assaulted her in July 1881. At around that time she would have been about two months' pregnant with Parnell's first child, the short-lived Claude Sophie. Back in 1890, while a man could divorce his wife for infidelity, a woman was required to prove her husband guilty of cruelty as well as adultery.

There has always been a question mark surrounding the O'Shea divorce. The repercussions ended the political career of Charles Stewart Parnell and divided the IPP for a decade.

Cui bono?

There were numerous beneficiaries, but all, other than O'Shea himself, might merely have benefited from that haphazard piece of legislation, the law of unintended consequences. Did the Tories and Liberal Unionists, who had striven to neuter or obliterate the threat of buoyant Irish nationalism, simply profit from a supreme stroke of good fortune, when O'Shea, 'the outraged valet', sued for divorce? Or was O'Shea bribed, cajoled or threatened into making a move at which he had baulked since he first became aware of his wife's affair almost a decade before?

The simple answer to this conundrum is that we do not know, and probably never will.

The personal papers of all the principals involved have been subjected to almost a century of scrutiny, so unless an entirely new tranche of documents were to emerge, this will remain as one of the great 'known unknowns' of Irish history.

The humiliation and downfall of Parnell might be Act III of a drama that began with the 'Jubilee plot'. However, it might equally be an example of casual serendipity. Was O'Shea a lone wolf or a cunning conspirator?

Bolstering the 'lone wolf' argument, O'Shea (a Roman Catholic whose church was opposed to divorce) had a catalogue of ulterior motives for maintaining his pragmatic silence until, Scrooge-like, he filed his divorce petition on Christmas Eve 1889. This was a month after the last gasp of the expiring Special Commission and at a time when it was abundantly clear that the three commissioners were not about to banish Parnell to political purgatory. However, chief among the incentives to stay O'Shea's hand was the glacial pace of Aunt Ben's crossing of the River Styx. In 1881 she was ninety years of age, widowed (since 1845) and ailing. Katharine O'Shea (née Wood) was her favourite niece and, in effect, her carer. Katharine would inherit a sizeable chunk of the estate of an exceptionally wealthy woman,* who, logic dictated, was not long for this world. O'Shea simmered but bided his time, in the expectation that Mrs Wood's demise would bring him, via his estranged wife, a portion of that estate. In the interim he could get on with the job of blackmailing and 'milking' Parnell for political advancement. Financial prosperity could wait a few months. And wait it did. Aunt Ben defied expectations and held on for almost another decade.

During which time the gravy train piloted by a vulnerable Parnell was derailed. This was inevitable, after the abstention of the captain in the vote on Gladstone's Home Rule Bill in June 1886. This petty act of betrayal was Parnell's reward for jeopardizing his reputation by forcing O'Shea on the Galway electorate earlier that year. O'Shea, unloved by his dismissive IPP colleagues, chose the embrace of his unionist political mentor, Joseph Chamberlain, over that of the leader coerced into becoming his political pimp. From June 1886 onwards it only remained to be seen whether O'Shea's patience would erode to the extent that he would hit back at Parnell and Katharine O'Shea even before Mrs Wood's death. This, despite the potential for gratifying the captain's antipathy to his former party leader, was always unlikely. Advertising the affair would scandalize the nonagenarian Mrs Wood into cutting her niece (and, by default, her nephew by marriage) out of her will.

When Aunt Ben finally expired and left her entire estate to Mrs O'Shea – to the fury of Katharine's siblings – the captain was not rewarded for his deferred gratification. So he now had

*Her fortune was in the region of £140,000 to 150,000, the equivalent of *c.*£25 million in 2026.

a multitude of motives, beyond the political, to sue for divorce in 1889.

However, O'Shea also had numerous disincentives to sue for an end to his marriage. There is little doubt that he was susceptible both to blackmail and to a substantial bribe to stay his hand. A complicating factor with the latter course of action lay in the fact that Parnell passionately desired an O'Shea divorce. He did not want the whole affair brushed under the carpet again after the captain had been bought, or scared, off. That still left the option of a substantial secret cash settlement and a petition for divorce on the part of Katharine O'Shea. Persuading O'Shea to admit to adultery and cruelty in open court would be expensive. There would be no political redemption for the captain were he to admit to being a philanderer and a wife beater in a divorce court.

Even before it became clear that his estranged wife – because of the legal challenge to Aunt Ben's will – was not going to be in a position to buy him off, was the prospect of revenge and potential political rehabilitation proving to be more attractive than a sum of money that would allow for a contented retirement in Spain? O'Shea was capable of acting in a manner that seemed to contravene his best interests. However, even in the case of the obvious self-harm of his Home Rule Bill abstention, there had been an upside. He had preserved his all-important relationship with Joseph Chamberlain, who, even while in the post-Home Rule wilderness of his own making, held out some slim hope of political rehabilitation to the captain. There is a fair to even chance that O'Shea made the same calculation in 1889 as he had in 1886. Whether Chamberlain was constantly in his ear urging him to sue for divorce; merely passing casual hints; or feigning complete indifference, O'Shea was aware of the personal gratification with which his political mentor would greet the gelding of the Irish nationalist threat that must follow the downfall of Parnell.

Such gratification, it must also have occurred to the ambitious captain, would be shared by a grateful Tory government, over which Chamberlain's influence was growing. The establishment would be in his debt. Surely a safe Tory or Liberal Unionist constituency was little enough to ask in return for the downside to a divorce suit that could come seriously unstuck based on his own infidelities, his long collusion in his wife's affair, in addition to the animosity of Parnellite supporters in possession of riding crops and shotguns and who were not afraid to use them. He deserved a prize of some kind for a gamble that could lead to political rewards or to perdition.

Cui bono?

Pointedly, O'Shea made no attempt to conceal the fact, among the influential members of his circle of acquaintances, that he was contemplating a suit for divorce. Chamberlain was aware of O'Shea's intentions by the middle of October 1889, at the latest, and probably well before that date. 'Now to *revert* [my italics] to the other business,' the captain wrote to his mentor on 13 October 1888, 'owing to some recent circumstances it is under consideration whether some strong action should not be taken by me, and I am anxious that you (and a few others) should be rightly informed.'[8]

One of those who was also aware of the impending action was the nation's top spy, Nicholas Gosselin. On 12 December 1889, less than a fortnight before the lodging of the divorce petition, Gosselin wrote an unsolicited and gossipy letter to William Henry Joyce. 'The Gosling' alleged that Katharine O'Shea had been responsible for the transfer of a large sum of her aunt's money, which had now gone missing. 'O'Shea is going for a divorce. The relatives are going for the money. Mrs. O'Shea expects to become Mrs. Charles Stewart Parnell … this is enough for one letter, but please burn at once as it contains hanging matter.'[9] Thankfully Joyce did not comply with Gosselin's request. In his revealing memorandum Joyce speculated that Gosselin had not come by this knowledge accidentally. He was certain that the resources of the secret service were being used to back up O'Shea's case for a divorce, in much the same way that Joyce himself had been employed to bolster the *Times*'s case before the Special Commission.[10]

If indeed there was a 'Plan C' – a *grand*, or even *petit* strategy to associate Parnell with immorality, to compensate for the clandestine, journalistic and political failures thus far – then Gosselin was central. He was keeping Balfour up to date. In January 1890 he reported to the Irish chief secretary about the background to the O'Shea divorce petition, lodged a week earlier, while adding that the petitioner was 'in a great state of terror'. Should O'Shea be intimidated from proceeding with the suit, Gosselin advised Balfour that there was 'abundant evidence' of adultery that could be used to bring down Parnell in other ways.[11] Meanwhile Chief Inspector Littlechild was also gathering evidence of the cohabitation of Parnell and Katharine O'Shea and was reporting his observations to Robert Anderson.[12] Should O'Shea's courage fail him, it looked like there was a backup plan.

When it came to the divorce petition, Parnell himself had little doubt that his real nemesis lurked in the shadows behind O'Shea, rather than in the person of the cuckold himself. Liberal MP John Morley wrote in his memoir *Recollections* of a meeting with Parnell in Brighton in November 1890. In the course of a long conversation Morley delicately touched on the impending divorce proceedings. Parnell was insouciance personified. He dismissed the prospect of his undoing, observing that, 'The other side don't know what a broken-kneed horse they are riding'.[13] O'Shea was the obvious candidate for the role of rickety nag, but the 'other side' is just as clearly the Conservative/Liberal Unionist alliance – with Chamberlain in the vanguard – that had been trying unsuccessfully to bring him down since coming to power in 1886.

In an interview with the *Freeman's Journal*, which appeared within a week of the filing of O'Shea's petition, Parnell repeated his conviction that concerted unionist forces were behind the divorce suit. Parnell also told the *Journal* that 'Captain O'Shea ... has known that Mr. Parnell constantly resided there [Eltham] from 1880 to 1886.'[14] This was as close to a public admission of adultery and 'criminal conversation' as it was possible to make. Such an admission 'would not normally have been received in nationalist Ireland with any high degree of approbation,' Conor Cruise O'Brien observed euphemistically in his biography of a political movement, *Parnell and his Party*.[15]

Parnell also advanced a plausible and elegant conspiracy theory of his own. The divorce petition was a friendly gesture towards *The Times*, with whom Parnell's libel action was still pending. What better way to paint the newspaper in a positive light before a libel jury than by besmirching the reputation of its antagonist? Could *The Times* actually be the establishment entity bent on the destruction of Parnell? The newspaper certainly did not lack for motivation, but would it have gone cap in hand to O'Shea? There is evidence in the captain's surviving papers in the National Library of Ireland that he assisted the newspaper in its search for examples of Parnell's signature.[16] In addition, the ubiquitous Inspector Thomson alternated between working for *The Times* and gathering evidence for the O'Shea divorce.[17] This, however, only offers insubstantial reinforcement rather than attaching a convincing proof of Parnell's own theory.

However, despite Parnell's beguiling *Times* smokescreen, Joseph Chamberlain remains the more likely ringleader of any conspiracy to extract maximum benefit from O'Shea's invidious situation. In his account of the last five years of Parnell's life, Alfred Robbins, the parliamentary correspondent of the newspaper that was practically Chamberlain's 'in-house' journal, the *Birmingham Daily Post*, recalled being consulted by 'one on the inside of the Liberal Unionist "machine" whether Parnell would be politically ruined by a divorce … Capt. O'Shea, it was added, being believed to be willing to take proceedings.'[18] It does not take much imagination to deduce the identity of this mysterious Liberal Unionist 'insider' approaching the political correspondent of a Birmingham newspaper.

Robbins logged this conversation as having taken place in September 1889, while the Special Commission was still in session, and more than three months before O'Shea sued for divorce. Clearly the captain was not hiding his leverage under a bushel. Nor was he being discouraged from pulling the trigger by a certain Birmingham Liberal Unionist whose loathing of Parnell exceeded even that of the Irish leader's longer-standing adversaries in the Conservative Party.

Liberal Unionist antagonism did not begin and end with Chamberlain either. Lord Hartington, brother of the slain Lord Frederick Cavendish, who had a long-running extra-marital affair of his own with the Duchess of Manchester and might have been expected to display at least a modicum of sympathy, revelled in Parnell's downfall. 'I never thought anything in politics could give me as much pleasure,' he confessed to Queen Victoria herself.[19] The *schadenfreude* was probably just as evident in the House of Saxe-Coburg and Gotha as in that of the Cavendish/Devonshire dynasty.

It has always been pointed out by those who are sceptical of any notion of a 'grand' conspiracy to conjure *O'Shea v. O'Shea and Parnell* into being, that there is no smoking gun. No letters passed between the two men in which Chamberlain urged the captain forward or whipped him back into line at the first sign of procrastination. This is undeniable, unless Chamberlain's response to a letter from O'Shea in which he 'reveals' his marital difficulties constitutes a subtle form of coercion. Chamberlain replied to O'Shea's *cri de coeur* with the advice that, 'I fear that these things cannot be hushed up in the days of "P.M. Gazettes" & "Stars"* & I am not sure that the boldest course is not always wisest.'[20] Chamberlain was clearly edging O'Shea towards the divorce court, but his unsolicited advice hardly constitutes an unmannerly shove.

*The London evening newspaper the *Pall Mall Gazette*, edited by the pioneering journalist W. T. Stead and the *Star*, edited by T. P. O'Connor MP. Both were early manifestations of the so-called 'New Journalism', which prized sensation above all else.

The correspondence between the two men that does exist from the latter half of 1889 would have us believe that O'Shea became aware of the infidelity of his wife only in June 1887, and that Chamberlain knew no more on the subject than O'Shea had confided in him. Both assertions are arrant nonsense. O'Shea had known about, and even encouraged, his wife's liaison with Parnell since 1881. Chamberlain had been aware of the affair since the spring of 1882.* Henry Harrison refers to this short sequence of pre-divorce O'Shea–Chamberlain correspondence as 'show letters' – a contrived exercise in whitewashing designed to obscure Chamberlain's role in the divorce. The exchange of letters of mid-October 1889 give him the appearance of a sainted sepulchre who was innocent of all knowledge of his great rival Parnell's complicated love life. Chamberlain's assertion to O'Shea – banging on the doors of implausibility – that 'I have never listened to scandalous reports affecting my friends & in your case I have heard nothing & know nothing beyond what you have told me'[21] adds force to Henry Harrison's assertions that much of the relevant correspondence between the two was contrived for public consumption should the need arise to publish (it did not), and should not be taken at face value.

The sensational uncontested evidence heard in *O'Shea v. O'Shea and Parnell* led on to the divorce of Katharine O'Shea and her marriage to Parnell at the earliest legal opportunity. They were married on 25 June 1891, four months before his death. However, it also led to Parnell becoming either a laughing stock

*When Liberal Home Secretary William Vernon Harcourt announced at a meeting of cabinet members in 1882 that O'Shea might not be an ideal intermediary in the Kilmainham Treaty negotiations of that year because he was the husband of Parnell's mistress, Harcourt added, for good measure, that O'Shea had backed off filing for divorce as early as 1881 because of Katharine's 'discovery of adulterous relations of her husband which put him in her power'. (F. S. L. Lyons, *The Fall of Parnell, 1890–91* (Toronto, 1960), 63, and Dungan, *The Captain and the King*, Chapter 13.)

or an object of censure and contempt, depending on the level of one's prurience. While most Irish nationalist newspapers held their fire or rallied to his side – for the time being at least – the British press either mocked or reproached him. The unionist *Daily Telegraph* was oddly plaintive in its insistence that Parnell had no option other than to stand down from the leadership of the IPP:

> He must cease, for the present at any rate, to lead the nationalist party. Conscious as we are of the loss our opponents will sustain by his resignation, we trust that they will believe us when we say that we are in no mood to exult … it is no satisfaction, to us to feel that a political adversary whose abilities and prowess it was impossible not to respect, has been overthrown by irrelevant accident, wholly unconnected with the struggle in which we are engaged.[22]

The Times, however, *was* in a mood to exult. If 'revenge is a dish best served cold' Walter and Buckle must have annexed an icehouse for the newspaper's triumphant editorial, heralding what it hoped would be the demise of Parnell's political career. The newspaper extracted the last full measure of validation from the one-sided farce played out in the divorce court. 'No statesman aspiring to control a powerful party could survive the blow of having such a charge proved against him,' 'The Thunderer' thundered on 18 November 1890, safe in the knowledge that this time no defamation suit would follow.

Henry Harrison's *Parnell Vindicated*, published more than four decades after Parnell was felled by Lilliputians – as the author would have seen it – is a lengthy thesis outlining the political role played by 'the Chamberlain-O'Shea combination'[23] in the downfall of the man whom Harrison had served so loyally. He describes O'Shea as suffering from 'covenanted blindness' in disregarding his wife's affair, and of being a 'follower and agent of

Mr. Chamberlain'.[24] He paints a portrait of 'Judas' Chamberlain 'toiling in the wilderness as the unrewarded auxiliary of the Tories', a man who needed a coup of some kind to revive a career 'that seemed to be immobilised'.[25] Chamberlain had taken nitroglycerine to his bridges with the Liberals, and yet his radical background made him an uncomfortable bedfellow for the Tories.

The Special Commission, which Chamberlain played a major part in engineering, augured well if it could neutralize the sizeable bloc of Irish nationalist votes in the Commons, and even magically restore to life those extinct species, the Irish Liberal and the Irish Conservative MP. When that implausible strategy fizzled out in the banality of the Commission report in 1890 – which barely laid a glove on the Parnellites – Chamberlain stared irrelevance in the face once again. But if *O'Shea v. O'Shea and Parnell* could achieve what the Special Commission had promised and failed to deliver, Chamberlain's prospects became more rosy. Once he could brag, privately and humbly of course, that he was an actor in the downfall of Parnell, through his coaxing of O'Shea, then his prospects would improve. Any uptick in the fortunes of Chamberlain might also herald the return to political life of that other endangered species, Captain William Henry O'Shea. Hence the suspicion that, as Harrison observed, O'Shea acted as Chamberlain's 'agent' in the divorce case:

> Considerations such as these were not hid from Captain O'Shea, who had long since attached himself to Mr. Chamberlain's fortunes and who no longer had any political prospects or any political affiliations apart from Mr. Chamberlain.[26]

Seven years after the publication of *Parnell Vindicated*, Harrison was prepared to go even further in alleging a collusive plot between Chamberlain and O'Shea. In the interim, J. L. Garvin's biography of the Birmingham radical, based on hundreds of letters now lodged in the archives of the University of Birmingham, had been published. In this work, at least according to Harrison, the biographer was 'anxious to keep the skirts of his hero's coat as free as possible from spatterings of O'Shea's mud'.[27] In his 1938 riposte to the Chamberlain biography, *Parnell, Joseph Chamberlain and Mr. Garvin*, Harrison alleged a covert plot to dethrone the Uncrowned King and promised to 'point the finger of logical inference and reasonable surmise towards Chamberlain as the moving spirit behind the plot'.[28] However, a phrase like 'logical inference and reasonable surmise' immediately induces a sinking feeling that Harrison did not in fact have any more evidence to back up his suspicions in 1938 than he had in 1931. O'Shea, he asserts, had nothing to gain in divorcing his wife 'except, indirectly, in his capacity as friend, follower and henchman of Joseph Chamberlain'.[29] However, just because *he* had much to gain does not mean that Chamberlain was Iago to Parnell's Othello. Harrison does not close his case. We are left with suspicion, speculation and a modicum of circumstantial evidence.

And, when it comes to the *cui bono* issue, if Chamberlain was indeed the evil mastermind behind the fall of Parnell, the Tories took their own sweet time in delivering his reward. He did not become Secretary of State for the Colonies until 1895. The price of his belated entry into the Salisbury cabinet, almost a decade after his defection from the Liberals, was a retooling of his radicalism and the maturation of his innate jingoism. The former might have irked him, but by 1895 the latter came naturally. Similarly, if O'Shea himself was due some political reward, it too failed to materialize. No knighthood, no safe seat, no sinecure, not even an OBE.* Poor reward indeed for the personal risks he incurred in taking on the might of the Irish Party.

On the other hand!

*Ironically, Henry Harrison was awarded one in 1919, but O'Shea, who died in 1905, was not alive to grind his teeth in frustration at this elevation of a loathed antagonist.

Chamberlain was au fait with O'Shea's intentions. When, as Gosselin claimed in his note to Balfour, O'Shea began to shy away from pursuing his case, was it Chamberlain who stepped forward to stiffen his sinews? The Liberal Unionist leader had seen his good friend and radical ally, Charles Dilke, ruined by an 1886 divorce case in which the aggrieved husband, Donald Crawford, was a fellow MP. He can have had little doubt about how the information to which he was privy, detrimental to Parnell's career, would play out in the divorce courts and subsequently in the court of public opinion.

Parnell's biographer F. S. L. Lyons is *ad idem* with Harrison, in part at least. The motivation for the divorce, he asserts, was 'to retrieve the disaster to the unionist cause of the miscarriage of the special commission'.[30] Lyons also contends that Chamberlain's political passage into the ranks of the Conservative Party largely depended upon his ability 'to break up the Liberal-Parnellite combination'.[31] However, in his classic work *The Fall of Parnell*, which predated his definitive biography of the fallen leader, Lyons, while inclined to accept Harrison's thesis, still maintained that 'he has not unearthed any conclusive documentary evidence to show that the two men, or either of them, planned to use the divorce in the way he has said it was used'. Lyons, however, acknowledges that 'it is of course, likely enough that even if such a scheme had been hatched, no evidence of it would have been put on paper – or allowed to survive if committed to writing – because of the disastrous consequences if it ever came to light. If this is what happened, then we shall probably never know the truth.'[32]

One can only concur. The Tories and the Liberal Unionists, soon to become one and the same, had tried everything to blacken the name of Parnell and to neutralize the effectiveness of the movement he had created. They, and their allies in the police and security services, had failed repeatedly. Was the O'Shea divorce their final throw of the dice, or was it just a happy accident? Despite the suspicion, and some circumstantial evidence, that

O'Shea v. O'Shea and Parnell was a continuation of subversion by other means, and the nagging persistence of the *cui bono* question, the thesis that the O'Shea divorce constituted 'Plan C' leads inexorably to the unsatisfactory Scottish verdict of 'not proven'.

14

LOOSE ENDS

'Here is the real conspiracy to which the attention of every elector should be directed. Here is the Tory government revealed as being in trade and traffic with the employers of an avowed forger and confessed swindler. And for what end? To accomplish the moral assassination of a political opponent, to defeat the cause of home rule.'[1]

'Pigottism and *The Times* or "Parnellism and Crime" Exposed', *Pall Mall Gazette*, Extra No. 46, 2 March 1889

10 Downing Street, London, 6 December 1921, 2.15 a.m.

The exhausted plenipotentiaries had finally put pen to paper. Weeks of negotiations had resulted in a historic compromise. Twenty-six of the thirty-two counties of Ireland had achieved Dominion Status, becoming a sort of eastern Canada in the process. The bitter three-year Anglo-Irish war was at an end.

The atmosphere, however, was more rueful than triumphant. The treaty had been signed by the Irish delegates under the threat from the leader of the British coalition government, Lloyd George, of 'terrible and immediate war'. The British Lord Chancellor, the Tory barrister and savage wit, Lord Birkenhead, a champion of the unionist wing of the Conservative Party, was hardly ebullient. He famously observed that he feared the document to which he had just appended his signature would be his political death warrant. Michael Collins responded sombrely that it was more likely to be his *actual* death warrant. Collins and Arthur Griffth knew that they had a lot of explaining to do. Even persuading some of the other members of the Irish delegation to sign the document had not been easy. It was an earnest of the difficulties that they faced in selling the outcome of their labours to Dáil Éireann on their return to Dublin. The rhetorical flourish of the treaty being 'the freedom to achieve freedom' may already have been quietly coined by the Sinn Féin Finance Minister and Director of Intelligence shortly after signing the document.

Because what had been agreed between the representatives of Sinn Féin and the government of the United Kingdom was not the 'freedom' for which a majority (as it transpired) of the members of the Irish Republican Army had fought. It was more than Home Rule, but far less than a Republic. But it was certainly the 'Irexit' – presided over by a notorious Welsh radical who had been anathema to Conservatives a decade before – that the previous generation of Tory leaders had fought vigorously to avoid. Were the unionists of Salisbury's generation correct? Would this unprecedented concession to Irish nationalism really be the thin end of the wedge? Getting rid of the 'bolshie' Irish was no great loss, but where would it lead? Under the terms of the treaty, the (southern) Irish were only semi-detached at best, still owing allegiance to the British monarch. But would the qualified success of their bloody-mindedness, and their tenacious engagement with a numerically superior military force, encourage far more valuable and less expendable regions of the Empire to follow the Sinn Féin example?

In the medium term, the answer was 'Yes'.

Ultimately the fears of the Marquess of Salisbury came to pass. The British Empire went the way of the Roman Empire (Holy and secular), the Mongols, the Hapsburgs and the Romanovs. It took little more than a decade for the anodyne 1922 Irish constitution, which maintained the controversial oath of allegiance to the Crown, to be replaced by the thoroughly separatist 1937 model. This new template, devised by Eamon de Valera, consigned king and Governor General to oblivion. 'Good riddance' was by then the prevailing sentiment in both camps. Collins had been right. The Anglo-Irish treaty had indeed offered 'the freedom to achieve freedom', although his deadly rival, de Valera, was hardly about to acknowledge the fact.

By 1937, the mutual aggression of the IRA and the 'Black and Tans' had been sublimated into a hostile tariff regime. But with the 'Economic War' between the two states on the verge of resolution, for the UK the 'Six Counties' was quite enough 'Ireland' to be going on with. Salisbury was turning in his grave, but glacially at this point. However, he must have begun to spin more rapidly when the imperial rot spread to India (which became an independent republic two years before Ireland). He continued to rotate, with increasing violence, as, one by one, the Asian and African colonies were detached and allowed to drift off into independence. He would have seen through the threadbare but reassuring cover offered by the creation of the Commonwealth.

By the mid-1960s, barely forty years after Ireland, the first domino, had fallen, Robert Gascoyne-Cecil, 3rd Marquess of Salisbury, would have been entitled to exclaim bitterly, 'I told you so.'

Caveat emptor

> 'It was a trial without a jury, and a political trial, too, in the home of Magna Charta [*sic*]; the cause of the trial a half-successful revolution, with the tribunal and its defined jurisdiction constituted by our political adversaries.'[2]
>
> Michael Davitt, *The Fall of Feudalism in Ireland* (1904)

The Special Commission fell short of introducing an abiding neologism into Hiberno-English. For a while after the dissection of Pigott in the witness box in February 1889, the word 'hesitancy' (spelled correctly) acquired a new currency, as a term of abuse in Ireland. However, just as the slightly older insult 'Carey'* was

*After the Invincible 'approver' James Carey.

not handed down to posterity, neither did 'hesitancy' endure as an offensive slur. By the time the purveyors of 'Pigottism' and the protectors of Carey had abandoned the jurisdiction, the ranks of those who might have been aware that they had been mortally insulted if either term was directed at them had dwindled appreciably. However, in the raw aftermath of the onslaught of *The Times* and their Tory mentors, a muttered and rasping 'hesitancy' – with its underlying implication of 'West Britishness' and chicanery – was intended to sting. It reflected the rancour of nationalist Ireland, a reaction to the sight of their leaders being placed in the dock by a newspaper, read only – in Ireland at least – by unionists, place-seekers and *shoneens*.

Lies, evasion, misdirection, illusion. It might be a catalogue of the bag of tricks of the stage conjurer. Until, that is, you add surveillance, forgery, special pleading, felon-setting and misinformation. All of which brings us back to the Salisbury administration and its agitated response to the threat of Irish Home Rule. A grim overreaction to the revolutionary insipidity of William Gladstone's 1886 Government of Ireland Bill.

There are no statues to Gladstone in Ireland.* There should be at least one monument to the man who introduced the Church Disestablishment Act of 1869, the Land Acts of 1870 and 1881, and the Home Rule Act of 1886. He tried again, and failed better, in 1893. Although his bill did pass the House of Commons by a vote of 301–267, it fell at the insurmountable fence of a Tory-populated House of Lords, mustering only 41 votes there. It was a stark reminder of Tory antipathy to Irish aspirations and an unsatisfactory curtain call for the Grand Old Man, who took himself off to retirement in Hawarden, North Wales shortly afterwards.

The Tories, meanwhile, discovered an unexpected mellow side, although their administrative démarche was 99 per cent

*One was planned for Dublin in 1909 but after the Great War it was diverted to the Gladstone family's Hawarden estate in Flintshire. (*Irish Times*, 10 December 2025).

pragmatism, 1 per cent compassion. After the disastrous Parnellite 'split' of 1891 and the spectacle of Irish nationalists taking sizeable chunks out of one another, a kinder, gentler Tory phoenix was allowed to rise from the ashes of its snarling predecessor. This benevolent bird then spent most of the next fifteen years trying to buy off Irish nationalism by ridding the country of the burden imposed by its devoted allies among the Irish landlord class. Create a snug and satisfied Irish peasantry, the reasoning went, and you legislate against the emergence of any further O'Connells or Parnells. Throw in a decent measure of devolved government at some nebulous point in the distant future (pallid enough so as not to offend the loyalists of north-east Ulster) and the thirty-two counties of Ireland might have become Scotland or Wales, rather than twenty-six of them holding out for what turned into eastern Canada.

So the turn of the century was the era of 'killing Home Rule with kindness'. Legislation in 1885, 1891, 1896 and (especially) 1903 transformed the country's landlords into a threatened species and created an Irish peasant proprietary, complete with its own privileged *kulak* class of wealthy graziers. But for the intervention of the Great War and the virtual cessation of land transfers, the policy might have succeeded in undermining the Irish separatist spirit far more readily than the punitive and clandestine efforts of the late 1880s. But the project began to falter. The wartime coalition government, led first by Asquith, then by Lloyd George, put paid to the emollient approach. The sanguinary response to the Easter Rising of 1916, and the self-inflicted wound of the 1918 Conscription crisis, united nationalists of all stripes and frustrated any British inclination to substitute conciliation for coercion.

Of course, long before Lloyd George's ill-advised attempt to press-gang Irish men into the British Army,* the Tories, in opposition, had reverted to type in the face of even the qualified victory of Home Rule during the 'crisis' of 1912–14. The party of

*There was even a proposal that they be allowed to join the French Army.

Andrew Bonar Law, who replaced Balfour as Tory leader in 1911, set about undermining not just Irish democracy but the legitimate government of the United Kingdom. The 'Ulster will fight, and Ulster will be right' rubric of 1886 gave way to the far more sinister 'There are things stronger than parliamentary majorities', in 1912.[3] While clearly seditious, this soundbite was merely a logical extension of the conspiracy of the 1880s. The essential difference was that, in 1912, when a newly minted Home Rule crisis threatened the Empire, the Tories were in opposition. This time they lacked the levers of government to enforce their will.

The fall of a charismatic (if somewhat autocratic) Irish leader, followed by the Parnellite split, was a utopic moment for the Tories. Ironically it offered Salisbury and his nephew an opportunity to recalibrate, to set aside the cosh and to try compromise. The coercive, manipulative and subversive plot to strangle moderate Irish separatism at birth was replaced by the era of conciliation. The rogues' gallery of 'Bloody Balfour', Pigott, Anderson, Gosselin, 'Red' Jim McDermott, Millen, the *agent provocateur* and black propaganda accompanied by 'ops' of the same colour gave way to the Congested Districts Board and later to George Wyndham and the Land Purchase Act. The comprehensive 1903 legislation, designed to create a contented and malleable Irish electorate and banish any tendencies towards separatist recalcitrance, almost succeeded. The country was still overwhelmingly rural in the early twentieth century. But for the fact that the intervention of the Great War left more than 100,000 frustrated tenant farmers retaining the unwanted status of tenant, who knows how things might have gone?

The Marquess of Salisbury might even have been permitted to rest in peace, the Empire safe from that destructive Sisyphean rock that Irish nationalists threatened to roll down the hill.

However, the onslaught of the Cecils, uncle and nephew, was ultimately counterproductive, although only the latter was alive to see that first domino teeter and fall in December 1921. Because the 1880s 'Plot against Ireland' succeeded only in cultivating a residual siege mentality within Irish nationalism that ensured the survival of a militant republican ethos, awaiting its moment. All in spite of the switch to the gentler imperialism of the 1890s. Irish nationalists never quite put aside the resentment of the intended humiliation of the *Times* Commission and a distinct unease associated with the lengthy jail sentences meted out to men who, though hardly innocents, had often been seduced into terrorism by agents of the Crown. Thomas Clarke begat Séan Mac Diarmada, MacDiarmada begat Michael Collins, and Collins begat chaos. Call it facile, but just as there is an irritating grain of truth in the notion that the Fenians have some claim to be the founding fathers of modern Canada, Salisbury and Balfour have an equally counterintuitive claim to being godfathers to modern Ireland.

Viewing his handiwork in the 1920s, Balfour observed of the newly independent fledgling state that 'it was the Ireland that we made'. By 'we' he meant the Tories and the policies that had brought about peasant ownership of Irish land. However, were he to cast his mind just a little further back, to the era of coercion and conspiracy that preceded 'constructive unionism' and the ecstasy of land purchase, he may have spoken even truer than he knew.

Acknowledgements

My sincere thanks are due, as in previous instances, to my esteemed and jovial agent, Jonathan Williams, for both his pre- and post-production work on this volume. Little or nothing escapes his eagle eye. My gratitude is due, once again, in huge measure, to my editor Neil Belton, of Apollo/Head of Zeus. His faith in me – which I hope has been rewarded – and his diligent culling, tweaking and exhortation, have been vital components now of three consecutive works on aspects of Irish history. Our last outing together spanned three hundred years. Although this volume covers little more than three years, it demanded just as much of both of us. I would also like to express my gratitude to Neil's colleagues Megan Harris and Neil Burkey for their work on the text. This book could not have been written without the thorough and inspired work of historians of this space and period such as the late Shane Kenna, Owen McGee and Christy Campbell, and the custodians of the National Archives of Ireland and Britain, the National Library of Ireland, the British Library and the manuscript room of the library of Trinity College Dublin. My gratitude also to Patrick Power for access to material in his private collection and to my regular 'comrade in arms' Ultan Courtney for some invaluable detective work. Finally, my affection and eternal gratitude to my wife Nerys Williams, who was grappling with a far more serious work of her own downstairs while I ploughed ahead upstairs. And to my children, Amber, Rory, Lara, Ross and Gwyneth as well as their offspring, to whom the book is dedicated.

Bibliography

Manuscript and Documentary Sources

British Library

Althorp papers
Balfour papers
Gladstone papers

The National Archive, Kew

Foreign Office Series Five: The Fenian Brotherhood
Home Office HO 144 series
PRO 30/60 series (including Balfour secret service papers)

Trinity College, Dublin

Michael Davitt papers

National Library of Ireland

John Devoy papers
Timothy Harrington papers
Memorandum and copies of documents by a Mr Joyce, one-time official under Balfour, dealing with the role of the British government in the Anti-Parnellite conspiracy 1889–91
Memorandum for the information of the Executive Council by William Henry Joyce
William Henry O'Shea papers

National Archives of Ireland

Chief Secretary's Office Registered Papers, Police and Crime Division Reports

University of Birmingham

Joseph Chamberlain papers

University of Chicago

The O'Gorman Mahon Papers

University College, Cork

William O'Brien papers

Private collections

Patrick Power papers

Official Papers and Reports

House of Commons debates

House of Lords debates

Report of the Departmental Commission to Enquire into the State, Discipline and Organization of the Detective Force of the Metropolitan Police, 1878, London, HMSO, MPS Library

'Note on the Proposed Establishment of a Central Criminal Investigation Department' by Sir Andrew Fraser, 25 April 1903, 6–7. British Library, Oriental and India Office Collection, L/PJ/6/670/(493/4)

Report of the trials of Alexander M. Sullivan and Richard Pigott for libels on the government at the City of Dublin Commission

Sir Charles Russell, *The Parnell Commission: the opening speech for the defence delivered by Sir Charles Russell* (London, 1889)

The Special Commission, Report of the proceedings before the Commissioners appointed by the Act, vols 1–11 (1890)

The Special Commission, Report of the commissioners (1890)

Newspapers and Magazines

Adelaide Advertiser

Annual Register

The Citizen

Daily News

Daily Telegraph
Evening Mail
Freeman's Journal
Illustrated London News
Irish World
Labour World
Macmillan's Magazine
Morning Advertiser
New York Herald
New York Times
New York World
Pall Mall Gazette
Punch
Reynolds's Newspaper
Reynolds's Weekly
The Times
United Ireland
United Irishman

Contemporary Works

Philip H. Bagenal, *The American Irish and their influence on Irish politics* (Boston, 1882)

Frederick Moir Bussy, *Irish Conspiracies: Recollections of John Mallon (the Great Irish Detective) and Other Reminiscences* (London, 1910)

Dick Donovan, *The Crime of the Century* (London, 1904)

Andrew Dunlop, *Fifty Years of Irish Journalism* (Dublin, 1911)

St John Ervine, *Parnell* (Boston, 1925)

Rudyard Kipling, *Barrack Room Ballads and Other Verses* (London, 1892)

Henry Lucy, *A Diary of the Salisbury Parliament 1886–1892* (London, 1892)

John MacDonald, *Diary of the Parnell Commission: Revised from 'the Daily News'* (London, 1890)

John T. McEnnis, *The Clan-na-Gael and the Murder of Dr. Cronin* (San Francisco, 1889)

John Morley, *Life of Gladstone* (London, 1908), 2 vols

John Morley, *Recollections* (New York, 1917) 2 vols.

R. Barry O'Brien, *The Life of Lord Russell of Killowen* (London, 1901)
James O'Connor, *Recollections of Richard Pigott* (Dublin, 1889)
'Pigottism and *The Times* or "Parnellism and Crime" Exposed', *Pall Mall Gazette*, Extra No. 46.
H. B. C. Pollard, *Secret Societies of Ireland: Their Rise and Progress* (London, 1922)
Alfred Robbins, *Parnell: The Last Five Years* (London, 1926)
Algar Labouchère Thorold, *The Life of Henry Labouchère* (London, 1913).
Patrick J. Walsh, *William J. Walsh, Archbishop of Dublin* (Dublin & Cork, 1928)

Memoirs

Robert Anderson, *Sidelights on the Home Rule Movement* (New York, 1906)
Robert Anderson, *The Lighter Side of My Official Life* (London, 1910)
Henry Brackenbury, *Some Memories of my Spare Time* (Edinburgh & London, 1909)
Joseph Chamberlain, *A Political Memoir, 1880–92* (Connecticut, 1954)
Edward Clarke, *The Story of My Life* (London, 1918)
Thomas Clarke, *Glimpses of an Irish Felon's Life* (Dublin, 1922)
Michael Davitt, *The Fall of Feudalism in Ireland* (London & New York, 1904)
John Devoy, *Recollections of an Irish Rebel* (New York, 1929)
Tim Healy, *Letters and Leaders of My Day* (London, 1928), 2 vols
Henri Le Caron, *Twenty-Five Years in the Secret Service* (London, 1895)
John George Littlechild, *The Reminiscences of Chief-Inspector Littlechild* (London, 1894)
Maurice Moser, *Detective Stories* (New York, 1890)
William O'Brien, *Evening Memories* (Dublin, 1920)
T. P. O'Connor, *Memoirs of an Old Parliamentarian* (New York, 1929), 2 vols
Frank Hugh O'Donnell, *A History of the Irish Parliamentary Party* (Washington, 1970), 2 vols

Jeremiah O'Donovan Rossa, *Rossa's Recollections 1838–1898* (Shannon, 1972; first published New York, 1898)

Katharine O'Shea, *Charles Stewart Parnell, His Love Story and Political Life* (New York, 1914)

Richard Pigott, *Personal Recollections of an Irish Nationalist Journalist* (Dublin, 1883)

Dr Mark Ryan, *Fenian Memories* (Dublin, 1946)

John Sweeney, *At Scotland Yard: Being the Experiences During Twenty-Seven Years Service of John Sweeney, Late Detective-Inspector Criminal Investigation Department New Scotland Yard* (London, 1904)

Alfred E. Turner, *Sixty Years of a Soldier's Life* (London, 1912)

P. J. Tynan, *The Irish National Invincibles and Their Times* (London, 1894)

Secondary Sources

Stephen Ball (ed.), *A Policeman's Ireland: Recollections of Samuel Waters, RIC* (Cork, 1999)

Paul Begg and Keith Skinner, *The Scotland Yard Files* (London, 1992)

Michael Bentley, *Lord Salisbury's World: Conservative Environments in Late Victorian Britain* (Cambridge, 2007)

Paul Bew, *Ancestral Voices in Irish Politics* (Oxford, 2023)

Frank Callanan, *T. M. Healy* (Cork, 1996)

Christy Campbell, *Fenian Fire: The British Government Plot to Assassinate Queen Victoria* (London, 2003)

J. A. Cole, *Prince of Spies: Henri Le Caron* (London, 1984)

A. B. Cooke and John Vincent, *The Governing Passion: Cabinet Government and Party Politics in Britain 1885–86* (Brighton, 1974)

Ultan Courtney, *Sons of Fire: the Murder of Thomas Hodgett* (privately published, 2022)

Anthony Cronin, *The Identity Papers* (Dublin, 1979)

L. P. Curtis Jr, *Coercion and Conciliation in Ireland: A Study in Conservative Unionism* (Princeton, 1963)

Dictionary of Irish Biography (Cambridge, 2009)

Myles Dungan, *Land is All That Matters: the Struggle That Shaped Irish History* (London, 2024)

Myles Dungan, *The Captain and the King: William O'Shea, Parnell and Late Victorian Ireland* (Dublin, 2009)
J. L. Garvin, *Life of Joseph Chamberlain*, 3 vols (London, 1933), vol. 2.
Terry Golway, *Irish Rebel: John Devoy and America's Fight for Irish Freedom* (New York, 1998)
Peter Gordon, ed., *The Red Earl: The Papers of the Fifth Earl Spencer*, vol. 1 (Northampton, 1982)
J. L. Hammond, *Gladstone and the Irish Nation* (Connecticut, 1974)
Henry Harrison, *Parnell Vindicated: The Lifting of the Veil* (London, 1931)
Henry Harrison, *Parnell, Joseph Chamberlain and Mr. Garvin* (London, 1938)
John Juxon, *Lewis and Lewis: The Life and Times of a Victorian Solicitor* (London, 1983)
Julie Kavanagh, *The Irish Assassins: Conspiracy, Revenge and the Phoenix Park Murders that Stunned Victorian England* (New York, 2021)
Robert Kee, *The Laurel and the Ivy* (London, 1993)
Shane Kenna, *War in the Shadows: the Irish-American Fenians who Bombed Victorian Britain* (Kildare, 2014)
Shane Kenna, *Jeremiah O'Donovan Rossa: Unrepentant Fenian* (Dublin, 2015)
Algar Labouchère Thorold, *The Life of Henry Labouchère* (London, 1913)
Sara Lodge, *The Mysterious Case of the Victorian Female Detective* (New Haven and London, 2024)
F. S. L. Lyons, *Charles Stewart Parnell* (London, 1977)
F. S. L. Lyons, *The Fall of Parnell, 1890– 91* (Toronto, 1960)
Philip Magnus, *Gladstone, A Biography* (London, 1954)
Donal McCracken, *Inspector Mallon: Buying Irish Patriotism for a Five Pound Note* (Dublin, 2009)
Owen McGee, *The IRB: the Irish Republican Brotherhood from the Land League to Sinn Féin* (Dublin, 2005)
T. W. Moody, *Davitt and the Irish Revolution, 1846–1882* (Oxford, 1981)
Stanley Morison, *The, History of The Times*, vol. 3 (London, 1947)
R. Barry O'Brien, *The Life of Charles Stewart Parnell* (London, 1910)
Conor Cruise O'Brien, *Parnell and his Party* (Oxford, 1957), 281.
William Ó Broin and Desmond Ryan, *Devoy's Post Bag*, 2 vols (Dublin, 1948), vol. 2

Leon Ó Broin, *Fenian Fever: An Anglo-Irish Dilemma* (Ireland, 1971)

Leon Ó Broin, *Revolutionary Underground* (Ireland, 1976)

Leon Ó Broin, *The Prime Informer: a Suppressed Scandal* (London, 1971)

Margaret O'Callaghan, *British High Politics and a Nationalist Ireland* (Cork, 1994)

Bernard Porter, *The Origins of the Vigilant State: the London Metropolitan Police Special Branch Before the First World War* (London, 1987)

Bernard Porter, *Plots and Paranoia* (London, 1989)

Patrick Quinlivan and Paul Rose, *The Fenians in England, 1865–1872* (London, 1982)

Bruce Robinson, *They All Love Jack: Busting the Ripper* (London, 2016)

James Paul Rodechko, *Patrick Ford and His Search for America: A Case Study of Irish-American Journalism* (New York, 1976)

Paul Rose, *The Manchester Martyrs* (London, 1970)

K. R. M. Short, *The Dynamite War: Irish-American Bombers in Victorian Britain* (Dublin, 1979)

Algar Labouchère Thorold, *The Life of Henry Labouchère* (London, 1913)

Charles Townshend, *Political Violence in Ireland* (Oxford, 1983)

B. M. Walker (ed.), *Parliamentary Election Results in Ireland, 1801–1922* (Dublin, 1978)

Niall Whelehan, *The Dynamiters: Irish Nationalism and Political Violence in the Wider World, 1867–1900* (Cambridge, 2012)

T. Desmond Williams (ed.), *Secret Societies in Ireland* (Dublin, 1973)

Theses

Lindsay Clutterbuck, *The Evolution of Counter Terrorism Methodology in the Metropolitan Police from 1829 to 1901, With Particular Reference to the Influence of Extreme Irish Nationalist Activity*, PhD thesis, University of Portsmouth, 2002

Articles

Lindsay Clutterbuck, 'The Progenitors of Terrorism: Russian Revolutionaries or Extreme Irish Republicans?' in *Terrorism and Political Violence*, vol. 16, no. 1 (2004)

Lindsay Clutterbuck, 'Countering Irish Republican terrorism in Britain: its origin as a police function', in *Terrorism and Political Violence*, vol. 18, no. 1, 2006.

E. R. R. Green, 'The Fenians Abroad' in T. Desmond Williams (ed.), *Secret Societies in Ireland* (Dublin, 1973)

Richard Hawkins, 'Government versus secret societies: the Parnell Era' in T. Desmond Williams (ed.), *Secret Societies in Ireland* (Dublin, 1973)

F. S. L. Lyons, 'Fenianism 1867–1916' in T. W. Moody (ed.), *The Fenian Movement* (Dublin/Cork, 1968)

Patrick Maume, 'Parnell and the IRB Oath', *Irish Historical Studies*, vol. 29, no. 115 (May 1995).

James McConnel, '"Fenians at Westminster": The Edwardian Irish Parliamentary Party and the Legacy of the New Departure' in *Irish Historical Studies*, vol. 34, no. 133 (May 2004)

T. W. Moody, '*The Times* versus Parnell and Co., 1887–90' in *Historical Studies*, vi (1968), pp. 147–82

John O'Beirne Ranelagh, 'The Irish Republican Brotherhood in the Revolutionary Period. 1879–1923' in D. G. Boyce, (ed.), *The Revolution in Ireland, 1879–1923* (London, 1988)

Leon Ó Broin, 'The Invincibles' in Williams (ed.), *Secret Societies in Ireland* (Dublin, 1973)

Margaret O'Callaghan, 'Richard Pigott, the Fringe-Fenian Press and the Politics of Irish Nationalist Transition to Parnellism' in Fearghall McGarry and James McConnel (eds), *The Black Hand of Republicanism: Fenianism in Modern Ireland* (Dublin, 2009)

Eunan O'Halpin, 'The Secret Service Vote and Ireland, 1868–1922' in *Irish Historical Studies*, vol. 23, no. 92 (November 1983)

T. Desmond Williams, 'John Devoy and Jeremiah O'Donovan Rossa' in T. W. Moody (ed.), *The Fenian Movement* (Dublin/Cork, 1968)

Image Credits

p.xx Print Collector / Contributor / Getty Images
p.xxiii Hulton Archive / Stringer / Getty Images
p.16 Hulton Archive / Stringer / Getty Images
p.52 Licensed under the terms of CC-BY 4.0, The Board of Trinity College Dublin
p.76 Classic Image / Alamy
p.92 The Reading Room / Alamy
p.145 From the British Library archive / Bridgeman Images
p.161 The Print Collector / Alamy
p.174 Pictorial Press Ltd / Alamy
p.188 National Gallery of Ireland Collection, NGI.6214
p.229 Historic Collection / Alamy
p.239 Courtesy of the National Library of Ireland
p.247 Look and Learn / Illustrated Papers Collection / Bridgeman Images
p.270 Classic Image / Alamy *(top)* and Courtesy of the National Library of Ireland (*middle and bottom*)
p.272 Classic Image / Alamy
p.294 The History Collection / Alamy

Notes

Introduction

1 Michael Bentley, *Lord Salisbury's World: Conservative Environments in Late Victorian Britain* (Cambridge, 2007), 65.
2 Michael Davitt, *The Fall of Feudalism in Ireland* (London & New York, 1904), 531.
3 Robert Taylor, *Lord Salisbury* (London, 1975), 117.
4 *Ibid.*, 118.
5 T. W. Moody, '*The Times* versus Parnell and Co. 1887–90', *Historical Studies VI* (London, 1968), 147.
6 Paul Bew, *Ancestral Voices in Irish Politics* (Oxford, 2023), 142.
7 Taylor, *Lord Salisbury*, 120.
8 Moody, '*The Times* versus Parnell and Co.', 167.
9 Margaret O'Callaghan, *British High Politics and a Nationalist Ireland* (Cork, 1994), 107.

Prelude

1 Shane Kenna, *War in the Shadows: the Irish-American Fenians who Bombed Victorian Britain* (Kildare, 2014), 200.
2 John Devoy, *Recollections of an Irish Rebel* (New York, 1929), 210–11.
3 The National Archives, Home Office 144/1537/1, 30.10.83, Robert Anderson secret report to Home Secretary.
4 *Annual Register*, 13 December 1884.
5 *Reynolds's Weekly*, 21 December 1884.
6 Edward Jenkinson to Earl Spencer, 17 December 1884, Althorp papers, British Library, Add. MSS 77035.
7 John Sweeney, *At Scotland Yard: Being the Experiences During Twenty-Seven Years Service of John Sweeney, Late Detective-Inspector Criminal Investigation Department New Scotland Yard* (London, 1904), 24.
8 *Annual Register*, 13 December 1884.
9 Sweeney, *At Scotland Yard*, 26–8.

1: *Status quo ante bellum*: Fenians, Home Rulers and Land Leaguers

1 Leon Ó Broin, *Fenian Fever: An Anglo-American Dilemma* (New York, 1971), 23.
2 *Ibid.*, 19.
3 J. A. Cole, *Prince of Spies: Henri Le Caron* (London, 1984), 146.
4 James McConnel, 'Fenians at Westminster: The Edwardian Irish Parliamentary Party and the Legacy of the New Departure', *Irish Historical Studies*, vol. 34, no. 133 (May 2004), 42–64.
5 F. S. L. Lyons, 'Fenianism 1867–1916' in T. W. Moody (ed.), *The Fenian Movement* (Dublin/Cork, 1968), 39.
6 John O'Beirne Ranelagh, 'The Irish Republican Brotherhood in the Revolutionary Period. 1879–1923', in D. G. Boyce (ed.) *The Revolution in Ireland, 1879–1923* (London, 1988), 137–56.
7 Myles Dungan, *Land is All That Matters: the Struggle That Shaped Irish History* (London, 2024), 416.
8 *Dictionary of Irish Biography*, vol. 2, 438–9.
9 P. J. Tynan, *The Irish National Invincibles and Their Times* (London, 1894), 249.
10 *Dictionary of Irish Biography*, vol. 4, 641–2.

2: Bombing Britain

1 Philip H. Bagenal, *The American Irish and their influence on Irish politics* (Boston, 1882), 213–14.
2 Henri Le Caron, *Twenty-Five Years in the Secret Service* (London, 1895), 269.
3 John MacDonald, *The Daily News Diary of the Parnell Commission* (London, 1890), 120.
4 Sweeney, *At Scotland Yard*, 151.
5 MacDonald, *Daily News Diary*, 120.
6 Le Caron, *Twenty-Five Years in the Secret Service*, 270.
7 The Special Commission, Report of the proceedings before the Commissioners appointed by the Act, vol. 2, 146.
8 MacDonald, *Daily News Diary*, 137.
9 John T. McEnnis, *The Clan-na-Gael and the Murder of Dr. Cronin* (San Francisco, 1889), 110.
10 John Devoy papers, National Library of Ireland, MS 18,015/2/119.
11 H. B. C. Pollard, *Secret Societies of Ireland: Their Rise and Progress* (London, 1922), 71.

12 Christy Campbell, *Fenian Fire: The British Government Plot to Assassinate Queen Victoria* (London, 2003), 126.
13 Leon Ó Broin, *Revolutionary Underground* (Dublin, 1976), 60.
14 Devoy, *Recollections*, 329.
15 *United Irishman*, 21 May 1881.
16 *Irish World*, 25 March 1876.
17 *The Citizen*, 22 December 1883.
18 *Labour World*, 11 October 1890.
19 Shane Kenna, *Jeremiah O'Donovan Rossa, Unrepentant Fenian* (Dublin, 2015), 168.
20 *United Irishman*, 7 June 1884.
21 Niall Whelehan, *The Dynamiters: Irish Nationalism and Political Violence in the Wider World, 1867–1900* (Cambridge, 2012), 87.
22 Kenna, *O'Donovan Rossa*, 143.
23 *Ibid.*, 145.
24 Lomasney to Devoy, 18 February 1881, in William O'Brien and Desmond Ryan (eds), *Devoy's Post Bag*, vol. 2 (Dublin, 1948), 40.
25 Terry Golway, *Irish Rebel: John Devoy's Fight for Irish Freedom* (Dublin, 2015), 134.
26 Lomasney to Devoy, 23 February 1881, *Devoy's Post Bag*, vol. 2, 44.
27 Lomasney to Devoy, 26 January 1881 and 11 February 1881, *Devoy's Post Bag*, vol. 2, 33, 37.
28 T. Desmond Williams, 'John Devoy and Jeremiah O'Donovan Rossa' in T. W. Moody (ed.), *The Fenian Movement* (Dublin/Cork, 1968), 95.
29 Kenna, *War in the Shadows*, 130.
30 The Special Commission, Report of the proceedings, vol. 2, 131.
31 William O'Brien, *Evening Memories* (Dublin, 1920), 142.
32 Sergeant Patrick McIntyre, 'Scotland Yard: Its Mysteries and Methods', *Reynolds's Newspaper*, 3 March 1895.
33 John George Littlechild, *The Reminiscences of Chief-Inspector Littlechild* (London, 1894), 95–6.
34 K. R. M. Short, *The Dynamite War: Irish-American Bombers in Victorian Britain* (Dublin, 1979) 232.
35 Sweeney, *At Scotland Yard*, 22.
36 *Ibid.*, 22.
37 *Ibid.*, 29.
38 Owen McGee, *The IRB: the Irish Republican Brotherhood from the Land League to Sinn Féin* (Dublin, 2005), 133.
39 Jenkinson to Spencer, 25 January 1885, Althorp papers, BL, Add. MSS 77035 and memorandum, 26 January 1885, TNA, HO 144/721/110757.
40 *United Ireland*, 31 January 1885.

41 Donal P. McCracken, *Inspector John Mallon: Buying Irish Patriotism for a Five Pound Note* (Dublin, 2009), 138.
42 Lindsay Clutterbuck, *The Evolution of Counter Terrorism Methodology in the Metropolitan Police from 1829 to 1901, With Particular Reference to the Influence of Extreme Irish Nationalist Activity*, PhD thesis, University of Portsmouth, 2002, 196.

3: The War of the Three Kingdoms: Ireland and the Growth of the British Secret Apparatus

1 Bernard Porter, *The Origins of the Vigilant State: the London Metropolitan Police Special Branch Before the First World War* (London, 1987), 26.
2 McIntyre, *Reynolds's Newspaper*, 3 March 1895.
3 Major Nicholas Gosselin, cited in Short, *The Dynamite War*, 235.
4 *Irish Times*, 19 April 1884.
5 Short, *The Dynamite War*, 88.
6 Richard Hawkins, 'Government versus secret societies: the Parnell era', T. D. Williams (ed.), *Secret Societies in Ireland* (Dublin, 1973), 106.
7 Jenkinson to Spencer, 1 July 1885, Althorp papers, BL Add. MSS 77036.
8 TNA, HO 144/721/110757. This entire file includes a litany of complaints from Monro to Sir Charles Warren and others about Jenkinson's London freelancing.
9 Jenkinson to Spencer, 1 July 1885, Althorp papers, BL Add. MSS 77036.
10 Jenkinson to Harcourt, 31 May 1884, cited in Charles Townshend, *Political Violence in Ireland* (Oxford, 1983), 164.
11 Jenkinson to Harcourt, 10 December 1884, cited in Townshend, *Political Violence in Ireland*, 165.
12 McGee, *The IRB*, 133.
13 Davitt, *The Fall of Feudalism in Ireland*, 427.
14 Jenkinson to Spencer, 20 December 1885, Althorp papers, BL, Add. MSS 77036. 'I am a strong advocate for Home Rule, and believe that we must face the question now, without loss of time.'
15 *Labour World*, 27 September 1890.
16 Davitt, *The Fall of Feudalism in Ireland*, 432.
17 Memorandum of Michael Davitt, Davitt papers, Trinity College, Dublin, MS 9441/3127/2.
18 Statement of Matthew O'Brien, Davitt papers, TCD, MS 9441/3216.
19 Davitt papers, TCD, MS 9365.
20 Davitt, *The Fall of Feudalism in Ireland*, 433–4.
21 *Ibid.*, 434.
22 Statement of Matthew O'Brien, Davitt papers, TCD, MS 9441/3216.

23 Whelan to Davitt, 17 September 1883, Davitt papers, TCD, 9441/3148.
24 Jenkinson to Spencer, 7, 23, 31 August 1883, Althorp papers, BL, Add. MSS 77031.
25 Consul Clipperton to Granville, 30 September 1884, The National Archives, Foreign Office 5/1930.
26 Sara Lodge, *The Mysterious Case of the Victorian Female Detective* (New Haven and London, 2024), 186.
27 Davitt, *The Fall of Feudalism in Ireland*, 438–40.
28 Davitt, 'Notes by an amateur detective', Davitt papers, TCD, MS 9551.
29 Porter, *The Origins of the Vigilant State*, 78.
30 Anderson memorandum, 30.3.1881, HO 144/721/1537/1.
31 Harcourt to Spencer, 16 March 1883, cited in Clutterbuck, *The Evolution of Counter Terrorism Methodology*, 202.
32 Stephen Ball (ed.), *A Policeman's Ireland: Recollections of Samuel Waters, RIC* (Cork, 1999), 59.
33 Porter, *The Origins of the Vigilant State*, 73.
34 Jenkinson to Spencer, 12 April 1884, Althorp papers, BL, Add. MSS 77033.
35 Table showing charges, offences, sentences and other particulars relating to treason felony prisoners, TNA, PRO 30/60/12.
36 Farndale memorandum, 13 December 1887, HO 144/193/A46664B/13.
37 Nicholas Gosselin memorandum, HO 144/193/A46664B/11.
38 McGee, *The IRB*, 181.
39 Davitt papers, TCD, MS 9551.
40 *Dictionary of Irish Biography*, vol. 6, 507–8.
41 Lionel Carden, Chargé d'Affaires, Mexico City to Foreign Office, 17 May 1885, TNA, FO 5/1932, f.24.
42 Carden to Foreign Office, 23 May 1885, TNA, FO 5/1932, f.32.
43 Jenkinson memorandum, 30 May 1885, TNA, FO 5/1932, ff.45–51.
44 Carden to Foreign Office, 3 September 1885, TNA, FO 5/1932, ff.94–6.
45 Carden to Foreign Office, 11 July 1885, TNA, FO 5/1932, ff. 65–7.
46 Millen to Carden, 14 October 1885, TNA, FO 5/1932, f.172.
47 Jenkinson to Spencer, 15 December 1884, Althorp papers, BL, Add. MSS 77035.
48 James Monro, unpublished memoir (1903), 73, cited in Clutterbuck, *The Evolution of Counter Terrorism*. The original copy of the memoir is in private hands and the only known copy now resides in the Metropolitan Police Service Museum, where it is currently not available to researchers. (Author's correspondence with Metropolitan Police Service Museum 23–4 April 2025.)
49 Monro memoir, 49, cited in Clutterbuck, *The Evolution of Counter Terrorism Methodology*, 27.

50 Jenkinson to Spencer, 21 May 188, Althorp papers, BL, Add. MSS 77036.
51 James Monro to Evelyn Ruggles Brise, Parliamentary Private Secretary to Henry Matthews, 3 December 1886, TNA, HO 144/721/110757.
52 Charles Warren to Hugh Childers, 24 May 1886, TNA, HO 144/721/110757.
53 McIntyre, *Reynolds's Newspaper*, 5 May 1895.
54 Edward Jenkinson to Henry Matthews (Home Secretary), 28 October 1886, TNA, HO 144/721/110757.
55 Jenkinson to Spencer, 24 September 1888, Althorp papers, British Library, Add. MSS 77037.
56 Le Caron, *Twenty-Five Years in the Secret Service*, 272.
57 Jenkinson to Gladstone, 11 December 1885, Gladstone papers, British Library, Add. MSS 56446.
58 Eunan O'Halpin, 'The Secret Service Vote and Ireland, 1868–1922', *Irish Historical Studies*, vol. 23, no. 92 (November 1983), 348–53.
59 £28,371.15.7 to be precise. Jenkinson to Spencer, 25 June 1885, BL, Add. MSS 77036.
60 Jenkinson to Henry Matthews, 28 October 1886, TNA, HO 144/721/110757.
61 Home Secretary (Matthews) to Edward Jenkinson, 10 December 1886, TNA, HO 144/721/110757.
62 *Ibid.*
63 Jenkinson to Spencer, 1 March 1885, Althorp papers, KS 250, cited in Campbell, *Fenian Fire*, 165.
64 Jenkinson to Spencer, 4 September 1884, Althorp papers, KS 250, cited in Campbell, *Fenian Fire*, 154.
65 O'Callaghan, *British High Politics*, 118.
66 Robert Anderson, *Sidelights on the Home Rule Movement* (New York, 1906), 89.
67 Robert Anderson, letter to *The Times*, 30 April, 1910.

4: The Bombshell

1 House of Commons Debate, 18 April 1887, vol. 313, c.1225.
2 John Morley, *Life of Gladstone* (London, 1908), 2 vols, vol. 2, 474.
3 Stanley Morison, *The History of The Times*, vol. 3 (London, 1947), 57.
4 Moody, '*The Times* versus Parnell and Co.', 156.
5 St John Ervine, *Parnell* (Boston, 1925), 242.
6 *The Times*, 18 April 1887.
7 Morison, *The History of The Times*, vol. 3, 51.
8 *Ibid.*, 50.
9 *The Times*, 7 March 1887.
10 Morison, *The History of The Times*, vol. 3, 51.

11 HC Deb, 10 March 1887, vol. 311, cc.1752–4.
12 Whelehan, *The Dynamiters*, 77.
13 *The Times*, 10 March 1887.
14 *The Times*, 14 March 1887.
15 *Ibid.*
16 *Ibid.*
17 *Ibid.*
18 *The Times*, 18 March 1887.
19 *The Times*, 12 April 1887.
20 *The Times*, 18 April 1887.
21 HC Deb, 8 May 1882, vol. 269, c.323.
22 *Punch*, 30 April 1887.
23 Katharine O'Shea, *Charles Stewart Parnell, His Love Story and Political Life* (New York, 1914), 120.
24 Alfred Robbins, *Parnell: The Last Five Years* (London, 1926), 43.
25 HC Deb, 18 April 1887, vol. 313, c.1225.
26 Davitt, *The Fall of Feudalism in Ireland*, 534.
27 HC Deb, 18 April 1887, vol. 313, cc.1226–7.
28 *The Times*, 21 April 1887 & Ervine, *Parnell*, 242–3.

5: 'The Jubilee plot': Fishing for a Red Herring

1 Robert Anderson, *The Lighter Side of My Official Life* (London, 1910), 117.
2 *Reynolds's Newspaper*, 20 September 1896.
3 Le Caron, *Twenty-Five Years in the Secret Service*, 255.
4 Luke Dillon to John Devoy, 7 February 1887, *Devoy's Post Bag*, vol. 2, 299.
5 McEnnis, *The Clan-na-Gael*, 77.
6 Anderson, *The Lighter Side*, 117.
7 Dillon to Devoy, 7 February 1887, Dr John McInenry to Devoy, 13 February 1887, Michael Breslin to Devoy 14 March 1887, *Devoy's Post Bag*, vol. 2, 299–302.
8 Anderson, *The Lighter Side*, 169.
9 Luke Dillon to John Devoy, 7 February 1887, *Devoy's Post Bag*, vol. 2, 299.
10 Monro to Foreign Office, 19 May 1887, PRO/TNA, FO 5/2044.
11 *The Times*, 1 June 1887.
12 Anderson, *The Lighter Side*, 117.
13 Kenna, *War in the Shadows*, 262.
14 *Ibid.*, 270–1.
15 Cf., for example, two memoranda dated 13 August 1885 in which Julian Pauncefote refers to being 'directed by Marquis of Salisbury' (f.89) and 'the Secretary of State wishes …' (f.88). TNA, FO 5/1932.

16 Hawkins, 'The Parnell Era' in *Secret Societies in Ireland*, 102.
17 Monro to Anderson, 4 November 1887, TNA, HO 144/1537/2.
18 Anderson, *Sidelights*, 118.
19 Short, *The Dynamite War*, 233.
20 *New York World*, 29 January 1893, cited in Campbell, *Fenian Fire*, fn.369.
21 *Morning Advertiser*, 17 June 1887.
22 Le Caron, *Twenty-Five Years in the Secret Service*, 256.
23 Copy of the unpublished memoirs of James Monro, cited in Kenna, *War in the Shadows*, 276.
24 Davitt papers, TCD, MS 9551.
25 *The Times*, 20 April 1888.
26 James Monro, unpublished memoir (1903), 73, cited in Clutterbuck, *The Evolution of Counter Terrorism Methodology*, 262.
27 Monro memorandum re. 'Jubilee plot', 4 November 1887, TNA, HO 144/1537/2.
28 *New York Times*, 27 October 1887. The newspaper's account refers to Harkins throughout as 'Hawkins'.
29 *Daily News*, 27 October 1887.
30 James Monro, unpublished memoir (1903) 78, cited in Clutterbuck, *The Evolution of Counter Terrorism Methodology*, 261.
31 *New York Times*, 27 October 1887.
32 *The Times*, 20 April 1888.
33 Clutterbuck, *The Evolution of Counter Terrorism Methodology*, 328.
34 *Ibid.*, 330.
35 Frederick Moir Bussy, *Irish Conspiracies: Recollections of John Mallon (the Great Irish Detective) and Other Reminiscences* (London, 1910), 161.
36 Porter, *The Origins of the Vigilant State*, 89.
37 Lady Gwendolen Cecil, *The Life of Robert, Marquis of Salisbury*, 4 vols (London, 1921), vol. 2, 38 & 40.
38 Andrew Roberts, *Salisbury: Victorian Titan* (London, 1999), 358.
39 Cecil, *Salisbury*, vol. 3, 75.
40 *Quarterly Review*, October 1883.
41 Taylor, *Lord Salisbury*, 189.
42 Roberts, *Salisbury*, 383.
43 L. P. Curtis Jr, *Coercion and Conciliation in Ireland: A Study in Conservative Unionism* (Princeton, 1963), 103.
44 Cecil, *Salisbury*, vol. 3, 302.
45 Roberts, *Salisbury*, 384.
46 Curtis, *Coercion and Conciliation*, 104.
47 *Ibid.*
48 Roberts, *Salisbury*, 446.

49 *Ibid.*, 515.
50 *Ibid.*, 448.
51 Taylor, *Lord Salisbury*, 121.

6: The 'Bloody Puddle': The Special Commission Convenes

1 HC Deb 18 April 1887 vol. 313, cc1226.
2 Davitt, *The Fall of Feudalism in Ireland*, 543.
3 MacDonald, *Daily News Diary*, 2.
4 J. L. Garvin, *Life of Joseph Chamberlain*, 3 vols (London, 1933), vol. 2, 336.
5 HC Deb, 24 July 1888, vol. 329, c.351.
6 *The Times*, 31 July 1888.
7 Henry Lucy, *A Diary of the Salisbury Parliament 1886–1892* (London, 1892), 98.
8 *Ibid.*, 100.
9 Garvin, *Chamberlain*, vol. 2, 388.
10 *Ibid.*, 404.
11 *Ibid.*, 384.
12 *Ibid.*, 384.
13 Frank Callanan, *T. M. Healy* (Cork, 1996), 186.
14 Garvin, *Chamberlain*, vol. 2, 385.
15 Frank Hugh O'Donnell, *A History of the Irish Parliamentary Party* (Washington, 1970), vol. ii, 225.
16 Henry Harrison, *Parnell, Joseph Chamberlain and Mr. Garvin* (London, 1938), 163.
17 *The Times*, 10 July 1888.
18 Edward Clarke, *The Story of My Life* (London, 1918), 274.
19 *The Times*, 5 July 1888.
20 *The Times*, 5 July 1888. The word 'hesitancy' was correctly spelled in that day's issue of *The Times*. The misspelling was in the actual letter from which Webster was reading.
21 HC Deb, 6 July 1888, vol. 328, c.577.
22 *The Times*, 6 July 1888.
23 *The Times*, 12 July 1888.
24 HC Deb, 9 July 1888, vol. 328, cc.742–3.
25 Davitt, *The Fall of Feudalism in Ireland*, 536.
26 Morley, *Life of Gladstone*, vol. 2, 473.
27 Curtis, *Coercion and Conciliation*, 277–8.
28 Morley, *Life of Gladstone*, vol. 2, 476.
29 F. S. L. Lyons, *Charles Stewart Parnell* (London, 1977), 395.
30 Joseph Chamberlain to Mary Endicott, 7 July 1888, cited in Garvin, *Chamberlain*, vol. 2, 386.

31 Garvin, *Chamberlain*, vol. 2, 386–7.
32 Lyons, *Parnell*, 393.
33 HC Deb, 11 March 1890, vol. 342, c.524.
34 Joseph Chamberlain, *A Political Memoir, 1880–92* (Connecticut, 1954), 283.
35 HC Deb, 24 July 1888, vol. 329, c.353.
36 Joseph Chamberlain to Mary Endicott, 25 July 1888 cited in Garvin, *Chamberlain*, vol. 2, 388.
37 HC Deb, 12 July 1888, vol. 328, c.1102.
38 Taylor, *Lord Salisbury*, 122.
39 Curtis, *Coercion and Conciliation*, 280.
40 T. P. O'Connor, *Memoirs of an Old Parliamentarian*, 2 vols (New York, 1929), vol. 2, 177.
41 HC Deb, 20 July 1888, vol. 329, c.46.
42 Labouchère to Gladstone, 27 October 1888, Gladstone papers, BL, Add. MSS. 56449, f.208.
43 Davitt, *The Fall of Feudalism in Ireland*, 498–9.
44 Morison, *The History of The Times*, vol. 3, 48.
45 Bew, *Ancestral Voices*, 142.
46 O'Connor, *Memoirs*, vol. 2, 151.
47 Davitt, *The Fall of Feudalism in Ireland*, 544.
48 O'Connor, *Memoirs*, vol. 2, 137.
49 Curtis, *Coercion and Conciliation*, 280.
50 O'Connor, *Memoirs*, 139.
51 Clarke, *The Story of My Life*, 274–5.
52 *Ibid.*
53 Harrison, *Parnell, Joseph Chamberlain and Mr. Garvin*, 168.
54 Salisbury to Smith, 4, 9, 15 September 1888, cited in Curtis, *Coercion and Conciliation*, 282.
55 R. Barry O'Brien, *The Life of Lord Russell of Killowen* (London, 1901), 212.
56 O'Brien, *The Life of Lord Russell*, 216.
57 Arthur Conan Doyle, *The Casebook of Sherlock Holmes* (London, 1974), 16.
58 John Juxon, *Lewis and Lewis: The Life and Times of a Victorian Solicitor* (London, 1983), 223.
59 Morley, *Life of Gladstone*, 482.
60 Morison, *The History of the Times*, vol. 3, 62.
61 The Special Commission, Report of the proceedings, vol.1, i.
62 Morison, *The History of The Times*, vol. 3, 62.
63 Leon Ó Broin, *The Prime Informer: a Suppressed Scandal* (London, 1971), 83.
64 MacDonald, *Daily News Diary*, 2.
65 Curtis, *Coercion and Conciliation*, 279.
66 The Special Commission, Report of the proceedings, vol. 1, 41.

67 *Ibid.*, 48.
68 *Ibid.*, 194.

7: The Captain, the Forger, the Spy and the Bagman

1 *United Ireland*, 3 November, 1888.
2 *Punch*, 10 November 1888.
3 Robbins, *Parnell*, 67.
4 Juxon, *Lewis and Lewis*, 219.
5 The Special Commission, Report of the proceedings, vol. 1, 378.
6 MacDonald, *Daily News Diary*, 9.
7 The Special Commission, Report of the proceedings, vol. 1, 153.
8 These details of O'Shea's life are extracted from the author's *The Captain and the King: William O'Shea, Parnell and Late Victorian Ireland* (Dublin, 2009).
9 Joseph Chamberlain to Mary Endicott, 22 October 1888 cited in Garvin, *Chamberlain*, vol. 2, 393.
10 *Dictionary of Irish Biography*, vol. 7, 1071–87.
11 Katharine O'Shea, *Charles Stewart Parnell*, vol. 1, 134.
12 *Dictionary of Irish Biography*, vol. 7, 1071–87.
13 Dungan, *The Captain and the King*, 63.
14 *Dictionary of Irish Biography*, vol. 7, 945–6.
15 *United Ireland*, 22 May 1886.
16 Ó Broin, *The Prime Informer*, 95.
17 Davitt papers, TCD, MS 9549/10.
18 The Special Commission, Report of the proceedings, vol. 1, 153.
19 *Ibid.*, 155.
20 A. B. Cooke and John Vincent, *The Governing Passion: Cabinet Government and Party Politics in Britain 1885–86* (Brighton, 1974), 389–90.
21 The Special Commission, Report of the proceedings, vol. 1, 155.
22 *Ibid.*, 157.
23 *Ibid.*, 158.
24 Davitt Papers, Trinity College, Dublin, MS 9365
25 Davitt papers, TCD, MS 9441, 3200–1 – also McIntyre, 'My resignation from the force', *Reynolds's Newspaper*, 26 May 1895.
26 McIntyre, *Reynolds's Newspaper*, 26 May 1895.
27 The Special Commission, Report of the proceedings, vol. 1, 158.
28 Robbins, *Parnell*, 71.
29 McGee, *The IRB*, 126.
30 The Special Commission, Report of the proceedings, vol. 1, 161.
31 Davitt papers, TCD, MS 9441, 3198.
32 The Special Commission, Report of the proceedings, vol. 1, 159.

33 *New York Times*, 1 November 1888.
34 The Special Commission, Report of the proceedings, vol. 1, 147.
35 Robbins, *Parnell,* 68.
36 The Special Commission, Report of the proceedings, vol. 1, 165.
37 O'Shea to Chamberlain, 1 November 1888, Joseph Chamberlain papers, University of Birmingham, JC 8/8/1/114.
38 Chamberlain to O'Shea, 2 November 1888, Chamberlain papers, JC 8/8/1/115.
39 *United Ireland*, 3 November 1888.
40 The Special Commission, Report of the proceedings, vol. 1, 159.
41 *Punch*, 10 November 1888.
42 *New York Times*, 1 November 1888.
43 Ervine, *Parnell,* 260.

8: The Strange Pilgrimage of Richard Pigott

1 Anthony Cronin, *The Identity Papers* (Dublin, 1979), 192.
2 James O'Connor, *Recollections of Richard Pigott* (Dublin, 1889), 24–5.
3 Pigott to unknown correspondent, 28 March 1879, Devoy papers, NLI, MS 18,010/28/4.
4 Richard Pigott, *Personal Recollections of an Irish National Journalist* (Dublin, 1883), 80.
5 O'Connor, *Recollections of Richard Pigott*, 9.
6 McGee, *The IRB*, 44.
7 *The Irishman*, 23 & 30 November 1867.
8 *Report of the trials of Alexander M. Sullivan and Richard Pigott for libels on the government at the City of Dublin Commission*, 208.
9 Margaret O'Callaghan, in Fearghall McGarry and James McConnel, *The Black Hand of Republicanism: Fenianism in Modern Ireland* (Dublin, 2009), 154.
10 *Dictionary of Irish Biography*, vol. 8, 120.
11 Davitt, *The Fall of Feudalism in Ireland*, 133.
12 O'Connor, *Recollections of Richard Pigott*, 11.
13 Richard Pigott to The O'Gorman Mahon, 9 March 1880, The O'Gorman Mahon Papers, University of Chicago, Folder 22.
14 O'Callaghan in McGarry & McConnel, *The Black Hand of Republicanism,* 155.
15 McGee, *The IRB*, 45.
16 *Ibid.*, 45 & 64.
17 O'Connor, *Recollections of Richard Pigott*, 22–3.
18 Dick Donovan, *The Crime of the Century* (London, 1904), 30.

19 Donovan, *Crime of the Century*, 29.
20 *Ibid.*, 227.
21 O'Connor, *Memoirs*, vol. 2, 136.
22 Donovan, *Crime of the Century*, 229.
23 Pigott to David Murphy, undated, Davitt papers, TCD, MS 9441/3281 & 3282.
24 Richard Pigott to William E. Forster, 9 June 1881, The Special Commission, Report of the proceedings, vol. 5, 577.
25 O'Connor, *Recollections of Richard Pigott*, 14.
26 Richard Pigott, 'The Irish Question', *Macmillan's Magazine*, vol. XLV, November 1881–April 1882, 168, 175.
27 *Ibid.*, 169.
28 Pigott to Forster, 30 July 1882, The Special Commission, Report of the proceedings, vol. 5, 587.
29 *Ibid.*, 587.
30 *United Ireland*, 3 December 1881.
31 Davitt, *The Fall of Feudalism in Ireland*, 571–2.
32 *Ibid.*, 572.
33 B. M. Walker (ed.), *Parliamentary Election Results in Ireland, 1801–1922* (Dublin, 1978), 354 & 339.
34 The Special Commission, Report of the proceedings, vol. 5, 382.
35 Davitt, *The Fall of Feudalism in Ireland*, 563.
36 *Ibid.*, 563–4.
37 *Dictionary of Irish Biography*, vol. 1, 608–9.
38 MacDonald, *Daily News Diary*, 148.
39 MacDonald, *Daily News Diary*, 151.
40 *Ibid.*
41 Donovan, *Crime of the Century*, 309–10.
42 Davitt, *The Fall of Feudalism in Ireland*, 574.
43 New York Mayor's office to Richard Pigott, 20 May 1886, Davitt papers, TCD, MS 9386/1347.
44 Pigott to Egan, 12 January 1879, Devoy papers, NLI, MS 18,010/28/10.
45 Tim Healy, *Letters and Leaders of My Day* (London, 1928), vol. 1, 271.
46 Sir Joseph West Ridgeway to Arthur Balfour, 15 November 1888, Balfour papers, British Library, Add. MSS 49809, ff.21–4.
47 Labouchère to Gladstone, 27 October 1888, Gladstone papers, BL, Add. MSS 56449, f.208.
48 The Special Commission, Report of the proceedings, vol. 5, p.484.
49 Davitt, *The Fall of Feudalism in Ireland*, 582.
50 Davitt Papers, TCD, MS 9551, 29.
51 *Ibid.*, 31.

9: 'A Thing, a Reptile, a Monster': The Exit of Richard Pigott

1 O'Connor, *Memoirs*, vol. 2, 181.
2 Archbishop Walsh to Richard Pigott, 17 September 1885, Davitt papers, TCD, MS 9386/1346.
3 Patrick J. Walsh, *William J. Walsh, Archbishop of Dublin* (Dublin & Cork, 1928), 393–4.
4 *Ibid.*, 395.
5 *Ibid.*, 397.
6 *Ibid.*, 400.
7 Davitt papers, TCD, MS 9551, 38.
8 O'Shea to Chamberlain, 28 December 1888, Chamberlain papers, JC 8/8/1/117.
9 *Reynolds's Newspaper*, 3 March 1889.
10 MacDonald, *Daily News Diary*, 139.
11 The Special Commission, Report of the proceedings, vol. 5, 326.
12 MacDonald, *Daily News Diary*, 142.
13 *Ibid.*, 142.
14 *Ibid.*, 141–2.
15 *New York Times*, 22 December 1889.
16 MacDonald, *Daily News Diary*, 144.
17 The Special Commission, Report of the proceedings, vol. 5, 348.
18 *Ibid.*, 349.
19 *Ibid.*, 371–82. Russell's cross-examination runs from 385 to 443.
20 James Monro to Charles Warren, 3 November 1886, TNA, HO 144/721/110757.
21 MacDonald, *Daily News Diary*, 147.
22 *Ibid.*, 150.
23 Davitt, *The Fall of Feudalism in Ireland*, 575.
24 O'Brien, *The Life of Lord Russell*, 227.
25 *Ibid.*, 229.
26 MacDonald, *Daily News Diary*, 151.
27 Robbins, *Parnell*, 87.
28 MacDonald, *Daily News Diary*, 154.
29 The Special Commission, Report of the proceedings, vol. 5, 501.
30 Robbins, *Parnell*, 89.
31 The Special Commission, Report of the proceedings, vol. 5, 502–7
32 Robbins, *Parnell*, 88.
33 O'Connor, *Memoirs*, vol. 2, 166.
34 MacDonald, *Daily News Diary*, 161.
35 The Special Commission, Report of the proceedings, vol. 5, 545.

36 *Ibid.*, 550–2.
37 Davitt, *The Fall of Feudalism in Ireland*, 581.
38 Lyons, *Parnell*, 420.
39 Andrew Dunlop, *Fifty Years of Irish Journalism* (Dublin, 1911), 246.
40 MacDonald, *Daily News Diary*, 164.
41 The Special Commission, Report of the proceedings, vol. 6, 31–2.
42 MacDonald, *Daily News Diary*, 168.
43 The Special Commission, Report of the proceedings, vol. 6, 33.
44 MacDonald, *Daily News Diary*, 166.
45 *Ibid.*, 165–6.
46 *Reynolds's Newspaper*, 3 March 1889.
47 *Times*, 4 March 1889.
48 Healy, *Letters and Leaders*, 303.
49 Ó Broin, *The Prime Informer*, 86.
50 Donovan, *Crime of the Century*, 316–17.
51 O'Shea to Chamberlain, 9 March, 1889, Chamberlain papers, JC 8/8/1/121.
52 Anderson, *The Lighter Side*, 134–5.
53 Bruce Robinson, *They All Love Jack: Busting the Ripper* (London, 2016), 770.
54 *Dictionary of Irish Biography*, vol. 8, 120–4.
55 Davitt, *The Fall of Feudalism in Ireland*, 617.
56 McIntyre, *Reynolds's Newspaper*, 10 March 1895.
57 Davitt, *The Fall of Feudalism in Ireland*, 617–18.
58 *Ibid.*, 618.

10: From Checkmate to Stalemate: Endgame at the Commission

1 Rudyard Kipling, 'Cleared – in Memory of a Commission', *Barrack Room Ballads and Other Verses (1892)*.
2 HC Deb, 31 July 1888, vol. 329, c.1059.
3 MacDonald, *Daily News Diary*, 285.
4 The Special Commission, Report of the proceedings, vol. 9, 554.
5 *Evening Mail*, 8 July 1889.
6 John McCarthy to P. C. McGough, 29 November 1888, NLI, MS 8579.
7 HC Deb, 12 September 1887, vol. 321, cc.286–7 and HC Deb, 28 February 1889, vol. 333, cc.577–8.
8 MacDonald, *Daily News Diary*, 286–7.
9 Davitt, *The Fall of Feudalism in Ireland*, 609.
10 Anderson, *The Lighter Side*, 164.
11 The Special Commission, Report of the proceedings, vol. 4, 535.
12 MacDonald, *Daily News Diary*, 123.

13 Davitt, *The Fall of Feudalism in Ireland*, 609–10.
14 MacDonald, *Daily News Diary*, 137.
15 *New York Times*, 13 February 1889.
16 *New York Times*, 14 February 1889.
17 Porter, *The Origins of the Vigilant State*, 94.
18 Anderson, *Sidelights*, 6.
19 HC Deb, 20 March 1889, vol. 334, cc.276–7.
20 MacDonald to Anderson, 10 January, 1899, cited in Robinson, *They All Love Jack*, 783.
21 *Reynolds's Newspaper*, 12 May 1895.
22 Sheridan to British Minister, Washington DC, 13 March 1886, TNA, FO 5/1932, ff.31–2.
23 Lionel Sackville-West memorandum, 21 March 1886, FO 5/1975, f.33.
24 Davitt, *The Fall of Feudalism in Ireland*, 553.
25 19 November, 1888, Kirby to Soames ('Mohawk' to 'Assert'), HC Deb, 4 March 1890, vol. 341, c.1858. Copies of the deciphered telegrams are also to be found in the Timothy Harrington papers, National Library of Ireland, MS 8579.
26 Davitt, *The Fall of Feudalism in Ireland*, 551.
27 Healy, *Letters and Leaders*, vol. 1, 297–8.
28 Ó Broin, *The Prime Informer*, 92.
29 Statement of P. J. Sheridan, 28 May 1889, *New York Herald*, 12 January 1890, cited in Davitt, *The Fall of Feudalism in Ireland*, 557.
30 5 April 1889, Birch to Soames, HC Deb, 4 March 1890, vol. 341, c.1862.
31 R.Barry O'Brien, *The Life of Charles Stewart Parnell*, (London, 1910), 453.
32 19 June 1889, 21 June 1889, 5 July 1889, HC Deb, 4 March 1890, vol. 341, c.1864.
33 Joyce, Memorandum, NLI, MS 11119, cited in Ó Broin, *The Prime Informer*, 90.
34 Patrick Maume, 'Parnell and the IRB Oath', *Irish Historical Studies*, vol. 29, no. 115 (May 1995).
35 Campbell, *Fenian Fire*, 318.
36 MacDonald, *Daily News Diary*, 349.
37 13 December 1888, Thomson to Soames, HC Deb, 4 March 1890, vol. 341, c.1856 and Harrington papers, NLI, MS 8579.
38 *Labour World*, 11 October 1890.
39 Gosselin memorandum to Matthew White Ridley, 7 October 1896, TNA, PRO 30/60/13/2.
40 Thomson to Soames, 1 April 1889, Harrington papers, NLI, MS 8579.
41 Soames to Thomson, 8 April 1889, Harrington papers, NLI, MS 8579.
42 *New York Times*, 13 April 1889.
43 *Devoy's Post Bag*, vol. 2, fn.304.

44 Michael Breslin to John Devoy, 14 March 1887, *Devoy's Post Bag*, vol. 2, 302.
45 MacDonald, *Daily News Diary*, 212.
46 Sir Charles Russell, *The Parnell Commission: the opening speech for the defence delivered by Sir Charles Russell* (London, 1889), 4.
47 Russell, *The Parnell Commission: the opening speech for the defence delivered by Sir Charles Russell*, 24.
48 Lyons, *Parnell*, 427.
49 The Special Commission, Report of the proceedings, vol. 7, 245–7.
50 *Ibid.*, 258.
51 *Parnell Commission Report* (London, 1890), 66.
52 *Ibid.*, xv.
53 Lyons, *Parnell*, 429
54 *Parnell Commission Report*, 146.
55 Lyons, *Parnell*, 432.
56 Morison, *The History of The Times*, vol. 3, 89.
57 Lyons, *Parnell*, 431.
58 Morison, *The History of The Times*, vol. 3, 89.

11: Theatre of the Absurd: The Wardour Street Snake Pit

1 Labouchère to Herbert Gladstone, 3 November 1888, cited in Callanan, *T. M. Healy*, 202.
2 O'Shea to Chamberlain, 28 December 1888, Chamberlain papers, JC 8/8/1/117.
3 Nicholas Gosselin memorandum to Matthew White Ridley, 7 October 1896, TNA, PRO 30/60/13/2.
4 O'Connor, *Memoirs*, vol. 2, 152.
5 Chamberlain to O'Shea, 31 December 1888, William Henry O'Shea papers, National Library of Ireland, MS 5752.
6 Ervine, *Parnell*, 256.
7 Davitt papers, TCD, MS 9366.
8 Davitt, *The Fall of Feudalism in Ireland*, 612.
9 Davitt papers, TCD, MS 9551.
10 Davitt, *The Fall of Feudalism in Ireland*, 611.
11 Robert Kee, *The Laurel and the Ivy* (London, 1993), 494.
12 Davitt papers, TCD, MS 9551.
13 *Ibid.*
14 Sir Joseph West Ridgeway to Arthur Balfour, 15 November 1888, Balfour papers, BL, Add. MSS 49809, ff.21–4.
15 Davitt papers, TCD, MS 9551.

16 Davitt, *The Fall of Feudalism in Ireland*, 615.
17 *Ibid.*, 616.
18 Callanan, *T. M. Healy*, 199.
19 *Dictionary of Irish Biography*, vol. 8, 120–4.
20 Davitt papers, TCD, MS 9386/1357.
21 Davitt papers, TCD, MS 9365.
22 *Ibid.*
23 Davitt, *The Fall of Feudalism in Ireland*, 612.
24 *The Repeal of the Union Conspiracy; or, Mr. Parnell, M.P., and the I.R.B.* (London, 1886), 3.
25 *Ibid.*, 62.
26 *Ibid.*, 82.
27 *Ibid.*, 81 fn.
28 *Ibid.*, 92–6.
29 *Ibid.*, 96.
30 *Freeman's Journal*, 4 May 1886.
31 *United Ireland*, 10 July 1886.
32 Hoare to Salisbury, 18 February 1887, TNA, FO 5/2044.
33 Davitt papers, TCD, MS 9441/3165.
34 *Ibid.*, 9441/3169.
35 *Ibid.*, 9441/3199.
36 Houston to O'Shea, 6 March 1889, Chamberlain papers, JC 8/8/1/122.
37 Parnell to Alfred Webb, 15 October, 1884, MS 35996, National Library of Ireland.
38 Parnell to the Manager, Press Association, London, 16 July 1888, MS 50,065, National Library of Ireland.
39 O'Connor, *Memoirs*, vol. 2, 131.
40 Anderson, *Sidelights*, 144 & 213–14.
41 Mallon to Talbot, 14 December, 1881, National Archives of Ireland, CSORP, Police and Crime Division Reports, III, Compensation Cases, Crimes Act, 1882–3, Carton 6, 1881/45113.
42 Chamberlain memorandum re. meeting with O'Shea, 1 August 1888, Chamberlain papers, JC 8/8/1/92.
43 Davitt papers, TCD, MS 9551.
44 Egan to Labouchère, 2 December 1888, cited in Algar Labouchère Thorold, *The Life of Henry Labouchère* (London, 1913), 346.
45 Tevis to Davitt, undated 1888, Davitt papers, TCD, MS 9441/3223.
46 *Dictionary of Irish Biography*, vol. 5, 733–9.
47 Tevis to Davitt, undated 1888, Davitt papers, TCD, MS 9441/3224.
48 Maud Gonne to Davitt, 30 November 1888, Davitt papers, TCD, MS 9441/3225.

12: The Reluctant Archivist: William Henry Joyce Colludes with 'The Forger'

1 William Henry Joyce, 1923 memorandum to the Free State government re. 'Sidelights on British Conspiracies', NLI, MS 11119.
2 HC Deb, 31 July 1888, vol. 329, cc.1013–14.
3 'Pigottism and *The Times* or "Parnellism and Crime" Exposed', *Pall Mall Gazette*, Extra No. 46, 16.
4 Curtis, *Coercion and Conciliation*, 284.
5 Salisbury to Balfour, 22 August 1888, BL, Add. MSS 49689.
6 J. L. Hammond, *Gladstone and the Irish Nation* (Connecticut, 1974), 594.
7 Callanan, *Healy*, 190.
8 Curtis, *Coercion and Conciliation*, 285.
9 Davitt, *The Fall of Feudalism in Ireland*, 616.
10 TNA, HO 144/926/A49962/39.
11 Thomas Clarke, *Glimpses of an Irish Felon's Life* (Dublin, 1922), 27–32.
12 *Dictionary of Irish Biography*, vol. 6, 852–3.
13 The Special Commission, Report of the proceedings, vol. 3, 522.
14 MacDonald, *Daily News Diary*, 98.
15 The Special Commission, Report of the proceedings, vol. 3, 544.
16 Davitt, *The Fall of Feudalism in Ireland*, 616.
17 *Adelaide Advertiser*, 14 November 1890.
18 Davitt, *The Fall of Feudalism in Ireland*, 616–17.
19 Bussy, *Irish Conspiracies*, 221.
20 *Ibid.*, 225.
21 *Ibid.*, 226.
22 *Ibid.*, 227.
23 Parliamentary question minute, 8 April 1910, TNA, HO 144/926/A49962.
24 James Monro to Eugene Wason, 9 April 1910, TNA, HO 144/926/49962/35.
25 Anderson, *Sidelights*, 26.
26 Paymaster General's Office to Leon Ó Broin, 23 December 1960, NLI, MS 31667.
27 *Dictionary of Irish Biography*, vol. 4, 1083–4.
28 Joyce, memorandum to Free State government, 15 December 1923, NLI, MS 31698.
29 Diarmuid Fawsitt to Leon Ó Broin, 25 March 1961, NLI, MS 31667.
30 Moody, '*The Times* versus Parnell and Co.', 162.
31 *Ibid.*, 163.
32 *United Ireland*, 19 August 1889.
33 *United Ireland*, 16 March 1889.

34 Ridgeway to Balfour, 15 May 1888, cited in Curtis, *Coercion and Conciliation*, 285.
35 Ó Broin, *The Prime Informer*, 55.
36 Joyce, memorandum to the Free State government, NLI, MS 11119.
37 *Ibid.*
38 Ó Broin, *The Prime Informer*, 68–9.
39 *Ibid.*

13: The O'Shea Divorce: Plan C?

1 *United Ireland*, 4 January 1890.
2 Taylor, *Lord Salisbury*, 123.
3 Divorce trial details from *The Times*, 17 & 18 November 1890.
4 *United Ireland*, 4 January 1890.
5 Joyce, memorandum to the Free State government, 15 December 1923, NLI, MS 31698.
6 Affidavit of Dr Charles Bader, 4 May 1888, from the private collection of Patrick Power.
7 High Court of Justice, Probate, Divorce and Admiralty Division, Affidavit #3419, *O'Shea v O'Shea and Parnell*, 24 July 1890, from the private collection of Patrick Power.
8 O'Shea to Chamberlain, 13 October 1889, Chamberlain papers, JC 8/8/1/127.
9 Gosselin to Joyce, 13 December 1889, NLI, MS 11119.
10 Ó Broin, *The Prime Informer*, 95.
11 Gosselin to Balfour, 12 January 1890, PRO 30/60/13/2.
12 Report of Inspector Littlechild, 19 November 1889, HO, 144/1538.
13 John Morley, *Recollections* (New York, 1917) 2 vols, vol. 1, 250 & 254.
14 *Freeman's Journal*, 30 December 1889.
15 Conor Cruise O'Brien, *Parnell and his Party* (Oxford, 1957), 281.
16 Soames to Paul Askin, 9 October, 12 October 1888, 16 February 1889, NLI, MS 17815.
17 O'Shea to Chamberlain, 19 March 1890, Chamberlain papers, JC 8/8/1/137.
18 Robbins, *Parnell*, 132.
19 Philip Magnus, *Gladstone, A Biography* (London, 1954), 387 & 391.
20 Chamberlain to O'Shea, 14 October 1888, Chamberlain papers, JC 8/8/1/126 & 129.
21 Chamberlain to O'Shea, 14 October 1888, Chamberlain papers, JC 8/8/1/129.
22 *Daily Telegraph*, 17 November 1890.
23 Harrison, *Parnell, Joseph Chamberlain and Mr. Garvin*, 201–4.
24 Harrison, *Parnell Vindicated: The Lifting of the Veil* (London, 1931), 134.
25 *Ibid.*, 407.

26 *Ibid.*, 408.
27 Harrison, *Parnell, Joseph Chamberlain and Mr. Garvin*, 227.
28 *Ibid.*, 228.
29 *Ibid.*, 228–9.
30 F. S. L. Lyons, *The Fall of Parnell, 1890–91* (Toronto, 1960), 59.
31 *Ibid.*, 61.
32 *Ibid.*, 66–7.

14: Loose Ends

1 'Pigottism and *The Times*, *Pall Mall Gazette*, Extra No. 46, 2 March 1889, 16.
2 Davitt, *The Fall of Feudalism in Ireland*, 544.
3 Andrew Bonar Law, Blenheim Palace speech, 12 July 1912.

Index

Page numbers for illustrations are in *italics*.

Abberline, Insp Frederick 39
Aesop 249
agent provocateur 42, 50, 61, 95, 98–9, 122, 266
Alexander II, Tsar 45
Allen, William Philip 6, 31, 178
American Civil War (1861–65) 4, 63, 286
Ancient Order of Hibernians 26
Anderson, Robert, *The Lighter Side of My Official Life* 99–100, 104–8
  on *agent provocateurs* 95, 99
  CID head 289
  'Fenian hunter' 57–8
  Jenkinson and 67–8, 70
  Joyce and 285, 291
  'Jubilee plot' 123, 124
  Le Caron's handler 35, 44, 122, 230, 231, 234–5
  Millen and 101, 102, 111, 119
  Mulqueeny and 165–6
  O'Keeffe and 273
  Pigott and 176, 216
  RIC and 49
  Times and 283–4
  undervalued 71–2
Anderton's Hotel, Fleet Street 200, 213–15, 216
Anglo-Irish Treaty (1921) 286, 312–14
Archbishop's palace, Dublin 199–202
Archibald, Edward 5, 62
Ashbourne Act (1885) 82
Ashbourne, Edward Gibson, Baron 82, 187
Asquith, Herbert H. 148, 204, 205, 248–9, 283–4, 316

Bagenal, Philip Henry Dudley, *The American Irish and their influence on Irish politics* 21, 258, 265, 266, 268
Balfour, Arthur J. 80–1
  'Bloody Balfour' 317
  Crimes Act and 93
  Gosselin and 303
  on Ireland 318
  Joyce and 289–91
  Monro and 116
  O'Donnell and 133
  plot to kill 119
  Salisbury and 278
  Thomson and 244
  West Ridgeway and 195, 260, 287
Barrett, Michael 6–7
Barry, Tom, *Guerrilla Days in Ireland* 209
Beach, Thomas *see* Le Caron, Maj Henri, Twenty-Five Years in the Secret Service
Behan, Brendan 24, 25
Biggar, Joseph Gillis 8, 77, 86, 146, 148, 160
'Birch' (negotiator) 241–2

Birkenhead, Lord 312
Birkenhead Railway Station (1884) 42–4, 60–1
Birmingham 59–60
Birmingham Daily Post 304
Blennerhassett, Sir Rowland 191, 219
'blocked toilet' incident 120
Boland, Michael 25, 27, 63, 65, 100, 105, 111, 112, 123
Bonar Law, Andrew 317
Boycott, Capt Charles Cunningham 11
Boyton, Michael 85, 86, 146
Brackenbury, Sir Henry 46
Brennan, Thomas 85, 86, 146, 152
Breslin, John J. 192–3, 194
Brett, Charles 6
Bright, Maria 120, 123–4
British bombing campaign (1880s) 21–41
British Empire 313–14, 317
British Secret Service xxii
'Brooklyn Dynamite School' 29–30, 34
Buckle, George 79, 84, 143, 267, 307
Buller, Gen Sir Redvers 266
Burke, Edmund 247
Burke, Ricard O'Sullivan 6, 51, 80, 165
Burke, Thomas H. 16
Burton, Harry 39–40
Bussy, Frederick Moir 124, 282
Butt, Isaac 7, 11, 189
Byrne, Anne 225
Byrne, Frank 87, 146, 165–6, 191, 268, 279

Callanan, Frank 279
Callan, Philip 164, 259–61
Callan, Thomas 109, 115, 119–21, 123, 124, 268, 279
Campbell-Bannerman, Sir Henry 143
Campbell, Henry 203, 256, 261, 271
Canada 4, 35, 52–3, 103, 127
'Captain Moonlight' 10, 14
Carden, Lionel 64, 106
Carey, James 87, 314–15
Carnarvon, Henry Herbert, 4th Earl of 18, 263
Casement, Sir Roger 285
Casey, Joseph 6, 207, 236, 264–5
Casey, Patrick 51–2, 264–5
  Davitt and 263
  Hayes and 261, 274, 280
  'indispensable' 56
  IRB and 6
  McIntyre and 236
  Millen and 104
  Mulqueeny and 165, 262, 268, 274
  newspaper warning 109
  O'Shea and 168
  Pigott and 194, 198, 207, 214
  Reynolds and 269
  Russell and 164
Cassidy, Patrick Sarsfield 100, 105, 110, 111, 114, 123
Catesby, Robert 41, 96
Cavendish, Lord Frederick 15–17, 80, 94, 165
Cavendish, Lucy 15
Cecil, Lady Gwendolen 125–6
Cecil, Robert, 1st Earl of Salisbury 96, 97
Chamberlain, Joseph 130–2, 304–6, 308–10
  'backdoor' negotiations 14–15
  Commission and 138–9, 141
  Home Rule Bill, 19
  influence on Smith 147–8
  "Judas" 170
  M. O'Brien and 224
  on O'Shea 156, 274

O'Shea and 130, 132, 159, 161, 163, 202, 255, 283, 301–10
O'Shea writes to 221
Chester Barracks attack (1881) 32
Chicago Clan *see* Clan na Gael
Childers, Hugh 67
Churchill, Sir Randolph 140–1, 199, 266
Church of Ireland 7
cipher telegrams 238–40, *239*
Clan na Gael 23–4, 25–41
cipher code 26
'cipher telegrams' 238–40, *239*
Devoy and 9
'effective' 57
extreme members xxiv
'Fenian' 45
'General Hailing Sign of Recognition' 26
M. O'Brien and 224
Revolutionary Directory 27
under Sullivan 87
Triangle faction 27, 100, 105, 116
United Irishmen rivals 12
See also Fenian Brotherhood (FB)
Clarke, Richard 30–1
Clarke, Sir Edward 135, 147, 295
Clarke, Thomas, *Glimpses of an Irish Felon's Life* 280
Clarke, Tom 36, 37, 318
Clerkenwell prison bombing (1867) xxii–xxiii, 57
Coercion Act (1882) *see* Prevention of Crimes (Ireland) Act (1882)
Cohen, Joseph 109, 115, 117–18, 121, 123
Coleridge, Lord 134, 137, 146
Collins, Michael 312–13, 314, 318
Conrad, Joseph, *The Secret Agent* 57
Cork Fenians 51
Corridan, John Joseph (*aka* Corydon) 178
Cowell, Peter 166, 257, 259, 260, 261
Cox, Joseph 228
Crimean War (1853–86) 20, 78
Crimes Act (Ireland) Act (1882) 17, 93
Criminal Law and Procedure (Ireland) Act 1887 133, 205
Cronin, Anthony, *The Identity Papers* 172
Cronin, Dr Patrick 27, 240
Cruise O'Brien, Conor 304
Cullinane, James 228, 229
Cunningham, James Gilbert 38–9, 40
Curtis, L. Perry 138, 278

Daily Telegraph 307
Daly, John 42–4, 57–62, 265, 280, 289
Davis, Eugene 51–2, 56, 191, 193, 260, 264

Davitt, Michael, *The Fall of Feudalism in Ireland* 8–9, 10–11, 88
on Beach/Le Caron 230
Capt Stephens and 56, 266
on 'cipher telegrams' 240
closing address 250
on the Commission 314
defence 148
Delaney and 282
Golden Lion crowd 258–61
Hayes and Stephens 262
on Hoare 244
on ILPU 190
investigative work 62–3, 104, 162–3, 165, 221, 223, 224–5, 226–7
J. Casey and 236
Jenkinson and 50
Le Caron and 262–3
Louden as witness 227
McDermott and 51–2, *52*, 54
mild adverse finding against 251

Davitt, Michael (*cont'd*)
on Millen 110
on Mulqueeny 274
O'Shea divorce and 298
Parnell and 94, 129, 137, 148
on Pigott 179, 186, 194
Pigott and 197–8, 208, 216–17
Reynolds and 269
Sheridan and 241, 242–3
Tevis and Gonne 275–6
Times–Tories dilemma 141–2, 146
Day, Justice 211
Day, Sir John Charles 147
Delaney, Patrick 237, 281
d'Esterre, John 159
de Valera, Eamon 313
Devoy, John 26–9, 32–3
Breslin and 192
Clan na Gael and 9
Fitzpatrick and 246
indicted 146
L. Dillon and 98
Le Caron and 231
letters from followers 100
on Lomasney xxii
Millen and 63
Dickens, Charles 175
Dillon, John 17, 18, 83, 146
Dillon, Luke 37, 39–40, 77, 98
Disraeli, Benjamin 7, 8
'Donovan, Dick' (James Edward Muddock), *The Crime of the Century* 181–3, 191, 192–3
Doterel, HMS 29
Dublin Castle 11, 44–50, 51, 65–8, 261
Dublin Metropolitan Police 50
'G' Division 13, 55–6, 274
Duffy, Charles Gavan 10
Dunlop, Andrew, *Fifty Years of Irish Journalism* 214
'dynamitards' 12, 29, 40, 55, 111, 122, 164, 230
'Dynamite Saturday', London (1885) 12, 38–40

Easter Proclamation (1916) 36, 280, 316
Egan, Patrick 90–1, 173–4
background 11
correspondence with Parnell 191, 213, 217
Daly stays with 59
Delaney and 281
evidence against 61, 77, 190
flees to USA 17
indicted 146
'Invincible' 16
IRB treasurer 180
Le Caron and 36, 231, 232
Parnell and 136, 141, 243
Pigott and 12, 75, 184, 272, 275
writes to Labouchère 275
'Emergency Fund' (*Irish World*) 33
Endicott, Mary (*later* Chamberlain) 131, 132, 138, 139, 156

Farnara, Giuseppe 45
Farndale, Joseph 61
Fawkes, Guy 95, 96–7
Fenian Brotherhood (FB) 3–6, 24–5, 100, 102, 103, 105
Fenianism 3, 9, 10, 23, 25, 45, 57, 185
Fenian Rising (1867) 6
Finerty, John 28
Finigan, Lysaght 279
Fitzgerald, P. N. 146
Fitzpatrick, Maj Rudolph 246
Flag of Ireland, The 179, 180
Flanagan, John Woulfe 83–8
Fleming, John Lomasney, William Mackey
Foley, Con William 113, 115

Ford, Patrick 12, 28, 33, 86–7, 146, 248
Foreign Office, Whitehall 35, 64, 65–8, 162, 246
Forster, William E. 13, 14, 15, 16, 176, 181, 185, 212
France 51, 107–8, 191
Freeman's Journal 12, 265, 303
Freemasons 25–6, 232
Fremantle Prison, Western Australia 27, 192
Froude, J. A. 247

Gallagher, Dr Thomas 36, 37, 224
Garvin, J. L. 308–9
'Gentle Torpedo' *see* Millen, Gen Francis Frederick
Gladstone, Catherine 215
Gladstone, Herbert 19
Gladstone, William E. 12–13, 14–15, 46–7
  becomes PM 7
  Chamberlain and 163
  conversion to Home Rule 18–19, 79, 144, 187
  Jenkinson and 68
  Labouchère and 196
  legacy 82, 315
  'Parnellism and Crime' 89–90
  seat bombed 39
  Tory coercion measures 93
Glasgow bombing campaign (1883) 34
Goethe, Johann Wolfgang von 142
Golden Lion, The (Soho) 166, 256, 257–66, 267, 275
Gonne, Capt Thomas 275
Gonne, Maud 275–6
Gordon, P. J. 85, 146, 152
Gosselin, Maj Nicholas 43–4, 58–61
  Balfour and 303
  Hoare and 244
  Joyce and 289, 302
  Mcdermott and 54
  Monro and 66
  O'Brien works for 196, 224
  on the secret service 255
  Soames and 269
Government of Ireland Bill (1886) 81
Great Famine (1845–9) 3, 10, 37, 78, 205
'Greek fire' 98–119
Gresham Hotel, Sackville Street 54–6
Griffith, Arthur 285, 313
Grosvenor, Lord Richard (*later* Baron Stalbridge) 189, 258
Gunpowder Plot (1605) 95–7

Hall, Sydney Prior 22
Hannen, Sir James 147, 149, 215
Harcourt, William Vernon 57–8, 66–7
  on Anderson 72, 234
  Home Secretary 44, 45
  on Ireland 42
  Jenkinson and 49, 68
  Joyce and 288
  on O'Shea 306
  on Salisbury 127
  Smith and 278
Harkins, Michael 109, 112, 115–16, 120–1, 123, 124
Harrel, David 283
Harrington, Timothy 17, 82, 83, 93, 146, 238
Harris, Matthew 77, 85, 111, 112, 141
Harrison, Henry, *Parnell Vindicated*, 271, 306, 307–8, 309
Hartington, Lord 15, 207, 305
Hayes, John P.
  Jenkinson and 59, 207
  MacDonald and 263
  O'Shea and 166–7

Hayes, John P. (*cont'd*)
P. Casey and 236, 261, 268, 274, 280
Stephens and 259, 262
Healy, Tim 17–18
defence 148
evidence against 77, 146
on the government 226
Labouchère and 195
on 'Mrs Tyler' 54
on O' Donnell 134
O'Shea and 160, 163
on Pigott 220
on Sullivan 240
Herds League 227–8
History of The Times, The 84–5
Hoare, Gen William 223, 244–6, 266, 282
Hodgett, Thomas 230
Holbeche House, Staffordshire 96
Home Office, Whitehall xxiv, 44–50, 65–8, 162
Home Rule Bill, First (1886) 19, 40, 68, 71, 126, 160, 163, 168, 187, 265, 300, 301, 315
Home Rule crisis (1912–14) 315–16
Home Rule League 7–8, 11
homicide rates 14
Hôtel des Deux Mondes, Avenue de L'Opéra, Paris 172–4, 193, 194, 206
House of Commons 12, 36, 55, 61, 80, 112, 119, 129–32
House of Commons bombing (1885) 39
House of Lords 20, 95–7
Houston, Edward Caulfield 173–4, 189–90, 192–4, 203–4, 206–8
Joyce and 287
Le Caron and 232
O'Shea and 269
Pigott and 187, 217, 235, 267
portrait *188*
Reynolds and 269
Reynolds's on 218

Illustrated London News xxiii
Inglis, G. S. 142, 203–4
Invincibles, the 15–17, 34, 80, 91, 94, 146, 165, 191, 237, 279
Irish Church Act (1869) 7
Irish Loyal and Patriotic Union (ILPU) 76, 173, 185, 187, 188–94, 198, 206, 287–8
Irishman, The 5, 11–12, 172, 177, 178, 180, 183, 184
Irish Nation 27, 32, 63
Irish National Brotherhood 100
Irish National Land League (INLL) 11–15, 75, 77, 87, 141, 144, 146, 152, 179, 184, 185, 227, 251
Irish National League (INL) 17, 51, 84–5, 90, 160
Irish National League of America 63, 67, 88
Irish Parliamentary Party (IPP) 13, 17–18, 21–4, 68, 79–80, 87, 144, 187–8, 251, 279
Irish People, The 4, 177–8
Irish Republican Army (IRA) 40
Irish Republican Brotherhood (IRB) 3–6, 7–10, 101–2
Clan na Gael and 33
infiltrated 62, 71
J. Stephens and 182
Millen and 111
O'Shea and 167
Pigott as treasurer 76, 180–1, 183
structure 264
Supreme Council 8, 10, 24, 59, 101
See also Irishman, The
Irish Times 214
Irish World 12, 28, 33, 86, 88, 248
Ives, Chester 63

Jack the Ripper 39, 222, 256
James I, King 96
James, Sir Henry 142–4, 147–8, 152–3, 229, 234, 243, 250, 283
Jenkinson, Edward 45–50, 53–62, 66–8, 69–72, 104–7
  counter-terrorist chief xxiv, 40, 108
  Harcourt and 44
  Hayes and 59, 207
  informers/agents 165, 167, 256, 259
  'Jubilee plot' 123
  Millen and 103, 104, 105, 106
  M. O'Brien and 223
  Monro and 112
  O'Neill and 43
  ousted 101
  Parnellite informant 163
John, Benjamin 120
Johnson, John *see* Fawkes, Guy
Joyce family murders (1882) 226–7, 251
Joyce, Myles 226–7
Joyce, William Henry, 'Sidelights on British Conspiracies' 17, 220, 242, 277–92, 296, 302
'Jubilee plot' (1887) 95–128, 245
Junior Carlton attack (1884) 37

Kelly, Thomas J. 6
Kenna, Shane 105
'Kennedy, Miss' (Moroney's companion) 113, 114–15
Kernoff, Harry 267
Keys, Mrs Elizabeth 115
Kickham, Charles, *Knocknagow* 3, 8, 9, 10, 43
Kilmainham Jail 13–15, 169, 273
'Kilmainham Treaty' (1882) 14, 17, 155–6, 159, 237, 273, 306
Kipling, Rudyard 226
Kirby, J. F. ('Mohawk') 238, 240–2

Labouchère, Henry 196–7
  Egan writes to 275
  Healy and 195
  O'Brien and 224, 243
  on Parnell 255, 261
  Pigott and 216, 268
  Pigott's confession to 214, 215, 218, 262
  Pigott visits 204, 208
Labour World 244
Ladies Land League 14, 146, 274
Land Acts 186, 316, 317
Land Courts 13, 14, 186
Land Law (Ireland) Bill (1881) 13, 15, 82
Land League of Great Britain 87
Landlord and Tenant (Ireland) Act (1870) 7
Land Purchase Act (1903) 317
Land War (1879– 82) 10, 15, 16, 82, 89, 159–60
Langham, Samuel 117–18
Larkin, Michael 6, 31, 178
Le Caron, Maj Henri, Twenty-Five Years in the Secret Service 22–4, 34–6
  Anderson handles 44, 58, 68, 284
  Beach becomes 230–6
  contribution from 41
  on Cronin 240
  Davitt on 262–3
  gives evidence 21, 35, 36, *229*
  Kenna on 105
  Monro and 104, 122
  on Moroney 109
  Reynolds and 269
  on the secret service 98
  Sullivan and 102
Lecky, W. E. H. 247
'Letter No. 2' (Parnell *'facsimile letter'*) *76*, 79–81, 85, 89, 93–4, 143–53, 156, 161, 169–70, 236, 241, 268–73, *270*, *272*

Lewis, George 148–9, 196, 213, 214, 216
Littlechild, Ch Insp John George 36–7, 114, 118, 280–1, 303
Liverpool 60, 81
Liverpool Police Barracks attack (1881) 32
Liverpool Town Hall attack (1881) 32
Lloyd George, David 312, 316
Local Government Board 19, 34
Lockwood, Frank 210, 294, 296
Lomasney, William Mackey xxi–xxv, 31–2, 38
London bombings (1883) 34
London Bridge attack (1884) xxi–xxv, 38
London Daily News 150–1, 163, 230, 247
London Underground bombings (1883) 37
Louden, John J. 227–30
Luby, Thomas Clarke 3
Lynch, Hannah 146
Lynch, Sarah 166, 257
Lynch, William 36
Lyons, F. S. L. 139, 249, 251

Maamtrasna murders, Co. Mayo (1882) 226–7, 251
McCabe, Dr Edward 200
McCafferty, John 146, 266
McCarthy, Justin 17, 88, 146, 159
McCracken, Donal 17
MacCurtain, Tómas 230
McDermott, Jim 'Red Jim' 50–4, *52*, 99, 223
Mac Diarmada, Séan 318
MacDonald, John Cameron (*The Times*) 143, 203, 205–6, 218, 267
MacDonald, John (*London Daily News*) 150–1, 234–5
  Davitt on 263
  on James 243
  on Le Caron 23
  on Louden 227
  on Pigott 191, 204, 208, 209
  reporting on Special Commission 129, 163
  on Soames 203
McEnnis, John T., *The Clan-na-Gael and the Murder of Dr. Cronin* 23–4, 98
McGee, Owen 50, 105
McGonagall, William Topaz 199
McIntyre, Sgt Patrick 36, 42, 67, 95, 235–6, 255
Macmillan's Magazine 185–6
MacNeill, Eoin 285, 286
McParland, James 244
Maguire, Prof Thomas 173–4, 193
Mahon, Colonel James P. O'Gorman 157
'Major Yellow' (agent) *see* Stephens, Capt Darnley Stewart ('Major Yellow')
Mallon, Peter xxi–xxv
Mallon, Supt John 282–3
on Anderson 124
  arrests Parnell 13, 17
  Egan and 17
  'Lydia' and 182
  O'Keeffe and 274
  Sheridan and 237
  surrounds Gresham Hotel 55
Manchester Martyrs' 6, 178
Mansion House failed attack (1881) 32, 33
Matthews, Henry 70, 99, 105, 124, 289
'Melville, Joseph' *see* Moroney, James. J. (*alias* 'Joseph Melville')
Melville, William 108
Metropolitan Police xxiv–xxv, 38–40, 232
  CID 49, 56, 66, 67, 72, 104

'Section D' ('Special Secret Branch') 104
'Mezzeroff' (Richard Rogers) 29
Millen, Gen Francis Frederick 4–5, 62–5, 101–13, 122–4, 243–6
  Anderson and 99, 100, 119
  death 248
  indicted 146
  Jenkinson and 68
  meets Moroney 114, 115
  pursuit of 236–46
Millen, Kitty and Florence 111–13, 246
Millevoye, Lucien 275
Monro, James 66–8, 106–8, 114–19, 121–3
  Anderson and 70, 99–100, 283–4
  becomes Met Commissioner 289
  Hayes and 207
  Jenkinson and 49, 112
  Kenna on 105
  Millen and 104, 109–10, 113
  Pigott and 216
Monteagle, Lord 96
Moody, T. W. 286
Mooney, Thomas J. (James Moorehead) 34
Morley, John 75, 127, 138, 149, 298, 303
Morning News 63
Moroney, James. J. (*alias* 'Joseph Melville') 109, 111–12, 113–15, 117–19, 122–3
Moser, Det Insp Maurice 56, 57
'Mrs Tyler' (agent) 54–6
Mullett, James 146
Mulqueeny, George 164–8, 170, 259, 262, 263, 268, 274–5
Murphy, David ('Denis Fagan') 183–4
'Murphy, Maurice' (negotiator) 174, 191–2, 209
Nally, P. W. 281
National Land League of Mayo 10–11, 13
National League *see* Irish National League (INL)
Nation, The 177
New Law Courts, London 21–4
New York Herald 63
New York Times 30, 170
Nolan, Joseph 111–13, 118, 119, 121
'No Rent Manifesto' (1881) 14
Northcote, Sir Stafford (Lord Iddesleigh) 106, 258

O'Brien, Matthew ('Sinclair') 196, 223–5, 242–3, 244, 275
O'Brien, Michael 6, 31
O'Brien, Peter 'The Packer' 288
O'Brien, Richard Barry 148, 209, 241
O'Brien, William, *Evening Memories* 35–6
  evidence against 77
  execution 178
  indicted 146
  influential MP 83, 111–12
  INL and 17
  journalist 12, 13, 184, 186
Ó Broin, Leon, *The Prime Informer: a Suppressed Scandal* 284–5, 286
O'Callaghan, Prof Margaret 179, 262
O'Connell, Daniel 159
O'Connor, James, *Recollections of Richard Pigott* 172, 178, 179, 180, 182, 184, 211
O'Connor Power, John 8
O'Connor, T. P. 81, 147, 256, 271, 305
O'Donnell, Frank Hugh, *A History of the Irish Parliamentary Party* 133–7, 146, 203, 207
O'Donnell (Head Constable) 228

O'Donnell v. Walter (1888) 133–7, 146, 203, 207, 250, 268
O'Donovan Rossa, Jeremiah 26–32
arrested 4
Hayes on 59
indicted 146
McDermott and 51, 53–4
Millen and 64
'skirmishers' and 12
A. Sullivan and 177
O'Gorman Mahon, Col James P. 157, 180
O'Halloran, Maurice 228
O'Halpin, Prof Eunan 69
O'Keeffe, Arthur 273
O'Kelley, Edward 183–4
O'Kelly, James J. 8, 13, 136, 264
O'Leary, John 3, 8, 9, 30, 146
O'Mahony, John 3, 4
O'Malley, Bernard 152–3
O'Malley, James 52
O'Neill, Daniel 43, 59, 60, 62
O'Neill, Gen John 34–5
O'Shea, Capt William Henry 155–71
background 157
Capt Stephens and 259, 275
Chamberlain and 130, 132, 202, 255, 283, 301–10
Chamberlain on 156, 274
Davitt suspects 260, 261
divorce case 13, 252, 293–311
gives evidence 153, *161*
Houston and 269
'Kilmainham Treaty' 14–15
M. O'Brien and 224
Mulqueeny and 262, 268, 274–5
Parnell and 91, 139
Pigott and 220–2, 274
Punch on 154
stands for election 180
United Ireland on 154
O'Shea, Gerard 296
O'Shea, Henry 157
O'Shea, Katharine (*née* Wood) 92–3, 157–9
children 295, 296, 297, 299
divorce case 252, 293–311
left 'Aunt Ben's' fortune 296, 300, 301
portrait *294*
relationship with Parnell 13, 14, 19, 82, 91, 135, 161, 169
O'Shea v. O'Shea and Parnell (1890) 252, 293–311

Pall Mall Gazette 278, 305, 312
'panic of 1873' 10
Paris 30–1, 62–3, 235–6, 264–5
Casey/Mulqueeny meet in 165, 274–5
Egan/Le Caron meet in 36, 231
Jenkinson/Millen meet in 64–5, 106
Le Caron in 22
McDermott in 51, 52
Millen in 101, 103, 108, 111
Moroney in 113–14
Pigott in 216–17, 222–3, 268–9
Pigott/'Maurice Murphy' meet in 191–3
Pigott/Millen meet in 112
Stephens in 6, 56
Tevis in 110
See also Hôtel des Deux Mondes, Avenue de L'Opéra, Paris
Parnell, Anna 14, 146
Parnell, Charles Stewart 8–9, 13–15, 17–19
Capt O'Shea and 195, 256–7
Chamberlain and 130–2
on the Commission report 251
correspondence with Egan 191, 213, 217
Daily Telegraph on 307
defamation payout 252
'defence fund' 54
'dynamitard' 280

Egan and 243
evidence against 77, 146, 173–4, 190
'facsimile letter' *76*, 79–81, 85, 89, 93–4, 143–53, 156, 161, 169–70, 236, 241, 268–73, *270*, *272*
giving evidence 154–6, *247*, 248–9
INLL president 11, 40, 263
Jenkinson on 71
Katharine O'Shea and 13, 14, 82, 91, 92–3, 135, 158–9, 161, 169
Labouchère on 261
Le Caron and 36, 231–3
Lomasney and 31
O'Shea divorce case 295–311
personal correspondence 271
Pigott and 196–7
Sheridan and 242
signature 269–75
speeches 75
supporters of 77–8
suspected to be the Ripper 256–7
The Times and 79–94
See also Special Commission on Parnellism and Crime
Parnell, Clare 295
Parnell, Claude Sophie 299
Parnell family 8
'Parnellism and Crime' articles xviii, 72, 81, 84, 86, 89, 134, 141–4, 152, 174, 201, 210, 263, 277, 284, 292, 297
Patton, Dr George Valentine 173
Percy, Thomas 96
Pethers, Caroline 295–6
Philidor, François-André 250
'Philidor position' (chess) 249–50
Phoenix Park Murders (1882) 16, 33, 46, 91, 94, 173
Pigott, George 177
Pigott papers 150, 153
Pigott, Richard, *Personal Recollections of an Irish National Journalist* 75–7, 143–4, 146, 216–25, 265, 267–9
'Black Pamphlet' and 263
buys *The Irishman* 5
Callan and 261
Capt Stephens and 259
Casey brothers and 264
children 225
Davitt suspects 260, 261
Dickensian life of 175–98
Egan on 275
exit of 199–25
flees to Madrid 219, 220–2
gives evidence *174*, 208–15
Golden Lion visits 261–3
Labouchère and Sala 236
letters to Walsh 200, 210–11
loses newspapers 11–12
'Lydia' and 182, 191, 192–3
meets Houston 206
Millen and 104
Millen family and 112
and 'Murphy' 174, 191–2
O'Shea and 220–2
in Paris 172–4
Parnell and 166, 272
Parnellism Exposed" 263
Russell and 163–4
spelling errors 136, 204, 210, 213, 272
strange pilgrimage of 172–98
suicide of 176, 194, 202, 219–20
visits Daly 280
warrant for arrest 216
Pinkerton, Allan 25
Pinkerton National Detective Agency, USA 25, 116, 224
Pinkerton, William and Robert 244
'Plan of Campaign' (1886–91) 19, 82–3, 90
Police News *145*
Polti, Francis 45

Powell, Enoch 69
Power, John O'Connor 279
Prevention of Crimes (Ireland) Act (1882) 33
Protection of Persons and Property (Ireland) Act (1881) 12, 13, 17
Punch magazine 91–2, *92*, 170

Quinn, Insp Patrick 113, 114, 121
Quinn, Thomas 279

Redmond, John 88, 146, 285
Reform Act (1884) 18
Repeal of the Union Conspiracy, The (anon) 263–4, 266
Reynolds's Newspaper xxiv, 36, 202, 218, 235
Reynolds, W. J. 269
Ribbonmen, the 10, 227, 249
Richmond Prison 4, 5, 51, *52*
Rising Sun, The 38
Robbins, Alfred 155, 169, 304–5
Roberts, Andrew 126
Robinson, Bruce, *They All Love Jack* 222–3
'Rory of the Hills' 10
Rossa, Jeremiah O'Donovan *see* O'Donovan Rossa, Jeremiah
Royal Irish Constabulary (RIC) 15, 48, 49, 59, 69, 107, 155, 227, 230, 278–9
Russell, Sir Charles 164–6, 168–70, 208–9
  closing address 247–8
  cross-examines Houston 206–8
  cross-examines Le Caron *229*, 231–3
  cross-examines Pigott *174*, 210–13, 267
  cross-examines Soames 203
  Delaney and 282
  Le Caron and 23, 230
  O'Shea and 153, 155–6, 163, 167, 221
  Pigott and 195, 204, 216
  Soames and 290
  The Times and 237
  Walsh and 201
Russell, William Howard 78

Sackville-West, Lionel 238
Sadleir, John 175–6
St James's Square bombings (1884) 37
Sala, George Augustus 214, 215, 217, 262
Salford Barracks bombing (1881) 30–1, 32
Salisbury, Robert Gascoyne-Cecil, 3rd Marquess of 124–7
  Ireland and 313, 314
  Millen and 106
  on Parnell 94
  as PM 18, 19, 69, 133, 278–9
  replaced by Bonar Law 317
  targeted 97
Sayre's law 25
Sayre, Wallace Stanley 25
Scotland Yard *see* Metropolitan Police; Special Irish Branch, Scotland Yard
Sexton, Thomas 17, 77, 141, 146, 229
Shamrock, The 179
Shannon, W. J. 214, 215, 216, 217, 268
Sheridan, P. J.
  background 15
  evidence against 146
  flees to USA 17
  Land League organizer 16, 77, 85, 86, 87, 141
  pursuit of 236–46
Sigerson, Dr George 178
Sinn Féin 285, 313
Skirmishing Fund 28, 29, 33, 57, 86
Smith O'Brien, William 205
Smith, Sir A. L. 147

Smith, W. H. 137–41, 147, 278
Smyth, P. J. 177–8
Soames, Joseph 197–8, 203–4
  Gosselin and 269
  James and 143
  Joyce and 285, 290
  Kirby and 240
  letter to Joyce 286
  McIntyre and 236
  M. O'Brien and 224, 225
  Pigott and 220
  Quinn and 279
  Reynolds and 269
  Russell and 290
  Shannon and 214
  Sheridan and 211, 212
  Thomson and 243
  United Ireland and 286
  visits Daly 280
  Webster and 203, 215–16, 218
  West Ridgeway and 287
Special Commission on Parnellism and Crime 21–4, 138–53, 162–71, 280–3
  Davitt's information 50, 62
  endgame at the 226–52
  Houston evidence 190, 206–8
  Le Caron evidence 21, 35, 36, *229*
  O'Shea evidence 153, *161*
  Parnell evidence 154–6, *247*, 248–9
  Pigott evidence *174*, 191, 208–15
  Police News *145*
  report 249–52
  The Times takes the stand 202–25
  two tons of files 17
Special Irish Branch, Scotland Yard 58, 72, 108, 162
Special Irish Branch (SIB), Scotland Yard 36, 37–8, 39, 40–1, 44–50, 65–8
Spencer, Earl 18, 46, 49, 57–8, 60, 61, 66, 68, 71
Spencer, Lord Lieutenant, Earl xxiv
'Stack' (*aka* Dunne) 121–2
Stead, W. T. 207, 276, 305
Steele, Anna 298
Stephens, Capt Darnley Stewart ('Major Yellow') 56–7, 166, 258–60, 263, 265–6, 268, 275
Stephens, James 3, 4–5, 6, 24, 26, 30, 146, 182, 191
Stewart, Augustus 189
Sullivan, Alexander 32–3, 178–9
  betrayed 123
  Davitt and 240
  indicted 146
  J. J. Moroney and 109
  'Jubilee plot' 111, 123
  Le Caron and 35, 36, 102
  McEnnis and 23
  Millen and 63, 65, 101
  O'Donovan Rossa and 177
  suspicious of the Parnellites 112
  'Triangle' faction 25, 27, 34, 87, 100
Sweeney, Insp John xxv, 23, 37, 38, 45

Taylor, Robert, *Lord Salisbury* 140, 293
Tenant League 10
Tenniel, John 91–2, *92*
Tevis, Gen Charles Carroll
  betrayal of 35, 103
  Davitt and 110, 275–6
  extremist 264, 265
  Kenna and 105
  Millen and 104
  O'Shea and 166–7
  Parnell and 100
  P. Casey and 268
Thomson, Insp James and Martha 107, 243, 244, 304
'3 Fs' 9, 13
Three Kingdoms, The 44–50

Times, The 19–20, 21–2, 77–94, 133–7
'Behind the Scenes in America' 103, 107, 133, 235, 283, 285
bent on destruction of Parnell 304
editorials 307
employs Mulqueeny 167
endgame at the Commission 226–52
Gonne and 276
Joyce and 'The Forger' 277–92
letters to 194–5, 195–7, 214, 235–6
on liberty 95
Parnell *'facsimile letter'* *76*, 79–81, 85, 89, 93–4, 143–53, 156, 161, 169–70, 236, 241, 268–73, *270*, *272*
takes the stand 202–25
See also 'Parnellism and Crime' articles; Special Commission on Parnellism and Crime
Tone, Theobald Wolfe 25
Tower of London bombing (1885) 12, 38–9
'Tracy' ('witness') 228
Trevelyan, George Otto 56
Tynan, P. J. 17, 122, 146

Ulsterman, The 177, 182
Ulster Protestants 19
United Brotherhood *see* Clan na Gael
United Ireland
Balfour on 81
boxes of files 288
editorials 170, 286–7
'Forger's' business 277
Jenkinson and 40
Joyce and 290
McDermott visits 51
O'Keeffe employed by 273
O'Shea and 154
on the O'Shea divorce case 293, 295
Pigott and 186
'A Plan of Campaign' 82
The Times and 86, 265
on Whelehan 228
W. O'Brien editor 12, 13, 184
United Irishman, The 27–8, 30
United Irishmen of America 12, 29, 51, 53, 100, 105

Viceregal Lodge (*now* Áras an Úachtaráin) 16, 46
Victoria, Queen 29, 78, 95–128, 305
Victoria station bombing (1884) 37

Walsh, Dr William 199–202, 210–11, 240
Walsh, John 146
Walter family 20, 78, 235
Walter, John 78
Walter, John III 79, 133, 138, 143, 278, 307
Wardour Street, London 255–76
Warren, Sir Charles 67, 99, 289
warring kingdoms 65–8
Waters, Insp Samuel 58
Webb, Alfred 270
Webster, Sir Richard 135–6, 151–2, 163–8, 248–9
Anderson and 234
concedes 'facsimile' letter is a forgery 268
Harrel and 283
Harrington and 238
Houston and 206
James and 148
Mallon and 282–3
O'Connor on 147
O'Shea and 155, 156, 169
Pigott and 208–10, 217–18
Soames and 203, 215–16, 218
Weekly News 178
Westminster Abbey 109–10

Westminster Crypt bombing (1885) 12, 39
Westminster Palace 56
West Ridgeway, Sir Joseph 195–6, 260–1, 261, 287
Whelehan, Gerald (RIC Head) 228–9
Williamson, Supt Adolphus 'Dolly' 49, 58, 108, 110
Windsor Castle 29, 56
Winter (*alias* Dawson) 67
Wood, Anna Maria 'Aunt Ben' 158, 161, 162, 168, 297–8, 300–1
Wood family 158, 161–2, 168, 297, 298, 300

Yeomen of the Guard (Gilbert and Sullivan) 202, 225
Young irelanders Rising (1848) 3–4, 6, 205

About the Author

Myles Dungan is a broadcaster and historian. He presents *The History Show* on RTÉ Radio 1, was a Fulbright scholar at the University of California, Berkeley and is an adjunct lecturer in the School of History and Archives, University College, Dublin. He has also compiled and presented a number of award-winning historical documentaries. He is the author of numerous works on Irish and American history and holds a PhD from Trinity College, Dublin.